MARS BY 1980

The Story of Electronic Music

David Stubbs

FABER & FABER

First published in 2018
by Faber and Faber Limited
Bloomsbury House
74–77 Great Russell Street
London WC1B 3DA

Typeset by Ian Bahrami
Printed in the UK by CPI Group (UK) Ltd, Croydon CRO 4YY

A CIP record for this book
is available from the British Library

ISBN 978-0-571-32397-5

To Roshi, Dara and Alisha

CONTENTS

PART FOUR

PREFACE I

In writing this book, I realised I was taking on an exciting but also invidious, some might even say impossible, task. I wanted to take in the full range of electronic music, rather than home in on one particular aspect, beginning with its very earliest manifestations at the turn of the twentieth century and its apparent global domination in the popular music of the twenty-first, with EDM challenging rock's long-held dominance as the default form of stadium music entertainment.

I wanted to take in its vast sweep, across a range of genres, create an account at once intimate and aerial in its perspective, at once personal and historical. It's not, however, intended to be exhaustive. This is not a directory. I can see now fans of particular electronic musicians, or even the musicians themselves, reaching for this book, heading immediately for the index and finding, to their dismay, no mention of their heroes (or themselves). I can hear the voices of anguish. Why no mention of Super Collider and their sinuous blend of fractal electronics and neo-soul vocals? Where is Todd Rundgren, whose synth-driven *A Wizard, a True Star* blazed a lightning trail through the 1970s? Why the omission of the brilliant Tod Dockstader and Arne Nordheim from the musique concrète list? Were they not French or female enough?

Or where is Halim Abdul Messieh El-Dabh, the Egyptian American composer born in 1921 who experimented with wire recorders in the early 1940s, composing music made from field recordings in Cairo that, albeit tentative in their technology and outcomes, pre-date Pierre Schaeffer by half a decade, and who died in 2017 having seen the electronic music he prefigured spread arterially throughout the body of modern music? Or Jean-Jacques Perrey, early adopter of the Ondioline, who used the techniques of musique concrète to splice together a gleefully de-solemnised, populist take on the genre, eventually going on to work with Luke Vibert on the album *Moog Acid* (2007), aged eighty? Of neither of these is there a single mention in the entire book.

How come no Jean-Michel Jarre, a more serious student of electronic music than his rather son et lumière style suggests? Or Vangelis, whose soundtrack for the 1981 film *Chariots of Fire* was, in retrospect, an inspired choice for a period film about the 1924 Olympics, where a lazier, safer choice would have been an opulent, *Downton Abbey*-style orchestral soundtrack?

Where are Space? Hot Butter? Sarah Brightman and Hot Gossip's 'I Lost My Heart to a Starship Trooper'? And how could you possibly write an entire book of this nature and completely ignore Kraftwerk? (It's all right, Kraftwerk are in here.)

No judgement is intended on those omitted. As I say, this is a personal and selective account that is more about aspects and angles, patterns and trails than encyclopaedic completism. Nor is it a 'techie' account. It's more about the meanings and resonances of electronic music, how the shapes it has taken, the successes it has achieved and the failures it has suffered reflect the hopes, fears and loathing it has inspired in humanity. It refers outside of music into the realms of sport, TV, philosophy, the visual arts, non-electronic music, politics, national identity, race. But predominantly it refers to the music, made using the medium of electricity, but not guitar-based. That's important. That such music feels less 'real', less organic, less heroic, more schematic and heartlessly methodical to those wary of it is one of the underlying themes of *Mars by 1980*.

The book stretches into the twenty-first century but, as the title implies, it alludes also to something that was lost in the twentieth century at some unspecified, pre-postmodern moment: an idealism about the future and all that it might contain, from socialism to space travel, dreams that now seem laughably antique or agonisingly extinct. Mark Fisher, my late friend and colleague, felt something along these lines. While not hoping to emulate his own cultural and philosophical investigations, there are smatterings here and there of his influence, not least in his abiding belief that the oppressive school of thought established in lieu of Mars circa 1980 – that there is No Alternative to the prescriptions of capitalism and the free market – is merely a rhetorical sleight of hand. Electronic music has been a carrier of malignant ideas, of date-stamped fictions and a means of disseminating mediocrity on an industrial scale – in every gym, all the time, for a start. However, at its best, it has opened up great vistas of possibility as to what human beings can do with their invention and imagination, when unshackled from fear, custom and conservatism.

'No alternative' was the neo-liberal mantra; 'no future', as jeered by Johnny Rotten of the Sex Pistols in 1977, was the concurrent cry of despair that punk bequeathed, which, whether it meant to or not, helped scotch the flowery, futuristic dreams of a new Age of Aquarius as dreamt by the hippies. No future. We're still suffering the aftershock of that particular Song of Experience, the cynical refrain of the post-space age, of our postmodern times in which we are too clever, too afraid to speculate wildly on a better future of expanded horizons. This is the historical vantage point from which *Mars by 1980* surveys over a hundred years of electronic music and theory and the context in which electronic music is made today. There are a thousand good reasons to give way to despair, but what is there to lose by attempting to rediscover in the electronic music of the past not merely a glow of nostalgia but the glow of possible dormant futures that have merely been deferred?

A further note: although the book proceeds broadly chronologically, its chapters are thematic in a way that militates against an orderly timeline. There's a little bit of leaping about back and forth between the 1950s and '60s, 1970s and '90s, and back – but we reach the twenty-first century in the end.

For their valuable assistance, guidance and illumination I'd like to thank the following: Dave Watkins, Ian Bahrami, Lee Brackstone and all at Faber, as well as my agent, Kevin Pocklington; Jono Podmore, Simon Reynolds, Dan Hancox, Robin Rimbaud, all at *The Wire* magazine, where I worked for two years, a brief but packed era of immense discovery and exposure to new musics, and a chance to meet their creators; the commissioning editors of the late *Melody Maker*, *Vox* and *Uncut*, including Allan Jones and Jerry Thackray, who allowed me to meet childhood (and adult) heroes in the flesh; Neil Mason, Rudi Esch, Uwe Schütte, Mark Wernham and Push at *Electronic Sound* magazine; Luke Turner and John Doran at *The Quietus*; Clive Harris, Graham Dowdall and my partner, Roshi Nasehi.

PREFACE II: ONE SUMMER

July 1977. Britain. A late Sunday afternoon. A dormitory village, several miles from Leeds. A lane. A bedroom in an extension above a garage. A bedside table. A fifteen-year-old boy on the bed, bedroom-bound by adolescence. A boy holding a microphone connected to a cassette recorder next to a transistor radio, a fuzzy mono transistor radio with a soft grey speaker. Customarily, this radio sits in the kitchen, accruing a coating of brown grease from the cooking fat billowing around the clock. Customarily, it's an instrument of oppression, broadcasting *Waggoners' Walk*, *The Archers*, Vince Hill, *Sing Something Simple*, all of which give the lie to the supersonic seventies – the sallow fifties, more like.

On a Sunday afternoon there's nothing to do except homework, to while away the hour until the velveteen Tom Browne presents the suspenseful Sunday chart show, the first breaking news of the hit parade in any week. This is too important to be broadcast solely on Radio 1, with its barely adequate, interference-addled signal, so, for one hour a week only, there's pop on Radio 2, rather than the customary bow-tied crooners and *Semprini Serenade*. Unfortunately, it's preceded by Charlie Chester and his *Sunday Soapbox* – 'With a box full of records and a bag full of post, it's radio soapbox and Charlie your host!' It's impossible for a fifteen-year-old to make sense of. He's billed as 'Cheerful' Charlie, but it's cheerless fare indeed, like being obliged to look on as an old uncle shows you his yellowing collection of World War II bobbins and cigarette cards, with the threat of a slap on the head if you're not paying attention. These were the 1970s as lived, still coated with dark-brown war-surplus paint, barely relieved.

This was the context into which a new single crash-landed like Skylab.

1976. Musicland Studio in Munich, home to the communes that gave rise to Amon Düül but now host to an emerging disco factory. Among the musicians are Keith Forsey, a drummer who, like Can's Jaki Liebezeit, rejects the ostentatiousness of soloing in favour of the discipline of keeping time with thudding, machine precision. There's Pete Bellotte, a shy English expat who is good at framing albums conceptually and song structure. There's engineer Robbie Wedel, keeper of the secrets of the Moog synthesizer, some of which, it turns out, are unknown even to Mr Moog himself. Finally, there's the grand master and surveyor of the mixing desk, Giorgio Moroder. To the fifteen-year-old, his name speaks of sports cars, of aftershave cool, of suave, go-ahead European Teknik. Later, his moustache, hair and shades will make him look like a Eurodisco grotesque, but for now he exists primarily in the fifteen-year-old's imagination. Motorik, mobile Moroder.

Finally, there's Donna Summer herself, an American ex-cast member from the musical *Hair* who will later refuse to limit herself as 'merely' a disco singer, as well as unwisely alienate a vast segment of her audience when she gets religion and decides to condemn the gay lifestyle. For now, however, she's Donna Summer – wide-eyed, energetic, gossipy, full of love and fun, a gift from heaven. This team helped put together the epic, sensual 'Love to Love You Baby', but it was banned on release for its overt sexuality. The boy had no means of hearing it at the time, merely hearing *about* it. It was as mythical to the fifteen-year-old as sex itself.

This new track is an afterthought – an addendum to a concept album conceived by Bellotte, an Anthony Powell-esque dance backwards and forwards through pop history and prehistory with the ironically nostalgic title of *I Remember Yesterday*. It's a showcase for Summer's immense versatility, harking back to 1940s swing, then the Motown era, then early-1970s badass soul, then disco as constituted in the present day with 'Take Me' – and then, with 'I Feel Love', the tomorrow that was 1977.

The track is built like a new car, the body first. Its apparently impossible electronic repetition and velocity is achieved by Wedel syncing two tracks in a way that feels superhuman. It's another feat of German ingenuity, following the composer Paul Hindemith's experiments in 'motorik' music, the investigations of Herbert Eimert and Karlheinz Stockhausen, and, later, the inventions of Klaus Dinger, Ralf Hütter, Jaki Liebezeit and engineers like Kurt Graupner during the Krautrock era.

'So You Win Again' by Hot Chocolate is at number one. The boy resents its fatalism, which seems to infect the pedestrian pace of the song. 'Ma Baker' by Boney M is in there somewhere, another West German confection. Emerson, Lake and Palmer have ballooned into the Top 10 with 'Fanfare for the Common Man', as corny an example of prog rock's pretensions to classical status as ever deigned to touch down in the charts, but snapping further back somewhere is 'Pretty Vacant'. Two new holes are being ripped in pop's arse this week, and this is one of them. The other . . .

Practically the moment it beams down, 'I Feel Love' feels like first contact: the slow opening of the spacecraft door, the blinding shaft of green light. This is . . . what is this? Brian Eno hears it and rushes straight into David Bowie's studio, claiming to be holding the future in his hands. Sparks hear it and promptly decide to ditch their band, hit up Moroder and function as an electronic duo. And that's just the start.

What is this? Pure, silver, shimmering, arcing, perfectly puttering hover-car brilliance. Space's 'Magic Fly' to the power of ten. Seven inches have become twelve. Keyboards are played with unheard-of, bionic, rotor-blade capability. It glides the way scissors do when you achieve that perfect synergy between mind, hand and blade, cutting through the dreary brown curtain of 1970s entertainment and revealing space. Space 1977. No exhaust, no vapour trails, no strings, no frills, this is take-off. People will be left behind, people will be laid off. May you never hear rock music again. May you never hear light orchestra music again. May you never see *Happy Days* again.

Meanwhile, Donna Summer's vocals fall like petals from robot heaven. The machine, threshing immaculately, owns this song; it's for her to glide diaphanously around it, strew it with vocal grace – minimal subject matter. The words 'I feel love', applied with a mild, synthetic treatment, sound like she is channelling the voice of machinery that has experienced an epiphany, like *Star Trek*'s Commander Data discovering emotion. Except there is something coolly indifferent about this sonic craft, indifferent even to Donna Summer as it glides onwards and upwards, for minute after minute, powered on something far more durable than mere human stamina. Even as the record fades away, you sense it is still out there, puttering pneumatically away, cruising at cirrus level.

In 1973, the boy had received a five-year diary as a Christmas present. Flicking forward through its empty pages, he reached as far away as 1977. Maybe it was the way the two sevens clashed, or maybe it was the chevron-like effect of the two numbers in conjunction, but as a year it felt especially futuristic. What will life be like in 1977? Even decades later, the feeling somehow still holds. 1977 was *Star Wars*, Skylab, *The Six Million Dollar Man*, the Sex Pistols, Summer. The Apollo mission had closed a few years earlier, but no matter. Mars. Mars by 1980, surely. The boy was still growing, the world was still growing. Colour television had arrived only months earlier, in the boy's household at any rate, and now electricity had arrived, the electricity that would take us to uncharted space. 'I Feel Love' felt like the launch of an exploratory mission, an advance probe to delineate the decades that would take us to the twenty-first century, by which point the boy would be thirty-seven years old with his whole life behind him.

Decades later, the boy would still ask himself, 'What will life be like in the year 1977?'

INTRODUCTION

In January 2017, to test the notion that electronic music is pretty much the fabric of twenty-first-century post-pop, I decided to listen to the UK Top 20 of what used to be called singles. Well into the mid-1990s, when *Top of the Pops* was still extant, the charts were like the weather: you knew who was riding high, what was dominating the airwaves, and when Wet Wet Wet had a prolonged period at number one with 'Love Is All Around', you couldn't help but feel it and know it, like a prolonged spell of drizzle.

In 2017, knowing who or what is in the singles charts feels more like undertaking a piece of journalistic investigation – or sneaking furtively into a teenager's bedroom and switching on a computer to try to find out what's going on in their young minds. Not that this sort of pop estrangement is confined to those of a certain age – pop itself is in the process of being supplanted by YouTubers, fizzy twenty-somethings who have bypassed the irksome requirements of the music business to become stars purely on the basis of their effervescent audience, chatting about stuff from the edges of their beds to infatuated teens and pre-teens. Nonetheless – and despite 'sales' being an issue when it's the simplest matter to download illegally, rip YouTube videos to mp3 or simply make do with Spotify – there are charts that reflect the prevailing tendencies, the state of things.

Not everything in this Top 20 has an electronic component. ZAYN and Taylor Swift's 'I Don't Wanna Live Forever' is a virtuous thing of acoustic purity; even today, there remains a hint of subtle reproach on the part of 'real' music-makers in an over-processed pop environment. Swift is certainly deemed to stand out from her peers in this decade, purer of heart and purpose. Meanwhile, although its intro sounds like it's heading towards Massive Attack's 'Safe from Harm' before taking a different turn, Rag'n'Bone Man's 'Human' positively agitates with signifiers of flesh-and-blood authenticity, from the lyrical entreaties of the refreshingly bulky singer to his moniker and the song title. Perhaps the most convincing note of naturalism, however, is struck by Little Mix, one of four acts to have two hits in the Top 20, in what feels like a remarkably stagnant hit parade compared with ages past. For all their manufacture and gloss, their defiant, chanty, abrasive, girls-on-the-razz attitude bursts through, reminiscent of the Spice Girls or Shampoo.

Overall, though, the experience is one of horrifying, suffocating homogeneity, punctuated by flashes of electronic wizardry that remind you, in an age when analogue is the resort of the avant-garde conscientious, of the potency of state-of-the-art digital technology and its ability to wreak unheard-of permutations and microsounds. The machines are doing great. It's when the human factor kicks in that the problems start. So, Sage the Gemini's 'Now and Later' boasts a buzzing, minimal bass to have died for thirty years ago, but which is now just a drop in the pop ocean, punctuated by what sounds like the shard of an accordion sample. The rap, however, is tediously glazed, routinely Auto-Tuned and normative, the sound of someone determined to say and do whatever it takes to be at the party.

Occupying the top two positions is Ed Sheeran. Again, he seems to owe something to his perceived ordinariness: physically he looks agricultural, the sort of bloke who between making pop songs carries his sandwiches to work in a bucket. 'Shape of You', however, lilts to a dancehall beat, clearly the pop tinge *du moment*, a cocktail indeed of marimbas and house tropicalia. Sheeran's vocal, meanwhile, follows almost exactly the same cadence as TLC's 'No Scrubs', but given that Sheeran was only eight when that single was released, all the way back in the twentieth century, you wonder just how conscious a lift this is.

The content of the 2017 charts is no more designed to speak to me as a middle-aged man than are the YouTubers so beloved by my twelve-year-old daughter. Still, as one who first started following the charts in the late 1960s, when pop provided practically the sole source of colour and electric jolt in a childhood whose furnishings, ambience and media environment were still very much of the 1950s and earlier, I'm at least in a position to compare and contrast. What is strongest – stronger than in pop's twentieth-century heydays, the 1960s, '70s and '80s – is the feeling of a generation gap. Back then, pop was much more an inclusive family affair, in which each generation was catered for, from tots to grannies. Period programming from the 1960s tends to reach straight for Jimi Hendrix and Cream, but the likes of Engelbert Humperdinck were more dominant, while the biggest-selling UK solo singles artist of the decade was Ken Dodd. There are no Mr Blobbies or Lena Martells in today's charts, while the still hugely grossing veterans, from Zeppelin to Elton John to Paul McCartney, also give them a wide berth. There is no ridiculous, no sublime either, merely an efficient, faultlessly studio-conceived conveyance of tunes meticulously designed to converge on the predictable from the outset.

In 2011, Daniel Barrow wrote in *The Quietus* about what he termed the 'soar', which he described as follows:

a move that's been creeping into ubiquity in pop songwriting – that surge from a dynamically static mid-tempo 4/4 verse to a ramped-up major-key chorus, topped, in the case of female singers, with fountaining melisma; the moment the producer deploys the riff, the synth-gush, the shouted vocal-hook for which the whole of the rest of the song is a mere appendage, a prologue and epilogue that only the chorus validates. If you've heard it – and rest assured, you have – it's because it developed, as a trope, in some of the most inescapable songs of the last few years: 'I Gotta Feeling', 'Empire State of Mind' (both Jay-Z-enhanced and solo versions), 'Tik Tok', Flo Rida's 'Club Can't Even Handle Me Yet', 'California Gurlz'.

2011 was a long time ago, however, and in this Top 20 at least there is only a single, faint instance of the 'soar'. At one level, as the first generation to be steeped in rock'n'roll, Alan Freed and the *Six–Five Special* reach their late seventies, there is a huge nostalgia industry, in which stars of yesteryear continue to be active and, in some cases, make millions annually. The charts, though, comprise an almost eerie, history-less monoverse in which all that matters are the trends and tempos established over the last year or so, in which everyone is careful to keep in step with one another, share notes at all times. That said, this has been the overall condition of pop for most of this century.

What's also striking, and similarly depressing, is that pop hasn't been this non-queer since the days of Rosemary Clooney, the early 1950s. Gay culture had always been one of the great underground drivers of rock and pop, from Little Richard right through to Hi-NRG, often necessarily coded in a world that was institutionally homophobic. And yet today, when gay rights, while by no means universally accepted, are more established in the Western world than ever before, queer pop has disappeared. The charts in 2017 are primarily an idyll of young, photogenic, heterosexual love, preferably experienced in a seaside environment.

What's also lacking is the sense of irony and artifice that makes ABC's *The Lexicon of Love*, for example, perhaps the greatest pop album ever made and accounts, frankly, for the higher levels of intelligence at work in the post-punk/new pop of the early 1980s. Today, pretty much every song makes an ardent play for sincerity, a smooth-talking 4-realness, in part to make a strong impression as a suitor but also as a means of signalling humanity and authenticity in the face of strong suspicions that modern pop is an Auto-Tuned studio confection. They protest too much, however: the greater the need to ascend to ever more emotional heights, the greater the requirement for Auto-Tune's harnesses.

There is a sense of guilt and recrimination over the fact that studio technology and machinery are stifling true talent and expressiveness, providing artificial enhancements. And yet the problem is not the technology itself, which continues to yield fascinating details and capabilities, albeit incidentally at times in suffocatingly banal productions; it's the conservatism and timidity and pragmatism of those using it. The three sins of modern politics are also the sins of modern pop.

What's interesting also, watching the adverts preceding some of these tracks on YouTube, is how much more thrilling and innovative the electronica-soaked soundtracks to the ads are, how much more audacious and atmospheric than the rather stiff pop offerings that follow them.

An exception to all of this is Daft Punk, who feature in two of this particular week's Top 20 hits, in conjunction with The Weeknd: 'I Feel It Coming' and 'Starboy'. In truth, these are not the French duo's finest offerings, but 'Starboy' is at least preceded by a moment of bracing Daft Punk kitsch: an electronic fanfare that sounds like it was culled from a 1970s son et lumière festival, followed by a series of synth dynamite explosions to herald the main event, The Weeknd himself, though he disappoints a little with the by-the-book cadences of his vocal.

Daft Punk have longevity. I interviewed them in Los Angeles in 1997, following the release of their debut album, *Homework*. I loved the record, although I regarded it as a magnificently precious piece of kitsch, an uncanny achievement by two boys from a country whose international pop pedigree had been pretty much

non-existent a few years earlier. I did not envisage that they would
be global superstars in the year 2017. I probably did not give the
year 2017 a single thought. As I had done for years, as I would
do for years to come, I assumed the pop cultural clock to be at
about five minutes to midnight. In one of my first-ever reviews
for *Melody Maker* in 1986, I referred to 'this late hour'. It always
felt late. Daft Punk felt *très* 1997, an immaculate conceit, harking back to the days of Chic, Italo-disco, Telex, bouncing 4/4
grooves, wah-wah vocoders and novelty robo-bands like their fellow countrymen Space, who had a 1970s hit with 'Magic Fly'. I
should have seen the signs, however: in the record stores on Sunset
Strip, dead, white grunge had been supplanted in the displays by
a British wave of electronica, including the Prodigy, Underworld
and the Chemical Brothers – and now, Daft Punk. A new electronic era was being birthed.

The sheer unassuming modesty of Daft Punk was deceptive
also. The duo's Thomas Bangalter was dismissive of the luxury art
deco surroundings of the Argyll hotel. 'If it had been up to us,
we would have stayed in some little sleazy motel, y'know, out of
town,' he said. 'Some place with atmosphere. That would have
been more us.' It was hard, also, to be in awe of their magnitude
when I knew that they owed their name to a phrase from a review
by a colleague of mine, the late Dave Jennings at *Melody Maker*,
who had reviewed them in their previous, lo-fi guitar incarnation
Darlin': 'daft punk', he declared. They kept the record industry
at arm's length. Instead of management, they had a 'mate' who
acted as a go-between. When Virgin France needed to liaise with
the band, they were forced, in those relatively primitive days of
telecommunication, to trawl the likeliest Parisian cafes and bars
to track down said mate. The band themselves appeared to show
no appetite for superstardom, deliberately masking their faces
for photoshoots. A few weeks after I interviewed them, I was at
a record-company bash. Though I had spent an hour in their

company, when Bangalter flagged me down to say 'Hi' there was a mortifying second or so before I remembered who he and his partner, Guy-Manuel de Homem-Christo, were.

Daft Punk, however, had a grasp on the immediate future.

'Today, it's possible to make a record in your bedroom at a cheap price,' said Bangalter. 'Our album, *Homework*, is cheaper than nearly any rock album. No studio expenses, producers, engineers. We're not saying there is a right way or wrong way to go about things, but this is certainly a way. When we started to make music, we were just trying to form the teenage band everyone wants to be in.'

I mumbled something about the Internet being just around the corner. At that point, the Web was mostly dial-up, an optional bolt-on for *Wired*-reading nerds who spent altogether too much time staring at screens talking to strangers in discussion groups. Daft Punk, however, saw the transformative effect the Internet was about to have, as the future was finally upon us.

'The Net makes things more accessible, too,' enthused Bangalter. 'You can have the same access on a small site as a big site. You can sell records without leaving your bedroom, and you don't need a set of big producers. You won't need to go knocking on the doors of record companies, or A&R people or magazines with piles of tapes they never listen to.'

'It all sounds like it's going to put me out of a job,' I mumbled. Eighteen months later, I was made redundant.

Meanwhile, despite constantly protesting against the hype around them and the privilege heaped upon them, so intense was their distrust of the music industry, Daft Punk went from strength to strength in the twenty-first century. Unlike their peers, their music is steeped in retrospection: George Duke, Barry Manilow, guitar synthesizers, Buggles, Zapp all drift through on the relentless 4/4 of their dancefloor productions. They have a DJ-literate aware-ness of the pop past that has sustained them into their early forties.

Unlike the parallel retrograde fare of their popular rock peers in this post-rock era, however, there is something uncanny about their replications and rearrangements of the past. From 'Digital Love' to 'Lose Yourself to Dance' they have created a continuum, a utopian mechanism that with the routine perfection of an automaton distils the mess, the extraneous dross and frills of 1970s and '80s pop, makes unlikely finds in its more obscure and neglected regions and preserves its vital flashes of brilliance. The sample of clipped funk guitar from Chaka Khan's 'Fate', boosted and isolated on 'Music Sounds Better with You', Bangalter's Stardust project, is a case in point. As fine as the original, Arif Mardin-produced track sounds, it is diminished by comparison with the track that lifts from it. Whatever virtue there is in originality is shrunken into irrelevance by the inspiration of the steal and the use to which it is put, as it threshes through 'Music Sounds Better with You' like a remorseless, freshly stropped funking blade.

Furthermore, at a time when there is much fretting and pooh-poohing about the overuse of vocal treatments, Daft Punk make unabashed use of the vocoder. They don't use it, like others, as a form of vocal make-up to conceal blemishes, but rather they revel in its artificiality. Indeed, there is a far more emotional tug to Daft Punk's vocoderisation than that achieved by common-or-garden pop Auto-Tuners. They achieve a sense of vulnerability, of alienation, a sense of longing to be fully human.

Although they are very different types of outfits, only Kraftwerk match Daft Punk in their perfect balance of the retro and the futuristic, in their supreme belief in their operational skills that gives them the confidence to appear ridiculous to the public. Daft Punk, however, wear masks or, later, helmets for the same reason Kraftwerk project robot versions of themselves on stage: to preserve their privacy, to invest all in the product, not to waste energy on the banal soap opera and public autobiography required by the celebrity glare. It has worked. Where flesh-and-blood

contemporaries have withered away, they, like Kraftwerk, are preserved throughout pop time.

With Daft Punk, it's possible to imagine, from our sorrowful
position in the post-space age, that it is for ever 1980. Imagine if we
left behind the strife of earth, reached Mars and built discotheques
there, dancing our nights away in a state of cartoon perfection.

Although its beginnings were in the nineteenth century, and harbingers of it earlier still, the story of electronic music is the story of
most of the twentieth century. By the turn of the millennium, we
were, to all intents and purposes, pretty much where we are now in
2018. Electronic music, whose history is one of suspicion, oblivion,
fear and loathing, as well as futurism, utopianism and speculation
on a cosmic scale, is ubiquitous. We have been post-rock since the
mid-1990s. EDM (electronic dance music) supplanted it as the
new stadium rock, as popular guitar music reached a creative terminus, its intrinsic capabilities for expansion exhausted. There are,
have been extremists, including Wolf Eyes and Sightings, as well
as players such as Fred Frith and Derek Bailey, among others, who
have investigated the outermost possibilities of the instrument,
but they have been unable to reach beyond the periphery of public
attention, the public's appetite for abstract extremism in music not
matched by their appetite for its equivalent in the visual arts.

Electronic music is the natural stuff of now, though even within
the genre there is revulsion at the invisible digital nature of production, not unlike the smartphones and laptops whose dull thrall
keeps each of us in our individual spaces, interacting only virtually,
the supposed billions of options and connections of the Internet
leaving many feeling enervated, disconnected and helpless, with
no options at all. Others call for analogue and its too easily discarded equipment because of its more visible means of production,
as a protest against the planned obsolescence and because of the
liberation that can come through ostensibly 'limited' kit. As Sean

Booth of Autechre remarked to me in 2003, 'Everyone adheres to this idea that you've got to throw an old bit of technology away when something new comes along. Why? When do you decide that something's obsolete?'

Paradoxically, it is electronic practitioners who are leading the most pertinent charge against the supposed hegemony of electronics in the modern age. In some ways, the subtext is 'We want the twentieth century back.' A case in point is the group Metamono, featuring Jono Podmore, who has worked with Irmin Schmidt and the late Jaki Liebezeit of Can, among others. Podmore invited me to his flat to have a go on his vintage equipment, a classic, pre-keyboard valve synthesizer – part of Metamono's 'instrumentarium', which includes such antique equipment as a theremin, a wireless and a Mu-Tron III+. His co-band member, fine artist and fellow antique enthusiast Mark Hill (Paul Conboy makes up the trio) purchased a Korg MS-20. On stage, performed in real time, these instruments recreate the romance, the sense of grappling and engagement with electronic equipment that has been lost in an era when an electronica performance might consist merely of a single person on stage lit up by the dull glow of their laptop, its logo casting a forlorn beam into the audience.

Podmore asserts that there is a durability about the older equipment that is lacking in the post-Jobs era: 'The technology may date back to the 1920s in some cases, but it has been developing ever since and retains an audio quality far in advance of the paltry trickle of normalised data dribbling out of the headphone socket of the generic laptop masquerading as a musical instrument on stage right now in cities all over the globe.'

Metamono play according to the diktats of a self-penned manifesto designed to reinvigorate a music that has become a 'flaccid shadow of the power it once was'. A corollary to Matthew Herbert's more famous manifesto on the use of sampling, Metamono promise that:

metamono will never

– use a microphone
– use digital sound generation or sampling
– use mechanical sound generation
– use digital sound processing
– make overdubs
– remix
– be afraid of mono

metamono will only

– use analogue electronic sound generation
– use analogue electronic sound processing
– use digital recording and basic editing when no alternative
  is available
– compose and mix simultaneously
– build their own or play used instruments

For Futurists like Luigi Russolo, as well as visionary composers such as Busoni, Varèse and, later, Stockhausen, new electronic
modes of music-making weren't novelties, conveniences, cost-
cutting devices or objects of tinkering fascination for gadget nerds
who were less than human in their make-up. They were the means
whereby music would exceed the bounds of mere scripted notation,
explore infinite possibilities in tandem with a world whose technological leaps and bounds seemed limitless. In their wildest dreams,
they truly believed that electronic music could soundtrack, or even
by some occult means be the source of, an expansion of mankind's
capabilities. We could take to the air, the moon, the stars even.
Parallel advances in science demanded a soundtrack that did more
than merely modify the orchestral equivalent of nineteenth-century
empires whose collapse had been hastened by the machine age.

Others, however, feared – indeed, continued to fear – that
mechanisation would simply put mankind on the dole; moreover,

that machinery, in the form of uncanny automata, would take on human characteristics, including the desire to dominate and enslave, much as the machines themselves had been put to work as unpaid servants in a notional immediate future. There was, as we shall see, a racial component to this fear, one which perhaps accounts for the differing levels of reluctance between black and white people to embrace innovation in music technology.

Music was certainly a contested area. Technologies of all kind were in development in the early part of the twentieth century. On the one hand, there was the technology of dissemination. The microphone would radicalise vocal delivery, supplanting the crudity of the hand-held megaphone and making a star of Bing Crosby, who from the 1920s onwards understood how to take advantage of the device to develop a more intimate, nuanced vocal style that bridged the gap between audience and performer from yards to mere inches.

And then there was the gramophone. In one of its earliest editions, in 1926 *Melody Maker* ran a concerned editorial expressing the fear that with the rise of this popular new contraption, which merely encouraged listening rather than playing, the supply of musicians would give out. Under the headline 'What Will Music Be Like in 1935?', editor Edgar Jackson wrote:

> These are the days of mechanical music.
> Even the home piano is allowed to get out of tune and stiff from lack of use. The family is now gathered round the wireless set or the gramophone and the whole library is out of date.
> What will our children be like in 1935? Is there not a tangible danger that in these ten short years there will be a glut of critics and a dearth of performers?
> The Mozarts of 1926 are now jazzing to the gramophone instead of creeping with hope to the organ. Instead of earning

proud salaries in 1935, they will, unless they wake up, be the
merest automatons . . . still demanding entertainment from
the musicians of today.

In a sense, Jackson had a point. On the one hand, there are more
people having a go at, and succeeding in, making music worthy
of attention than the market can possibly bear today. No reviews
editor of a music magazine, their desk groaning with new releases
only a fraction of which could possibly be drawn to the attention
of their readerships, would dispute this. On the other hand, *Melody
Maker*'s earliest editions were largely devoted to sheet music for
an audience assumed to consist principally of musicians, the vast
majority of whom would have played for home entertainment
rather than harbouring dreams of stardom. There was evidently a
shift towards consumerism with the arrival of record players.

Fears were further exacerbated in the 1930s, during the 'robot
hysteria' of that decade. In 1930, in the *Bakersfield Californian*, an
item credited to the American Federation of Musicians appeared
in protest at the use of canned mechanised music in theatres,
accompanied by an illustration of a comely female harpist in a
diaphanous white gown who unmasks herself to reveal that she is
a robot. 'Is the Robot Fooling YOU?' demands the caption, urging readers to join the thousands who have already signed up to
the 'Music Defense League' by signing, cutting out and mailing a
coupon printed next to the article.

It's not hard to see why the intoxication of the early Futurist
manifestos, whose authors urged us to cast aside wholesale the
trappings of the nineteenth century and embrace the dynamism
of the twentieth-century industrial age, stalled somewhat after
the war, which the Italian art movement had greeted with such
retrospectively grisly and misguided relish. It was harder to warm
to the boons of technology when so many had been slaughtered
by recently introduced mechanical means in the Great War.

Meanwhile, the mass unemployment of the Great Depression hardly engendered an appetite for labour-saving.

The issue of labour, or the perceived effort required, has been another long-standing bone of contention in electronic music. Does one sweat honestly in its production? Does producing it induce the sort of facial contortions that denote an impassioned act of creativity? During the post-punk era, there was a contrast between the tangible physical exertion of players like New Order's Stephen Morris, insufficiently skilled to give off the air of effortlessness, applying himself to his kit as he generated handmade drum riffs, and those electropopsters, probably incapable of five consecutive press-ups, who simply flicked the switch on a drum machine. Their lack of physical application invalidated them in the eyes of many, confirmed their note-from-Mummy-to-get-out-of-PE effeteness. During the rave era, this became an increasing problem for *Top of the Pops*, as even the pretence that the miming musicians were 'doing something' broke down. The stasis of a house artist had to be countered with an energetic dance troupe to give some visual assurance that the expenditure of energy was in some way connected with this music. The Orb simply didn't bother when they appeared on the show in 1992 to 'play' their hit 'The Blue Room'. They undermined the expectation of hard work simply by sitting and playing chess for the song's duration, a switch having been thrown to initiate its transmission.

The objections of the Musicians' Union to synthesized music were understandable. Donna Summer's 'I Feel Love' arrived in 1977, its supersonic sequencer effects suggesting that the days of disco, supplemented by the flourishes of multiple players in an orchestra pit, were numbered. Who could not sympathise with the union's concerns that their members were in danger of being put out of work? And yet who cannot giggle at online footage of Summer performing the single that year, accompanied not by Moroder's synthesizer but by an orchestra of bow-tied musicians, sawing away frantically at their stringed instruments in a doomed attempt to simulate the effects of Moroder's sequencer?

Technically, there could have been electropop in the 1930s. In 1932, in the Soviet Union, Evgeny Sholpo and Nikolai Voinov worked on the Variophone photo-electrical synthesizer, which used a system of rotating discs capable of generating Stylophone-like renditions of popular and classical tunes that sang out artificially in harmony with a new, sodium-lit, electrically powered age. There was, however, absolutely no appetite for its development, nor for Russolo's noise intonators, which were taken up by zero composers, not even Varèse. Composers like Paul Hindemith made tentative efforts to devise a notional 'motorik' music (more of that later), while John Cage explored the possibility of vinyl as a musical instrument as early as 1939, but otherwise the mid-twentieth century was a fallow period indeed for electronic music. The 1930s and '40s were dominated by the mass participatory phenomena of big-band music and swing, with its high turnover of dance styles.

With the arrival of the post-war years came a frightening understanding of the capabilities of atomic science and the profound existential retrospection prompted not just by the trauma of war but the hideous depths to which mankind could sink with the assistance of railways and industrial equipment – the Holocaust. Gadgetry and labour-saving devices abounded, but also a terrible sense that thanks to hare-brained, tinkering boffins who couldn't let things lie, science would wipe out humanity. The 1950s were a golden age for musique concrète, music made from found sounds assembled from magnetic tape recordings and cut up and manipulated in the studio, but it neither sought nor gained any popular traction in that decade, any more than the obscure findings of a chemical laboratory caught the public imagination. Insofar as electronic music did impinge, it was in the use of instruments such as the theremin and ondes Martenot to denote the ominous whirl of flying saucers or aerial-sprouting aliens on TV shows or B-movies that functioned as projections of American paranoia.

The 1960s were heralded in pop by Joe Meek, a British producer who was among the first to grasp the potential of what would later become a truism – the studio as musical instrument. Meek was, in effect, an engineer/auteur who, on hits like John Leyton's 'Johnny Remember Me', brought a CinemaScopic sense of breadth and depth to the pop single; the female cry of the song's title seems to resound for miles across cowboy country as the hero gallops reluctantly towards the sunset. Meek revelled in the resonances of rock'n'roll, the shake and the rattle, the sonic ripples it created. From childhood, he had been fascinated by electronic components, radio valves, the nuts and bolts of emerging technology. He spent his obligatory stretch of National Service working as a radar technician. He was obsessed with studio space but also outer space, celebrating the nascent space programme on 1962's 'Telstar'. As the earth turned and 1959 became 1960, he released *I Hear a New World*, an EP (later album) recorded with the Blue Men, a skiffle group he brought in to provide the acoustic matter to which he could apply his studio treatments. We know that the sound effects he used were achieved using everyday items such as milk bottles, straws, spoons and kitchen sinks rather than yet-to-be-invented or unavailable electronic equipment. As with the BBC Radiophonic Workshop, however, which similarly made do with humdrum domestic objects, the effects achieved remain unearthly and unmatched, signifying lost hopes and a scarcity of resources that would be lost once technologies like the Moog synthesizer became widespread. With cuts like the title track, Meek intended to paint pictures of outer space, on whose distant orbs human beings seemed on course to be touching down very soon. In retrospect, what he depicts is the awestruck credulity of a nervous but excited generation who sensed they were on a pre-dawn cusp and had absolutely no idea what the 1960s would bring, be it thermonuclear war or first contact with aliens, but for whom the future was rising like a giant sun.

What Meek himself didn't anticipate, sadly, was the Beatles. He heard a demo tape of the Fab Four that was presented to him by Brian Epstein and told him not to bother with them. Perhaps he felt that guitar bands were indeed about to be supplanted by something more sonically expansive. Essentially, however, and despite the key inventions in electronic music, the 1960s would be the decade of the Beatles and of the guitar.

As the decade progressed, Meek went into a decline. There are shades of Joe Orton and Alan Turing about his eventual tragedy. Much of this was down to his own personality: he was beset with paranoia, carried away with a belief that one could communicate with the dead, including Buddy Holly, to which end he set up equipment in graveyards, and was arrested for 'importuning' in a public toilet and fined £15. He was later implicated in a crime dubbed 'the Suitcase Murder' on account of his known homosexuality. Tarnished by association and beset by business woes, including the freezing of his royalties for 'Telstar' following a legal dispute, in 1967, in a fit of despair, he murdered his landlady with a shotgun before killing himself.

Although a denizen of the late-1950s rock'n'roll scene who was superseded by subsequent trends, you sense that Meek was too far ahead of his time, that the new world he envisaged in his studio innovations was too long a time coming – not unlike the verdict in the 'Telstar' lawsuit, which was awarded in his favour following his death.

The Beatles were not only the biggest group of the 1960s but also at its vanguard, with John Lennon, Paul McCartney and George Harrison all taking an interest in the tape manipulations inaugurated by Pierre Schaeffer and taken up by composers like Karlheinz Stockhausen, whose 1967 epic *Hymnen* was received appreciatively by at least some members of a radicalised,

psychedelicised rock audience, as well as players including Frank
Zappa, the Grateful Dead and Pete Townshend, all belatedly
catching on to the mind-expanding properties of musique concrète. The Beatles made widespread use of tape manipulation on
tracks like 'Tomorrow Never Knows', 'Strawberry Fields Forever'
and 'I Am the Walrus'. One of Brian Epstein's last acts as Beatles
manager was to send a frantic telegram to Stockhausen urgently
asking permission, granted in the nick of time, to use his photo
as part of the collage/pantheon on the cover of *Sgt Pepper's Lonely
Hearts Club Band*. McCartney claimed that despite his reputation as the grannies' Beatle, it had been him who first introduced
Lennon to Stockhausen, his favourite piece being *Gesang der
Jünglinge*. Although Lennon had said that 'avant-garde was
French for bullshit', meeting Yoko helped open his mind and
he put together what is without doubt the most widely heard
musique concrète piece of all time: 'Revolution 9' on the *White
Album*. That piece is a creditable enough montage, though with
distinct signs of amateurishness in its composition. When I first
heard it, however, the piece terrified me, as I read it in conjunction with Vincent Bugliosi's book *Helter Skelter*, which told the
story of how Charles Manson had trawled the *White Album* for
coded messages urging him and his followers to venture on the
killing spree he hoped would spark a race war. 'Revolution 9' had
been the inspiration for an act of racist, homicidal madness.

The Beatles' enthusiasm for electronic music didn't really expand
beyond this point, either during the remainder of their group
years or their solo careers, in which they settled into conventional
songwriting grooves, the electronic experiments left behind like a
youthful dalliance. Another stalling.

Retrospectively, electronic music should have enjoyed more of a
flowering than it did in the late 1960s. Historians make much of
the albums made during that period by groups like Silver Apples,
United States of America and so forth. And then there was White

Noise, a group formed in 1968 that included a young classical bass player with a scientific background called David Vorhaus, who teamed up with Delia Derbyshire and Brian Hodgson of the BBC Radiophonic Workshop.

Vorhaus's Camden flat is a veritable museum of vintage electronic equipment, though having lived through the privations of early synthware, he has no truck with the current analogue vogue. 'I know lots of people like that, wanting to buy VCS3s with all the knobs on. No, my God, no! I had nothing but that for ten years, instruments that wouldn't stay in tune and you could only play one note at a time! I would say thank God for programs like Reactor, a tool where you can build your own gear on a computer. The potential there is astronomic. I've been working on mine for over ten years. I've converted all my old equipment onto my computer. In the old days, we used to go off to places like Amsterdam with a whole carful of gear. One time we went and we were missing a single module, without which we couldn't do anything. We literally had to mime to my album. So I thought, "Fuck this." Now I've built everything into just this laptop.'

Vorhaus has witnessed the entire sweep of electronica in his lifetime, but when he first met Derbyshire and Hodgson, following a chance encounter at the Camden Roundhouse, he had no idea, despite being a musician with a working knowledge of electronics, that the two could somehow combine.

'The pinnacle of one's career would have been to join the LSO as a bass player. Music was meant to be a hobby. Physics was going to be my career. It was a pure fluke that I should have met them that night.'

An Electric Storm was recorded in 1968 and released in June 1969. Its use of tape-splicing, varispeed, pitch-shifting and bending, as well as the early use of the EMS Synthi VCS3, made for an experience that could and should have realised the inner experiences of any self-respecting acid head of the era. Objects and voices rear and uncloak like Romulan vessels in the mix, colours erupt, shapes shift, attack, taunt and recede, all within the context of regular pop songs. 'Love Without Sound', in particular, which owes so much to the then unsung Derbyshire, is in terms of sheer freakology aeons ahead of anything issued by the mainstream psychedelic rock artists of the era.

White Noise received a generous advance from Chris Blackwell's Island label; however, the album stiffed initially, selling only a couple of hundred copies before slowly, very slowly wending its way to cult status over the years.

Given the great, mind-expanding transitions of the 1960s – the shift from black and white to colour, in both TV and culture, the awe inspired by the Apollo missions and the eventual moon landings, the utopianism and insurrectionary spirit of the age – the arrival of Robert Moog's modular synthesizer, unveiled in 1967, might have been expected to herald a giant leap for music-kind. But was it?

At the first-ever Moog Symposium, held at the University of Surrey in 2018 and featuring performances by Throbbing Gristle's Chris Carter and Chris Watson, formerly of Cabaret Voltaire, Thom Holmes, perhaps the world's leading expert on Moog synthesizers, discussed his obsession with the instrument, one that led him to build a collection aiming to consist of every record featuring a Moog ever made. The Moog, he said, was the instrument which took electronic music 'out of the laboratories and onto the desktops of musicians and recording companies'.

At the end of his lecture he played an extended montage of the welter of records on which the Moog appeared in the period between 1967 and 1970, before it was supplanted by the mini-Moog. The instrument managed to embed itself everywhere, albeit hard to notice at times – from cinema and advertising soundtracks to the often pointlessly byzantine prog of Emerson, Lake and Palmer to soul records such as the Four Tops' 1970 album *Still*

Waters Run Deep. It was a delightful selection, ranging from the would-be commercial to the fiercely non-commercial, exciting a gamut of responses, from wonder to laughter. There were fiercely experimental outings, such as Douglas Leedy's album *Entropical Paradise* and free jazz by Burton Greene and Sun Ra. There were interventions on popular songs, such as Simon and Garfunkel's 'Save the Life of My Child' (from the 1968 album *Bookends*), on which Moog himself played the instrument. However, much of the music seemed only to simulate rather than supplant existing styles and instruments. Wendy Carlos's *Switched on Bach,* for example, merely replaces the wood from which the original Bach works are hewn with luminous plastic. It triggered a number of follow-ups, including *Switched on Rock* and even *Switched on Country*, in which old standards are given fuzzy, dayglo Moog coatings. There were cover versions, including one of 'What's New Pussycat?' (by Christopher Scott, from the album *Switched on Bacharach*), in which the Moog mewls imitatively. MOR artists such as American orchestra leader Hugo Montenegro, with his 1969 album *Moog Power*, also embraced the instrument. Rather than groundbreaking, however, this eruption of Moog music seems to create a kitsch coating. The instrument's tones feel very much of their era, like Tupperware parties, hot pants and the Mini Moke. While there certainly are sunken Moog treasures from the late 1960s and early '70s that are still worthy of investigation and plunder, so often the sound of the Moog feels like not so much a harbinger of the imminent demolition of rock, more a novelty, a fashion accessory, signifying a Robbie the Robot-style future, but one which is a long way away as yet.

This was not for want of trying on the part of Bernie Krause and his musical partner Paul Beaver, Moog's 'representatives' on the west coast, who offered their musical services to some two hundred and fifty artists in the late 1960s, including the Monkees, whose 'Daily, Nightly' is believed to be the first record to feature the instrument. The Monterey Pop Festival of 1967, at which the Moog was unveiled, certainly led to a surge in musicians exploring to some degree the possibilities of synthesized sounds. George Harrison was among them. He recorded the album *Electronic Sound* on the Zapple Label, the experimental wing of Apple. If parts of it sound like a demonstration of Moog technology, that's because that's precisely what it was. Krause had offered to demonstrate the Moog synthesizer to Harrison, who recorded the demonstration and put it out as side two of the album, with the credit 'assisted by Bernie Krause'. An enraged Krause took legal action.

Although the Moog features on *Abbey Road*, on 'Maxwell's Silver Hammer' and 'Here Comes the Sun', it's peripheral, as was the Moog's impact on the Beatles' later output and the rock of the era as a whole. The Rolling Stones couldn't muster any interest at all for the new instrument. There's comical footage from that era online of a stoned-looking Keith Richards messing somewhat cluelessly with the input leads of a custom-built modular synth; it's like watching an infant playing with Lego for the first time. Mick Jagger actually owned a Moog synthesizer but later sold it, with the instrument eventually falling into the hands of Tangerine Dream at a cost of $15,000. Pete Townshend achieved some great arpeggiated effects on 1971's 'Baba O'Riley', but ultimately he became exasperated by the cumbersome and temperamental nature of the instrument. Frank Zappa's early albums with the Mothers of Invention make occasional forays into musique concrète, a conscious homage on the part of a rock artist unusually conversant with twentieth-century developments in classical music. As his career wore on, however, he became more preoccupied with jazz-rock and guitar soloing.

Resistance was cultural also. For all its futurist credulity and open-mindedness, 1960s rock culture had a strong, romantically agrarian streak. The truth lay in the fields, among the daisies and the trees. Synthesizers did not sit well in such dreams. Furthermore, the individual expressionism of the era came to fullest flower in rock-guitar prowess. The axe-wielding heroes were the gods of the day: great, pretty much exclusively male players who were yet to experience the interrogative rigours of feminist deconstruction, uninhibited by as yet unspoken accusations of phallic symbolism in their playing. Page, Clapton, Beck and, of course, Hendrix were judged by their dexterity and virtuosity. They played electric, but had they expressed themselves through knobs, dials, tape loops and keyboards, they would have forfeited their prestige somewhat. Synthesizers, then as now, had little to do with 'virtuosity' in the time-honoured sense. They required a different skill set, one that struck diehard rockists as suspiciously passionless and schematic. Guitar heroes, men whose stardom depended on striking poses of sinewy passion, eschewed them. Pink Floyd created 'On the Run' for *Dark Side of the Moon*, a scurrying piece that involved feeding an eight-note sequence into an AMS synthesizer, but this felt more like a brief demonstration of stereophonic modernity rather than any serious exploration of a new instrumental dimension in which guitars would be forsaken or their hegemony destabilised. Queen made a point of stating on their album sleeves that they did not use synthesizers. Like many 'proper' rock musicians of the era, they regarded them as a form of cheating.

(That said, Jimi Hendrix's *Electric Ladyland* is perhaps the closest we have to an album that combines electric-guitar virtuosity with electronic invention, which is one of the reasons why, to my mind, it is the greatest rock album ever made. '1983 . . . (A Merman I Should Turn to Be)' is as much a feat of soundboarding as fretboarding, with engineer Eddie Kramer a co-participant in a real-time creative process that saw him 'flying around the mixing desk', tweaking and adjusting Hendrix's playing; the result is a piece of honorary electronica, conveying in a way no live electric guitar could the sense of immersive, fantastical, oceanic descent described in the song's lyric.)

The 1970s saw the gradual encroachment of synthesizers and electronics. The West German Krautrock movement, which included Kraftwerk, Faust and Tangerine Dream, embraced electronics out of a deep-seated cultural need to create a new sense of national cultural identity rather than subsist on the imposed rock'n'roll 'Marshall Plan' of Anglo-American rock and beat music. Elsewhere, and way beneath the attention of most music critics, female artists like Annette Peacock and Suzanne Ciani were undertaking expeditions into the expressive possibilities of synthesizers; being ignored at least enabled them to develop their work in an untrammelled, uncompromised, freely exploratory way. Meanwhile, Brian Eno was making his own forays into ambient, bringing among other things a visual art sensibility to bear on music-making.

The late 1970s also saw an abrupt spike in activity thanks to the mass production of cheap synths, exported from Japan in particular, and a sudden proliferation of terse, spitting proto-electropop that was antithetical to the somewhat cathedral-like, ostentatious splendour of keyboard-driven 1970s prog. There was no stalling now, no touching back down on hippy earth. Kraftwerk, Robert Rental, Cabaret Voltaire, Giorgio Moroder and others represented between them the launch of the perma-electric.

Japan's role in determining the technological course of the remainder of the twentieth century was personified by the Yellow Magic Orchestra. Ryuichi Sakamoto declared that they 'invented technopop'. They didn't. However, on albums such as 1981's *Technodelic* they did introduce a range of new electronic timbres and techniques, thanks to their ground-floor exposure to breakthroughs in synth technology in their own country. As Kraftwerk did with Germany, so YMO played with obliquely Western perceptions of Japan. Their origins were in kitsch, paying homage to the exotica soundtracks of Martin Denny and the like. Their expert use of new synths added a shimmering, modernistic sheen to their witty, cartoon, oriental otherness, implying that the new electronic age was bathed in the light of a sun rising in the East.

One of the first groups to provide a jolting reminder in my fourth-form days that 1980 was imminent was the American group Devo, who with singles like 'Jocko Homo' burst in on the common-room tribes of punks, metalheads and Genesis-lovers like comedy jumpsuited aliens who had tumbled down from a wormhole. But theirs was a message born out of despair for mankind's hopes, antithetical to Kraftwerk. As Devo's Jerry Casale told me, the origins of the group were not in speculative dreams of life in the year 1983 but in actual events that took place in the year 1973, the year of the massacre of demonstrating students at Kent State University, to which Casale and fellow group member Mark Mothersbaugh had been witnesses.

'That crystallised it for me in all seriousness,' Casale said. 'When the National Guard started shooting at people, I was in the middle of it. And those students they shot at were eighteen, maybe nineteen, just middle-class kids objecting to Nixon expanding the war into Cambodia. And they just sprayed that crowd with live 16mm bullets.

'We were all just running – and I saw an exit wound come out of one student lying on the ground dead, the size of a coffee saucer. That snapped me – how brute force and power control the planet, control information, control spin.'

'Snap' is the word. Devo had about them a certain punitive urgency, particularly evidenced on 'Whip It' (1980), which, like Heaven 17's '(We Don't Need No) Fascist Groove Thang', parodied the accelerated martial air that marked the sharp right political turn at the beginning of the decade. (It wasn't an S&M song.) 'We were being criminal with the synthesisers,' agreed Casale. 'We like the primal energy of rock'n'roll, we just disliked the artifice and convention of mid-1970s arena rock – we wanted to bring it back down to something like a paramilitary group.

'We were trying to show teamwork and precision rather than the cult of individuality. There were other groups using synths in a way that was pretty, spacey and saccharine. We wanted to use them in a nasty way, mixing them in with guitar music.'

'You Thought Devo Were Weird? Time You Met the Residents', read a headline in *Melody Maker* in 1978. Only 'meeting' the Residents was apparently impossible. They took the depersonalisation of electronic music to extremes, refusing to divulge their identities, appearing in press photos in staged shots with giant eyeballs over their heads – the gaze of pop reversed. Their masterpiece was 1979's *Eskimo*, made with the assistance of Don Preston, a former Mother of Invention, on synthesizers. Each track was accompanied by a text outlining a short story purportedly concerning the everyday lives or legends of the Inuit people of the Arctic. The tracks themselves, made using home-made instruments, chants and electronic effects, would represent an exact sonic transcription of each of these narratives. Take 'Arctic Hysteria', for example, in which (mostly) female Inuits are driven temporarily insane by their environment. In burgeoning, circling, whited-out tones, the synths vividly depict the cruelly overwhelming ambient conditions. Like the *Hörspiel* mooted by Delia Derbyshire and Barry Bermange on their 1960s collaborations, this was a whole new mode of electronic expression that was never fully explored subsequently.

Cheap synths and post-punk electropop, the sudden toppling of assumptions about the superiority of white Anglo-American rock, Donna Summer, the rise of microchip technology, Kraftwerk's *The Man-Machine* – all of this amounted to a spike for twentieth-century electronic music, a point at which it seemed both ubiquitous and strange. For me, its impact felt most severe when it cut diagonally through rock music – angular, abstract interventions. Faust had specialised in this: for example, the sudden analogue dental-drill shriek that erupts in their otherwise pastoral

'It's a Bit of a Pain', from 1973's *Faust IV*. Others followed. PiL, for example, who had their post-punk sensibility honed in 1978, while Joy Division were still in gestation as Warsaw. They frequently adopted a hostile stance towards their audiences, which often comprised lumpen punksters who expected lead singer John Lydon to carry on in *Never Mind the Bollocks* vein. They had other ideas, however, such as giant video screens erected at gigs, ideas intended to taunt and confound, deconstruct/reconstruct, (post) modernise rather than crudely 'destroy'.

Key to this was Keith Levene's use of the Prophet 5 synthesizer. It's most stark on the PiL live album *Paris au Printemps*, released in 1980 and comprising recordings made at Le Palace in Paris in January of that year, wheeling massively through the closing stages of 'Theme' and coming to earth with a jackhammer impact, grinding to a halt, then dying in a rippling, analogue detonation, its reverberations resounding around the room. Or on the live version of 'Careering', grinding and breaking tarmac, intervening with huge, zigzag sirens. The synths feel like deliberate, aggressive broadsides, intended to galvanise and challenge their audience, with whom it feels PiL are in a stand-off, bordering on hostility. Electric-shock treatment.

Allen Ravenstine had a similar role in Pere Ubu, as evidenced on their great trio of late-1970s albums, *The Modern Dance* (1978), *Dub Housing* (1978) and *New Picnic Time* (1979). He had been a noisehead since 1971, when he was also a pothead, sitting around an apartment in Lakewood, Ohio, listening with an artist friend to the sounds generated by oscillators adapted from fuzztones plugged into a stereo. He then moved on to a four-track player and, later, flush from a trust fund left to him by his parents, who had died when he was in his teens, an EMS synthesizer.

It was this instrument, beyond the means of most garage/punk groups starting out at the time, that he used in Pere Ubu. Tracking the wavering, gibbering emotions of vocalist David Thomas, the sliding contours of Tom Herman's guitars and the rumbling, hollowed percussion of the rhythm section, Ravenstine's role is to deploy his array of patches to supplement these songs in a variety of ways: as an escape valve for their inner energies, like the steam-kettle effect on 'Non-Alignment Pact'; to sketch their neurological workings; to mirror them in the abstract; to render them in wave patterns. All of this he achieved through a series of shrieks, chatters, bubbles, rattles, bleeps and boosts that sound like what Russolo could only have wished to achieve when he applied the levers on his primitive intonarumori back in 1913.

The likes of PiL and Ubu apart, however, electronics overhauled pop and rock in the 1980s in what was a serene and bloodless coup, as evidenced by the sheer pop efficiency with which, say, Orchestral Manoeuvres in the Dark went about their work, led by the Kraftwerk-inspired Andy McCluskey. Far from being alien, quirky or novel, he and OMD showed that electronics were the natural language of new pop and, as if to prove his point, he later became a successful songwriter for Atomic Kitten, among others.

The rewiring was complete by the 1980s. Even Bruce Springsteen and Leonard Cohen felt obliged to smatter their albums with synth effects, so as not to appear anachronistic. Devo, ironically, suffered as a result of this ubiquity and were dropped in 1985.

'We were visual artists using music,' said Casale. 'We only used that stuff in the first place because it fit those ideas. We weren't even trying to do what ended up being done, that candified Flock of Seagulls-style electropop. At one point we didn't quite know where to go. It gets ugly. It gets weird. Business does you in. I wanted to make huge, primitive, frightening Led Zeppelin-style songs but with the same lyrical content. But we didn't go there as a band. Some of the other guys weren't comfy with it and the record company were saying, "Give us another 'Whip It'!"'

The ubiquity of electronics also affected Kraftwerk, who, their foundational work done, duly withdrew from recording further albums, though they have carried on as an increasingly successful live operation since. With rave, the emphasis shifted from electropop bands to a stream of vinyl, from the urbane to the peripheral – a revisitation of the hippy fields again, as raves took place beyond the M25 and tripping clubbers rediscovered the intoxicating joy, in abeyance for years, of gathering en masse.

The 1990s saw the rise of techno and drum 'n' bass. This seized the imagination of a group of Warwick University-based academics, led by Sadie Plant and Nick Land, self-described cyberpunks who, with almost mystical fervour, saw in the new electronically driven dance movements the possibility of 'accelerationism' – the soundtrack to capitalism hastening its own demise. Forget those fusty old bearded college Marxists sitting around waiting for capitalism to die of its own contradictions; rather, let it crash and burn as a result of its own turbo-charged momentum. Drum 'n' bass's fast-cut, hyperspeed backbeats felt like accelerationism embodied. Vocals were tweaked once more, à la Joe Meek, to Pinky & Perky-style falsettos, as if to suggest the sudden fast-forward pace of things.

Cyberpunk got it wrong. So bent were its leaders on defying leftist orthodoxy that some of them, including Plant, embraced aspects of Thatcherite ideology, such as opposition to the welfare system, which, Plant felt, maintained an inertia among the lower classes. In the early 1990s, cyberpunk must have felt like a theoretical way forward, a wormhole to a post-capitalist idyll. However, the future did not pan out that way. Drum 'n' bass, far from opening up a new expanse of techno-rhythmical options, rapidly became codified, its tropes surprisingly easy to assimilate. Before long, even gardening programmes seeking to add an injection of hipness reached for the simple option of incorporating a snatch of drum 'n' bass into their theme tunes. Nor did cyberpunk anticipate the dampening, ubiquitous effects of the Internet, which has been a dominant cultural force since the switch from dial-up to broadband in most homes around the turn of the millennium.

The current century – the post-rock and post-pop century – is harder to read. There has been a mushrooming of activity, a rhizome-like effect of underground interconnections, a proliferation that can only be done justice through mixed metaphors. Microsounds and disintegration, 50 million shades of ambient, retro-futurism, minimalism, maximalism; conversely, a superstar elite of DJs and EDM artists like Skrillex who have created a heavy-metal-style, major language out of electronic music, cranking up the decibels, blackening every pixel, accentuating the directness and the simplicity, filling arenas and stadia; though even EDM, cranked perpetually to the max, may be on the wane, having allowed itself no further place to go.

Where now? A million pathways to the future. Or maybe no future. A super-saturation, or maybe a sense that nothing is happening, or likely to happen. This sense of paradoxical cultural malaise has been with us for a while; maybe it's the permanent condition. But there have never quite been times like 2017 – so scarily unpredictable, yet pregnant with possibilities. The far right seems to be on the rise; polemical Canadian hip-hoppers Consolidated's crunching 1992 anthem 'This Is Fascism' suddenly feels less like dystopian hyperbole, more a horribly apt précis of the state of play at the time of writing.

What is certain, however, is that as the long echo of the twentieth century continues to resound, electronic music has built up a heritage, one that pre-dates rock and even jazz; a musical one whose implications, indeed whose very existence has only recently become clearer. It's a history of daft fears and lost hopes, cul-de-sacs and vistas, of taboos and transcendence; it is the ultimate means whereby music makes it, exceeds itself in previously untold ways, and those who play it exceed themselves. Pierre Boulez, the post-war composer and conductor, and founder of IRCAM in Paris, described the classical world of tonal music and thought as reflecting pre-twentieth-century science, in which the forces of gravity and attraction played a defining role. He described twentieth-century serial music as a system defined by a universe in 'perpetual expansion'. The same could be said for electronic music, which used serial music as a jumping-off point.

Electronic music has been dogged by fascist connotations. Luigi Russolo, author of the founding manifesto of electronic, noise and futurist music, was a fascist. The accusation has reared up again in the era of industrial/dance music, with some artists and listeners dangerously seduced by the tyranny of the beat. And yet electronic music at its most open-ended and experimental, conceptually ambitious and paradigmatic is the ideal soundtrack for the anti-fascist liberation mindset – a liberator of gender and race from dull-earth dogma, offering imaginary alternatives to every sort of stifling, oppressive orthodoxy and prejudice, scrambling the signals and imperatives bombarded at us on a daily basis, subtly seeking to influence our behaviour in the ongoing war between us and the increasingly elusive, almost abstract powers that be. The music of infinite colour and free choice. A music of the twentieth century that could yet provide the architecture for the imagination of the twenty-first. A music whose long past speaks about a future that might not be as forfeited as postmodern despair can make it seem.

PART ONE

1

ELECTRONICS: A PREHISTORY

We have also sound-houses, where we practise and demonstrate all sounds and their generation. We have harmonies, which you have not, of quarter-sounds and lesser slides of sounds. Divers instruments of music likewise to you unknown, some sweeter than any you have, together with bells and rings that are dainty and sweet. We represent small sounds as great and deep, likewise great sounds extenuate and sharp; we make divers tremblings and warblings of sounds, which in their original are entire. We represent and imitate all articulate sounds and letters, and the voices and notes of beasts and birds. We have certain helps which set to the ear do further the hearing greatly. We also have divers strange and artificial echoes, reflecting the voice many times, and as it were tossing it, and some that give back the voice louder than it came, some shriller and some deeper; yea, some rendering the voice differing in the letters or articulate sound from that they receive. We have also means to convey sounds in trunks and pipes, in strange lines and distances.

This passage, a copy of which Daphne Oram nailed to the wall in her workplace, is the founding stone of electronic music practice, its first articulation. It's by Francis Bacon, written in his utopian text *New Atlantis*, published posthumously in 1626 and set on the fictional island of Bensalem, which is peopled by a society of devotional inhabitants whose days are spent in praise to God and in futuristic research towards a new enlightenment. Bacon may not have written the works of Shakespeare, but he did experience and set down this fleeting mental illumination, which anticipates the musical element that we at times take drearily for granted today. It's a passage which shows that the dreams and desires ingrained in electronic music, derided in its time as flat, automated and emotionless, aren't merely the product of the mechanical age that made the music possible; that they have glowed faintly, repressed and unrealised, in the mind of humanity for centuries. Bacon's passage is a rare foretelling of the shape of sound to come, anticipating loop pedals, samplers, synthesizers, studios and the primacy of instruments even in an era when instruments of any kind were considered lowly, man-made, peasantly contraptions and choral music the highest and nearest-to-Godly mode of expression.

'Music is the electrical soil in which the soul lives, thinks and invents. I myself am of an electrical nature. Everything electric stimulates the spirit to fluent, precipitous, musical creation.' This quote has been attributed to Beethoven, though it may in fact have come from his friend Bettina von Armin, corresponding to Goethe's mother. In Beethoven's time, the word 'electricity' had gained traction following Michael Faraday's bold experiments around 1752 with a wet kite to demonstrate the electrical nature of lightning, electricity's most spectacular manifestation in the pre-technological world. Certainly, some of the jolting, tempestuous phrases that punctuate Beethoven's most famous works sound lightning-like in their thunderous, luminous brevity, breaking like epiphanies across the troubled skies of the Romantic era. The eighteenth century also brought us Mary Shelley's *Frankenstein; or, The Modern Prometheus*, which involved galvanism, whereby a muscle contracts when stimulated by an electrical current. Beethoven tried galvanism in a vain attempt to cure his deafness; the use of electricity as a means of physical therapy was very much in vogue at the time, with rumours of miracle cures rife. For the composer, however, the treatment amounted to a series of unpleasant shocks. What he suffered feels like a metaphor for later generations' exposure to the first bracing assaults of electronic music.

Proto-electronic instruments began to appear tentatively at this time. There was the Denis d'or, invented by Václav Prokop Diviš (1698–1765), an 'electro-acoustic' instrument where the piano strings are vibrated using electromagnets, and a prototype of the later orchestrion. However, it is suspected that the qualities of this instrument were attributed retrospectively and that in fact it was merely a prank device whereby the inventor could administer electric shocks to anyone who tried to play it. Later came the clavecin électrique, constructed by Jesuit priest Jean-Baptiste Delaborde in Paris in 1759, a keyboard instrument that used a static electrical charge to make metal bells vibrate, creating an organ-like effect. Drawings show an elaborate loom-like device. Despite its prescience and aeolian pretensions, it seems that its effects were more trouble to create than they were worth – the instrument wasn't developed further. The Swiss inventor Matthäus Hipp was credited in 1867 with an 'electromechanical piano', possibly based on the workings of a tuning fork, but never bothered to develop the instrument commercially.

It was in America, alongside the invention of player pianos, that the commercial possibilities of electrically driven instruments first made significant headway, thanks to the prodigal talent and prodigious energy of one Thaddeus Cahill, a Washington-based, 115-pound hyper-metabolic human dynamo whose business instincts matched his scientific acumen. It was 1893, and Cahill, a child prodigy, had been working on various inventions since his late teens, specialising in keyboards (he was in the process of developing an electric typewriter). It occurred to him that the tones produced by conventional musical instruments could be produced with electrical dynamos, tones generated from some central device that could simulate all of the qualities of instruments such

as violins and pianos but mechanically iron out their defects. He
was influenced in his thinking by the German scientist Hermann
von Helmholtz, whose 1862 book *On the Sensations of Tone* had
been translated into English in 1877. Essentially, von Helmholtz
showed that there was more to a musical note than was suggested
by the seemingly irreducible black symbol written on a piece of
paper; that it was made of component parts – harmonics – that created distinguishable 'tone colours', which were what distinguished
different instruments playing the same note. This was vital knowledge to those, like Cahill, who were in the business of devising
machines to synthesize sound. It brought music into the realms
of science and engineering, opened it up as a potential palette
rather than a mere notational system. The technicolour twentieth
century was at hand. Von Helmholtz himself even constructed a
simple 'synthesizer' to help illustrate his point. Moreover, with the
invention of Alexander Graham Bell's telephone, Cahill envisaged
that his instrument would have the power to replace entire orchestras and be broadcast telephonically across the country, bringing
classical music and opera to the masses.

The name of Cahill's instrument would be the Telharmonium,
which would go through various versions, with its inner workings
ensuring it weighed in at 200 tons. As Reynold Weidenaar wrote
in his 1995 study *Magic Music from the Telharmonium*:

> His guiding vision was twofold: a machine that could produce
> scientifically perfect tones, and absolute control of these tones
> to a mathematical certainty by mechanical means. Such fine
> control should allow the player to express all his spellbinding
> emotion with the surging power and intensity of a violinist
> – with as little mechanical impediment as possible. The tone
> should be sustained indefinitely, like an organ, but should
> yield willingly to the musician's touch with absolute sympathy
> and sensitivity. The instrument must of course retain the chord

capacity of the piano or organ. Thus could the defects of the three great domesticated musical instruments – piano, organ, and violin – be consigned to oblivion.

All of this would come at a cost, however – $200,000. And so Cahill and his business partners put on a demonstration for a group of businessmen in Baltimore. He arranged for them to hear a performance of 'Handel's Largo', played in Washington and broadcast by phone via a horn attached to the receiver. The gambit was successful and they agreed to put up $100,000 as a first instalment for the licence to distribute Telharmonic performances and construct the first commercial version of the instrument.

News of the Telharmonium spread, even across the Atlantic to Britain's Lord Kelvin, whose scientific endeavours included an early attempt to determine the age of the planet earth. He invited Cahill to deliver a paper on the subject of the Telharmonium in London. Meanwhile, work began on the huge rotor mechanisms required to develop the instrument and create 'tonal pigments' to simulate the sounds of orchestral instruments. Finally, in 1905, the Telharmonium was up and ready to be installed in New York, and for its sounds to be broadcast to thousands of hotels, theatres and restaurants across the country. These establishments were only too keen for a musical broadcast system, having had to work with large human orchestras to supply discreet music to their patrons, not always very discreetly or inconspicuously.

The initial feedback in response to the Telharmonium was mixed. There were complaints that its broadcasts were interfering with the telephone wires used for domestic calls. One man, it was said, had phoned his wife one evening to say he was working late at the office, only for the interfering Telharmonium strains of 'William Tell' to strike up on a crossed wire, convincing his angry spouse that he was making whoopee at some good-time joint. There were complaints too from the musicians about the immense difficulty of playing the instrument's complex rig of keyboards, despite their supposed labour-saving properties. Meanwhile, orchestral musicians themselves naturally viewed the new machine with great suspicion, regarding it not unreasonably as a device to catapult them onto the breadline. Others found the sounds generated by the Telharmonium a touch . . . synthetic. They missed the authentic rasp of traditional instruments, whose 'defects' they regarded as integral to their character.

Others, however, appreciated the unnaturally sweet, sonorous sounds produced by the Telharmonium, as well as being astonished by the sheer fact that they were attending to live sounds broadcast from many miles away. Mark Twain, on hearing the Telharmonium, declared, 'The trouble about these beautiful, novel things is that they interfere so with one's arrangements. Every time I see or hear a new wonder like this I have to postpone my death right off. I couldn't possibly leave the world until I have heard this again and again.' The writer Ray Stannard Baker was an early enthusiast for the machine, especially its ability to bring music, once the sole province of the wealthy, to everyday people, thereby 'democratising' music the way libraries had with books and galleries with art. He acknowledged the effect this would have on working musicians but noted as a positive that this would mean fewer strikes; furthermore, those specimens of antiquity who had to scrape a living sawing on bowstrings and parping into wind instruments would in the future have a niche appeal to those who appreciated their olde worlde charm, persisting as candelabras and horses did in the electric light and automobile age.

By 1907, however, the Telharmonium was in desperate trouble. In terms of revenue Cahill and co. weren't reaping anything like enough to cover their maintenance costs and salaries. 'The times are hard, applicant is poor, the expense is burdensome,' groaned Cahill. The arrival of other technologies, such as player pianos and Wurlitzers, with wireless radio also heaving in from the horizon, made the Telharmonium, for which dispensation had been granted to lay its own cable system just a short while earlier, seem very old, obsolete and unwieldy hat. The Telharmonium was a harbinger of the future, but its own future was shadowed by a mountain of debt. Bankruptcy followed. The Telharmonium was a dinosaur of the pre-Futurist age, laid low by its 200-ton ambitions, high maintenance, immobility and inability to adapt.

Cahill persisted passionately with the Telharmonium long after the game was clearly up; it was his life's passion, one which superseded his cooler business instincts. And yet it is not easy to root for him. He seems to have lived and died by the sword of obsolescence. One of the deeply ambivalent motifs of the history of electronic music is the impact it has had on the livelihood of musicians. Cahill was untroubled by this. Furthermore, Cahill himself does not seem to have been overly interested in the possibilities represented by his invention for the expansion of music as an art form. His interests were technical niceties, patents, mass broadcast and production. As for the stuff produced by the Telharmonium, he was quite happy for it to consist of no more than the long-established popular classics, merely disseminated with an electrical component.

When news of the instrument reached Europe, however, its Futurist aesthetic possibilities were immediately seized upon. In his *Sketch of a New Esthetic of Music*, written in 1906, the same year that Picasso's *Les Demoiselles d'Avignon* effectively inaugurated modern visual art, the Italian composer Ferruccio Busoni embraced the concept of the Telharmonium, which he'd read about in Ray Stannard Baker's recent article. He rhapsodised on its possibilities for liberating the composer from traditional systems:

Who has not dreamt that he could float on air? And believed his dream to be reality? Let us take thought, how music may be restored to its primitive, natural essence; let us free it from

architectural, acoustic and aesthetic dogmas; let it be pure
invention and sentiment, in harmonies, in form, in tone-
colours (for invention and sentiment are not the prerogative
of melody alone); let it follow the line of the rainbow and vie
with the clouds in breaking sunbeams; let Music be naught
else than Nature mirrored by and reflected from the human
breast; for it is sounding air and floats above and beyond the
air . . .

Florid and orotund as his prose was, it expressed the possibility of instruments like the Telharmonium enabling music to take
flight from the elaborate classical apparatus that had built up by
the late nineteenth century and realise a Promethean liberation
first posited in the early part of that century.

In 1916, Edgard Varèse fetched up in America. A future inspiration to Frank Zappa, among others, he spent most of his career
as a composer awaiting the instruments that would truly articulate the 'noise' of the twentieth century and the deeper, elemental
forces their unleashing signified. He was naturally keen to hear the
Telharmonium and made directly for West 56th Street, where the
latest version of the instrument was stationed. By this time, however, it was effectively a museum piece. The composer whose music
anticipated technologies yet to be invented had the misfortune to
arrive in New York in the post-Telharmonium age. He was disappointed by the machine, and perhaps little wonder: sound-wise,
its most direct bequest has been the humble Hammond organ. In
principle, though, it represented something quite new, quite else
and quite vast to come.

2

FUTURISM AND THE BIRTH OF NOISE

In October 2016, the French newspaper *Le Figaro* is a typically staid, urbane European newspaper, its cover featuring a selection of smartly dressed men and women caught in the act of negotiating Europe's uncertain future. The main image is one of a female, arms crossed to show she means business, the main headline referring to a new cold war between France and Russia, accompanied by a photograph of Nicolas Sarkozy and Vladimir Putin in grim conference. Back in 1909, *Le Figaro* was even more staid, its pages barely encumbered with photographs at all. However, on 20 February of that year, readers of the journal would have been stirred to peruse on that edition's front page a manifesto, composed by one F. T. Marinetti, whose aim was to shatter like crockery and sweep aside like yellowing lace tablecloths every time-honoured assumption about the world as it was presently cosily and elaborately constituted. This was the *Founding and Manifesto of Futurism*, the latter a word that has become common coinage in ways even its author couldn't have imagined, unless premonitions of Tubeway Army materialised in his fertile, speculative imagination. Its desire was to electrify, and electrify, ultimately, it did.

It loses nothing in translation. Above all else, Marinetti was a master of prose whose every giddy swerve of phrase has the power to intoxicate, even more than a century later. Its opening passages are aromatic with fervour, designed to seep insidiously into the nostrils of the ardent young aesthete. Rather than getting down to the bullet points of the manifesto, or abiding by any newspaper sub-editor's style guide about the information to be set out in the opening paragraph of a front-page story, he sets the scene amid the sumptuous, even decadent surroundings of his quarters. Marinetti had been brought up in Alexandria, Egypt, and was accustomed to a world of exotic imported privilege. Indeed, it was only with the assistance of an old friend of his father from the Alexandria days, the Pasha Mohammed el Rachi, an Egyptian ex-minister who resided in Paris and owned a large number of shares in *Le Figaro*, that Marinetti was able to pull off the improbable stunt of placing the manifesto of an avant-garde art movement on the front page of one of Europe's most respectable mainstream newspapers.

'We had stayed up all night, my friends and I, under hanging mosque lamps with domes of filigreed brass, domes starred like our spirits, shining like them with the prisoned radiance of electric hearts. For hours we had trampled our atavistic ennui into rich oriental rugs, arguing up to the last confines of logic and blackening many reams of paper with our frenzied scribbling.'

Thereafter, the atmosphere thickens, the air pervaded and enriched by the stench and noise of trundling trams and locomotives, their mechanical force representing the unbound energies of a new century. The more putrid stench of the old world abides too: the 'old canal muttering its feeble prayers'. Next moment, Marinetti and his friends set out on an early-morning adventure: an automobile ride, exhilarating and richly metaphorical. This is no mere joyride; they are in pursuit of Death itself, 'its dark pelt blotched with pale crosses as it escaped down the vast violet living and throbbing sky'.

Marinetti comes a cropper in his car as two wobbly cyclists approach like a 'stupid dilemma', their lack of certitude causing the author to skid into a ditch. Such an incident did actually befall Marinetti, but in this manifesto he proudly presents it as a rebirth. The mud he swallows is as life-giving as 'the blessed black breast of my Sudanese nurse . . . When I came up – torn, filthy, and stinking

– from under the capsized car, I felt the white-hot iron of joy deliciously pass through my heart!' With the help of passers-by he revives the car like a 'big, beached shark', and with a single caress it snorts back into life. Engine roaring once more, his readership – those willingly swept up in his prose at any rate – are presented with the points of the manifesto. These celebrate virtues, some of which he has already demonstrated so thrillingly: 'aggressive action, a feverish insomnia, the racer's stride, the mortal leap, the punch and the slap. We affirm that the world's magnificence has been enriched by a new beauty: the beauty of speed.'

All of these are brought into play to obliterate all artistic and cultural achievement hitherto, which has settled into a complacent, senile inertia. Marinetti and the Futurists reserved a deep contempt for those artistic guardians who set on high the stuff of pre-industrial art – its peasantry, glades and bowls of fruit on rustic wooden tables – while regarding with sniffy disdain the products of the machine age even as they enjoyed the comforts and conveniences they brought. All of this was dismissed with the contemptuous epithet 'passéism'. Italy, the primary consideration of the nationalist Marinetti, needed to be freed from passéism's curators, 'its smelly gangrene of professors, archaeologists, *ciceroni* and antiquarians'.

As well as grandly celebrating himself and his little band of artists as conjurors of 'primordial elements' summoning forth a lava of modernity that would drench the mass graveyard of the heretofore, Marinetti celebrated with convincing and uncritical poetic exuberance the industrial age, the 'vibrant nightly fervour of arsenals and shipyards blazing with violent electric moons; greedy railway stations that devour smoke-plumed serpents; factories hung on clouds by the crooked lines of their smoke; bridges that stride the rivers like giant gymnasts . . . and the sleek flight of planes whose propellers chatter in the wind like banners and seem to cheer like an enthusiastic crowd'.

Amid this came the most provocative, troubling and, to many, including the poet Gertrude Stein, obnoxious elements of the manifesto: 'We will glorify war – the world's only hygiene – militarism, patriotism, the destructive gesture of freedom-bringers, beautiful ideas worth dying for, and scorn for woman.' By 'woman', it was later argued, Marinetti meant the shackles of domesticity, though he himself married and the Futurists themselves were fathers to daughters, lovers, as well as women themselves in certain instances, while enthusiasts like the beautiful heiress Luisa Casati, who declared her desire to be a 'living work of art', functioned as a muse to the movement.

However, Marinetti also declared himself dead against 'moralism, feminism and every other form of utilitarian cowardice', and stated that art should 'be nothing but violence, cruelty and injustice'. He would try to clarify this in a later essay, *Scorn for Women*, a somewhat convoluted tract in which he seemed to honour the merits of womankind while nonetheless concluding, 'Feminism is a political error. Feminism is an intellectual error on the part of women, an error which their instinct will eventually recognise. IT ISN'T NECESSARY TO GIVE WOMEN ANY OF THE RIGHTS DEMANDED BY FEMINISM. TO ACCORD THEM THESE RIGHTS WOULDN'T PRODUCE ANY OF THE DISORDERS SOUGHT BY THE FUTURISTS, BUT ON THE CONTRARY WOULD BRING ABOUT AN EXCESS OF ORDER.'

Such a man was Marinetti: anarchist, visionary, poet, emancipator, prose genius, showman, artistic benefactor, herald of modernity, nationalist, reactionary, the man who provided the rhetorical framework that would initiate electronic music in the twentieth century, fascist.

Unlike previous or concurrent art movements such as cubism, Futurism had a programme for the entire transformation of society. Italy would come first, of course, but then civilisation as a whole would tumble to the forces already scraping their metallic hooves and snorting fire. The visual arts would be looked after by artists like Umberto Boccioni, who would make dynamism and synaesthesia a factor in their works. Then there was architecture (Antonio Sant'Elia), men's clothing (of which Giacomo Balla took care in his *Futurist Manifesto of Men's Clothing*, calling for the abolition of 'passéist clothes, and everything about them which is tight-fitting, colourless, funereal, decadent, boring and unhygienic'), cuisine – and music, which was the province of the composer and musicologist Francesco Pratella. However, it was hard to discern anything particularly Futurist about his compositional efforts, which, like Pratella himself, are mostly forgotten. The true Futurist, and the one whose legacy has most endured, was one of the movement's relative dilettantes, albeit a determined autodidact.

Luigi Russolo was frankly a mediocre painter. His efforts to convey synaesthesia on his canvasses by means of billowing coloured ribbons emerging from a keyboard are more banally illustrative than mind-blowing. But it was with his *Art of Noises* manifesto that the twentieth century was declared open – to the prospect of music, noise, environment, machine crashing together to create the waves whose motions are the stuff of our daily lives.

Published in 1913, *The Art of Noises* is presented humbly to Russolo's colleague 'My dear Pratella', with the artist signing off as 'Luigi Russolo – painter', as if graciously to stress that his ideas are being imported into the medium of music by an outsider, rather than arising from any formal classical training. Fraternally, he recalls standing shoulder to shoulder with the composer, fists and canes flying, at a typically fractious Futurism event in Rome, where a tear-up with the audience was considered absolutely essential to the occasion; polite applause, the like of which they received when they brought their roadshow to the UK, was considered by Marinetti to represent failure.

He then outlines the epiphany that leapt to his 'intuitive mind'
– a new art for a new century:

> In antiquity, life was nothing but silence. Noise was really
> not born before the nineteenth century, with the advent of
> machinery. Today noise reigns supreme over human sensibility.
> For several centuries, life went on silently, or mutedly. The
> loudest noises were neither intense, nor prolonged nor varied.
> In fact, nature is normally silent, except for storms, hurricanes,
> avalanches, cascades and some exceptional telluric movements.

All this had changed with the advent of the machine age:

> [We] are approaching noise-sound. This revolution of music is
> paralleled by the increasing proliferation of machinery sharing
> in human labour. In the pounding atmosphere of great cities
> as well as in the formerly silent countryside, machines create
> today such a large number of varied noises that pure sound,
> with its littleness and its monotony, now fails to arouse any
> emotion.

There followed a passage that would surely have met with the
Futurist leader Marinetti's approval, so closely did it accord with
his own consciously outrageous, sweepingly iconoclastic style:

> For years, Beethoven and Wagner have deliciously shaken
> our hearts. Now we are fed up with them. This is why we get
> infinitely more pleasure imagining combinations of the sounds
> of trolleys, autos and other vehicles, and loud crowds, than
> listening once more, for instance, to the heroic or pastoral
> symphonies.

He invites Pratella to take a tour with him in the modern city, now
a veritable symphony of unprecedented noises crying out for its
corollary in music: 'We will have fun imagining our orchestration
of department stores' sliding doors, the hubbub of the crowds,

the different roars of railroad stations, iron foundries, textile mills, printing houses, power plants and subways.' Furthermore, he adds optimistically, modern warfare now offered the bonus of a fresh panoply of machines of large-scale massacre. He quotes a poem written by Marinetti from the battlefields of the Balkan wars then raging, a jubilant phonetic spree of 'Tamtoumb's and 'taratatatatatatata's. Later, when World War I broke out, Russolo spent much of his downtime on the front making notes about the various noises of war, with a view to incorporating them into his intonarumori.

He outlines the machines he envisages, which will score and regulate harmonically and rhythmically this new variety of noises. They will not merely reproduce the sounds of the city, he says. Rather, these noises will provide an index, a resource for his machines to create sounds, gloriously impure, myriad, compound sounds. 'With the endless multiplication of machinery, one day we will be able to distinguish among ten, twenty or thirty thousand different noises. We will not have to imitate these noises but rather to combine them according to our artistic fantasy.'

It would have been understandable if Russolo had confined himself to casting his manifesto onto the winds of speculation in the hope that some designer or engineer would be inspired to take up his ideas and render them into something mechanically work-able. This was a task, however, that Russolo, despite his utter lack of training, took upon himself.

The intonarumori was cased in a rectangular box, with a large trumpet horn on its front and a crank on its rear that put a wheel in motion. The faster the machine was cranked, the more intense the noise. On the top of the machine was a lever that moved on a graduated scale and was able to vary the tone. One of the most striking features of the machine was its ability to 'glide' between pitches; 'glissandi' would go on to become a distinctive feature of twentieth-century classical music, as used by Ravel, for example.

Glissandi were key to the Futurist principles of dynamism and continuity, the idea of an energy flow between notes, rather than a division between them. Russolo was determined to overcome what he called the 'stupid barriers of the semitone', using the manual controls of the intonarumori to achieve what he called 'enharmonic gradations' instead.

It was Russolo's intention to assemble in the intonarumori sound box a 'family of noises', categorised as follows:

1. Roars, Thunderings, Explosions, Hissing roars, Bangs, Booms
2. Whistling, Hissing, Puffing
3. Whispers, Murmurs, Mumbling, Muttering, Gurgling
4. Noises obtained by beating on metals, woods, skins, stones, pottery, etc.
5. Voices of animals and people, Shouts, Screams, Shrieks, Wails, Hoots, Howls, Death rattles, Sobs
6. Screeching, Creaking, Rustling, Buzzing, Crackling, Scraping

He always stressed that the new music he sought to usher in wasn't merely banal, figurative representations of everyday sounds: 'As I conceive it, the Art of Noise would certainly not limit itself to an impressionistic and fragmentary reproduction of the noises of life.' Rather, these noises would become 'malleable matter', a clay from which the artist would 'transform it into the element of emotion', forging something quite new. Russolo could have been talking about today's samplers, in which the sounds do not merely reference themselves but, mechanically processed, become unrecognisable from their source, a 'fantastic association of the different timbres', as opposed to the ploddingly regular timbres of ordinary instruments.

This idea of utter transformation went for the Futurist movement as a whole. Thanks to Marinetti's taunts and provocations, Futurism could easily be regarded as early-twentieth-century art's equivalent of *Top Gear*, celebrating speed and motor vehicles with amoral élan and wilful macho philistinism. However, despite the trappings of their manifestos, the Futurists, not least Russolo, were concerned not merely with the material but with the spiritual. As Italian scholars such as Luciano Chessa have noted, they were deeply attached to the ideas of the occult.

Today, those who embrace such ideas are considered anti-scientific, refusing to put their beliefs in divination, magic, auras, ghosts and the spiritual world to the sort of rigorous double-blind tests demanded by modern scientists that would either vindicate or, perhaps more likely, expose them. However, at the turn of the twentieth century, such a dichotomy did not necessarily exist. Much as Newton had practised alchemy as well as establishing the laws of gravity (indeed, he was far more interested in his work as an alchemist than his discoveries on gravity, which he kept in a drawer for years), so did many scientifically minded people believe that the ideas of the occult were on the threshold of becoming demonstrable reality, that a new inner-spatial realm of 'spiritual science' was at hand. Mediumism, telepathy, astrology and magnetism were, wrote Arnaldo Ginna in 1915, the 'sciences of tomorrow'. All that was needed was further research and experimentation.

The invention of the X-ray machine, for example, seemed like a tremendously exciting pointer in this direction. The occult, after all, meant that which is hidden. Here we had a machine that was able to reveal, for the first time, that which had been hitherto invisible, interior. It represented a new form of clairvoyance, one that might go on to pick up such phenomena as auras or the residual traces left by body movements, which were integral to the Futurist principle of dynamism and perpetual movement, as represented in their images of walking dogs that appeared to have twenty legs, of the universe consisting of vibrations of varying degrees of intensity in the ether. Surely the X-ray machine, in tandem with all of the other astonishing strides science was taking, was a sign of the inexorable upwards trajectory of scientific progress? The Futurists certainly believed so.

In 1911, Marinetti envisaged that by force of 'exteriorised will', man would be able to fly. He further believed that humankind would be replaced by mechanised versions of themselves, minus the feeble defects of the flesh, and would achieve mastery over space and time. Such prophecies seem both ridiculous and eerily prescient today, as we continue to fret over the prospect of AI. But given how life on earth had been transformed so rapidly with the arrival of the machine and the industrial age, with flying machines dawning why not assert that the skies would be rife with metal flying men by, say, the year 1950? Fevered and poetic as Marinetti's speculations were, who was to say that they were unreasonably far-fetched?

Some of the Futurists' ideas may not have materialised, but they do not seem unfeasible – like metaphors for the sensations of today's media environment. The painter Umberto Boccioni believed that oils and canvasses on walls would soon prove too inadequate a spectacle to stimulate the voracious masses. He envisaged 'whirling musical compositions of enormous coloured gases, which on the scene of a free horizon, will move and electrify the complex soul of a crowd that we cannot yet imagine'.

Russolo was convinced that his intonarumori would not just be a novel means of generating new permutations of sound but that it would summon forth the forces at work between mind, body and spirit, give 'skeleton and flesh to the invisible, the impalpable, the imponderable, the imperceptible'. The microtonal possibilities afforded by the instrument would enable the artist to take the myriad noises available to them as rude matter, mere material, but then transform them in ways that transcended the mere material, the known, precedented world of matter, and through exquisite artistic sensitivity and channelling convey and expose the latent spiritual energies in tangible forms; render, in other words, the spiritual as material. The artist in this process was more than a mere slapper or dauber or grinder or sawer or hacker; rather, a clairvoyant, a medium. Such was the power of the intonarumori, believed Russolo, that it could pipe forth the spirits of the dead: languishing between this world and the next but given tangible form by a noise artist working at a higher plane of consciousness.

Doubtless, Russolo would have explained all of this at great length and with much technical detail appended at the instrument's first unveiling in prototype form at the Teatro Storchi in Modena. One imagines him with his eyes cast into the beyond, oblivious to the curled lips and restive grunts of his seated audience, many of whom were all too aware of the provocative nature of Futurist events and more than willing to play their own robust part in the performance art. However, much like a comedian who prefaces his routine by informing the room that they are about to hear the funniest joke they have ever heard, having given his machine the big build-up, Russolo was on to a loser the moment he ceremoniously pulled the lever of the machine – and nothing happened. And then nothing happened again.

These malfunctions were greeted with ribald amusement rather than polite sympathy. The third time, the intonarumori sputtered into action, and Russolo and his collaborator Ugo Piatti began to hand-crank its strange, muffled noises, which gradually grew in volume. So did the crowd, some of whom, one suspects, had come with the sole purpose of heckling. 'To the asylum!' some jeered. It was hard for the intonarumori to make itself heard above the cackling and jesting.

'There is a trick, there's a trick! Open the box! You want us to appreciate an imitation, while we can easily enjoy the original!' It was too much for the compère, Marinetti, who bellowed, 'You have the sceptical attitude of farmers!' And with the audience overwhelming the sounds of the machine with their exercise of a more traditional art of noise, Russolo was forced to give up and the curtain fell on the evening. 'I perfectly knew – Marinetti shouted at the audience while people were leaving – that donkeys wanted the monopoly of noise!'

The instrument received its first proper airing in April 1914, in Milan. Marinetti had warned that although the instrument would excite 'pleasant feelings', in order to 'get' the intonarumori 'religion' would be required; in other words, faith in its capabilities. This countered the accusation among those who reiterated that all the instrument seemed able to generate was a series of threeps, groans and more clamorous noises, which did not live up to the billing it had been given by Russolo in both his manifesto and accompanying lectures. The concert was greeted with riotous derision by many, but others were enthralled. Stravinsky is said to have rocketed from his chair when he first heard the instrument, casting around the room to check that its sounds weren't coming from some other source.

The truth is, tirelessly omnivorous student of the arts, sciences and humanities that he was, brilliant visionary, versatile in the skills to which he applied himself, Russolo was a mediocre artist. He was a mere demonstrator, and certainly not of the calibre likely to conjure up representations of the spiritual world.

In time, other musicians would devise instruments based on the same principles as the intonarumori. However, no composer of stature was willing to dispense with conventional instruments in order to work with them; not even Varèse, who had befriended Russolo and seen his invention at work.

Russolo carried on adding to his series of intonarumori, introducing various modifications and developments, but although in principle they represented an advance on the conventional orchestra, in other ways they sounded feeble and inept by comparison. A sole recording made in 1921 of the intonarumori backed with a regular orchestra is fascinating. 'Serenata per intonarumori e strumenti' features the strange, swilling, wheezing noises of the instrument, which suggest any number of comparisons, from a giant, rheumatic sea slug to the groan of a dredging machine that has developed some power of mechanical speech. Infinite variety but limited capability – and yet it also feels like the instrument is actually being propped up by the orchestra it is supposed to supplant. If in competition, the intonarumori would have been swept away like balsa wood by the power of a full conventional orchestra, which despite the notational constraints of the music it played was still able to convey formidable nuance, heft, colour, energy and sheer volume, making a Wagnerian mockery of poor Mr Russolo tugging away at his strings and levers.

The decline of Russolo and of interest in his *Art of Noises* went hand in hand with the decline of Futurism. The movement persisted right up until World War II, only petering out with the death of its founder, Marinetti, in 1944, and Russolo himself in 1947, just too soon for him to learn of the arrival of electronic music and musique concrète – the next, belated phase of his noise-music dream. Given the apparently hectic pace of change at the turn of the century, could he have anticipated that progress in mechanical sound-making would fall into such abeyance? Futurism, meanwhile, was supplanted by successive 'isms': first Dadaism, which borrowed its tactics of outrage and words-in-freedom; and then surrealism, at which point (despite the official communist sympathies insisted upon by surrealism's leader, André Breton) modern art became less a movement for absolute social change, more a market commodity, with Salvador 'Avida Dollars' Dalí its first shameless celebrity. 'The oldest of us is thirty: so we have at least a decade for finishing our work,' Marinetti had written in his original Futurist manifesto. 'When we are forty, other younger and stronger men will probably throw us in the wastebasket like useless manuscripts – we want it to happen!'

Futurism hadn't merely become passé, however; it had become morally, philosophically and politically discredited. Its glorification

of the 'hygiene' of war rang bitterly hollow following the dreadful
and unforeseen scale of the carnage of World War I. Among its victims had been Sant'Elia and Boccioni, the latter thrown, in sadly
bathetic manner, from a horse in 1916. Still more shamefully, the
Futurists were doggedly allied with the fascists. Revisionists have
attempted to pass this off as an unfortunate early romantic dalliance that was abruptly abandoned when the brutal realpolitik
of Mussolini and his henchmen became clear, and certainly there
was a schism between Marinetti and the party in 1920. However,
by 1927, Marinetti, Russolo and co. were involved in openly fascist art exhibitions and maintained that allegiance for the duration
of the regime. This is inescapable; when becoming inebriated on
the irresistible revolutionary fervour and declamatory prose of the
Futurists, fascism is one of the toxins you are imbibing.

This wasn't just a coincidental political sympathy. Futurism has
inherently fascist traits, not just in the fervent nationalism of its
leader Marinetti but also in its cold-steel certainties, its brutal desire
to sweep away the old, the cherished, the weak and feeble in favour
of a more mechanically determined, superhuman (for which read
less than human) dynamic imperative. Its totalitarian desire to
create new and utterly impersonal structures from scratch has an
undeniably avant-garde frisson but was sincerely meant. The violence, cruelty and injustice of which Marinetti boasted wasn't just a
brilliant, pertinent rhetorical conceit but an apt description of the
bad seeds lurking in the soil of the Futurist/modernist aesthetic.

For all that, Marinetti comes across historically as a pathetic
figure in his dotage. His dogged stream of manifestos, including
a 1930 manifesto on Futurist cooking, seems risible; one thinks
of P. G. Wodehouse's Sir Roderick Spode, would-be leader of the
Black Shorts, as reimagined by Clive Exton in the TV comedy
Jeeves and Wooster, puffed up and solemnly addressing a humiliat-
ingly small band of devoted followers, outlining his plans to give
over the county of Lincolnshire to the cultivation of turnips.

Fascism probably accounts for the overall mediocrity of Futurist art and its inability to make good on its own visionary claims. Fascism impeded Futurism because fascism gets things wrong. There's a lack of empathy, a lack of true perception and lasting acuity amid its grand schemes and discredited occultist follies. There are a few good works that apply the Futurist principle: Boccioni's *Those Who Leave/Those Who Stay*, for example, in which dynamic brushstrokes render palpable the emotional state of those embarking on a railway journey and the well-wishers they leave behind, saddened at their departure. There's a humanity, an eternal truthfulness about *Those Who Leave/Those Who Stay* that is fundamentally lacking in Futurism as a whole.

The same 1933 home encyclopaedia in which I looked up the definition of Futurism said that the movement had had no discernible lasting effect. So it might have seemed. None of Russolo's noise machines survived: some disappeared; one was destroyed in 1930, supposedly while exhibited in the foyer of a Paris cinema screening *L'Age d'Or*, where an audience enraged by the film's anti-Catholic content smashed it to pieces. Futurism seemed smashed to pieces, an Italian folly that had been overtaken by progress in science – fast joining the dots and moving away from the mystical groping in the dark of the occultists – as well as the arts.

And yet when the smoke of the century began to clear, Futurism, for all its grave flaws and limitations, took its proper and vital place in the timeline. It provided an aesthetic vision, a vista, a vital, jolting ignition, as well as providing an electric light for all subsequent innovators. Ravel, Stravinsky and Cage – as well as Varèse, despite his sceptical remarks – were all informed by Futurism to some degree or other.

Furthermore, there were other Futurisms with a musical component. In Russia, for example, there had been a Futurist movement of sorts since 1908, inaugurated by Velimir Khlebnikov's prose work *Iskusenie Gresnika*, followed by a 1912 manifesto entitled *A Slap*

in the Face of Public Taste, whose authors, including Khlebnikov
and the poet Vladimir Mayakovsky, urged readers to 'throw
Pushkin, Dostoevsky, Tolstoy, etc., etc. overboard from the Ship
of Modernity'.

Come the Revolution, and prior to Stalin's crushing, reactionary
insistence on the figurative kitsch of socialist realism, the Russian
avant-garde was all too willing to be pressed into the service of
the Soviet state. Dziga Vertov's 1930 sound film, bracingly entitled
Enthusiasm! The Dombass Symphony, in some ways anticipates the
ideas of musique concrète: it's a splicing together of industrial noise,
a veritable workers' celebration of mines, furnaces and factories captured on a giant piece of recording equipment only available now
in the 'talkie' era, a hugely ambitious attempt to glorify, in the form
of sound art, Russia's workers in their collective effort. Prior to that,
in 1922, Arseny Avraamov had composed *The Symphony of Sirens*,
whose 'instrumentation' included the industrial sounds emanating
from the port city of Baku – its sirens, seaplanes, artillery fire, ships'
horns, steam engines – as well as a full choir delivering a stirring
paean to the virtues of the Russian proletariat. This symphony was
performed once, as a monumental nocturnal public event the year
it was composed; it was not recorded, however, and all that we have
is a recreation made by Leopoldo Amigo and Miguel Molina in
2003, based on the composer's notes and instructions, which goes
some way to conveying what a giddying spectacle this event would
have made, its simultaneism and confluence of man-made environmental sounds again prefiguring the work of later avant-garde
composers, including Luc Ferrari. One can only imagine how this
mode of industrial sound assembly might have developed had state
approval of such cultural activity somehow continued under some
imaginary benign alternative to Stalin; more importantly, as deep
sighs from socialist historians would attest, one can also only wonder how the fate of the international working classes might have
panned out under such a scenario.

Many years later, the ZTT label, co-founded by Paul Morley, paid the most direct homage to the movement. As a music journalist, Morley practised his own version of words-in-freedom, which poured implicit scorn on the passéist/rockist clichés of 1970s/'80s music press discourse, while producer Trevor Horn and the group Art of Noise would provide a more rigorous, durable, sizeable, dominant electropop architecture that would make all that preceded it sound tinny and Meccano-like by comparison. Horn productions like 'Relax', a recreation from scratch of the song presented to him by Liverpool group Frankie Goes to Hollywood, impacted on the chart like jet-black bouncing bombs, expansive yet elastic monuments to pop modernity that in terms of sheer looming volume would be unmatched until the heavy, heady days of EDM. This was Marinetti's dream of the human supplanted by a mechanised version of itself realised, through the 'exteriorised will' of Horn. In lieu of the band's doggedly but all too humanly inadequate original version of the song, Horn replaced their performances with MIDI-controlled electronic instruments that were pre-programmed on the MIDI sequencer. The original rhythm section of drums and bass was replaced by a beat provided by a sequenced Linn 2 bass drum. The bass was derived from a single sampled E note from the bass guitar and sequenced in absolutely perfect time.

Even so, with its moralism and feminism and its postmodern passéism, the 1980s would have disappointed the Futurists. They may have felt that their work had been in vain, their name taken in vain. Still, their verve, their fearless, reckless rejection of the vast, accumulated, overbearing, rotting weight of nineteenth-century civilisation was a vital, quixotic gesture. Wrong in so many ways, artistically disappointing in others, Futurism nonetheless anticipated with vivid, thrilling relish the astonishing, dangerous, wonderful, terrible world we live in today.

3

POÈME ÉLECTRONIQUE: THE LONG
WAIT OF EDGARD VARÈSE

Like many people, I first became aware of Edgard Varèse via
Frank Zappa referencing him on the back of the early Mothers
of Invention album sleeves. I first became aware of Frank Zappa
in the mid-1970s, thanks to my music teacher, Mr Phillips, who
spoke with a velvety, George Melly-esque growl, a chain-smoker
who had the constitutional air of a human ashtray. He was as
rigidly bored as we were by the music curriculum, which saw us
plodding up and down scales and across fretboards on a selection
of battered old instruments, the lessons enlivened only by chewing
bits of paper torn from exercise books and flicking them at one
another. Every now and again, however, Mr Phillips would haul
himself up and attempt to invigorate proceedings by wheeling the
school record player into the classroom and selecting a few discs
to edify us about the processes of modern music-making, trying to
impress on us that there were worlds of intrigue in contemporary
sound that extended even beyond what we then considered to be
the apex of modern excitement: facing each other on the dancefloor at the school disco, thumbs in belt loops and leaning into
each other rhythmically like glam-rock stags to the stomping beat
of Mud's 'Tiger Feet'.

On this occasion, Mr Phillips invited us to compare and con-
trast two 1960s artists: Cat Stevens and Frank Zappa. He followed
'Morning Has Broken' with Zappa and the Mothers of Invention's
'Help, I'm a Rock' from their 1966 debut *Freak Out!* The latter track

sounded like the work of a madman, a disorienting, extended piece featuring a stammering, repeated bass, before shape-shifting into free jazz and then some sub-doo-wop jabbering. And a lyric about a talking rock. You were allowed to do this? We were allowed to listen to it in school? At some level I realised that this plumbed fathoms of serious intent of some sort that the 'Ying Tong Song' by the Goons, the strangest record I had heard up to that point, did not.

It was one of a series of epiphanies that I experienced as a teenager. I filed it away, only to revisit it as a fifteen-year-old, suddenly suffused, thanks to exposure to the music press, by an intense consciousness of the purposes, meanings and hidden moral agendas that could be contained within rock music, moral, deep, intense meanings of which I had hitherto been mindlessly oblivious as a mere pop-chart consumer. I sought out that Mothers of Invention album and became a student of Zappa, mailing out a postal order in exchange for a book made up of old reviews, interview clippings and xeroxed photos pasted in chronological order, which I pored over several times.

At this point, in 1978, the early, and greatest, Zappa albums were still deleted. I had to acquire them from the Leeds City Record Library, whose perfunctory racks of well-thumbed vinyl discs of wildly varying quality I would paw through thrice weekly, past old Canned Heat albums and never-borrowed Ringo Starr solo albums, hoping albums like *Freak Out!* (and *Absolutely Free* and *We're Only in It for the Money*) weren't out on loan. Finally, I picked them out, one by one, committing them to C90 cassettes, the various scratches and occasional jumps of the library copies an ingrained part of my listening experience of these vital works. Exercising my newfound rock critical skills, I decided that 'Help, I'm a Rock', which Zappa said was a 'tribute to Elvis Presley', was a sardonic depiction of the existential quandary of the King and the genre over which he presided as monarch. It was also, I surmised, an insolent nod to Simon & Garfunkel's 'I Am a Rock', operating at a far more oblique discursive level than Paul Simon's honeyed little homilies.

Eventually, I came to decide that, the early Mothers apart, Zappa was an overrated figure, his sneering disdain for pop revealing more about his own overdeveloped superiority complex and ultimate incapabilities than the state of popular music. I also found his guitar noodlings clinical and his pseudo-orchestral arrangements frigid, fussy, soulless and pointless, failing to justify his blatant pretensions as a 'serious' musician. For a while, however, I was obsessed with Zappa, the ideal gateway artist for an adolescent on the threshold of taking music very seriously indeed. And I noted that not only did 'Help, I'm a Rock' feature a segment entitled 'In Memoriam Edgard Varèse' (the composer had died only months earlier, in 1965) but that on the back of each of those Mothers albums was inscribed the motto 'The present-day composer refuses to die', credited to the great man of whom I knew nothing. Zappa's use of concrète methods and studio electronics on *We're Only in It for the Money*, meanwhile, impacted on my mind like lightning bolts on a distant horizon.

I would have to seek out this Varèse. I was on a journey to the centre of the earth that started with Mud, then rock, then the deeper-than-rock stratum at which Zappa operated, and then, perhaps the heat source of the twentieth century, M. Varèse.

In the event, Varèse found me, via the BBC: a Radio 3 broadcast of one of his greatest works in a rather slim oeuvre – *Amériques*. Ironic, perhaps, that I'd been shepherded in my discovery of the counter-culture and avant-garde not by rebel, dropout mentors but by the benign institutions now under siege in today's neo-liberalism-ravaged Britain: secondary school, the city library, the BBC. This, for me, was classical music turned on its side and used as a battering ram on ancient assumptions, shock-haired, tumultuous, billowing with the giddy fragrances of the first dawn of modernity.

*

Edgard Varèse was born in 1883. A hundred years later, aged twenty-one, I found myself in Strasbourg while Interrailing, accompanied by a Sony Walkman cassette player featuring home recordings of his oeuvre, and chanced upon a festival to commemorate the centenary of his birth entitled 'Musica 83'. His works were being performed alongside those of his more useful successors in sonic architecture, including Iannis Xenakis. I bought a poster of the event that featured a photo of the composer taken in the year before he died, his grey hair still a raging brushfire poking in all directions, his lined face a study in compositional earnestness, his gaze penetrating deep into an unseen beyond. He would stare down at me thus from the wall of my college room, an ancient conscience, and would continue to do so for years afterwards – the present-day composer, still refusing death in all its myriad, stultifying forms.

For Varèse remains one of the key and still molten figures of twentieth-century culture, a man whose life intersected at various points with Lenin and Trotsky, Picasso, Le Corbusier, Erik Satie and Debussy, and later Charlie Parker and even a very young Frank Zappa, who was permitted to make a long-distance phone call to the composer on his fifteenth birthday in 1955. To Zappa's chagrin, he wasn't in, but the teenage unknown eventually contacted his idol and received a letter of encouragement from him. The composer's influence can be heard coursing through Zappa's music – in the dense, percussive clatter of 'Nine Types of Industrial Pollution', for example – less so in his subsequent, tightly scripted, jazz-rock peregrinations.

Varèse was born in Paris but was sent by his parents to be raised by relatives in the small village of Le Villars in Bourgogne, including his grandfather Claude, on whom he doted far more than his own father, an engineer and conventionally bourgeois nineteenth-century patriarch. It was here, in this sleepy, relatively noiseless and culturally inert little community, that the very young Varèse experienced a moment's interruption that would affect him profoundly and stay with him for the rest of his life. He was awoken by the sound of a train passing close to the village, its whistle emitting a high 'C' note as it roared on that arced through the night and embedded itself, for all time, in his consciousness. It seems to have awoken him to the new machine forces that would fire the coming century, beautiful, terrible and awesome, at once ultra-modern and yet elemental. It also awoke him to the possibilities of ambient noise as a musical component more powerful than conventionally arranged instrumentation.

Varèse developed his musical interest when he was forced to rejoin his parents in Turin (his father was Italian), studying at the local conservatory and writing his first opera when he was twelve. His father, however, was determined that Varèse should follow in his footsteps, insisting he enrol at Turin Polytechnic to study engineering and setting him at loggerheads with his son. When Varèse's mother died in 1900, their relationship worsened, as Varèse insisted on developing his career as a composer, and he struck his father during one tussle. It is ironic, perhaps, that engineering would play a role of sorts in his music, not just in his use of new technologies but in his music's precise calibrations and judgements of dynamism and tensions. There was tension aplenty, however, between Varèse and his father, whom he loathed for his attempted authoritarianism and lack of the softer paternal qualities of his maternal grandfather. This conflict, many felt, was responsible for the violent quality of his music, crashing and erupting, bursting against the obdurate dams of tradition ('Tradition is simply a bad habit,' was one of Varèse's better aphorisms). It also accounted for his inability to be a good father himself. He married an actress, Suzanne Bing, with whom he had a daughter, but he was too engrossed in his work to be an attentive family man. They were divorced a few years later.

In 1903, Varèse parted for good from his father and any chance of an allowance, leaving for Paris, where he took up music studies, before moving on to Berlin. He met the Italian composer Ferruccio Busoni, whose ideas had a deep impact on him; in 1908, Busoni wrote, 'I am more or less convinced that in the authentic new music machines will be necessary, and that they will play an important role. Perhaps even industry will have its role to play in the progress and transformation of aesthetics.'

Varèse experienced at first hand the tumult of the early twentieth century and met some if its instigators. Among them was Picasso, whom he sat and watched eat a meal, unable to bring himself to let on about his own penniless and desperately famished state. He had brief encounters with Lenin and Trotsky while they were still hatching the Russian Revolution. He studied with interest the manifestos of the Futurists, though he was shrewd enough to realise that for all its immense significance as a movement, it wasn't likely to produce great art. He took issue with what he saw as the superficiality of Russolo's *Art of Noises* manifesto. 'Futurists, why do you reproduce the vibrations of our daily life only in their superficial and distressing aspects?' he would write.

Especially distressing to Varèse was the outbreak of World War I, glorified and embraced by the Futurists as an act of 'hygiene'. For Varèse, the war was a tragedy, not least because it pitted two countries he loved against one another: France and Germany. He was mobilised in 1915, working as a bicycle messenger before contracting double pneumonia and being invalided out. But Europe was ruined for him by the Great War, and he couldn't bring himself to feel great animus for Germany, having been so steeped in, and influenced by, German music and culture, and having lived in Berlin. On 18 December 1915, therefore, he made what he believed would be a temporary trip to New York, leaving behind his manuscripts in his Paris apartment. It turned out, however, to be a permanent, inadvertently visionary and artistically fateful move. He was thirty-two. He had $90 to his name but only knew a couple of words of English. Very shortly after stepping onto the dock he was knocked down by an automobile and laid up for eleven weeks.

In New York, Varèse was exposed to the crosstown cacophony and incessant thrum of the world's most dynamic industrial city, which was still very much in the process of its own construction. His early orchestral works strongly evoke the everyday clanks and horn blasts and sirens and heavy machinery that were the soundtrack of Manhattan life, the industrial noise. If Gershwin wrote of the American in Paris, here was the resonant converse: a Parisian in America, bringing a deep-dyed but highly receptive classical sensibility to the young country. With his well-chiselled classical good looks and hair that looked as if it were set permanently on end by his restless cerebral cogitations, he looked every inch a blazing specimen from a European artistic tradition that it was in fact his intention to supplant. He was actually offered the chance to write popular orchestral music for Broadway productions, but loftily declared that he could not be 'both virgin and whore' and declined. He retained a disdain for the popular and the commercial. As his friend, the poet Alejo Carpentier, would write, 'For him, New York is neither jazz nor "musical comedy", nor even Harlem dives. He stands apart from those ephemeral characteristics of this new world but feels himself profoundly moved by the tragic meaning that he perceives in the implacable rhythm of its labour, in the teeming of the docks, in the crowds at noon, in the bustle of Wall Street.'

Varèse's music was more than merely imitative of the dawn of the industrial era. He sensed that new energies were in the process of being released, however, latent potentials, and that old walls were collapsing and the nineteenth-century way of doing things would be irrelevant in the new age. He saw himself as seeking the 'bomb' that would 'explode' the musical world and bring forth into it what had hitherto been regarded as 'noise' but which he saw as a legitimate element in 'organised sound'. This bomb, he foresaw, would be technological in nature. In his first interview in America, Varèse said, 'What I am looking for are new technical mediums which can lend themselves to every expression of thought and can keep up with thought.'

In July 1922, in an interview with the *Christian Science Monitor*, Varèse further said, 'What we want is an instrument that will give us a continuous sound at any pitch. The composer and the electrician will have to labour together to get it. At any rate, we cannot keep on working in the old school colours. Speed and synthesis are characteristics of our own epoch. We need twentieth-century instruments to help realise them in music.' Later, in 1930, in a roundtable discussion about the future mechanisation of music, he said that it was not a matter of reproducing existing sounds but 'making possible the realisation of new sounds in accordance with new conceptions . . . the present tempered scale system seems to me worn out'.

Although there were prototype electronic instruments available, they were imitative, gimmicky and did not have the capacity of which Varèse, in the 1920s and 1930s, could only dream. As early as 1905, however, he was aware of the siren, which would become a recurring motif in his compositions. His use of the noise device would dismay and anger some concert-goers, while others made the mistake of regarding it as no more than a signifier of modern New York street life. That it was, but Varèse also admired the 'parabolic' qualities of the sound it produced, its luminous purity and self-sufficiency, and the relationship between the siren and the human hand: you cranked it, but then the sound you produced took on a brief life of its own, before arcing downwards into decay. The siren interventions in his pre-World War II orchestral works certainly signified the new potencies of the machine age, but they also represented an invasion of the hitherto inadmissible into the echelons of art, of 'noise' as a new dimension of the musical lexicon, a component in its organisation, as well as acting as a collage of the sort Picasso had inaugurated in modern visual art, collapsing the arbitrary walls, those stuffy formal distinctions, between art and life.

Olivier Messaien said of Varèse's chamber and orchestral works that they were 'electronic' in nature before there was such a thing as electronic music, and so they were. Pieces such as *Offrandes* (1921), *Hyperprism* (1922–3) and *Octandre* (1923) are classical music hoist vertical, like skyscrapers under construction. Sounds coalesce and clash, move upwards like bars of lava, emissions of brass grind like heavy diggers. Attack, sustain and decay, all watchwords in synthesizer music, abound in Varèse's works, as well as looped *idées fixes*. These pieces do not progress harmonically but are endlessly and heatedly erupting, like the sun's surface seen close up. Among the many notable things about Varèse's music in this period is his extensive use of percussion, busy and irregular, whose use in classical music had been quite reticent and even taboo hitherto; indeed, *Ionisation* (1929–31) is composed exclusively for percussion instruments. This sort of thing was quite unheard-of. Conversely, strings are given much shorter shrift compared to the brass and woodwind sections, and in some pieces are dispensed with altogether. Varèse held a contempt for strings, regarding them as part of the passéist fabric of the pre-twentieth-century era.

Varèse's key ideas come together in his major works for (very) large orchestra, *Amériques* and *Arcana*. Both works contain nods and homages to his avant-garde contemporaries and predecessors: *Ameriques'* opening flute motif is clearly reminiscent of Debussy's *Prélude à l'après-midi d'un faune* (or perhaps Stravinsky's *Rite of Spring*); *Arcana* clearly alludes to Stravinsky's *Firebird*. But overall they are unmistakably the work of a composer who had established his own distinctive, impassioned and often paradoxical soundworld.

Both pieces are huge in scale but quite short, reflecting Varèse's lack of interest in composition as a mere means for narrative and storytelling. The structure, the architecture was all: *Amériques* is made up of a series of distinctive blocks. And yet the music also reflects Varèse's deep interest in the models and structures of nature, of crystal formations and the way currents of varying speed combine to make up the overall flow of a river.

Amériques is at once ultra-modern, an evocation of 1920s Manhattan, and yet seems to hark back to a volcanic age before the earth was fully formed. It is just twenty-five minutes long but each of those minutes is a New York minute, a simultaneist ebb and flow of soundclouds, traffic cacophony, multiple dramatic flurries, slapping rhythms, distant blasts, sirens, theatre-pit orchestras, machine labour, subway carriages, fretting pedestrians, skyscraper needles and the mournful drone of horns. One can imagine sounds of this nature drifting from the Hudson River through the window of his apartment as he wrote. However, the plural is key in the title. This is not merely the America as reflected in monochrome cine reels and jazz soundtracks but an imagination of multiple possibilities. Varèse spoke of 'discoveries – new worlds on earth, in the sky, or in the minds of men'. What might be the upshot of this upwards surge of energy that is twentieth-century urban America? What forms might it eventually take? How dangerous is this great, man-made eruption, this project drawing on the combined energies of ambitious, industrious immigrant dreamers?

Varèse was attending to the exterior world, which he conveys with unmatched vividness, but also to his interior musical visions. He once said that Beethoven had been lucky to have been deaf: it meant that he was able all the better to attend, undistracted, to his 'inner ear'. The motions of his music were further informed by scientific advances, with the general public beginning to acquire a more vivid grasp of the vocabulary of astronomy and atomic physics. In a radio interview, Varèse urged those listening to his music to think in terms of the processes of 'crystallisation', or to 'visualise the changing projection of a geometrical figure on a plane, with both plane and figure moving in space, but each with its arbitrary and varying speeds of translation and rotation'.

And yet, for all its Promethean passions, its at times over-whelming intensity that is somehow reconciled with the structural know-how of an extensively trained engineer, there is eventually a feeling of deep frustration. Varèse's orchestral music pines for undiscovered modes in which to express itself. Indeed, a more sceptical listener might say that his works in this period are much of a muchness, as if produced by a generator of some sort; that he grapples over and over with the same tropes and compositional issues. He did surpass himself, however, not just with *Ionisation* but also *Density 21.5* (1936), for solo flute. *Ecuatorial* (1932–4) makes use of both the theremin, the contact-free electronic instrument named after the Soviet Leon Theremin, who invented it in 1928, which sees the player manipulate the space between two metal antennae, and in a later revision of the piece, the ondes Martenot, invented the same year by Maurice Martenot, which achieves similar effects using vacuum tubes. The problem with both these instruments, however – retrospectively, in particular – is that while they perform functions of which conventional instruments are incapable, they are somewhat limited in expressive scope and, moreover, tainted by the association with novelty and their eventual use to signify the eerie or exotic in B-movies.

Varèse's productivity as a composer tailed off somewhat in the 1930s. He knew that in order to move forward, he required technological breakthroughs that were as yet unforthcoming. In desperation, he wrote in 1932 to the Guggenheim Foundation for a grant to work on expanding the possibilities and range of the Dynaphone, an instrument controlled with a pitch lever rather than a keyboard, to allow for 'the accurate production of any number of frequencies and consequently [enable it] to produce any interval or any subdivision required by the ancient or exotic modes'. The Guggenheim, quite possibly not having an earthly idea of what he was talking about, knocked him back.

He also approached a Hollywood studio in 1939 outlining at great length his ideas for 'organised sound' for soundtracks, rather than the usual classical prompts. He betrayed, however, a hint of unworldly scorn for the modern entertainment industry when he wrote that 'It seems to me that the motion picture industry might profit (even in the dollar sense in the end),' were it to take up his ideas. Hollywood did not.

It was only in 1949, with the availability of tape machines and their musical application, that Varèse, now in his late sixties, enjoyed the breakthrough for which he had longed. 'I can now piss in front of everybody!' he is said to have exclaimed when he realised that sound technology was at long last making the strides into the future of which he had long dreamt. He was granted the anonymous gift of an Ampex reel-to-reel tape recorder. This had been developed from the German Magnetophon system, which had been demonstrated as early as 1935. The Ampex was created at the bidding of Bing Crosby, of all people, who had already proven himself a trailblazer in his use of microphone technology to create a more intimate vocal style, and now led the way again in insisting on pre-recording his radio shows and mastering his commercial recordings onto magnetic tape. As he saw it, this would enable him to structure and edit his radio broadcasts in the way a Hollywood film was structured and edited, as well as to preserve them, rather than their being lost to the ether in a single live stream. He invested $50,000 in the Ampex company. As well as Varèse, another beneficiary of the Ampex recorder was Les Paul. Crosby gave his guitarist friend one of the first Ampex machines, and Paul took this equipment and ran with it, eventually conceiving multitrack recording. Bing Crosby as a key figure in technical and electronic innovation in the twentieth century? As his character in *High Society* would croon, 'Well, did you ever . . .'

In 1950, Varèse conceived his late orchestral masterpiece *Déserts*. Again, this was paradoxical. It drew on exterior American life for inspiration – the actual deserts of New Mexico he had visited during his time in his adopted country. However, he was also preoccupied with mental and spiritual deserts, which man wanders in solitude: 'Not only those stripped aspects of nature that suggest bareness, aloofness, timelessness, but also that remote inner space no telescope can reach, where man is alone, a world of mystery and essential loneliness,' as he put it. There is a moving thematic contrast between this piece and the similarly plural *Amériques*. The earlier piece implied a period of build-up, deadly or otherwise, whereas *Déserts* spoke to many of the civilised assumptions laid waste by such devastating mid-century phenomena as the Holocaust and the A-bomb.

There is a certain sobriety about the orchestral passages, a sombre delicacy in place of the grim, violent gusto of Varèse's more youthful works. Most sensational, though, are the seven minutes of 'Interpolations': taped electronic sections culled from field recordings made in various industrial settings – ironworks, sawmills, factories in Philadelphia. However, when as a young man Stockhausen met an excited Varèse, he had to restrain himself from voicing his opinion that the composer's methods seemed crude and lacking in technique.

And yet the 'Interpolations' in *Déserts*, recorded onto magnetic tape, even if they lack the sheer degree of development and application of a Stockhausen piece like *Gesang der Jünglinge*, remain miasmic, the more so with age, and obliquely, emotionally resonant – not just for the role they assume in the piece overall but as primitive relics of electronic sound. They sound like life imitating the art of Varèse: industrial recordings cut up, distorted, filtered and processed in a spliced arrangement that follows the familiar crests and plunges and multiple collisions of a Varèse piece. There's a palpable sense of metal on metal, of sparks and furnaces. There's something desolate and monochromatic about these pieces that makes you think about the world being forged at the dawn of time or the obscure clankings of some post-human activity three thousand years hence. Certainly, they're more than mere imitations of the hustle and bustle of modern life; they dare to use the stuff and noise of modern life as raw material, to create an environment that is somehow man-made and yet beyond man's comprehension, an environment of modern forces both awesome and terrible. *Déserts* is an ambient space for contemplation and reflection on what man has become, what is his lot, a representation of the post-war physical and moral landscape.

These were not the first electronic pieces, of course; what was unique about the 'Interpolations' in *Déserts* was that they were juxtaposed with acoustic orchestrated sections, sitting at odds with one another rather than integrated or blended. And it was this juxtaposition that would scandalise both critics and concert-goers when *Déserts* received its premiere at the Théâtre des Champs-Élysées, where Stranvinsky's *Le Sacre du printemps* had famously incited riots forty years earlier, among an audience unaccustomed to the shattering impact of impending modernity, which mirrored the violence and fragmentation of the Great War. Whether out of mischief or mishap, the programme saw Varèse's piece sandwiched between a performance of Mozart's Overture in B flat and Tchaikovsky's *Pathéthique* symphony, with the whole evening being broadcast, duly attracting a large (non-paying) audience to the theatre. They were immediately affronted by *Déserts*, the taped segments in particular, their restiveness growing from murmurs of disgruntlement to outright protest of the sort that used to enliven many a Dadaist soiree. But this was 1954, and Varèse himself was seventy-one years old. One Parisian critic, under the banner 'Broadcast Cacophony', wrote:

> A work written by a madman, grandiosely christened an
> 'electro-symphony' including a great deal of saucepan banging

and solos for flushing toilets with fanfares for stock cars
... The discussion continued out on the pavement. 'This
Monsieur Varèse ... needs a trip to the electric chair.'

The periodical *Le Monde* was more terse. *Déserts*, wrote its critic,
was 'a work composed by a lunatic'.

The nature of the programming made for a rare interface between
the wider population and the avant-garde. One can understand
how put out the critic and those concert-goers who took exception were. For them, the likes of Mozart and Tchaikovsky hung
high like chandeliers above the common fray of things, remote
and rarefied, their works made of precious, luminous matter. To
attend a classical concert, in white ties and finery, was to bask by
osmosis and in complacent repose in their superiority, to show
appreciation of the timeless verities of art, to take comfort in its
resolutions. Then along come fellows like this Varèse, depositing as
if from an upended dustcart the metal detritus of the low and sadly
actual world onto the hallowed confines of the concert floor. This
represented an act of vandalism, an absurdity, an insult to customers who had invested in this experience to have their sense of
distinction affirmed, not challenged. This was 1954, and it showed
that ideas proposed half a century earlier about what it was permissible to consider the stuff of art had yet to permeate widely. Some
sixty years further down the line, such irreverent ideas are accepted
reverentially in the world of visual arts, but *Déserts*, were anyone
to programme it for an unsuspecting audience rather than a niche
one, would almost certainly retain its power to offend purely for
daring to exist.

One shouldn't overstate Varèse's outsider status, however. Many
critics and observers saw the merits in his electronic works, while
his reputation had spread even to bebop circles: practitioners such
as the saxophonist Charlie Parker, for example, who around the
time *Déserts* received its premiere was stalking him shyly around

the streets of Greenwich Village, unable to find the courage to ask him to be his mentor.

The pioneering urban planner and architect Le Corbusier was another who retained a respect for Varèse, recognising in him a kindred spirit, despite working in a very different time. Both shared the same spatial, formal and material preoccupations, with the pre-eminence of form and function as priorities rather than the decayed, sentimental, old-world idea of quantity of content. When Le Corbusier was commissioned by the Dutch company Philips to create their pavilion at the 1958 World's Fair, he insisted on commissioning Varèse to compose a soundtrack to the construction he had in mind, and what's more that the composer be given absolute carte blanche to create as he pleased. Varèse took Le Corbusier at his word and even overruled the architect when despite himself he did make a couple of suggestions, including that he speak a few words over the piece.

With customary corporate courage, Philips quailed at Le Corbusier's insistence on Varèse. Given the resources at their disposal, they could have roped in a big composer – a Walton or a Copland. Varèse also suffered the attentions of an engineer in the Eindhoven studio who had his own ideas about the shape and form the piece should take. Varèse was of sufficiently truculent and stubborn a temperament to plough on regardless, not allowing such considerations as deadline and budget to affect his painstaking aesthetic visions. He finally emerged with the *Poème électronique*.

The interior of the pavilion conceived by Le Corbusier was stomach-like in shape, while the visuals projected onto its walls were, like the *Poème électronique*, grandiose and portentous, hinting at huge themes – from nature to love, from nuclear annihilation to the panoply of humanity – without touching down on any particular narrative thread. What it was 'all about' was deliberately vague. It was experiential. Varèse's eyebrows danced with excitement and mischief as he told of the three thousand people who shuffled into the pavilion every hour, to be assailed not just by the sequential images of skeletons, reptiles and mushroom clouds but by multiple loudspeakers on all sides broadcasting the composer's meticulous collage of sounds, whose 'routes' travelling through space were a new and vital aspect of the relationship between the listener and the sounds to which they were attending. These ranged from the concrète to the abstract, from grim, tolling bells to abstract electronic emissions, darting and hanging high in the ambience; from agonised murmurs like the undead souls of a catacomb to snake rattles and scrapings, which were as important to attend to as the sudden, rocket-like surges of compound noise. 'There was no applause,' said the composer, triumphantly. 'People left in a daze. No one said a word.' This, you feel, was his intention: not to walk the listener through the sound space but to push them into its disorienting darkness, the existential ghost-train ride it represented; to whisk from under their feet the old, traditional certainties of musical narrative and figurative representation and experience, if only for a few minutes, the terrifying exhilaration of the future that was already engulfing them of enlarged potentials, of which sputniks and satellites were merely tentative probes.

Despite forming part of a celebrated event for several weeks, *Poème électronique* was only retrospectively acclaimed as a milestone in the development of electronic music. Its effects didn't immediately alter the trajectory of the 1950s; it would have passed through the consciousness of the millions who saw it like a waking dream, a sensational but evanescent harbinger, rather than a practical, life-altering experience. Some critics respectfully embraced the experience, while others were bemused. Howard Taubman of the *New York Times* remarked that 'the sounds that accompany these images are as bizarre as the building'. Varèse wasn't able to capitalise on its success in his remaining years. He died, under protest to the last, in 1965.

Temperamentally utterly opposed to all attempts to impose on him any form of authority, Varèse refused to join any club, despite his intersections with the Dada movement and the major composers of the twentieth century. He refused the formal disciplines of the twelve-tone system and musique concrète, devising a mode of expression that might be described as Varèse-ese. He was a lone, pioneering soul in search of absolute liberation, rather than a pursuer of themes or political ideas. His music is neither utopian nor dystopian, but a means of expressing an unhindered creative force that sought to break the bounds of conventional representation, not so much out of a futuristic impulse, more to unleash forces that had lain repressed since the beginning of time. Nor was he merely providing a blueprint. Of course, he occupies a vital place in the timeline, which will later be dotted by the likes of Kraftwerk and the Aphex Twin, but simply to see him in terms of legacy is reductive. His works aren't merely a source of clues for what direction music was to take in the twenty-first century; they are worthy of embrace as mesmeric, vertiginous eruptions of a visionary and profoundly frustrated creative spirit. What works might he have produced had he had all the technological means currently available at his disposal? Still more brilliant ones? Not very good ones? Fine works, but lost in a vast lake of similar electronic excellence? It is impossible to say. Maybe his genius is contingent on his emerging when he did, when there was still a future to anticipate. One of the key midwives of that future was a French broadcaster, composer and musicologist, a brilliant but often prickly polymath easily given to haughty disregard for other composers, including this old Varèse fellow, who had travelled to Europe to work with him on *Déserts*, but whom he considered something of an amateur. Pierre Schaeffer did not always rub along well with other humans, but his way with machines would alter the course of music history in ways that were for a long time almost entirely unacknowledged. He would show that thanks to technologies that had emerged from Nazi Germany, of all places, you could now source music not just from instruments but from pretty much anything at all.

4

UN HOMME SEUL: PIERRE SCHAEFFER AND THE ART OF SCISSORS

There is no one instrument to play musique concrète. Instead, one must imagine an enormous machine, of a cybernetic type, capable of carrying out millions of combinations, and we haven't reached that point yet.
Pierre Schaeffer

In 1948, Pierre Schaeffer, director of the experimental Studio d'Essai in Paris, accidentally scratched a vinyl disc and underwent an 'illumination' that would have immense ramifications for future music. He played the damaged record and gradually became mesmerised by the lock groove, the same snatch of sound repeating over and over, detached from its original context to the point where it took on a new life and meaning of its own, became 'unlocked'. Later, the power of the lock groove would be more systematically explored by composers like Steve Reich on his 1966 recording 'Come Out', still later in the work of Liverpool turntablist Philip Jeck and, for that matter, across the entire genre of hip hop. For now, though, the lock groove offered Schaeffer a glimpse of a whole mode of making and sourcing music, liberated from its hitherto orthodox narrative. In old age, the exploratory but truculent and ever-dissatisfied and disappointed utopian Schaeffer, always the *homme seul*, would declare his life's work a failure, that much as the human condition was unalterable, there was no escaping from the 'Do-Re-Mi' hegemony in music, of which Bach was the once and forever daddy. However, Schaeffer's 1948 illuminations would represent the end of a long, dark age in which machine music had languished since the excited prophecies of the Futurists before World War I.

Pierre Schaeffer was born in 1910 in Nancy to a musical family. Despite the supposedly 'unmusical' nature of the work for which he is best known, he never developed any Futuristic scorn for the classical harmonic tradition, and disliked intensely such twentieth-century systemic innovations as serial music. In 1934, however, he took up the study of telecommunications, then very much a fledging field, at Supélec college, in Paris. He developed a fascination for the power of radio, the 'chamber of wonders', its untapped capabilities and what it meant for the relationship between music and the world, between sound and space. He'd been involved in one particular radical application of radio as a medium, prearranging a break in transmission on Radio Paris to herald the arrival of liberating Allied troops, with the blast of 'La Marseillaise' and readings from Victor Hugo triggering mass jubilation across the city. The world of sound effects, which he used extensively when collaborating on an eight-hour 'radio opera' series called *The Universe in a Shell* in 1948, also intrigued him. He foresaw a more expansive aesthetic purpose for these captured snippets of the sound environment, rather than them being mere theatrical props. He saw in them the possibility of reconsidering what constituted the stuff of music, with the scissors in the editing suite now a key instrument.

Schaeffer enjoyed rare access to an array of equipment for storing and assembling the looped sounds he collated, which ranged from snatches of vocal and orchestral work to a welter of everyday objects, among them crystal glasses, coconut shells, klaxons and bells. These included mixers and a direct disc-to-disc cutting lathe. He imagined an entire orchestra of turntables, perhaps, each playing a single note. All of this was in advance of the introduction of magnetic tape, which opened up great vistas of possibility for what he would dub 'musique concrète'. Already, however, Schaeffer understood that if for instance you hit a bell but push the 'record' button immediately after the initial strike, the oboe-like sound of its reverberation is wholly different when isolated and released as a thing in its own right. Now imagine a billion other objects, a trillion other permutations. It's just that as yet he could only imagine the 'cybernetic' machine that would be able to carry out the godlike task of processing all of this sound information.

The purpose of musique concrète, so far as Schaeffer was concerned, wasn't merely to add to the lexicon of music; it was also a new means of expressing the infinite variety of the human spirit as manifested in its relationship with the environment. He harboured, however, a mistrust for 'what the Germans pompously call "elektronische Musik". When I encounter any electronic music I react like my violinist father, or my mother, a singer. We are craftsmen. In all this wooden and tin junk and in my bicycle horns I rediscover my violin, my voice.'

Schaeffer decided to take his theory out into the field. One of his earliest recordings was *Étude aux chemins de fer* (Railway Study), eventually realised in 1948. In May of that year, he had travelled down to Batignolles station with a mobile sound unit and, in an exercise not dissimilar to Avraamov's *Symphony of Sirens*, asked the stationary drivers in each of the respective trains to unleash the sound of their engines. He found the results a little disappointing, despite the individual character of the noises from each train, and noted the bored expressions of the drivers once the initial novelty of the exercise had worn off. He realised that in order to achieve a result, he would have to resort to the editing studio and the record library to augment his stock of sounds, otherwise he had a dead loss on his hands. In his 1952 volume *In Search of a Concrete Music*, he revisits his diaries and the agonies and elations as he assembles a piece from his locomotive sources, creating something that doesn't merely replicate like a sound photograph but arouses subjective emotions, has its own internal rhythms of whose precise nature its maker is uncertain ('It's exciting, but is it music?'). Strangest of all for this pioneer to wrestle with was a musical creative process in which, as the writer Thom Holmes put it, 'material preceded structure' rather than the other way around, when a composer faced a blank sheet of paper. Schaeffer's prospect was a pile of unedited audio matter.

Working first alone and then with his fiery young assistant, Pierre Henry, Schaeffer made a series of recordings in the late 1940s and early '50s. Magnetic tape was now part of his toolkit, and he was also assisted by RTF's Jacques Poullin, who built him a series of machines to assist him further in his manipulations. Works from this period included various études, including his *Étude aux chemins de fer*, but also one for spinning tops, *Étude aux tourniquets*. He composed what might be considered the founding cornerstone of musique concrète, *Symphonie pour un homme seul*, a sonic drama of assembled sound that begins with what sounds like the jolting hammer of a fist against a trapdoor to the future, followed by a reverberant 'Ahoy!' yelled uncertainly into the uncharted darkness that lies beyond. Later followed *Orphée*, subsequently reworked by Pierre Henry as *Echo d'Orphée*, in which his use of varispeed, drones, delays, pitch-shifting, multiple tape heads, reworked snatches of vocals, instrumentation and environmental noise provided an index for future generations of samplers, turntablists and producers for whom the soundworld was no longer restricted to the musical scale but to whatever could be captured on a microphone.

By the mid-1950s, however, Schaeffer's recorded output dwindled. He was no longer the *homme seul*. Figures such as Stockhausen, Luc Ferrari, François Bayle and Bernard Parmegiani were now engaged in their own experiments at Paris's GRM (Groupe de recherches musicales), the collective founded by Schaeffer in 1958 dedicated to production, creation and new modes of musical communication. Schaeffer hosted these young composers, but there was an undercurrent of disdain, especially on the part of Pierre Boulez, whom Schaeffer later dismissed as 'a pretentious boy . . . a Stalinist'. By comparison with their own highly developed take on musique concrète, Schaeffer's work seemed a little primitive, the bashings of a '*bruitiste*'. Schaeffer, on the other hand, would eventually consider himself somewhat above the fray of the avant-garde. He was an administrator, a polymath, a philosopher who enjoyed jousting with the likes of Marshall McLuhan amid clouds of smoke on late-night TV panel discussions. The deeper he delved into the nature of sound, as in his voluminous 1960s tome *Traité des objets musicaux*, the more distant he became from the Futurist firebrands snapping at his heels. His remoteness and seniority were still more pronounced by the late 1960s, with the arrival of situationism and, worse, post-structuralism, whose relativist ethos was wholly anathema to a man like himself who had quite a definite sense of what was superior in this world, and who treasured the idea that the universe was not a free-for-all but was informed by deep-lying harmonic systems, as certain as the periodic table.

Towards the end of his life, Schaeffer could have surveyed the contemporary musical landscape and permitted himself a certain satisfaction that the machines and soundworld he had envisaged had come to pass, indeed were ubiquitous. However, in an interview published in 1986 with Tim Hodgkinson, formerly of the fiercely political avant-prog rock group Henry Cow, Schaeffer expressed only repudiation. His mind was as furious a lathe as ever, but he regarded his investigations as having yielded nothing of consequence. He offered little hope to new musicians, who, he said, should be reminded of what Dante wrote over the gates of hell: 'Abandon hope, all ye who enter here.'

He told Hodgkinson that there could be no 'new music' because, fundamentally, there is no progress. His concern was not for the dissemination of modern electronic music but for the preservation of old, primitive African musics, whose compositions could be instructive in the face of the 'barbarity' of Western culture but were in danger of going uncollated. He regarded popular twentieth-century music as essentially froth: he saw pop, jazz, the dance music of 'mass culture' as merely utilitarian, beneath his concerns. The notion that they reflected a changing world was, to him, a fallacy, because as the structuralist Claude Lévi-Strauss had shown, the 'world doesn't change'. Rock music? A mere undifferentiated blare of which he was only vaguely aware: 'My eighteen-year-old daughter listens to a lot downstairs, so I hear what comes under her door. It's enough.' It seemed to him, in his cursory experience, 'sad, and rather morbid', and the fact that it was realised through technological means only reinforced its inauthenticity: 'It's a cheat.' You can sense the rock musician Hodgkinson's chagrin that his own fastidious, rigorously underpinned work with Henry Cow was, as far as Schaeffer was concerned, much of a muchness with that of Deep Purple.

As for the practitioners of musique concrète, the genre Schaeffer had inaugurated, they could call their creations what they liked, but on one point he was definite: they were 'not music'. He confessed that in the midst of his studio explorations in the 1940s and 1950s, even as he was carrying out his études and defending his work against the theorists of 'pure' electronic music, such as Herbert Eimert, he was actually experiencing terrible guilt and self-loathing. He heard in his head the voice of his violinist father, a paternal conscience, asking him, 'What are you doing, little chap?' He laboured and laboured in the hope that working with turntables and tape, the tools of his trade, would see him arrive at music, but he did not. 'I couldn't get to music – what I call music. I think of myself as an explorer struggling to find a way through in the far north, but I wasn't finding a way through.'

'I think we've said enough,' says Hodgkinson, as the interview reaches this rather bleak terminus. Schaeffer added little to the topic after this – he died in 1995, aged eighty-five.

Pierre Schaeffer did not exactly disown his work, the earliest in the musique concrète canon, but he did consider it mere 'research' and dismayed his successors with what they saw as his scornful attitude to the genre he himself had initiated, as if they were fools for having taken up his own suggestions. 'If an object has something to say to us, it will not be through worn-out words, clapped-out symbols squeezed of all their savor. It will be like the stars and atoms whose whole poetry is in a new rigor in understanding,' he wrote in *In Search of a Concrete Music*.

I first heard Schaeffer's original *Orphée* at the music library in the Pompidou Centre in Paris in 1983, an old vinyl edition that I was able to take to a booth and listen to, and was never able to track down back in the UK. I knew nothing about him beyond his name and his reputation as an innovator. The music cascaded across my young mind like scalding liquid, as if from shattered glass tubes. I didn't try to analyse or decipher it, or place it in any sort of historical context; I was simply open to the liberties it took. I let it play freely in my head. I loved the way the sounds emerged from a strange nowhere, like the colours and shapes that come at you when you shut your eyes and press your fists against your lids. That I was unable to commit it to memory through subsequent repetitions makes it among the most cherished of my musical memories.

Later came a CD edition of his collected works, *L'Oeuvre musicale*. I don't marvel at it for being a prototype for subsequent music and an expansion of music's lexicon, nor do I share Schaeffer's own conclusion that it falls short of music. I have a different experience of it, in many ways beyond what Schaeffer could possibly have intended: the experience of listening to it in the early twenty-first century as a distant, weathered specimen of ancient modernity.

Take *Étude aux chemins de fer*. Its qualities are ghost-like: dissolving signal sounds decaying into nothingness, yet fixed for all time. Even their surface noise, which Schaeffer almost certainly didn't intend as a texture but had to accept as one of the limitations of sound reproduction in 1948, have a certain abiding crackling warmth about them, a poignancy exploited most effectively in our own time by Philip Jeck, especially on his contribution to the most recent version of Gavin Bryars's *The Sinking of the Titanic*: the paradox of the forever lost and the forever not lost – a decay that falls short of extinction. (It's no coincidence, I believe, that Schaeffer's memoir is entitled, in Proustian fashion, *À la recherche d'une musique concrète*.)

Other effects of the music, however, are wholly intended by its creator, such as the cinematic effect of environmental noise rendered from what feels like multiple angles, the result of rigorous judgements made in the editing suite. There is the sense of an untapped interior life realised through a new mode of sound assembly. As Schaeffer said of *Symphonie pour un homme seul*:

> The lone man should find his symphony within himself, not only in conceiving the music in abstract, but in being his own instrument. A lone man possesses considerably more than the twelve notes of the pitched voice. He cries, he whistles, he walks, he thumps his fist, he laughs, he groans. His heart beats, his breathing accelerates, he utters words, launches calls and other calls reply to him. Nothing echoes more a solitary cry than the clamour of crowds.

There is the feeling that technology has the potential to breed wholly new permutations, like the chance flickering when the sun plays on a flurry of water. And then there is the affecting consequence of sound released from its original, functional context through isolation and repetition, which as a result is lent a gratuitous spiritual inner energy of the sort dreamt of by the original

Dadaists – the ancient poetry of the objects that has awaited discovery since the beginning of time, speaking to us at last. As well
as being harbingers of future possibilities, these sounds, twisted,
strange, ectoplasmic and enigmatic, evoke a deep nostalgia for
something ethereal and primordial, pre-dating humanity, God
and order, taking place against a vast jet-black void of uncertainty.
If this is not music, then it is certainly art.

As if playing out traditional Franco-German enmity, however,
Schaeffer endured ideological rivalry from another school of modern musical thought emerging out of Cologne. Herbert Eimert
was a radio programmer and salaried employee of Cologne radio
station WDR after the war, when it was administered by the
British occupation forces. As a music student in the 1920s, he had
enraged his tutor with his embrace of twelve-tone, but he now saw
the opportunity to develop these ideas further in the newly emerging technological realms. He persuaded Cologne Radio to found
a Studio for Electronic Music. One of its first students would be
an orphaned teenager seeking to construct something anew, far
from the tragedy of war. Like Eimert, this boy initially shunned
concrète – after all, who would want anything to do with the stuff
and rubble of this fallen world?

5

STOCKHAUSEN: BEYOND THE COSMOS

When I was twenty-three, I became an intellectual in the extreme because everything was new to me. Until I was twenty-one or twenty-two, I hadn't much of an idea of what music was like. I played some music that I had heard on radios, but we didn't even have a record player at home, we had . . . nothing. Well, there was no home, that's the real explanation.

Karlheinz Stockhausen, by his own account, was a human *tabula rasa*, a clean slate of a young man, despite the depravity and adversity of the time and place in which he grew up. Born in 1928 in a rural community – the village of Mödrath in the Cologne region – Stockhausen was always extremely highly attuned to his environment: to the local church bells or the nocturnal sounds of the forest when his father took him out on hunting expeditions. Traumatic events opened up great fissures in his consciousness. His mother, who had played a little piano in the family home before the stress of bearing three children in quick succession broke her, was committed to a mental hospital. He recalled the aftermath of the nervous breakdown she suffered: 'I can still see my father bringing her downstairs, holding her tightly because my mother kept wanting to go to the window, shouting: "Just let me die!" Suddenly she pointed to the cellar door and shouted: "Down there is hell!" And then she pointed up the stairs and cried: "Up there is heaven. I want to go up to the loft."' Considered a

'useless eater', unfit to live in the Third Reich, she was extermi-
nated by the authorities in 1941. His father signed up for the war
and was killed in Hungary. From the age of thirteen, Stockhausen
was forced to fend for himself as a farmworker, learning Latin at
night, taking solace in its ancient truths and dictums. He worked
with an ambulance crew on the front line. There, his already
highly developed sense of spirituality was deeply affected by the
grisly spectacle of the Fall of Man: charred and strewn lumps
of flesh, the aftermath of air raids. He was struck by the awful
idea that in the midst of this carnage, amid bodies piled high at
hospitals, people's sexual impulses were heightened rather than
repelled, as they were reduced to the merely physical, 'disconnected from the divine'.

Yet despite their death-dealing capabilities, as a young boy it had
been the circling of planes across the sky that had sketched patterns
of possibility in his head as to humanity's technical capabilities and
the notion that he might too, in some as-yet-unimagined way, take
flight, ideas that would inform some of his wildly sanguine the-
ories about the unreleased potential of mankind. He himself was
certainly resilient and resourceful. After the war, while undertaking his music studies, he made a living as a pianist, bashing out
popular songs in Cologne bars and collecting butts and making
new cigarettes out of them to sell on the black market. He was
contemptuously aware of his guilty fellow Germans' sentimental
taste for familiar ditties, as if they could be redeemed by their saccharine, stearin innocence; the sort of banal, amnesiac German
music, codified as Schlager, that would prove far more popular
during the post-war years than the higher-minded efforts of himself and his colleagues at Darmstadt, where, from the early 1950s
onwards, the International Summer Courses for New Music generated a formidable barrage of serial music composition by Luigi
Nono, Bruno Maderna and Pierre Boulez, among others. That
said, in later years he kept a spinet piano at his home, on which

this often surprisingly down-to-earth man would play old ragtime tunes to entertain his children, and perhaps himself.

Aged nineteen, he began his studies at the Hochschule für Musik in Cologne. Today, glass casings exhibit like antique museum pieces the machinery with which he would eventually play his own remote, and not necessarily intentional, role in recasting modern music, both avant-garde and popular. He didn't just study music but also philosophy and 'Germanics'. Unlike many composers, Stockhausen wouldn't be exclusively immersed in the intrinsic scientific rigour of his music but would always see it in a wider context – in his case, universe-wide. He absorbed and took on board the most up-to-date thinking in composition, studying under Olivier Messaien, but this would ultimately be a jumping-off point for more wide-ranging studies, which included new technology and information theory under Herbert Eimert at the Studio for Electronic Music of the Westdeutscher Rundfunk (WDR), in Cologne. The studio housed a battery of electronic instruments: the Monochord and Melochord; a noise generator; an octave filter, which converted white-noise signals into octave-wide frequency bands; band-pass filters; a ring modulator, able to multiply two signals, including a sine wave; an oscilloscope, which could render sounds visible as they were generated; and a four-track tape recorder.

Stockhausen and Eimert worked on the periodical *Die Reihe*, in which they expounded on new musical theory and the potential role of electronics in modern composition, then in its infancy. The magazine, however, was blighted by infighting, disagreements, challenges to the authority of the senior Eimert from the younger Stockhausen, and derisive accusations from critics that the magazine's authors were guilty of pseudo-scientific blather, an accusation not without merit.

Stockhausen would come to be torn between two emerging schools emanating from two nations who, the recent war notwithstanding, were traditionally temperamentally at odds. As his recorded work shows, Eimert preferred the severe spotlessness of electronics, unsullied by recent history or the stuff of earth, a medium in which one could theoretically and materially explore the utterly new. It's not hard to see the appeal of this notion to post-war Germans, surrounded by the stench and mess and rubble of the old world and an utterly discredited, viciously reactionary Teutonic 'ideal'. It was an idea to which the young Stockhausen initially subscribed, inspired also by the Hermann Hesse novel *The Glass Bead Game*. However, over in France, Pierre Schaeffer had conceived the new medium of musique concrète, which, boosted by the invention of magnetic tape, enabled composers to incorporate into their compositions second-hand sonic matter, drawn from existing musical recordings or environmental noise.

Stockhausen visited Schaeffer's studio in 1952, where he made his first foray into musique concrète with *Konkrete Etüde*. He continued working with Eimert, however, and in 1955 composed the perennially astonishing *Gesang der Jünglinge* (Song of the Youths), a synthesis of pure, originally generated electronics and source material of a similarly 'unspotted' nature, as it happens: the 'youths' of the title were actually derived from a single voice – the virgin, unbroken voice of a twelve-year-old chorister, Josef Protschka. The work sated Stockhausen's desire for spiritual cleanliness. He regarded the work as akin to a sacred Mass, a devotional work of sorts from a man with profound religious hankerings. Catholicism, in particular, was his way of countering what he saw as the self-indulgent nihilism of his fellow post-war intellectuals. He regarded the cosmos not as an indifferent voice but as a heaven of possibility.

One could read into *Gesang der Jünglinge* a redemption of the word and concept of 'youth', which had been hijacked by the Nazis – as Stockhausen himself, conscripted by the Nazis, was painfully aware. The text sung by Protschka is from the Book of Daniel: the story of Shadrach, Meshach and Abednego emerging unharmed from the furnace into which Nebuchadnezzar cast them and singing thanks of praise to God. The contemporary relevances of this text were manifold. However, the piece also enabled Stockhausen to explore the perversions and mutations of the concrète method. The text was not delivered straight but as a fragmentary assault, with deliberately varied degrees of comprehensibility. This was Purity cracked and atomised, receding and showering like meteors, subdivided and multiplied, a piously, meticulously organised mathematical frenzy of sound particles, a cosmic dissemination infinitely more powerful than language. There was no 'structure' to the piece, which consisted rather of micro- and macro-evolutions of sound and shape.

Hearing it broadcast at the 'Rest Is Noise' festival at the Royal Festival Hall in 2013, its painstakingly assembled, finely chopped shoals of sine tones and real-life vocals showering from the rafters like an acoustic fireworks display, you could understand how musique concrète could at least make sense to a live audience who might otherwise have been puzzled by its seemingly arbitrary and irregular squiggles and eruptions. This was music that posited a new, more open relationship between sound and space, rather than the traditional fixed point of dissemination from a stage within a collective field of vision. *Kontakte*, composed by Stockhausen between 1959 and 1960, exhibits in even greater depth the idea of a music in which anything can come at you from anywhere, hoving in from infinitely deep space or exploding unexpectedly an inch from your nose – a new music for the dawning space age.

Kontakte was presented in two versions: one with the accompaniment of piano and percussion; the other – preferred by many, including the electronic duo Autechre – alone. As discussed by Stockhausen and others, the theme of *Kontakte* is its form. It is, for him, the ultimate work of serialism, a feat of total organisation in which 'timbre, pitch, density and duration are brought under a single control'. The control centre, in live performance, was a 'rotation table' surrounded by four microphones, from which the composer could manipulate, sending the sounds of the work arcing about the auditorium, placing them like long-range passes in the spots of his choosing via four loudspeakers situated in the four corners of the hall, thereby enabling an infinite variety of approaches between sound source and human ear. Total organisation, then, as a springboard for absolute freedom – an exciting or wholly unnerving prospect, depending on the listener's readiness to absorb music in 'darkness', and minus the footholds of certainty afforded by conventional arrangement and orchestration. To some, *Kontakte* might seem like the random flinging of toxic electronic filth by hidden miscreants. Such listeners were not in short supply and were often to be found in high places, as Stockhausen recalled in a 2005 interview with Réjean Beaucage: 'Karl Amadeus Hartmann, the extremely influential composer and president of the German section of the International Society for Contemporary Music, passed by me on leaving the hall and said, "Scheißen Stücke!" – "A piece of shit!" I was really hurt.'

Certainly, as a young man, I played my vinyl copy of *Kontakte* to friends as a sort of test, which I rather hoped they'd fail, enjoying a hollow and slightly pyrrhic feeling of superiority when they did. Even fellow music journalists regarded the music as a sub-*Clangers* farrago of sonic nonsense, cerebral snake oil perpetrated by mad Germans on po-faced, pseudo-intellectual dupes.

Some of them, though, have since come around, not least because the ubiquity of electronica and ambient has sophisticated the collective sound palate; or because of the undiminished capacity of the piece to astonish and impact. I'm playing it now as I type. In its deep background, a vastness murmurs; then, a sudden asteroid splash of concrète makes a crater in the cerebellum. Recessions, a nervous tinkle of percussion, a distant pulse like a receding spacecraft that, in a *trompe l'oreille*, is actually closing in.

Pianistic anxiety. Serrated fragments of metal, ancient drones, sudden fresh, cold waves. Whiplash intensity, particles illuminated by explosive flashes. Rumbles and signals from alien sources, unpredictable and irregular, but which seem premeditated, operating on a higher plane of thought. Long-extinct stars flickering obscurely. Diagonal bursts of radiation. Sudden catastrophes whose immolation leaves no afterburn, just a void. Single piano notes, isolated and disconnected from their original keyboard context, lost in space. Growling electric currents like approaching waterborne reptiles, changing course at the last second. Decelerations, then another crash-landing, sidelights whirling. Moons spinning off their axes. Cosmic birdsong. Oscillations, impossible droplets, curlicues, sparks.

Coiling sine waves, slowing and rearing like aliens right up in your face, probing and examining you as you try to remain stock still. A more regular broadside of events, constructions of stone and metal floating at speed from all angles, against a backdrop whose indifference and omnipresence is represented by a wispy perma-drone. Sabre squabbles, multiple collisions, scorched aftermath; a laser bolt between the eyes, the scatter of cerebral matter. Untranslatable alien exclamations writ large in carbon tags. Fresh Big Bangs, new universes. Inconsequential clatter, like spinning coins coming to rest. A dance of percussion and piano, brief echoes of Pierre Boulez's *Le Marteau sans maître*. Then, radioactive glitter in the eyes. An aluminium chorus, glass waves, siren calls, revolutions of light, varispeed. An ending, without resolution or arrival, whose fadeout merely indicates that we've been staring through the window at processes that are both permanent and infinite.

Kontakte was composed and presented at a time when the popular imagination of the Western world was still submerged in post-war dreams of imminent UFO invasion, as depicted in countless B-movies and parodied in Jerry Lewis movies and *The Phil Silvers Show*, as well as the prospect of human exploration of immediate space, with satellites having been launched into low earth orbit and Yuri Gagarin about to make the first manned space flight. When Stockhausen referred to *Kontakte*, he was referring, in academic terms, to the interface between certain musical elements, but the word resonates: one thinks of 'first contact', not just with alien life forms but with alien forms of music, extra-planetary, a long way from the ground on which previous musics had been founded, from the earth in which they had been tilled. It's a music that arrives just as the topography of the human imagination is beginning to expand into the outer cosmic unknown. The events hinted at in abstract/concrète terms in *Kontakte* – anxiety, wonder, unpredictability, adventure – should have reflected those of humanity on the verge of the space age, should have struck multiple chords; a sense of space coupled with a new spatial awareness. Yet in its own time at least, its impact was confined to a tiny coterie in the subsidised academic world of the European avant-garde. Elvis was still the main supplier of popular electricity.

That gradually changed, however, as the 1960s wore on and Stockhausen's reputation grew thanks to ever more prestigious commissions and his pioneering interest in multimedia events and music as part of broader environmental arts events, often brought together under the canvas of sponsored occasions such as Expo '70. He persisted with musique concrète and electronic music long after prestigious contemporaries such as Ligeti and Boulez had melted away from the genre, having lost interest in its possibilities.

Hymnen, composed between 1966 and 1967, represents Stockhausen's own apex in perhaps the greatest decade of the twentieth century, drawing together all of his preoccupations in an immense, globe-girdling work. Listening to it is like gloriously orbiting the planet from a hundred miles high, before crash-landing in remote charred deserts of the imagination in which only the intimacy of a human breath, perhaps that of the last man alive, remains audible. Such was my impression of the piece when

I first heard it, at least – Stockhausen's vivid electronic abstractions allow for a variety of Rorschach impressions.

Composed and assembled at the WDR in Cologne, *Hymnen* is subdivided into various 'regions'. The first plunges you immediately into the deep end already charted by John Cage on his 'Williams Mix' – the use of transistor radio as an instrument, the dial here manipulated by Stockhausen with uncanny virtuosity; within seconds of surfing the stations, a serendipitous occasion as the words 'United Nations' jump from the waves. This is in keeping with the work, through which are threaded recordings of various national anthems, subjected to varying degrees of fragmentation, interference and mutation. These are the most conspicuous concrète elements, highly recognisable reference points that enable the listener to recognise the extent to which Stockhausen treats and processes his source material. However, the pure radio waves are in delightful keeping with Stockhausen's cosmic and spiritual outlook: 'instant electronic music', he described them as in one interview, but what they also represent is that quality of the unsullied and unearthly that initially attracted him to the work of Eimert – the unexplored, untapped universe transmitting its constant, frantic, abstract message to mankind, if only we did not tune it out in favour of our own banal programmes. Radio waves – a glorious outpouring a mere tweak of a button away but regarded by most as mere interference.

Gradually, from region one (dedicated to Pierre Boulez) emerge grainy extracts of 'La Marseillaise', as well as 'The Internationale'. Was Stockhausen making some sort of political point about idealism or the hubris of nationalism? At one point, the sound of a flock of geese is mischievously tweaked to resemble the notes of the French anthem. But it's unlikely Stockhausen intended much in the way of direct social commentary. What is less deniable is that these musical signifiers of nation states and grand narratives must take their place, when viewed from afar, in the context of a new media environment, buffered, weathered and obscured by noise clouds, the unpredictable eruption of crowds and a whole host of sonic distractions rendered here in a panoramic sound snapshot. This is the world, shrunken by new technologies and also the increased consciousness of outer space. This is a new electric element in which Stockhausen exhibits the mastery of a Beethoven, with the same symphonic sensibility, the same sense of drama of when to attack and when to recede, the same overall sense of placement and architecture.

The drama is interrupted periodically by croupier-like announcements – '*Faites vos jeux, messieurs dames, s'il vous plaît*' – and one thinks back to *Kontakte* and Stockhausen as composer/ringmaster, at the hub of the wheel, ordering chance. Later, there's a fugal pause as he and his studio assistants chant the word '*rouge*'. Red, the roulette colour? Red, the political hue? In fact, it's a reference to the red in a paint tin, but the sudden switch from remote global vastness to this studio intimacy suggests we are suddenly in the cockpit with the gods.

The second region is dedicated to Henri Pousseur, composer and Stockhausen's co-worker at the Cologne studio in the 1950s, who many years later would create his own *Paysage planétaires*, whose weave of global ethnic styles feels like a nod to *Hymnen*. In the third region, the Russian anthem is manipulated, rendered electronically in analogue stretches that prefigure dark ambient noise of the early twenty-first century. The effect of this cybernetic perversion seems initially rather horrifying, as if flesh has melted away to reveal metal skeletons, but maybe all that's required is mere acclimatisation; the normal rules of gravity do not apply in Stockhausen's free-floating musical orbit. One becomes accustomed to the pulse and swell of his analogue electronics, whose fabric has simply supplanted the orchestral strings of the old world.

Finally, the fourth region, dedicated to Luciano Berio, in which the listeners find themselves suddenly adrift in another realm, no longer aboard a giant balloon taking in the world's anthems through a gauze of interference and irregular electronic mediation. Instead, Stockhausen co-opts a choral version of the Swiss national anthem, isolating its final chord on a tape loop that hovers like a dark organism throughout the piece. It was meant to form the basis of a utopian anthem, one whose respiratory motions are attuned to the breathing of the planet. However, there is a desolation, too, about the final region, with its isolated wails ringing across its plains, a moment of what sounds like crowd panic and, most powerful of all, a series of slow glissandos inspired by a visit Stockhausen made to the waterfalls at Yosemite Valley. These glissandos cascade throughout the piece, forever descending, forever renewing, at once spiritually cleansing and yet with the intensity of a firestorm that wipes out the humanity below. I first heard this section (in isolation, on the double album *Stockhausen's Greatest Hits*) aged fifteen and it filled me with terror, especially coupled with Stockhausen's warnings in the sleevenotes that mankind would very soon have to go through some sort of apocalyptic purge before it could be reborn.

'You see, usually we read about catastrophes that are to come,' he told the writer Jonathan Cott in 1971. 'But I find even talking to very conscious people that they always think in the back of their minds there might be an escape; perhaps they think it's just words and that the scientists who announce these catastrophes do so as an early warning in order to escape from these crises. They think it might not come. But it will come. We have to go through these crises at the end of the century and the beginning of the next . . . there is no other way.'

Hymnen, the composer confirmed, was a sort of musical therapy to prepare the listener for these dreadful but somehow redeeming events, the 'purifying shock' of a great war involving the Americans, the Russians, even the Japanese. You sense the Catholic Stockhausen at some level relishing this catastrophe, which would ultimately be for the improvement of mankind, a release of higher powers. Yet despite the absence, so far, of a World War III, Stockhausen's remarks resonate uneasily in an era in which most of us preserve our peace of mind by zoning out the repeated scientific warnings of the imminent dangers of global warming.

In his interest in studio equipment as a means of composition and sound-making – as a 'musical instrument', as the cliché would later have it – Stockhausen also attracted the attention of the world's biggest group, who, happily, were also its best and most adventurous – the Beatles.

John Lennon had been in contact by phone with Stockhausen and, on the *White Album*, would make an ambitious if slightly clumsy fist of musique concrète on the piece 'Revolution 9', whose sinister sound collages had the unintended effect of inciting the imagination of Charles Manson, who regarded the entire *White Album*, and 'Revolution 9' in particular, as a coded message, addressed to him personally, ordering him to carry out a programme of slaughter of selected white 'pigs', including Roman Polanski's wife Sharon Tate, thus precipitating a race war in which Manson and his followers would somehow emerge victorious. Not even Stockhausen had been prepared for, or even remotely anticipated, this catastrophe.

It wasn't just Lennon, however. Paul McCartney may have written the more MOR Beatles material but his natural curiosity (and bachelor freedom) drew him to art galleries and the avant-garde circuit, where he encountered Stockhausen's *Gesang der Jünglinge*, his favourite piece by the composer. 'What's often said of me is that I'm the guy who wrote "Yesterday" or I'm the guy who was the bass player for the Beatles,' McCartney told *Wired* magazine in 2011. 'That stuff floats to the top of the water, you know? But I'm also a guy who was really interested in tape loops, electronics and avant-garde music. That just doesn't get out there on a wide level, but it's true. I've really been fascinated by this stuff.'

Stockhausen duly found his place amid the pantheon of the *Sgt Pepper's Lonely Hearts Club Band* album sleeve, just above Tony Curtis and nuzzling on the neck of W. C. Fields. The navigator of the sonic firmament, he now found himself part of the firmament of influences refracted by the Beatles in the new psychedelic dawn, a mix of cabaret and culture, of high verse and slapstick comedy, of spiritual gurus and sex sirens. Frank Zappa, who parodied *Sgt Pepper* with his own masterpiece *We're Only in It for the Money*, also revered Stockhausen and, as he had done with Varèse, helped proliferate his name.

This was an age not only more open to highly experimental approaches to music-making than our early-twenty-first-century own, but also an era of greater credulity, in which anything was deemed possible. Mysticism was embraced rather than scoffed at for being mere wishful hippy vacuity touted by mind-addled, overprivileged hedonists in kaftans. The cosmos was regarded then as a potential bounty rather than, as in today's post-space age in which we gaze at vivid but impossibly distant galaxies through Hubble telescopes, an unexplorable and immense reminder of our own impotence. By 1980, we would be on Mars. Before then, however, as Stockhausen anticipated, aliens would propitiously decide that now was the right time in humanity's development to pay us a visit. His 1971 piece *Sternklang* was intended to serenade our new extraterrestrial friends as part of a welcoming reception on their arrival.

Stockhausen's mind was a brilliant one, operating with the strength of multiple lasers. He could speak – in detail and with a conviction lesser brains found hard to counter – of ancient Japanese ritual and musical custom, of horticulture, of Eastern mystical thought, of the all-embracing importance of spirals (an idea introduced to him by the English writer Jill Purce, with whom he liaised in the early 1970s), allude easily to philosophers like Pierre Teilhard de Chardin, as well as explain, to those with the ability to take it in, the workings of serial music, notions such as periodicity and harmonic perspective. He could out-converse most people across a range of topics, without even resorting to his first language.

And yet, for all his awesome grasp of a welter of material, for all his ability to peer beyond the conventions that bound lesser mortals, he was, not to put too fine a point on it, dead wrong about stuff. His refusal to accept that the boundaries of physics and science could not be as easily breached as the boundaries of classical music, as well as his faith in the properties of electricity, led him to a whole raft of, shall we say, sanguine ideas. Some of these were modest, the stuff of tomorrow's world: he suggested that using computer data, people could create their own 'silent zones' when out in public, special 'acoustical toilets' into which people could 'piss and shit . . . but they wouldn't be bothering anyone else with their acoustical garbage'. He believed that the study of cosmic rays and their impact should be part of the school curriculum, and that it was 'more important than writing and arithmetic'. He reckoned that headaches could be cured by simply shifting electrical energy from one part of the body to another using psychic effort. He held that such was the available power of electrical currents, if we were only to haul ourselves up by the bootstraps of our consciousness we could avoid death itself, 'if we were able to lead the current into the body and into all the limbs and their particles'. He believed that human beings would have to undergo some physical transformation of their bodies to endure thousands of years travelling at the speed of light, now that the era of space exploration was clearly here to stay. He believed that in his life and work he was guided by a series of angels.

Over time, and with age making him too grand a figure to be easily contradicted, Stockhausen gradually receded into the universe of his own beliefs. Eventually, he came to hold that, like Sun Ra, he was originally from another world altogether – that of

Sirius, the star system to which he paid homage in an electronic work composed between 1975 and 1977.

The most famous person to upbraid Stockhausen out of more than mere reactionary philistinism was his erstwhile musical colleague Cornelius Cardew, who in 1974 delivered a tract entitled *Stockhausen Serves Imperialism*, in which he took both himself to task for his involvement in the avant-garde and also its most famous names, John Cage and Karlheinz Stockhausen. Having founded the Scratch Orchestra in 1969, a free-for-all ensemble in which a willingness to participate and improvise was the main requirement of those who joined, Cardew was undergoing a crisis with regard to the 'elitist' nature of the difficult music to which he had dedicated his earlier life and its detachment from working-class tastes and concerns. He regarded its extremes as merely the decadent rot of a bourgeois musical form in the last throes of disintegration.

'The avant-garde period . . . is not the latest, but the last chapter in the history of bourgeois music,' he wrote. 'The bourgeois class audience turns away from the contemporary musical expression of its death agony, and contemporary bourgeois music becomes the concern of a tiny clique taking a morbid interest in the process of decay.' He at once decried Stockhausen as an obscurantist, working in the 'ivory tower conditions' of Darmstadt, and also as a showman/shaman/charlatan who had made a conscious effort in the late 1950s to peddle his music as a mystical snake oil, balm on a society riven in reality by class differences and injustices to which he was oblivious.

'In a recent interview, [Stockhausen] says that a musician when he walks on stage "should give that fabulous impression of a man who is doing a sacred service" [note the showmanship underlying that remark]. He sees his social function as bringing an "atmosphere of peaceful spiritual work to a society that is under so much strain from technical and commercial forces". Salesmen like

Stockhausen would have you believe that slipping off into cosmic consciousness removes you from the reach of the painful contradictions that surround you in the real world.' He condemned Stockhausen's mysticism, realised in his compositions, as part of 'a world outlook which is an ally of imperialism'.

Cardew's renunciation of the avant-garde took a wishful form. He embarked on what he called 'people's liberation music', populist ditties that could be bashed out on the piano at working men's clubs up and down the country and whose plain-spoken socialist lyrics and whistle-able tunes would prove a smash with the proletariat, tear up the 'hit parade' that was the musical province of the common man and trigger a revolution as their eyes were opened to social injustice via this base musical medium. The results were intriguing. 'Smash the Social Contract' is one of his more rousing numbers, though a sense of *déjà entendu* is confirmed when you realise that its chorus line bears an uncanny similarity to 'Funky Gibbon' by the Goodies.

For a man capable of such enormous complexity of thought, Cardew does not seem to have realised how simplistic the equation he used to arrive at his 'people's liberation music' was: revolutionary content plus the sugar pill of catchy pop melody = music to galvanise the masses into action. Of course, the dynamics between consumption, leisure, pop, politics and class struggle don't lend themselves to such easy solutions, and so it obdurately proved as Cardew gamely bashed at his keyboard to such little social avail.

Although imperialism was doubtless unaware of what a key servant it had in Stockhausen, there was a small grain of truth in Cardew's criticisms: mysticism was indeed a spurious balm that distracted rather than heightened consciousness, and while it garnered approval from Western onlookers it had done little or nothing to improve the lot of the countries from which it emerged and the struggles of their peoples against poverty and oppression.

As for Stockhausen himself, he made absolutely no concessions to populism. Moreover, as a conductor and arranger, he was rigidly authoritarian, as musicians would discover. It was their job to follow his exacting instructions to the last detail – a bracing challenge, no doubt, but one which left no room for their own input or suggestions. His way was the absolutely correct way. This meant that he was resolutely unflattered or ungratified by his supposed influence in paving the way for popular electronic music, most of which he saw as erroneous due to its over-reliance on repetition, which he regarded as a form of arrested articulacy: 'It is like someone who is stuttering all the time, and can't get words out of his mouth.' *The Wire* magazine ran an immortal piece in 1995 in which they presented to the composer for his scrutiny tracks by 1990s electronica artists, including the Aphex Twin, Plastikman and Daniel Pemberton. He clearly took the trouble to listen to each piece in turn but found them aberrant and simplistic. He upbraided 'Aphex Twin of Richard James' for indulging excessively in 'post-African repetitions' and urged him to vary his tempi, taking as his example his own *Gesang der Jünglinge*.

He returned to his theme when criticising Plastikman: 'I know that he wants to have a special effect in dancing bars, or wherever it is, on the public who like to dream away with such repetitions, but he should be very careful, because the public will sell him out immediately for something else, if a new kind of musical drug is on the market.' Robin Rimbaud, aka Scanner, whose samples eavesdrop on the telephone conversations of anonymous strangers, he liked a little more, but he still wished he would elaborate and transmogrify his sound sources, again citing by way of an example his own work – *Hymnen*.

Although technically and forensically accurate, and having done the courtesy of listening intently to the work of these young artists, Stockhausen reveals an amusingly high-handed disdain for popular music, whose imposed limitations he regards as inherent proof of its inferiority as a medium, and whose broad appeal is to him clear evidence that its appeal is narcotic rather than aesthetic. He's perhaps right to suggest that young electronica artists are more besotted by the sensational effects of his music, the 'unusual, the crazy', than by its rigorous methods and intentions. But clearly, to Stockhausen, the idea of any sort of cross-fertilisation between the low popular and the high classical is unthinkable, as is the idea that a piece of simple, repetitive popular music could achieve things besides and beyond the reach of any contemporary classical work, however great. In our own postmodern times this sort of snobbery is almost refreshing – almost. Certainly, you can imagine his inner voice screaming something along the lines of, 'I was not put on this earth just to pave the way for the bloody Aphex Twin!'

Scanner recalls his going-over by the old master, which also reveals Stockhausen's warmer, more human side. 'I actually came out better than some of the other musicians as their work was, and largely continues to be, based on issues of repetition, whereas mine has maintained a looser flow. He was even kind enough to send me some CDs in the post with a sweet card, and he had signed the CDs for me.

'I can't deny I found the entire episode both flattering and amusing, of course. I was familiar with *Hymnen* and it was little surprise to hear his very judgemental responses to the music. It wasn't that dissimilar to folks from another generation listening to the "young people's dance music" of today and failing to understand it in more ways than simply the sound, but all the cultural values invested in a form and style of music.'

Some sort of common touch might have helped Stockhausen in 2001, when he decided to discuss the terrorist attack of 11 September, in which thousands lost their lives. A simple expression of condolence would have sufficed. Instead, he was reported to have said, 'That characters can bring about in one act what we in music cannot dream of, that people practise madly for ten years, completely fanatically, for a concert and then die. That is the greatest work of art for the whole cosmos. Against that, we composers are nothing.' Stockhausen protested that he had in fact referred to the outrage as the work of 'Lucifer', but the remarks as reported caused sufficient upset for a series of concerts in Germany to be cancelled.

What could have prompted him to set out on such a train of thought? Is it possible that Stockhausen was still waiting for the global cataclysm that he had announced as impending some thirty years earlier and had taken the collapse of the Twin Towers as a key event that would tear a hole of opportunity, allowing for mankind's cosmic development? Certainly, he didn't develop his thoughts on this matter any further.

In the late 1960s and '70s, Stockhausen became a touchstone for some of the world's biggest artists, including the Beatles, the Grateful Dead, Miles Davis, Frank Zappa and, later, Kraftwerk, who understood his work at close hand, even if all they really had in common with the composer was that they used electronics as a means to effect a complete transformation of a genre. Stockhausen was also the butt of a certain scepticism, however, a high-profile signifier for modernist 'plinky-plonky' cacophonous excess. His own website features cartoons, including one from a 2004 edition of the *Guardian* showing a surgeon explaining to his patient on the operating table, 'No, it's not Stockhausen – we've just dropped a tray of surgical instruments.' Another shows a piano tuner asking the owner of a Steinway, 'When did you first notice that your Mozart sounded like Stockhausen?' Yet another cartoon features upstairs neighbours pogoing about, randomly smashing a ping pong ball hither and yon, as their downstairs neighbours complain, 'It sounds like those bloody idiots upstairs are playing their Stockhausen records again.' The lack of obligation felt by musical reactionaries to make their jokes at the avant-garde's expense remotely funny remains one of the wonders of the age.

It was Stockhausen for whom I reached when I wrote my book *Fear of Music: Why People Get Rothko but Don't Get Stockhausen*, in which I wondered aloud why twentieth-century avant-garde visual art was so enormously popular and well appreciated, while its musical equivalent remained neglected by comparison and was derided with impunity. There were various reasons for this, including the perpetual lack of exposure for new musical forms, exacerbating their sense of 'difficulty'. The public was more accustomed to modern art, not least because of frequent newspaper stories about how such-and-such a work had gone under the hammer for millions of dollars, accompanied by a picture of said work, its aesthetic value confirmed by its financial value. No such luck for avant-garde music, which had no equivalent of an 'original' to sell at Sotheby's.

Furthermore, there was the issue of time and scale. To visit a Rothko at the Tate Modern simply required turning up at the exhibition room and spending as little as a few minutes in sober contemplation of a piece of art that, despite the abstraction and scale on which Rothko worked, existed comfortably within its frame, within your field of vision. A few minutes, and then you could leave for the tea rooms, having ticked Rothko off your list of aesthetic chores. To attend a concert by Stockhausen, however, was a rather more daunting prospect, especially given his placement of speakers in the auditorium, which meant that sounds might catch you unawares from all manner of unexpected places. Furthermore, for a concert to be experienced in its entirety meant a stretch across time. Leave after a few minutes and you could hardly claim to have 'done' the composer; rather, you would have merely given up on the challenge.

For all that, Stockhausen is a far more appreciated figure in the Age of Electronica, feted by stars and tastemakers like Björk, the former members of Sonic Youth, Brian Eno, Portishead and many, many others. Plenty enough people met the challenge of watching him 'perform' his most famous electronic works, including *Kontakte* and *Hymnen*, at the Barbican in 2001, when he was dressed in what looked like a safari suit. He could have taken satisfaction from the fact that, via Kraftwerk in particular, the entire field of play in popular music was now electrified, while on the peripheries of pop, countless electronic practitioners were generating ambient, abstract noises from analogue and digital equipment that echoed his experiments from the 1950s and were made by young people who regarded him as a modern deity. As we have seen, though, he did not take any satisfaction from this proliferation. This was underdeveloped music, too reliant on repetition, and hardly following in his footsteps at all. He looked down from the mountaintop and saw only small dots of activity at the base. 'Why your repetition, your fixation on the same spot?' he might have wondered. 'Why don't you climb and develop and venture the way I did?' Kraftwerk once said, metaphorically, that they had 'no fathers', that they were remaking popular music as cultural orphans. Stockhausen might well have felt that he was artistically childless.

But then, was Stockhausen not pretty much away with the new-age fairies by the end of his life? What value could be placed on the achievements of a man who was so wrong about things – spirituality, religion, humanity's actual place in the cosmos, our true capacity for expansion, the real potential of electricity, the artistic worth of the 11 September attacks? What is the value in his work if it inadvertently serves not just imperialism, in its grandiose thematic attractions, but also the follies of an over-sanguine, overexcited, pre-Aquarian age? The answer to that lies in part in a response he gave to an interviewer who asked if he was a 'surrealist' composer.

'I recently gave six concerts in Norway, where I performed *Mittwochs-Abschied* [Wednesday Farewell, 1996], a work of electronic and concrète music,' replied Stockhausen, 'and I presented it as a music that was not only surreal, but transreal, in the sense that it creates expectations of events that could happen, but which turn into something completely different, strange, but it isn't the strangeness that is transreal; it is the miraculous nature of the musical transformation. Of course, there's a lot of surrealism in my music.'

Here's the thing, then: you do not have to subscribe to Stockhausen's outré beliefs, to subscribe to the joys and challenges of his works. The ideas he posits may not conform to physical or scientific reality, but they are, as he says, 'transreal'; they are tangible, triumphant additions to the musical lexicon. They reduce what was once considered irreducible. They fly by the nets of old classical structures, find air where there was once thought to be nothing. Like an intended explosion in the laboratory, they carefully and methodically tear giant fissures in the fabric of possibility. They chart new and limitless realms of inner space. They extend the imagination and obliterate prejudice. They are the products of an advanced musical language, to whose macro-scale and micro-details we might take decades, maybe centuries, to become fully accustomed. Far from being the giant decommissioned metal antiquities of a discredited modernist project, these are works whose potentialities and achievements will still be pored over, if there is anyone left to do any poring, in the thirty-third century, a music that's as eternal as God is dead. What seems impossible or improbable to a limited head like mine right now may seem rather less so then.

The notion of a Greatest Composer of the Century is more absurd than ever when it comes to the twentieth century. How do you compare a Stravinsky with an Ellington, a Cage with a McCartney? But for one man it's worth sticking one's neck out and defying the relativists to declare: Stockhausen was the greatest composer of the twentieth century.

6

4' 33" OF EVERYTHING: JOHN CAGE AND OTHER CONCRÈTE SOLUTIONS

Such is the dominance of Stockhausen, the vast, Germanic shadow of grandeur he casts, that it can be forgotten that he was one among many in his field. From afar, from the centre, he is still regarded by some as a maverick, an aberration even, whose folly deserves interring with the twentieth century, along with the Soviet Union and instant mashed potato. However, there were others who followed up on that which he hoped to inaugurate, while among his contemporaries were parallel thinkers making their own distinctive enquiries about the relationship between music, the world and new technologies. Among these was the man to whom he had dedicated the third region of *Hymnen*.

In early 1960, a tall, dapper, middle-aged fellow was invited onstage by host Garry Moore for the popular long-running American TV show *I've Got a Secret*. He was greeted cordially enough by the studio audience, but none of them had the faintest idea who he was. He introduced himself as John Cage, from Stony Point, New York, in his customarily effete tones, which were the stock-in-trade of many a comic character actor from the era. The audience was primed to giggle – the more so when Cage's 'secret' was that he was a composer who was going to perform one of his works, which would feature, among other things, a water pitcher, an iron pipe, a mechanical fish, a quail caller, a jug of roses and a watering can, as well as a tape recorder, radios and a grand piano. These items were listed on screen as the host recited them, eyebrows raising throughout, to the mounting mirth of the studio audience.

Cage permitted himself a kindly smirk; he wasn't new to prime-time television. He had already performed this piece on the Italian quiz show *Lascia o Raddoppia?* – a version of *Double Your Money* – while he was in Milan working with composers including Luciano Berio at the RAI studios. He'd attained further celebrity by participating in the show as a contestant, answering questions about mushrooms, a subject on which he had become expert during his rural sojourns at Stony Point.

'You know people are going to laugh?' the host warned Cage gravely – though that, of course, was the entire purpose of this TV exercise. Cage refused to play the stuffed avant-garde shirt. 'I consider laughter preferable to tears,' he said, to more laughter. The host referred to Cage as someone who dealt in 'experimental sound', only to be firmly corrected by Cage. 'Experimental music,' he said. He explained simply that since music was the production of sounds, and sounds were what he produced, then the result was music. It was that simple. He would demonstrate this to the audience with his presentation of 'Water Walk', so called because it featured the running of water and himself walking through the piece, event by event.

The host explained that Cage would be using a stopwatch 'because these sounds are in no sense accidental in their sequence'. Cage was known for enshrining chance as a determining factor in twentieth-century composition, but this did not mean he simply let things fall as they may. He began, striking a note on the pre-pared piano, whose reverberations ultimately would dominate this piece, buffeted by initial nervous laughter building to giddy gales of merriment from the studio audience. Oblivious, locked into his own organisational zone, Cage fiddles with a pressure cooker, toys with a rubber duck, applies a soda siphon, waters flowers in a bathtub, takes a drink of water, but the noises of all of these actions are dwarfed by the ongoing reverberations of the piano. Finally, Cage shoves his radios off their tables, an act of vandalism that brings a shriek of delight from the audience, although he had already explained that this was to resolve a dispute with the stage-hands' union as to their own participation in the making of this performance. 'Water Walk' is greeted not with a barrage of fruit or jeers but with fulsome applause from an audience sportingly appreciative of Mr Cage's gall in pulling off an elaborate gimmick.

Was this indeed a stunt of sorts, an act of attention-seeking on the part of a natural extrovert who, like Salvador Dalí, could not bear for long the introversion and obscurantism of twentieth-century art practice? To a degree, perhaps. He certainly looks as if he is enjoying himself, happy to trade off the barely concealed and uncomprehending derision of his hosts in exchange for getting to demonstrate his work, without compromise, to an audience of millions. The piece, however, is not mere gimmickry but illustrative of Cage's radical and deceptively complex artistic philosophy. He was, in this theatrical piece, 'testing of art by means of life', as his Zen teaching would have it, using everyday objects to show that art and music were not arbitrarily cordoned-off areas but that all was permissible for use. As he brandished his watering can he may even have had in mind the words of the film-maker Oskar Fischinger: that there is 'a spirit inside each of the objects in this world – all we need to do to liberate that spirit is to brush past that object and to draw forth its sound'. At another level, the 'Water Walk' is as simple as it sounds: a walk through the creative process, whose fluidity is represented by the various aquatic stages of the piece.

As well as for employing a vast battery of non-instruments in his repertoire, from brake drums and conch shells to tin cans and cricket callers, Cage is best known for the piece '4' 33"', which consists of a group of musicians not playing for the duration of the title. It was performed by the BBC Symphony Orchestra, who, in what they imagined was Cage's playful spirit, couldn't resist turning the thing into a comedy piece, with lots of barely contained grinning and antics from the conductor. '4' 33"', along with Marcel Duchamp's urinal, is ubiquitous in popular culture as the ultimate in anti-art pranksterism. There is, of course, more to it than that. Cage himself said, 'I didn't wish it to appear, even to me, as something easy to do or as a joke. I wanted to mean it utterly and be able to live with it.' He also asserted that 'I worked longer on my "silent" piece than on any other' – not slaving away on the score, of course, but in arriving at the concept, which had come to him first as a result of exposure to his friend Robert Rauschenberg's all-black and all-white canvasses. His calculations and thinking in arriving at the answer 'zero' were hard work indeed, work that he had done for us and made seem easy.

'4' 33"' is not about silence at all, in fact, but the impossibility of it. This was something he discovered on visiting an anechoic chamber at Harvard University, supposedly a sensory deprivation experience, but during which he was aware of two droning sounds, high and low. These were, the duty engineer told him, the sounds of his nervous system and blood circulation respectively. And so the point of '4' 33"' is that it is the ultimate ambient piece: it consists of whatever sounds happen to fill the listening space while the musicians do not play – a passing car or overhead plane, perhaps, a shuffle, a cough or simply the sound of the venue's central heating system. These sounds are now in the frame, just like the reflections of the observers of Rauschenberg's black and white canvasses became their (albeit transient) subject matter. All is now permissible as potential material in the realm of music. And, much as Duchamp implicitly questioned the authority of art curators and critics who presumed to say why this stuff here and not that stuff there could be dubbed art, so with '4' 33"' Cage questioned the whole elaborate apparatus of assumptions that upheld Western music and its sense of how, and of what, it should be composed. In terms of scoring and instruction, however, Cage hadn't finished there. With 1963's *Variations IV* he opened up matters still further, stipulating no more than that the work was 'for any number of players, any sounds or combinations of sounds produced by any means, with or without other activities'.

Electronic music and devices were naturally embraced by Cage, now that all was permissible. In 1952, and with the help of Bebe Barron and David Tudor in collating the source sounds that make up this short yet immensely packed piece, he produced 'Williams Mix', named after the funder of the project, Paul Williams, the African American architect who designed homes for Lucille Ball and Frank Sinatra, among others. Splicing together the piece, based on a 193-page score that was compared to a 'dressmaker's pattern book', proved extremely time-consuming; each second of the piece, whose contents include sounds of the city and country, musical instruments and '"small" sounds', is dense with sonic matter, more so than the musique concrète emerging from Europe at the time. This is distinctly American art. Indeed, the way this distributes itself across the canvas of its duration is a little reminiscent of abstract expressionist artist Jackson Pollock, delivering great splashes of chaos that on closer acquaintance are revealed to be methodical and patterned at a deeper level. Computers would later allow for the easier dissemination of alternative uses of the source material, in accordance with the open score laid down by Cage. He himself would embrace computers in later life, not least in their capacity as auto-generators in composition.

By the mid-1960s, however, having at least notionally laid low the grandiose architectural assumptions of Western classical music, having created great plains of possibility in which the wind chimes of Eastern philosophy now resounded, driven also by the great American thinker Henry David Thoreau and his urge to 'simplify, simplify', Cage, ironically, found himself painted into a corner. Though he carried on working, he had left himself with no further great leaps and bounds to make.

He did, though, live long enough to see the unexpected fruits of one of his earliest experiments. *Imaginary Landscape No. 1* was conceived by him in 1939, a work for two variable-speed turntables, frequency recordings, muted piano and cymbal.

'It's not a physical landscape. It's a term reserved for the new technologies. It's a landscape in the future,' said Cage, with justified faith in his own vision. So much of Cage is contained in the piece: the plucked, recurring motif is typical of the simplicity of his early work, while the percussive roar speaks of a composer who, like Edgard Varèse, understood the starring role percussion would play in rendering modern times. However, it's the use of variable-speed turntables and frequency recording discs, which he came by at the studios of the Cornish College of the Arts, in Seattle, which make this piece such an uncanny harbinger. They hover like unidentified flying objects in the mix, which is what they are – airborne arrivals from an alien sector of advanced thinking, here to change life on earth permanently. To have conceived of frequency recordings as possible musical elements rather than mere engineering tools, and of the record player as a musical instrument in its own right, placed him not only years ahead of Pierre Schaeffer and the musique concrète generation of the 1940s and 1950s, it also anticipated the innovations of DJs from Kool Herc onwards. Cage dissolved decrees regarding what was music and what was not music, set aside barriers whose absence we take for granted nowadays but which no one else even thought about removing in Cage's own time. *Imaginary Landscape No. 1* is the moment our world was created.

Luciano Berio formed part of a post-war Italian triumvirate that also included Bruno Maderna and Luigi Nono, all of whom made advances in electronic and concrète, working out of the Studio di Fonologia in Milan, which was attached to the RAI radio station. Nono's work was explicitly and instructively political, but while Berio had served briefly with the partisans at the end of World War II, he and Maderna in particular took a sensuous delight in the pleasures of this earth, from fine food and wine to chain-smoking and carousing. Berio cut an urbane figure in the arts world, his thick-rimmed black spectacles giving him the air of a Peter Sellers or a Harold Pinter. There's a certain sensuality that informs Berio's work, too, both orchestral and electronic, a certain jouissance that informs one of his most significant works, *Omaggio a Joyce*, written for his then wife, the American Armenian mezzo-soprano Cathy Berberian.

Written in 1958, *Omaggio a Joyce* follows Stockhausen's *Gesang der Jünglinge* in that it is composed of spliced, varisped, juxtaposed and cut-up recordings of a single human voice – that of Berberian, reciting with due feeling the opening passage of 'Sirens', a chapter from Joyce's immense *Ulysses*:

Bronze by gold heard the hoofirons, steelyringing imperthnthn thnthnthn.
Chips, picking chips off rocky thumbnail, chips.
Horrid! And gold flushed more.
A husky fifenote blew.
Blew. Blue bloom is on the
Gold pinnacled hair.
A jumping rose on satiny breasts of satin, rose of Castile.
Trilling, trilling: Idolores . . .

This lyrical, phonetically beautiful yet on the face of it impenetrably cryptic burst of prose is, in fact, a fragmentary series of pre-echoes of what is to come in the chapter, its events and emotions summed up in a stream of consciousness. It reveals how conventional prose, with its orderly syntax, fails to capture the mental condition, the process of thought, with its linguistic breaches, its synaptic explosions, its connective patterns, a consciousness that is both more and less than linguistic, yet nonetheless extremely vivid.

Think about how you think. It's like this. Still, *Ulysses* remains one of the relatively few monuments in the modernist canon of formal literary experimentation.

Berio uses this text as a launch pad for yet more formal departures. He saw language as merely 'arbitrary symbols' and musical thought as theoretically open to whole new realms of sound phenomena beyond the bounds of conventional notation. He regarded categories such as prose, poetry and music as too often consisting of works that merely provided 'assurances' to the reader/listener that what they were reading/hearing belonged in the category they supposed it to. Berio wished to blast all that. 'Verses, prosody and rhymes are no more an assurance of poetry than written notes are an assurance of music. We often find more poetry in prose than in poetry itself and more music in speech and noise than in conventional musical sounds,' he wrote in the notes to *Omaggio a Joyce*, faintly echoing his fellow Italian Russolo's *Art of Noises* Futurist manifesto.

Following Berberian's emotionally pitch-perfect reading of Daedalus's mental cloudburst, Berio presents his Studio di Fonologia treatment. The tapestry he splices and weaves from Berberian's voice, in the tedious, unreal time of the editing process, is a sensation that, as Joyce himself would have put it, 'flies by the nets' of both language and music, flying free in a whole new register of expression. Words and fragments of words rear and swirl like birds released from netting; vowels and exclamations are tweaked and subdivided, rush high and far away. The phonetics have taken on an unruly, multiple life of their own, receding far onto the sound horizon, then instantly gathering and smashing you in the face, massing like swallows, blackening the skies, or like parakeets luminous against the night sky. There's no predictability or resolution; and yet, spatially, dramatically, emotionally, *Omaggio a Joyce* makes supreme sense. Accept its challenge, refuse to be confounded by it, and it engages and exhausts your emotions in literally unspeakable ways, and is precisely calculated by a master composer to do so. Hundreds of brilliant decisions are sprinkled across this piece.

Berio wrote other pieces for Berberian, including *Visages*, another extended exercise in combining tape, scissors and electronics to exceed language. It's composed entirely of non-verbal vocal expressions, another demonstration of the limits of the merely verbal, a formal precursor in some ways to the work of Liz Fraser in the Cocteau Twins, whose cirrus cloud-like vocals reach far higher than mere spelt-out symbols. Around this time, Berio, without necessarily knowing it, left his educational imprint on music yet to come. In 1962, his students included future architect of minimalism Steve Reich and Phil Lesh, bassist of the Grateful Dead, whose love and knowledge of the music of Berio et al. would lend the Dead the wherewithal to conduct their own particular space-rock explorations. As for Berio, he followed his own course, disregarding more popular developments to which he might have been tenuously linked. Despite co-pioneering musique concrète, he did not uncritically embrace the electrification of modern music. He was particularly disdainful of synthesizers, which he described as 'pseudo-instruments'.

As for the Studio di Fonologia, it would close down in 1983, as Italian culture was trampled and laid waste by media mogul Silvio Berlusconi and his dancing girls. The counter-culture it represented was left to rot in the collective memory, regarded, if at all, as a folly of Italy's political flirtations with the far left, the Red Brigades and so forth. But Berlusconi's cultural and eventual political domination proved a syphilitic disaster for Italy. Today, Italians tentatively emerging from the wreckage of the *bunga bunga* years might yet reconnect with their immense twentieth-century legacy and find ways of contributing similarly to the twenty-first.

György Ligeti was born in 1923 in Transylvania, which had formerly been Hungarian territory but after World War I was ceded to Romania. His family were middle-class and Jewish, of pacific, socialist leanings. He himself was conscious of his Hungarian-ness and as a young man was deeply taken with Béla Bartók and Zoltán Kodály, both of whom had helped infuse twentieth-century classical music with a jagged, rhythmic earthiness drawn from their investigations into, and adaptations of, Hungarian folk music. He studied composition during the war but found his progress hampered by anti-Semitic educational policy. Hungary made a pact with Hitler, and Ligeti found many of his contemporaries joining up with Hungary's Iron Guard, their equivalent of the Hitler Youth, from which he was racially barred. By 1943, he had been pressed into a Jewish forced-labour unit and barely escaped with his life, finally fleeing in 1944 and hiding out in the woods, where invading Soviet troops eventually picked him up. His father and younger brother were both murdered in the concentration camps.

As a citizen of the Eastern Bloc, the end of the war did not bring outright liberation for Ligeti. By the early 1950s, the communist authorities were echoing the Nazis in their condemnation of modern art and music as decadent. Ligeti had heard by word of mouth about the electronic music emanating from Cologne in West Germany. The very idea of a music 'freed from the shackles of instruments [in which] sound can be synthetically produced from pure sine waves . . . fired my imagination. I absolutely wanted to go to Cologne.' Ligeti dreamt of swimming in the absolutely free compositional waters apparently afforded by electronic music, depthless oceans of infinite colour and variety and possibility. Despite the attempts of the authorities to jam them, he occasionally managed to hear indistinct radio broadcasts of electronic and musique concrète pieces from Darmstadt, which were dominated by their higher, shrieking frequencies. By 1956, Hungary was in revolt, but having initially appeared to be in retreat, the Soviet forces struck back. It was in the midst of street battles and gunfire on the night of 7 November that Ligeti boldly elected not to join his friends in the cellar of their Budapest house but remain upstairs so as to hear distinctly an unjammed broadcast of Stockhausen's *Gesang der Jünglinge*, heard by Ligeti as surely no one has ever heard it before or since, its cut-up, pealing fragments whizzing from all sides in tandem with actual bullets strafing Budapest.

Ligeti decided he had to leave the city. The young chorister of *Gesang der Jünglinge* was calling him like a siren. He and his girl-friend made a perilous trip to the Austrian border, evading the attentions of Russian troops, hiding out at a farm, then scrambling across minefields and ditches until an illuminated Christmas tree at a village church indicated that they had arrived, filthy, sodden and exhausted, in Austria.

Reaching Cologne in 1957, Ligeti immersed himself in the works of composers like Boulez, Xenakis and older masters like Anton Webern, as well as Stockhausen himself. He worked at the WDR and marvelled at mealtime conversations in which the young composers, full to the brim of themselves, devised *Glass Bead Game*-like schemes in which music and mathematics would combine to create a sonic architecture that would stretch upwards into space, casting a shadow over the lowly earthbound classical achievements of the past, which would seem like huddles of thatched medieval dwellings compared with the sky-scraping achievements they had in mind. Gradually, however, Ligeti became aware of the political culture of Cologne – the intrigue and infighting in which musical dogmas like twelve-tone composition still held sway. This wasn't very congenial to a young man who had experienced more than enough politics *in extremis* for a lifetime. Nonetheless, he was kindly received by Eimert in particular, who secured him work at the electronic studios, allowing Ligeti access to the whole candy store of 1950s equipment: pitch and noise generators, filters, echo chambers, ring modulators.

Ligeti's first piece was *Glissandi*, a playful enough, self-descriptive foray, but one that sounds like not much more than a greenhorn trying out the various dials on the machines he finds at his disposal, its electronic tones sliding and worming colourfully in and out of the darkness.

Artikulation, realised in 1958 with the assistance of Gottfried Michael Koenig and Cornelius Cardew, represents a vast evolutionary stride by comparison. Despite its brevity, *Artikulation* remains one of the most precious and brilliantly honed pearls in the entire canon of twentieth-century electronic music. On YouTube, it's best heard in conjunction with the visual score created retrospectively by Rainer Wehinger in the 1970s, but it's arguably better still to let the piece gently explode in your head and create its own synaptic patterns. Commencing with a watery rumble, like the processed, reverberant sounds of some rusty public urinal, it suddenly rears in the mix with a series of cheeky, echo-less, peek-a-boo flurries and almost-human phrases. After some moments of free, saucy play, gigantic clumps of aluminium come crashing down like satellite parts from the darkness above; creaks, groans ensue, tickling the eardrum physically. The toy box of noises collated by Ligeti is categorised by the composer as 'grainy, brittle, fibrous, slimy, sticky, compact'. Eventually, they recede on a luminous green tide, a highly entertaining cluster of furies who have decided to take their mischief elsewhere.

Amid the loftier, ambitiously overarching achievements of Stockhausen and Varèse, *Artikulation* bounces about imperishably, essentially like a rubber ball. It has all the energy of a *Looney Tune*, a crossover made explicitly by Raymond Scott, the popular US bandleader, who eventually dispensed with human players and resorted to machines of his own devising, but also perhaps less so by Stockhausen – there's a brief moment in *Kontakte* that seems to recall the opening ascending chord of the *Merrie Melodies* theme. Ligeti might have been expected to construct an electronic music more sombre and major in tone, one that sought to abolish the ruins of war and rise above the trauma of the dead past; instead, he created a miniature yet expansive masterpiece that revels in its resemblance to cartoon kitsch, yet has the spatial wit of a fast-rotating Alexander Calder mobile sculpture. As its title suggests, it's a sort of analogue to verbal expression; the sounds it presents are like a sort of chatter, the emissions of a fictional, alien language. It is, at a deeper level, a joyful expression of the absolute freedom for which Ligeti had yearned all his young life, a freedom brutally and almost fatally denied first by the Nazis and then by the Soviets. Grand themes, sobering gravitas and drones generated as if from some anti-banality machine are commonplace in electronica; far less easy to achieve is the sheer joy of a piece like *Artikulation*, which escapes both dogmatic snares and accusations of frivolity with its sheer resourcefulness, not unlike the resourcefulness Ligeti had to exercise more than once in his life to cheat death.

Ligeti attempted one more electronic piece, but then decided to abandon the genre altogether, deciding, simply, that it was no longer for him and that, despite the medium's apparently limitless potential, he had done within it all that he felt he could. Thereafter, he devoted himself to larger-scale works in the medium of conventional orchestra, which would remain undead despite the dreams of the Darmstadt children.

In a quiet nursing home near Copenhagen, an elderly Danish lady spent her final years and months surrounded by large items of obsolete-looking sound-making equipment and finding herself the object of attention of a procession of international journalists and contemporary musicians, from *The Wire* magazine to Jacob Kierkegaard. Her name was Else Marie Pade, yet another name to add to the substantial phalanx of women who worked as unobtrusive pioneers in electronic music, as ignored as switchboard operators in their own time, marvelled at decades later.

Pade was a sickly child and had to resort to patching together worlds from the sounds that trickled in through the window from the outside world as she lay bedridden and inactive. 'I was always thinking about sounds,' she told musician Jacob Kierkegaard. 'That is also why I chose to work with sound. For me it doesn't work with the voice, or if sound is just transmitted superficially with a little bit of echo. Then it is lost to me.'

Despite her infirmity as a child, Pade demonstrated immense courage when World War II broke out, joining an all-female Danish resistance group against the occupying Nazis. Aged twenty she was arrested for spying on German troop movements and spent many tedious, frightening months incarcerated at Frøslev prison camp. Deprived utterly of any stimulus, she fed her starved creative imagination as best she could by scratching musical scores onto the walls of her prison cell using the buckle of her garters. She made a promise to herself that, if ever released, she would dedicate her life to music-making.

Following her release, and a career as a housewife to which she was entirely unsuited, she took up studies in the nascent world of electronic music, following a chance radio broadcast of a piece by Pierre Schaeffer. She was the first Danish person, male or female, to do so. She thrived on the free rein the music afforded her, allowed to pursue it while attached to Danish Radio as a producer – the chance to realise in full technical and colour detail the sounds that had swum about in her head since childhood, the abstract sounds that represented her emotional response to the world. Her initial pieces were nuanced exercises in electronic impressionism – 1955's *A Day at the Deer Park*, for example.

It is the 1962 piece *Faust*, however, a highly personalised response to what she described as 'mentally charged material', which really sets her apart. Its warm but brooding, relentless, claustrophobic tones track the agitation of Goethe's drama; one confused young twenty-first-century listener wished to know how Pade had managed to transcribe the experience of tinnitus. Later works such as 'Se Det i Øjnene' ('Face It – Hitler Is Not Dead', 1970) were more extreme and severe, this piece in particular showing that her anger at the Nazis hadn't been allowed to dissolve into the mists of time. She would have to wait some forty years for her work to be recognised as a radical precursor to whole swathes of radical electronica, from Throbbing Gristle to Einstürzende Neubauten; for this soft-spoken little old lady living out her days amid the corridor footsteps of rubber-clogged nurses doing their rounds to receive her due as a *femme seule*.

In the annals of contemporary music, Luc Ferrari is a slight, deceptive figure of unassuming charm. If mentioned at all, he's often reduced to the footnotes of electronic-music history. Yet his innovations in what he called 'anecdotal music' posited a reshaping of the relationship between music and environment, made fresh claims for the artistic significance of the now commonplace practice of field recordings.

The first Ferrari piece I ever heard was 1969's *Music Promenade*, a recording of which I bought in 1981 while at university. Newly enriched by a student-grant cheque, I spent a quarter of it on sherry and biscuits, which I intended to live on for the entire first term purely because there was no adult in my life to tell me I should not; the remainder I rather more admirably spent on avant-garde albums, including this one by Ferrari. It impacted on my assumptions about musical perspective the way cubism did on my assumptions about visual art.

A work for multiple tape recorders, it exudes the warmth, sea breeze and hectic *joie de vivre* of a mid-century French holiday Sunday. It's a collage of recordings, sewn together with silvery passages of electric thread, whose recurring features include a somewhat meandering and out-of-tune brass band, fireworks, a posh prototype Sloane reminiscing with a neighing guffaw, 'First of all I was thrown in the water, hWAAAAHHH!!', a performance of *Macbeth*, the somewhat ominous barking of a sergeant major directing a military display, waltzes, as well as sundry ambient snatches of conversation and more desultory passages, obscure noises from beneath the boardwalk. Walking from one of these soundworlds to another is an experience I can only compare to the film *Russian Ark*, in which the protagonists find themselves condemned to wander the galleries of St Petersburg's Hermitage museum, the camera's unblinking eye following them through the galleries, each one hosting a different period of Russian history. Its own 'link' music is uncannily similar to Ferrari's.

There's a certain implied violence about *Music Promenade* in the abruptness of its juxtapositions and the bellicose tones of the director of the military display, among others, yet it represents lashings of sheer pleasure – everyday sounds heightened and bearing up to repeated listening by being framed as music. An essential work in Ferrari's canon, it's nonetheless one of his more 'composed' pieces. He went much further into the field, confounding and enraging even that great innovator of concrète, Pierre Schaeffer.

Born in 1929, Ferrari experienced his first fascination for the relationship between music and the everyday world when as a child he happened to hear a piece by Arthur Honegger, *Pacific 231*, on his father's Bakelite radio. The idea of 'an orchestra imitating noise' – in this case, the sound of a locomotive engine at full pelt – enthralled young Luc. He began to fixate on the distinctive sounds of automobiles, his ear training itself to distinguish different types of car engine. When the war came, with all its attendant tragedy and upheaval, it represented for the young Ferrari a fresh cornucopia of strange and wonderful noises: the dissonant strains of an out-of-tune piano the family was forced to acquire, having fled bombed-out Paris, as well as the Allied planes passing overhead – 'American Mustangs, Spitfires, British Lightnings'. 'Difficult' music would present no difficulty to someone with such cultivated and exacting ears as Ferrari, and his musical training drew him naturally towards the great post-war experimentalists.

He joined the GRM, but like a lot of young students he became disillusioned with the dogmatism and overbearing paternalism of senior figures like Schaeffer. In 1964, he presented *Hétérozygote*, a piece that used extensive and identifiable environmental sounds, gathered using newly available mobile recording technology. For Schaeffer, the identifiability of these sounds amid the metal abstractions of the magnetic tape passages were an offence, especially as the piece seemed to be built and shaped around them, rather than their being pulped for concrète, so to speak. Without irony, he flew into a rage at Ferrari, describing *Hétérozygote* as 'incoherent . . . formless . . . a noise'.

Ferrari, however, had struck upon a fresh configuration, one that he pursued further on his *Presque rien* series starting in 1968. This was received with still less sympathy than his previous work. Far more than concrète, which is concerned with commandeering everyday sounds for compositional purposes, *Presque rien* is almost pure field recording. Its sounds are the 'ready-made' ones of the environment; you might compare it to Marcel Duchamp declaring a bicycle wheel or a urinal a work of art, simply exerting his artistic authority to have these objects placed in the gallery. But Ferrari wasn't interested in mere Dadaist gestures. His presentation and framing of field recordings, whose artifice and arrangement he would carefully conceal – 'covering my tracks to make the process inaudible', as he put it – would be a lifelong pursuit.

The *Presque rien* series comprises recordings culled from beaches, agricultural engines and open-air community music, as well as an extended nocturnal sequence, rendered in a sort of aural night vision, in which Ferrari acts as a whispering narrator amid the incessant chirp of crickets. You can feel the heat rise and the verdant odours as you attend to these pieces; by encouraging close listening, you appreciate the natural music generated by the world we inhabit and potentially take the great political step of not taking the environment for granted. But these aren't mere unedited spools of field tape simply transferred to the recording studio. There is an extraordinary moment towards the end of the nocturnal sequence in which a storm begins to brew. As it does so, in an inversion of the oft-used device in which everyday recordings impinge on a piece of music, in this instance composed music impinges on a framed presentation of a natural soundscape: a brief, burgeoning passage of pastoral music before the breaking of a thunderstorm, later treated by Ferrari electronically to add a conspicuous black touch of hyperrealism.

Ferrari continued until the end of his life with his 'anecdotal music', everyday field recordings, treated only subtly, being the dominant feature of his compositions, which, albeit discreetly, remained compositions nonetheless. Only an unfortunate penchant for quaintly sexist cover images blights his reputation. He has made a unique contribution to a wide canon of 'field recording' artists that also includes, in their different ways, such figures as John Cage, David Tudor, Chris Watson and Bernie Krause. It's the minimal twists and little subversions of Ferrari to which I return, however; his work, and all that it wryly implies, deserves a much wider understanding and hearing.

Of all the *hommes* (*et femmes*) *seuls* who were the earliest adopters of electronic music in the post-World War II period, the case of Raymond Scott is among the strangest. How did this Juilliard-trained pianist of Russian Jewish descent, born Harry Warnow in 1908, a big bandleader famous for his frantic, breakneck jazz tunes that were the apt soundtrack for many a *Merrie Melodies* cartoon, come to die almost penniless in 1994, surrounded by the rusting electronic machinery of his own devising, which would go almost wholly ignored in the era in which it was made? How to explain his transition from wealthy populist, whose tunes were disdained as commercial and gimmicky by jazz aficionados, to an unsung precursor to the ambient and minimalist music that was the aural wallpaper of listening sophisticates at the time of his death?

During the long, strange arc of his lifetime, Scott intersected with, among others, saxophonist Ben Webster, Yul Brynner, Shirley Temple, Bo Diddley, Muppets creator Jim Henson, Devo's Mark Mothersbaugh and the late hip-hop producer J Dilla. He was a radio and TV fixture in the 1940s and '50s, but the music he made under the banner of the Manhattan Project, on instruments such as the Clavivox and Electronium, had to be rescued from their remote orbit like neglected satellites in the retro-futurist era of the early twenty-first century.

Scott was blessed with a sense of mischief and curiosity about the processes of modern sound-making, both of which infect his work. But he was also an emotionally distant man, both towards his children and those with whom he worked. He was self-contained and lacked trust in other people; these characteristics, too, would determine the unique zig and zag of his career.

He adopted the pseudonym Raymond Scott because he didn't want people to think he'd only landed his first job as pianist in the CBS Radio house band through nepotism – his older brother Mark conducted the orchestra. However, having got his feet over the pedals, he began to assemble his own band, a six-piece that he dubbed the 'Quintette' because he felt there was a certain syllable in the word 'sextet' that 1930s audiences might find distracting. Featuring such talents as the ill-fated alcoholic trumpet virtuoso Bunny Berigan, they began recording in 1937, cutting sides with such amiably quirky titles as 'War Dance for Wooden Indians', 'Reckless Night on Board an Ocean Liner' and 'The Penguin', which feel like forerunners of Frank Zappa. Like Zappa, though, Scott ran a tight ship musically, permitting only a limited amount of improvisation in his pieces before insisting that they follow the precise co-ordinates that he determined led to the finished version. This accounts for the genial sense of controlled clockwork chaos of his most famous hits: tight orchestration masquerading as mania. On Scott's official website there is excitement that Miles Davis once name-checked him in a record reviews column, but it's unlikely that he did so with very much affection. Whereas Davis's music is warm, pensive and open to input from the talented musicians in his employ, Scott's take on swing is action-packed, mechanical, highly scripted. He once auditioned Bo Diddley but found his playing 'too sloppy'. He sold in the millions, however.

It seems Scott was less interested in musicians, whom he regarded as mere tools, than music engineering. He got on much better with the guys behind the glass screen than those with whom he shared a stage, and better still with the technology itself. That said, in 1942 he did himself immense credit by putting together a mixed-race band, albeit for radio, and hiring, among others, Ben Webster and Charlie Shavers to join his various combos.

After the war, Scott receded from piano playing and combined pop projects, such as scoring a Broadway musical – *Lute Song*, starring Yul Brynner – and conducting the orchestra on the CBS show *Lucky Strike*, with more esoteric studio investigations, which would gradually come to monopolise his time. He dabbled with multitrack vocal recording, as popularised by Les Paul and Mary Ford. In 1946, he founded the enterprise Manhattan Research, whose name is eerily reminiscent of the concurrent Manhattan Project that produced the first American nuclear weapons. He unsuccessfully submitted the patent for an 'Orchestra' machine in the same year.

Ever since childhood, when he had spent hours honing his skills in competition with a 'Pianola', a player piano, in his father's store, Scott had had a predilection for the mechanical. He built a basic prototype of the sequencer, as well as a special 'keyboard theremin' for his daughter. His machines' names have the wonderful, sanguine, hand-cranked vibe of a time when a world of electronic music was a wishful and hopeful dream, redolent of antennae and Martian holidays and hovercars; the sounds they generated, for commercial use in adverts for companies like Bendix – 'The Tomorrow People' – are shot through with cartoon awe at the labour-saving, space-age devices the 1960s onwards would undoubtedly bring. He was also fully conversant, however, with the toolkit of Europe's musique concrète movement: Manhattan Research Inc. made available to the general public such imported devices as ring modulators and filters. Robert Moog met Scott in the late 1950s and was inspired to create the synth that bore his own name.

And yet, for all his apparently sure-fire commercial instinct, rich pedigree in the world of popular entertainment and appar-ent disregard for the remote aesthetic pretensions of the electronic avant-garde, Scott became more secretive and reclusive from the 1960s onwards, preferring life among the machines he could con-trol, indifferent to self-marketing, suspicious that his innovations would be ripped off if overexposed. He was a paradox. He used his ingenuity to bombard the general public with everyday items given an added electronic component, including electronic phone ringers and alarms and an ashtray that generated its own electronic tunes. In 1964, he released a series of albums titled *Soothing Sounds for Baby*. Achieved on the Clavivox, these therapeutically repet-itive pieces, with simple, plaintive, reverberant melodies, are at once child-friendly yet visionary and audacious in their deceptive lack of complexity. The tunes are, like Eno's, spare but exquisitely judged ambient sketches, immediately transfixing, seeming to push the exact buttons that transport the listener into another, untapped mental realm. That sense of profound nostalgia is, how-ever, coupled with the feeling that these records, despite their primitive electronics, sound like they were made in the year 2064, seemingly entirely at ease with their space-age desolation. (His son always believed that these albums were Scott's way of expressing, at a mechanically mediated remove, the affection he felt for his kids but was unable or disinclined to express personally.) Despite

Scott's pedigree, despite the cute tots that adorned the covers and their appealing, utilitarian intentions, these records sold next to zero copies. He even invented a prototype of the fax machine, but to no avail because no one else owned one, rendering the send and receive functions redundant. Here was Scott's problem: he was stranded in futurist space in the 1960s, having arrived too early, too ahead of a society that in the tumult of the decade had mentally deferred the dreams of the Tomorrow People.

There were one or two notable collaborations in the 1960s, despite his lack of recorded output. In 1967, Scott was impressed by some experimental movies made by a young Jim Henson, in his pre-Muppets phase, to which he added soundtracks that ping and reverberate with appropriately futuristic trepidation at such modern phenomena as the 'paperwork explosion' – the title of the Henson film – in modern offices. These are educative yet strangely unsettling films, Scott's music heightening the suggestion of unprecedented forces at work in the modern world. Meanwhile, in 1969, Motown supremo Berry Gordy got wind of Scott's experimentation and visited him at his Long Island studio, eager to see Scott's Electronium in action, a complex piece of kit involving vast banks of knobs and patch panels that was designed to preclude musicians altogether – the dream realised! – and function as a sort of 'ideas generator', an automatic composition machine capable of storing chords and rhythms that would be easily accessible by composers at the Hit Factory. Gordy was sufficiently impressed to retain Scott as head of Motown's electronic research department. Michael Jackson is said to have dropped by to take a curious look at the Electronium. The instrument, though, remained in a perpetual state of modification, with Scott reluctant, it seems, to release a finished article into the market place, despite an estimated million dollars being sunk into its development. Finally, and with no use of it made on any known Motown work to justify Scott's place on the payroll, Gordy let him go in 1977.

In the 1980s – ironically, the decade in which the synthpop he prefigured enjoyed its rise and eventual ubiquity – Scott suffered the greatest neglect of his life, his royalties dwindling and interest in his antique works-in-progress at near zero. He suffered a stroke in 1987, only semi-capable of enjoying the stirrings of a mini-revival he enjoyed in the early 1990s – of his jazz period.

Posthumously, however, Scott has enjoyed a resurgence in interest, with electronic music having aged sufficiently to take an interest in its own heritage. In 2006, J Dilla selected Scott's 'Lightworks' as part of his hip-hop montage *Donuts*. The track stands in a select group, one that also includes Daphne Oram's soundtracks to Lego adverts, of avant-garde electronic music put to commercial ends but emerging cleaner than clean from the process. Lightworks was the name of a cosmetics firm, and Scott recorded the jingle in the early 1960s. In it the (unidentified) female singer dutifully extols the virtues of the product: 'What is the magic that makes one's eyes sparkle and gleam, light up the skies?' she coos lightly. Over this, Scott's electronics also sparkle and gleam, but in a way that exceeds the brief: with its clusters of electronic rhythms, diaphanous, wispy effects and muted, luminous glow, 'Lightworks' transports the mind to dimensions way beyond the cosmetic. It offers a fuzzy, monochrome, too brief glimpse of the world of synth music that awaits far away over time's horizon. Tomorrow's music today, indeed, and the further we stretch into the tomorrow of the twenty-first century, the more precious the early sanguine intimations of a Raymond Scott feel. 'Lightworks' signals a future that came and went before it ever happened.

PART TWO

7

DISTANT GALAXIES, DEEP OCEANS: SUN RA AND MILES DAVIS

One of the most annoying myths about electronic music is that it is the preserve of a certain kind of white male: desiccated, cerebral, frigid. More than other genres, however, electronic music has, for a long time, migrated across race and gender, fluid and inclusive, a medium of expression for the outsider, the visionary, the stubborn anti-traditionalist. All of these have defied condescension and incomprehension to speak at times more intimately to future generations than their own, to whom they often seemed confoundingly alien or simply out of order.

Let's begin with a tale of two electrics.

Sun Ra was born Herman Blount in Birmingham, Alabama, the so-called 'Magic City'. His own sister was empirically certain of the fact. He had come into this world at his aunt's house near the train station in 1914, and she had watched the delivery through the keyhole – 'He's not from no Mars.' Ra didn't claim to come from Mars but from the planet Saturn. Though he could do nothing about his indiscreet sister, he systematically erased all the other details and documents pertaining to his life that he could, so that he could present himself in all solemnity to the world as Sun Ra, not a human, not of this earth. There are no photographs of Ra the child, a polite but reserved and deeply studious boy with an extraordinarily voracious appetite for literature of all kinds – or even as a young man. In 1941, we see a faded image of him in a suit, sitting at a piano and smiling innocuously.

The photo looks like it has survived an attempted arson attack.

Although he lived seventy-nine years on planet earth, Sun Ra had as little to do with it as possible. He was, in many ways, genuinely alien, and a lifelong sufferer from various physical ailments, the most severe of which was a hernia that inhibited his testicular development. He never displayed any sexual inclinations, openly denying his human physicality in that respect, and although his deep friendship with the Arkestra dancer June Tyson absolved him from outright misogyny, he felt that he could not be creative when women were around, regarding them, like an old-fashioned ship's captain, as a source of bad fortune. He did not follow conventional sleep patterns; he was an insomniac, though.

Living in the Deep South in the 1920s, he must have been at least anecdotally conscious of vicious racism, of lynchings and of the second-class citizenship endured by Americans of colour. If any such personal experiences of Jim Crow made an early, horrifying impression on him, however, they were expunged from his life's record. He lived, as it was possible to live, solely within his own black community, a life in which, if you kept your head down and, perhaps, your nose between the pages of a book, you could zone out the oppressive fact of white domination altogether. 'I've never been a part of the planet,' he claimed in one interview. 'I've been isolated from a child away from it. Right in the midst of everything and not being a part of it. Them problems people got, prejudices and all that, I didn't know a thing about it, until I got to be about fourteen years old.'

When young Herman did slip away from the protective cocoon of home and hearth, it was to hear the black bands that swung through Birmingham in the late 1920s. The more familiar jazz names of the era did not stop by that part of the world very often, but there was a local scene of less well-known outfits, with names like the Carolina Cotton Pickers, who made a deep impression on Ra. The way they dressed, the way they carried themselves, the way they played were, Ra realised, perhaps the only way for black people to represent themselves as agents of modernity, in a world in which they otherwise counted for nothing. For all its futurism, there is always the echo in Ra of these formative experiences, in the rough edges and large scales of the combos he put together, which were very old-style. The Arkestra was post-bebop but also pre-bebop. Big bands were generally considered to be cumbersome and out of fashion in the post-war era, by comparison with the smaller, speedier, more mobile outfits in which individualism and innovation could flourish. Ra distanced himself contemptuously from the earthly idea of 'freedom'. He believed in patriarchy, with figures such as himself at the helm, whose alien provenance afforded them the ability to guide humanity, or that portion of humanity they could influence, towards its true spiritual home: the realms of outer space, in which the bonds and illusions of planet earth, and the deathly masquerade of so-called life, would be dissolved.

Through poetry; through the theatre of the Arkestra, marching triumphantly from concerts while still playing as if to symbolise departure from this earth while still alive; through costume, which drew on ancient Egyptian iconography and myth, and the supposition that its culture was affected by visiting aliens; through the music, which created a joyful, anarchic noise – 'Great black music from the ancient to the future,' to borrow a slogan from the Art Ensemble of Chicago – Sun Ra fully realised an otherwise unrealisable philosophy in art, a tangible thing whose value, unlike his ideas, is beyond dispute. He nonetheless failed to feature in Ken Burns's epic ten-part history of jazz in 2000, magisterial as far as it went but conservatively curated by Wynton Marsalis.

Sun Ra considered himself too philosophically grand to be bothered by issues such as civil rights and black emancipation, of which he was openly scornful. For him, there were far bigger cosmological fish to fry. His indifference to earthly matters stretched to the financial and he often found himself in difficulties, including in meeting telephone bills, due to his habit of simply leaving the phone off the hook for long stretches of time in mid-conversation, racking up enormous charges. Band members who inquired about payment would be chastised by the great man for their sordid concern with petty earthly matters and invited to discuss more pressing issues, such as the stars in the night sky. And yet, despite making no pretence that the band he led was in any way democratic, he commanded lifelong loyalty from his players, some of whom approached him as talentless waifs in search of meaning and a collective roof, others of whom were players potentially the equal of Rollins or Coltrane – the likes of John Gilmore, Pat Patrick and Marshall Allen. In an interview with *Jazz* magazine, Pat Patrick described life in the Arkestra under Ra: 'You could say that we are less than his pupils – we're nobodies with the master.' Even after Ra's death, they would carry on with the Arkestra, carry on disseminating the music and message of their leader in life and the afterlife. It was unthinkable that they would ever have gone solo.

Sun Ra changed his name, but that was never necessary for Miles Davis, whose Christian name was a triumph of nominative determinism, as the great virtual expanses of his music would demonstrate time and again. Davis was born in 1926 in Illinois, into a very affluent African American family who owned a ranch near Arkansas; it was here that Davis would return to lodge when he endured his first bout of cold turkey, coming down off heroin. He was encouraged by his family to take up music and opted for the trumpet at his father's behest. At eighteen, he moved to New York to study at the Juilliard school of music and fell immediately into the city's burgeoning bebop scene, seeking out Charlie Parker and joining in the legendary jam sessions at Minton's that were the refuge of jazz players seeking to establish their own extended, individual voices in the post-big-band, post-swing era.

And yet although he accompanied Parker, having replaced Dizzy Gillespie, he realised early on not only that he would never be able to match these players' breathtaking virtuosity, but that there was little point in trying. Davis's entire musical career would have nothing to do with the modernist imperative to blow hard and fast, but instead was all about inverting jazz's energy – creating soundworlds, emotional ambiences in which invention depended on the reinvention of the collective setting, rather than pushing the envelope of individual extremism. He never had much time for Ornette Coleman.

Miles Davis was, as his autobiography makes clear, a shit. Unlike Sun Ra, he had no overriding cosmological message for humanity. Politically, morally, didactically and philosophically, he had pretty much nothing to say to humanity at all – except to impress upon them, through surliness and obnoxious deeds, that he was a tough, taciturn and intimidating man unafraid of using his fists and imposing his will through force of unpleasant character. He beat up women. He beat up his manager. He beat up fellow musicians. He was utterly charmless with audiences, on whom he turned his back while playing. He did not command lifelong loyalty from those who played with him – there are few, if any, constants in his recording career. Musicians like John Coltrane, Herbie Hancock, Bill Evans, Chick Corea, Cannonball Adderley, Keith Jarrett and Mtume drifted through his various line-ups before moving on to their own solo projects, graduates and beneficiaries of the experience, though doubtless thankful to have acquired the freedom to become prestigious solo artists in their own right. Davis seems to have been just as happy with this arrangement as they were. In his personal life, he went through a series of relationships with women, all of which were influential in his thinking, all of which ended, often with a legacy of violence.

And yet this is at the heart of what Davis actually did say to humanity – his great, unspoken emotional depths, which reached a far larger audience than Sun Ra, with women a significant percentage of their number. His wistful music, whether tonal or noisenik, spoke implicitly of loneliness and immersion, of the beauty and inescapability of the human condition. Whether his setting was rock fusion or the more formal modal setting of his classic *Kind of Blue* quintet, his trumpet voice was a constant – plaintive, abiding, gentle, warm, eloquent, buffeted, muted, vulnerable, tender, quietly strong. 'Miles' was the word – it was as if with his playing he was scanning the horizons. It represented for the most part a stark contrast with Davis as he presented himself in real life – surly, rasping, laconic, misanthropic, unsmiling, a wiry mass of small, nasty concerns, lewdly obsessed with female rear ends. It represented a hankering, essential solitude; in his own life's journey, he himself was the only constant. Abusive as he was towards the women in his life, he nonetheless spoke appealingly to the depths of womanhood; the pretty little cissy he'd been teased for as a child, which he suppressed through a lifelong machismo, had his say in his music.

Sun Ra was condemned to deal with the present day; his loneliness was that of a creature from a far more advanced and vibrationally pleasing spot in the solar system, unlike planet earth, with all its factiousness and failings. His mind, however, was fixed in the past and the future, his music a projection of the mental palaces he constructed, which enticingly exceeded the gruelling fare of the terrestrial. Naturally, he took a keen interest in twentieth-century technologies. He was an early adopter of tape recorders and had no qualms about inauthenticity when it came to studio treatments of his music. He was in search of a supreme authenticity, after all. Whereas other large music ensembles would, then and later, see the rise of electronic instruments as a threat, from the 1940s onwards Ra lectured his players that someday all instruments would be electric.

So slow, however, was the development of electronic instruments in the twentieth century, and so rigid the acoustic hegemony, that it was not until Ra was into his early forties that he began properly to investigate their properties, and not until he was well into his fifties that he voyaged to the extremes that made him such a guiding star for avant-garde rock listeners, as well as anathema to jazz purists. By his mid-sixties and the end of his life, whereas Davis had mellowed musically, arriving at an MOR acceptability of sorts, the electric heat of Sun Ra was at its most intense.

1956's 'India' is a gentle example of his early use of electric keyboards. He plays a Wurlitzer portable keyboard, introduced a year earlier. Electric keyboards weren't an absolute novelty, although they had previously been treated as such, as on Slim Gaillard's use of proto-synthesizer the Novachord on 'Novachord Boogie' in 1947. Ra's meandering soloing, across tropical, irregular thickets of percussion, lends 'India' an otherworldiness that is otherworldly even by comparison with the popular tropes of sci-fi soundtracking in 1950s America. No vibrating theremins to denote eeriness, but the assured tread of someone for whom these realms are home terrain.

By 1965, Ra's music was assuming a vastness, denoted by his use of keyboards such as the clavioline as instruments of navigation. It floats like a flying saucer across the skies of 'The Magic City', its wheeling movements, distant siren noises, hovering, wavering and firefly luminosity seeming to arouse unusual excitement in the clusters of acoustic instruments down below, as they tilt their extremities heavenwards.

Sometimes Ra could create alternative soundworlds simply with his arrangements and studio processing. 1966's *Strange Strings* is one of his 1960s high points, its primitive methods somehow adding to its timelessness. It's an example of the way he would use his players like a human synthesizer, programming them, hitting them like keys for intended effects, deploying their formidable range as part of a higher musical sequence. Their self-expression, or desire for self-expression if they had any such thing outside Ra's own plan, was of no consequence.

For *Strange Strings*, Ra raided music and cheap curio stores and put together a collection of stringed instruments, including kotos

and a Chinese lute, which he passed on to his horn and reed players and instructed them to play. That they had no training in these
instruments was very much the point. This was a Stockhausen-
esque exercise in putting formal training aside. He also deployed
Harry Partch-style home-made instruments, including a large
piece of sheet metal. When the players asked what they were supposed to play, Ra instructed them simply to play. The results are
a triumphant ebb of exploratory noise, premeditated by none but
Ra, the creator with a master plan, whose sheer lack of tonality is
exacerbated by the use of echo, reverb and distortion. Although
arrived at by very different and less democratic means, the results
bear comparison with the recordings of the improvisational collective AMM, just emerging in the UK at the same time and feted
by rock musicians such as Paul McCartney and Syd Barrett, for
whom Sun Ra was not yet on the horizon. It is another piece of
honorary electronic music.

In the late 1960s, when Robert Moog's new synthesizer hit the
market, Ra was naturally first among those keen to take it up.
He visited Moog's studios and found that he was having difficulty
operating one of the models. An assistant told him that sometimes
the machines responded differently to different people's skins. In
one of his flashes of underappreciated humour, Ra said, 'Even
machines can be racist! We gotta be ready for the space age!'

In the 1960s and '70s, others discreetly adopted the Moog,
either to create supplementary textures or to create a synthetic
slickness that showed their most banal and reductive possibility
– as ersatz orchestras. Ra's early mini-Moog pieces, sputtering,
irregular, anti-jazz emissions like 'The Code of Interdependence'
from 1970's *My Brother the Wind*, see him wrestling crudely with
the instrument, as if to wrest from it deeper possibilities, hidden
alien languages. In Ra's hands, the Moog sounds like a meteor
shower, or the sputterings of a recently crash-landed spacecraft,
or the sound of Atlantis rising from hitherto placid oceans, its

Futurist Luigi Russolo and his assistant demonstrate the intonarumori: 'noise makers' designed to generate the sonic ambiences of the new, machine-driven century.

Edgard Varèse, who had to wait until old age for the technology that would realise his visions as a composer.

Tangerine Dream. Despite the ambient foreboding of their music, the sheer spectacle of their lightshows and stacks of electronic instruments attracted large crowds.

Throbbing Gristle, who were described as 'wreckers of civilisation', saw it as their purpose to decondition audiences with their electronically enhanced barrages of sound.

advanced submarine people bringing the forty-third century to the twentieth. The Moog added to Ra's already outlandish arsenal a black box of new possibilities, come to threaten the orthodox shape and dimension of things.

Miles Davis spent most of the 1960s making tasteful, incremental advances on the high-water mark that was, and remains, 1959's *Kind of Blue*, an album of unmatched modal sobriety that represents one of jazz's supreme reflections on what it is to be human in the twentieth century. To hear it at any time is as if the clock has temporarily stopped, so perfect is the moment it captures and freezes. In Davis's own career it features like an evening stopover lakeside, an interlude of rueful but absolute clarity, before he gets back in his automobile and carries on travelling down the freeway. Davis stood slightly aloof from both the popular and radical developments of the 1960s, disdainful of free jazz and its atonal militancy, seemingly oblivious to jazz's displacement as a popular American genre by rock'n'roll and Beatlemania.

However, in every respect, Davis was always all about 'listening to the changes', and by the late 1960s, as the decade began to encroach upon his dress and narcotic habits and the attitudes of his girlfriends, whose outlooks affected his own phases, he began inevitably to attend to the impossible-to-ignore spirit of the age. He was struck by the sort of chopping precision number-one soul brother James Brown was producing as he went through his own 1960s evolutions, or the sheer, torrential outpouring of twisted colour with which former soul sideman Jimi Hendrix was flooding the world, burying the simple architecture of mid-1960s pop like Pompeii. 'I have to change. It's like a curse,' Davis told the *Washington Post* in 1969. But he was in his early forties by this point – no age today, although in his case it was coupled with the fact that he had been recording since the late 1940s and had assumed the sort of unassailable commercial position that can immure you from both the face of, and the necessity for, change. That he contemplated going electric flew in the face of jazz's particularly austere protocols and invited the accusation that he was making a crass and unseemly bid for populism. He had done enough in doing what others in his position had done before, have done since – simply weigh anchor. For daring to attempt his brand of fusion, he deserves great credit. Its success merits accolades beyond that.

Davis had his first taste of electric keyboards, the colour and limpidity they lent, when he heard his ex-sideman Julian 'Cannonball' Adderley's hit version of 'Mercy, Mercy, Mercy', written by the Austrian keyboardist Joe Zawinul. Before long, Zawinul was among the latest batch of players to join temporary forces with Davis, as composer as well as player; others would include Jack DeJohnette and Dave Holland, as well as Herbie Hancock and Keith Jarrett. Davis himself was often more of an overall architect and arranger than a composer, while the presence – and skills as a mixer and tape editor – of Teo Macero, whom he employed as producer, meant that when it came to his studio recordings, Davis was able to mess with the concept of time itself, often to the confusion of players, who were unsure whether what they were playing was a mere try-out jam or likely to end up on the final recording.

Among the first studio experiments that would see Davis drift into the electric was 'Ascent'. It was an altogether more placid outing than John Coltrane's *Ascension*, released in 1966, in which a collection of virtuoso contemporary jazz blowers goaded each other into dervish-like blasts of near-cacophonous frenzy. Much as *Birth of the Cool* had been an opt-out from the sheer iconoclastic velocity of the bebop years, so 'Ascent' hinted at a place of retreat from the 1960s revolutionaries. But the soundworld Davis delineated would be no less meaningful for that. 'Ascent' hints at the aqueous nature of his impending revolution. The track isn't exactly oceanic; its multiple electric keyboards are the sound of pebbles being skimmed tentatively across a still body of water to examine the overlapping effect of the ripples. It draws the ear inwards as it proceeds outwards, in circles. It's a new configuration for jazz – all-enveloping rather than blowing straight ahead.

In a Silent Way was Davis's first full-blown fusion album, released in 1969. Its personnel included Wayne Shorter on soprano sax (a holdover from his earlier line-ups), John McLaughlin on electric guitar, Dave Holland on bass, Tony Williams on drums and a trio of keyboardists – Chick Corea and Herbie Hancock on electric piano, and Joe Zawinul on organ. From 'Shhh/Peaceful', Davis isn't so much asking for calm but for a new mode of listening, in which pre-existing genres don't so much merge as dissolve into one another. Jazz-rock implies a marriage of major, noisy modern languages, but there is a circularity rather than a conventional twin-engine drive about *In a Silent Way*. The music drops like rain, or paint from Pollock's brush, into the ambient space created by its author. Organs and guitars exchange phrases in quick succession, electric keyboards bubble as if from the mouths of passing fish in an aquarium, Shorter's sax interventions rear like seahorses. Fears that this album would be a rock blowout are assuaged by the subtle brush of Williams's restrained but technically advanced playing; hopes that this would be a rock blowout are similarly dashed by the familiar monologue of Davis's playing, which, despite the odd studio treatment, is the voice he has steadfastly maintained since the bebop era.

Dismissed as 'droning aural wallpaper' by Stanley Crouch, one of the rearguard of critics employed on the Ken Burns jazz series who were too keen to preserve jazz as an all-American, everlasting flame of pure integrity, *In a Silent Way* proposes more than mere pleasantry. It anticipates such late-twentieth/early-twenty-first-century buzzwords as 'ambient' and 'immersion'. If Davis had any philosophy at all, it concerned music as the absolute be-all and end-all – 'The main thing that I love, that comes before everything, even breathing, is music.' Much as Sun Ra found a vast untapped realm of solace in the remote ringed-planet regions of outer space, so

Davis expounded, realised and coloured in a preternatural world of inner space, a state of grace, the amniotic waters of pre-birth; the rest was bullshit.

Bitches Brew followed in 1970. It feels like it has followed the skittering footsteps of evolutionary ancestors back into the ocean, but from the opening passages of Zawinul's 'Pharaoh's Dance' it is also clearly intent on a groove – the groove Davis insisted would be the most important aspect of his music as he moved into the 1970s. Added personnel on this album include Bennie Maupin on bass clarinet and Harvey Brooks, adding to the sacrilege on electric bass. It's an altogether more jagged, physical experience, as if we're no longer swimming but bumping and grinding along the irregular, jutting bed of the ocean floor, swinging down deep, coming face to face with the odd lurking demon. And it's as electric as eels.

Inevitably, the jazz establishment felt that Davis was guilty of multiple transgressions. Those who held to a notion of jazz as the unrivalled mode of popular music were still smarting from the feeling of being supplanted, rendered academic and/or antique by rock'n'roll, but it was a relatively new sensation. As a classical member of the old guard, better was expected of him. What was with the wah-wah pedals and the visor, the tentative Afro and the electric bass? Some sort of mid-life crisis? Or, worse, a sell-out at the expense of a genre struggling to retain its identity and relevance, to one very much in the ascendant: a crude, white, hairy perversion of the blues?

Worse, Davis's live music involved rock amplification. Jazz was supposed to be a conversation between players, for the edification of listeners. How could they be expected to be heard above one another in this blaring electric pandemonium?

Writing in 2006, critic Nat Hentoff suggested that Davis wasn't entirely without mercenary motivations during his fusion era. He'd come right out and said so. 'What Miles wanted from the music industry – and record buyers – was even more serious money that he merited for being so singular. Before *Bitches Brew* was made, I remember Miles saying of the rockers that "these white boys are making a lot of money with that, and I could do much more with that music than they can – and make more money." But that was not the primary reason he kept exploring rock, funk, and anything else that challenged him to transmute whatever interested him into Miles music . . . I doubt very much that fear of "decline" was part of his motivation. He was always listening ahead.'

But Hentoff had panned *Bitches Brew*, costing him his relationship with Davis. 'I listened to his "rock" recordings during that period, but seldom more than once. When I told him that, it caused the end of our friendship.'

Richard Williams, writing for *Melody Maker*, a weekly that maintained an informed perspective on both jazz and rock, was more laudatory about *Bitches Brew* and Miles's electric period in general. He was acute on the precision of Davis, whom he described as 'investing his brief phrases with all the pent-up power of a man trying to cut a diamond with a circular saw'. He also understood that, far from mongrelising, Davis 'wasn't a rock star, nor was he trying to be one. He had simply reached a new zone in his music, an area which allowed him to come through clearer and truer than ever.'

If there had been a separation between Davis's nasty, pugnacious side and the melancholy, pacific wanderings of his music, then even those disparate elements began to fuse in the early 1970s as the funk began to bite in his electric phase. In 1971, he released *Jack Johnson*, his soundtrack to Bill Cayton's 1970 documentary about the first black heavyweight boxing champion. Of the three great heavyweight boxing champions of the twentieth century, Davis would have identified most strongly with Jack Johnson. Joe Louis had depended on his white management to recast him as a 'credit to his race' and was a studiously deferential and uncontroversial figure. Muhammad Ali was a brilliant, lyrical extrovert who had used his success as a platform for political and religious proselytising and protest, and was, despite his beliefs, someone who appeared to take more pleasure in beating up black opponents than white ones. Johnson, like Davis, preferred to let his sense of racial injustice manifest itself in other ways and was combative and unapologetic; he took solace in the unheard-of pleasure of a black fist crashing against a white nose.

Although, unlike Sun Ra, Davis hired numerous white musicians, he had a seething sense of racial animus following an incident in which he was beaten up by a white cop for the mere crime of loitering outside a nightclub at which he was playing. At the conclusion of 'Yesternow', a voice intones, 'I'm Jack Johnson, heavyweight champion of the world. I'm black. They never let me forget it. I'm black all right. I never let them forget it either.' Johnson was all about 'unforgivable blackness', inviting open racism even from otherwise left-wing writers such as Jack London. He taunted the hapless series of great white hopes sent to dispatch the 'black peril' he represented in the ring. He strung out the fearful, sustained beatings he administered to them for round after torturous round, in particular the wretched Jim Jeffries, as if to avenge symbolically the fatal violence inflicted on African Americans during the Jim Crow era. Indeed, so enraged were whites by the slow, systematic dismantling and evisceration of their bloodied white hope Jeffries, called out of retirement to put Johnson back in his place at Reno, Nevada, in July 1910, that they ran amok, hunting down and lynching black men in a fetid aftermath of race riots that spread from Pittsburgh to St Louis.

In 1970, with boxing's race barrier long overcome and fighters like Ali and Joe Frazier dominant, it felt appropriate to recollect the trials of Jack Johnson with pride and anger. As if to add further insult to the injury he meted out to whites in the ring, Johnson did not always treat well the mostly white women whom he consorted with and married. However, that he should have been sentenced to a year in prison on spurious charges of 'transporting women across state lines for immoral purposes', because the white women in question were prostitutes with whom he had formed relationships, was clearly a monstrously unfair act of judicial racism.

1970's *A Tribute to Jack Johnson* is very much a record of two sides. The first, 'Right Off', is almost jaunty in its progress, with Davis blasting triumphant phrases over a choppy bed of rock-guitar riffing. It's as if it reflects the march of Johnson himself, smiling and joking as he carries the day against wretched, inferior white opposition, barely breaking sweat, revelling in his dominance and the unique privilege of racial role reversal it affords, flamboyant in furs and finery as he openly enjoys the spoils of his victories.

Side two, 'Yesternow', is, however, altogether more broody and inverted, marked by the slow retread of the bass riff from James Brown's 'Say It Loud – I'm Black and I'm Proud'. It's a piece located in a dark, interior space, one of ulcerous, festering rage against an injustice that can never be erased, nor the animus it creates. This builds to a crest, a writhing fury, as wah-wah guitars and anguished horn yelps tussle in a frenzy of bastardised noise, in which Chick Corea's electric keyboard is fed through effects pedals and a ring modulator. It's like furniture flying around a room, a terrifying fit of frustration.

Jazz critics of Davis continued to despair, as well as former sidemen like Bill Evans, all convinced he was making a frantic, cacophonous play for rock stardom. Well, in fairness, he was. He played a set at the Isle of Wight Festival whose unrelenting amplified barrage felt to lovers of his former modal elegance as akin to a dozen tractor engines revving at once. However, no one in rock, funk or jazz was sculpting or cooking anything like *Jack Johnson* in 1970. This inauthentic hybrid, this electrified, inorganic studio collage stewing in the blood of every known jazz sacred cow, was unique in its physicality, shading and mute eloquence.

1972's *On the Corner* was yet another skull-crushing act of black peril, and another calculated snub on Davis's part to the jazz critics, as well as the muso pedants who pored over sleeves for details of sidemen. Davis offered no personnel details on the album sleeve. Fuck your old white-man jazz protocols. This is something else. Electric 1970s black noise, funk rising like steam from the Harlem drains, or heat from the flap doors of a chophouse. The album begins pointedly in what is clearly mid-jam with an abstract, spitting funk-guitar riff, swimming in a gumbo of organ, tablas and electric keyboard. This is a New York minute that no one else in jazz, rock, pop or funk was capable of achieving: terse grooves, extended sidewalk debates, stacked, horny soul and hot pants. It's Bruegelian, simultaneist, an urban everything, street art that only a jazz orchestrator with a brilliant ear for newer forms could martial. It speaks about African American life in a way that's sacred and profane, life as actually lived in a fresh, supersonic era in which the pious monochromes of the Martin Luther King years and black-tie acoustic formalities of the Modern Jazz Quartet are now Black History and black life can be lived with stylish, sexual, unapologetic defiance. The mode of music had changed; the city was shaking.

It's interesting to compare Davis's jazz-rock with the most advanced white form, as composed by Frank Zappa – albums such as *Waka/Jawaka*, clearly influenced by Davis's electric phase. But all Zappa can achieve is a replication. He's too controlling, too tight in his scripting of his work, even down to the solos, so that the end result sounds like an immaculate parody. It's impressive but ultimately sterile, lacking wildness or burn, groove and soul. Zappa, like too many progressive white musicians of his era and their fans, felt he was rather above all that.

As for *On the Corner*, it's an assemblage. As ever, there's a distinct lack of direction from the often cryptic and Zen-like Davis, although he determined the overall scheme. Within that, musicians had to fend and think for themselves. None of the players to whom we're listening were aware of which of their labours would be used and which would hit the floor of the editing suite. They would only be presented with the music they were to play when they arrived at the studio – spontaneity was all. It's organised, highly accomplished chaos that succeeds not in terms of jazz integrity but as a super-bad end product whose creative sparks continue to fly upwards. It has retained its heat through the ages.

Between 1968 and 1970, when Davis first embarked on his electric phase, he was also going through a clean-living phase, working out with a personal trainer every day, eschewing drugs and alcohol, his diet co-determined by his vegetarian girlfriend. However, as he burned through the early 1970s, which also saw the release of the viciously heavy live album *Dark Magus*, it's as if the sheer heat he was generating as he ran the voodoo down and sweated out demons was taking a visceral toll. Illness and bad habits would again overwhelm him. There would be one more masterpiece before he relapsed into a toxic silence.

By the early 1970s, Sun Ra was achieving a cult notoriety in times that were halfway to catching up with him. He and his Arkestra found themselves revered in Europe, playing such prestige events as Nuits de la Fondation Maeght, where they would tear down joints and parade in their spangly plumage and headwear to thoroughly appreciative audiences who revelled respectfully in their otherness. There's footage of them playing in 1971 in West Berlin, encoring to a packed auditorium with a version of 'Shadow World', in which the hatted musicians build up from the piece's churning piano riff into a hilarious frenzy of celestial noise, musicians rotating in circles on the floor, smashing equipment, before a solo from John Gilmore that's like a dove frantically concussing itself in its attempts to burst through and fly free from the rafters. Ra then accompanies him, fingers dancing across his electric keyboard, unleashing notes like laser beams or deep-sea detonations. He was taking electric jazz to unexplored galactic, heliocentric realms.

Back in the US, he was a prophet without honour – and precious little profit, for that matter, playing free concerts in the park in North Philadelphia to audiences of literally zero. Nonetheless, in 1972, and despite continued penury, Ra was approached to make a documentary that eventually became a magnificently bizarre Blaxploitation C-movie entitled *Space Is the Place*, which indulged Ra's idea that he was a visiting prophet from another part of the solar system, from where he had travelled in a rocket ship fuelled by music. Although inimical forces ranging from a villainous pimp to the FBI force him to beat a hasty retreat back into space, the film swirls with a Sun Ra soundtrack, hoving in and out like radio static, as Ra preaches his message of 'another tomorrow', his words almost certainly destined to fall unattended like autumn leaves in the wind, despite, or perhaps because of, their cosmic urgency.

As the 1970s wore on, however, Ra's reputation grew among white avant-garde noiseniks, ranging from the Stooges to Sonic Youth's Thurston Moore to Chris Cutler of Recommended Records, who first introduced me to Sun Ra in the form of *Media Dreams* and *Disco 3000*, albums taken from sessions he recorded in Milan in 1978 with a reduced number of musicians and a phutting drum machine similar to that favoured by Suicide. These were huge, mind-exploding records, riding the Moog to places, and in ways, it had never been ridden before, not least on the title track to *Media Dreams* itself, gibbering like a twenty-mouthed alien bringing urgent cosmograms from distant planets. It's left a hole in my skull ever since. In terms of the sheer scale implied by *Media Dreams*, which I was lucky enough to hear at the impressionable age of fifteen, everything I've heard subsequently has been relative to its dimensions. This was jazz with unique, unprecedented Hubble vision. The contrast between Ra's staggeringly expansive playing and the tiny patter of the drum machine, like the ticking of a space shuttle engine, was crucial, as was the vicious Moog bass of 'Saturn Research'. Catch Ra in non-electric mode and he could seem surprisingly trad, almost Thelonious Monk-ish. His synth forays, however, were and remain as shattering as a meteor shower crashing through a window pane.

Two examples, both from 1980, when Sun Ra was already in his sixty-fifth year, the age Miles Davis was when he died: first, *Strange Celestial Road*, which features the sixteen-minute piece 'I'll Wait for You'. Its 'terrestrial' elements, the modestly pedestrian riff, June Tyson and Rhoda Blount's chanted vocals are overwhelmed like a hamlet by the aurora borealis of Ra's synths, which at four minutes in irradiate and atomise the listener like a transporter beam, before embarking on a galactic foray that has us plunging down wormholes and re-emerging in glittering, unknown regions of the cosmos, the sonic evocation of the trip away from earth that Ra promised mankind, one that he preached with heightened urgency as the 1980s ushered in a new cold war and the imminent prospect of nuclear annihilation once more.

Another example is from the film *A Joyful Noise* (based on the words of Psalm 98), Robert Mugge's film about Sun Ra, released in 1980. Its most explosive sequence sees a corpulent, sweating, sixty-something Ra in solo mode, perched over a tilted keyboard, physically rushing across it from side to side, creating juddering, turbulent bass vibrations like the birth pangs of a planet, twirling dervish-like with alarming alacrity and grace, facing away from the keyboard and creating twinkling effects with the skip of his fingernails. It's a performance that borders on the supernatural, almost seeming to prove that Ra was indeed channelling vast forces beyond human comprehension. Certainly, he was somehow wrenching potentialities from the circuitry of the Moog that were beyond the dreams of other users.

In 1991, I saw Sun Ra and his Arkestra at Ronnie Scott's. The leader was gravely ill, too ill even to sit at his keyboard. The Arkestra played without him, a typically rampant and colourful performance in which jazz, Afro brass and percussion, and

Egyptology were all on parade. At the end, Ra himself was assisted onto the stage. Reviewing that night, I'll never forget his contribution after he'd been lowered into the seat in front of his keyboard: sparing but devastating Moog notes like depth charges, tunings only available to his own antennae. By 1993, his stay on planet earth was over.

Miles Davis returned from an extensive sabbatical in 1981, a period sadly covered in Don Cheadle's 2016 film *Miles Ahead*, featuring Ewan McGregor as a fictional *Rolling Stone* journalist who gains access to the reclusive jazzman. One suspects Cheadle himself, excellent as Davis, had a much better film in mind than the risible caper that resulted on-screen following Hollywood studio meddling and insistence.

Davis's 1981 album *The Man with the Horn* marked a new change to mark a new decade: his crisp, detoxified phrasing was now accompanied by Yamaha CS30 synthesizer and Moog, courtesy of Robert Irving III and Randy Hall respectively. However, while *The Man with the Horn* twists and turns interestingly in places, reminding one fleetingly of David Byrne and Brian Eno and Jon Hassell's Fourth World Funk, it's also rained on by miserably excessive outpourings of heavy-metal guitar, the sort that gives jazz-rock a hideous name. By the time of 1986's *Tutu*, Davis had mostly given over responsibility for the writing and arrangement of the album to Marcus Miller. It's even more synth-based, featuring sequencers and drum machines also, but the chemistry is commercially orthodox rather than combustible. These are the sort of synths that had settled like a silver cloud over mid-1980s pop. Despite Davis's now outlandish appearance onstage – so colourful he could have taken his place in an Arkestra line-up with no questions asked – *Tutu* was largely the bland sound of a man who had quit fighting, content to blow out his days in his time-honoured style and collect a packet in the process – which he did.

Even now, however, Davis's divining skills enabled him to detect rare traces of brilliant melancholy coursing through the electric surfaces of 1980s radio pop, the stuff destined to live out an extended afterlife on the sort of stations favoured by minicab drivers taking you home across the empty city in the small hours. He covered Michael Jackson's 'Human Nature', Cyndi Lauper's 'Time After Time' and Scritti Politti's 'Perfect Way'. His own antennae weren't entirely defunct.

Ra and Davis were by no means the only artists to have made electric jazz. Paul Bley acquired a Moog years in advance of Sun Ra, though on 1970's *The Paul Bley Synthesizer Show*, on tracks like 'Parks', he plays the instrument in the manner of an ersatz piano, albeit expressively. However, Annette Peacock, with whom he worked, made 1972's *I'm the One*, in which synths feature like synaptic interventions, running commentaries on the drama and flux of songs like 'Pony', or like brainwaves, in a way that anticipates Allen Ravenstine's use of electronics with Pere Ubu. Her treatment of her own voice using the Moog serves only to super-humanise, rather dehumanise, her vocals, adding a feeling of multiple personae and perspectives.

Meanwhile, George Russell, who had relocated to Europe in despair at the lot of African Americans in the 1960s, cut *Electronic Sonata for Souls Loved by Nature*, a recording featuring European jazz luminaries such as Jan Garbarek. Driven across its two parts by one of the most motorik and propulsive piano riffs in modern jazz, it is soberly modal in its orchestrated phases but is shadowed by sheet waves of electronics and interpolations reminiscent of Varèse's *Déserts*, tapes of the ghostly reverberations of instruments treated and processed beyond recognition, portholes into the abstract. Russell was also overlooked in Ken Burns's jazz series – perhaps because he incorporated elements of the European avant-garde as well as European jazz players, therefore straying from the documentary's all-American narrative.

And then, in 1973, Herbie Hancock, clearly having benefited from his period with Miles Davis, released *Sextant*, whose opener, 'Rain Dance', immediately locates us in sputnik terrain, its bleeps and boosts part of a remote moon-raking armoury that includes the Hohner D6 clavinet, mellotron, ARP 2600, ARP Pro Soloist and Moog. It's a hybrid of the cosmic exploratory spirit of Sun Ra and the free-ranging fusion of Davis. Its effects were surprisingly far reaching – Boris Blank of Yello bought his first ARP synthesizer purely because he had seen it listed in the sleevenotes. The album's myriad inventions and suggestions, however, have been overshadowed by its immediate successor, *Head Hunters*, in which Hancock inaugurated a synth-based jazz–funk fusion that would see him become so successful that even his former bandleader Miles Davis found himself supporting him in concert.

All of these albums suggested possibilities for jazz to develop and breed further, having reached a terminus in terms of its own intrinsic development with Ornette Coleman and free jazz. They were considered deviant and promiscuous by jazz purists, deviations from the shining path that led all the way back to Buddy Bolden. By the twenty-first century, though, conversations between jazz and abstract electronics had become commonplace. *Trio × 3: New Jazz Meeting in Baden-Baden* (2002), featuring the late Steve Lacy and electronics from Bernhard Lang, is a single example among many, especially as free improv, with all its attendant lack of inhibitions, merged with jazz. There's a whole world of investigation to be had right there. However, those keen to defend jazz as some unsullied classical entity are in difficulties presently, unsure whether to celebrate its permanently evolving qualities and unique ability to speak to modern times, or to preserve the genre as a museum piece, glassed off from external influences.

Although both were contemptuous of categories and boundaries, Miles Davis and Sun Ra started musical life as creatures of jazz, for whom the electric was a means of evolution, escape and self-realisation. Their music was deeply personal yet represents mutant, eclectic legacies, worlds to explore, unique to jazz. Charlie Parker and Dizzy Gillespie represent high-water marks of pure jazz virtuosity; Ra and Davis represent entire ambiences.

The worlds they created and inhabited were products not just of their artistic and personal qualities but of their responses to the world as black men, though both to a degree were in denial about the indignities their sensitivities endured, and how it affected their artistic direction. It had been the same for Ellington and Armstrong, both of whom had coping strategies for their racial situation which at times made it seem like they were ingratiatingly oblivious to the issue of colour. Neither of them were, least of all Armstrong, despite accusations that his onstage antics showed him up as an 'Uncle Tom'.

Ra affected to disdain the issue of civil rights as banal by comparison with his higher cosmic aims for the black race. 'I'm not looking for liberty, I'm not looking for equality,' he insisted in *A Joyful Noise*. Yet it was clear that his yearning for anywhere other than this earth, a yearning that could only be realised through the extremes, electronic in particular, of his music, was connected with the unavoidable limitations imposed upon black Americans in the twentieth century, who would have to show ten times the resources of their white counterparts to achieve the same level of wherewithal and dignity. As Stevie Wonder once said, in relation to Muhammad Ali and how loud and hard he had to shout to assert himself, 'These things hurt – you, me.' Sun Ra felt he would have to traverse light years of space simply to feel at home.

As for Miles Davis, his taciturn truculence was merely a carapace, a means of dealing with the feeling of deep social inferiority which American society forced its black citizens to internalise. He was an intimidating presence – to journalists, fellow musicians, audience members, the women in his life – but at the height of his fame he himself was too intimidated even to book into a hotel, afraid he would suffer the humiliation of a colour bar. Not unlike Ra, rejected by this world he turned away and made his own, one that has enriched and emotionally informed us all.

Davis's last great piece was released in 1974, its thirty-two-minute-long highlight, 'He Loved Him Madly', an immensely sombre salute to Duke Ellington, who died that year. Davis had received a Christmas card from Ellington, which thrilled him no end. It read: 'Love you madly.' Ellington had sent similar cards to many of his friends – he knew his days were numbered.

'He Loved Him Madly' is like nothing else in Davis's electric canon. He himself chalks out its outlines with simple, spectral passages of organ, while Mtume maintains a low-level rumble of congas. 'We were playing off a mood,' Mtume said. 'Forget the chords, forget everything, it is all ambience.' Of course, Davis was guiding the sessions that comprised the eventual piece, which was so abruptly edited in places by Teo Macero as if to leave the listener under no illusion that this was not an embryonic jam but a pre-meditated and post-mediated piece, a concept, a collage.

The piece proceeds with the slow, deliberate pace of a New Orleans funeral march. Guitars chime in with occasional subdued murmurs, while bass sighs emanate from somewhere low in the mix, before Dave Liebman eulogises with a lengthy treated alto flute solo. Then, sixteen minutes in, Davis himself steps up to the podium with a lachrymose trumpet peal, one of his least complex yet most moving and cathartic solos, circling high in the heavens.

Ellington was dead; so were Louis Armstrong, Charlie Parker, John Coltrane, Billie Holiday, Clifford Brown, Eric Dolphy and Albert Ayler, among others. 'He Loved Him Madly' can be heard as the great ghost ship of jazz bobbing on dark waters, no one at the tiller, vital hands lost. Really, though, despite its elegiac feel, it represents a birth. It's been cited by Eno as vital to his thinking on ambient music, and from it, as well as the rest of Davis's electric period, so much has proceeded – the myriad mutant strains, from fourth world to broken beats to hip hop, that lie like a great reef below the ocean surface of twenty-first-century sound in the post-rock, post-jazz age.

8

DEUX FEMMES SEULES:
DERBYSHIRE AND ORAM

With her alliterative and impeccably English name, her prim
accent and roseate, unflappable, Quant-ish air of 1960s chic, Delia
Derbyshire, doyenne of the Radiophonic Workshop, has about her
all the makings of a fantasy figure. Indeed, German musician Felix
Kubin felt impelled to invent his own Teutonic Derbyshire equivalent, Ursula Bogner, to make up for the lack of any such figure
in the parallel German music scene. That Derbyshire was only
widely (re)discovered after her death in 2001 makes her a human
metaphor for the belated discovery by a new generation of electronic musicians and listeners of the legacy of musique concrète
long after its passing. It was this Delia, not jobbing TV composer
Ron Grainer (also responsible for the theme to *Steptoe & Son*),
who in effect realised the theme to *Doctor Who*, perhaps the piece
of electronic music that has imprinted itself most indelibly on the
historical and collective consciousness, in the UK at any rate.

In fact, Derbyshire was in many ways the antithesis of what she
appeared to be in the handful of now iconic photos of her at work
in the 1960s: cool in her headband and, it seems, her demeanour,
working methodically away. Her cut-glass pronunciation, as heard
in archive interviews, is slightly odd in its inflections ('sahnd'),
its strangeness not uncommon at a time when it was felt that in
order to get on, one had to suppress one's natural regional accent
(the England manager, Sir Alf Ramsey, was another case in point).
Although she won herself a place at Girton College, Cambridge,

she was originally from a working-class background: born in Coventry, father a sheet-metal worker. She alone was responsible for navigating herself to the upper echelons of Oxbridge, the BBC and the United Nations. Nonetheless, she suffered setbacks: Decca, who would later become infamous for turning down the Beatles on the grounds that guitar music was on the way out, would inform Derbyshire in 1955 that women were certainly not on the way into the world of sound recording, and her application to join their engineering department was rejected as it was considered no place for a young lady.

Temperamentally, Derbyshire was wayward, fiery and eccentric. Colleagues describe her as brilliant but infuriating to work with, prone to taking sudden offence at a seemingly innocuous remark or suggestion. Her work rate seems to have been variable in its pace. 'Some days, she didn't want to know,' says David Vorhaus, later her colleague in the proto-electropop 1960s group White Noise, whose 1969 album *An Electric Storm*, recorded clandestinely in the BBC's studios, is one of the lost milestones of the psychedelic era. She was analytical but unworldly; a story of her out cycling in Camden, near her home, only for her to fetch up in Vauxhall, on the south side of the Thames, with no idea how she got there, suggests a mind that was elsewhere. Her body of work consists largely of fragments of ideas, undeveloped pieces stored on a chaotic cache of tapes kept in cornflakes boxes that was eventually found by her partner in an attic after her death, suggesting that for all the painstaking labours required of her in the Radiophonic Workshop, she was more interested in processes than outcomes. There's a famous fragment of soundtrack, made in 1971 and discovered in her archive – a recording preceded by Derbyshire dismissing it in advance, 'Ah, forget about this, it's for interest only' – which sounds like a sudden plunge down a wormhole into the 1990s, an outtake by Autechre or Mike Paradinas or the Aphex Twin: a furious but regular jackhammer rhythm underpinning a brightly looming electronica motif. In 1971, Kraftwerk were already developing the drum machine-based minimal foundations of their eventual post-*Autobahn* canon – but, unlike Derbyshire, they knew they were on to something. She appears to have thought nothing of her futurist creation; just one more stone in the meteor shower of her electric imagination.

A desire to move swiftly on from idea to idea also accounts for her extreme annoyance at being asked by the BBC to tinker repeatedly with her theme to *Doctor Who*, requested from series to series to tweak it and jazz it up by department busybodies who didn't understand that the original needed no further gilding. Created from an organ, a stock recording of a plucked string, a melodica and edited excepts of white noise, and recorded on synchronised tape machines in a pre-multitrack age, it remains for millions of people the first and last word in musique concrète. It was certainly my first. Looking back at early episodes of *Doctor Who*, with their risible, lurching, fuzzy monsters and cumbersome Daleks, invulnerable to everything except staircases, I find it hard to believe that I, too, cowered in fear behind the living-room sofa as the Doctor yet again found himself under siege from growling extraterrestrial creatures. Much of that alluring dread, I realise, was the ripple effect of the Derbyshire theme, which felt like the skies being pulled apart like curtains and some giant cone-headed alien peering in, eliciting a Munch-like scream.

At the same time, Derbyshire's devotion to tonality and melody made the *Doctor Who* theme, albeit scary, as familiar to the 1960s experience as Tupperware. The future was coming some time soon, and *Doctor Who* was simply the headlong sound of us hurtling down the corridor in its direction, white chevrons receding at regular intervals in our wing mirrors. This was a given.

For Derbyshire, however, the everyday hidebound reality of working at the BBC was one of ostensible enlightenment hampered by budgetary cuts and institutional condescension. She sought out other outlets in frustration at being regarded as the 'sound effects girl', using her nimble aptitude with the scissors to play a vital back-room role in the overall broadcasting effort. Along with her colleague Brian Hodgson and engineer (and later founder of EMS) Peter Zinovieff, she set up Unit Delta Plus, an organisation dedicated to the promotion of electronic music and its artistic applications. Her work was presented at the 1966 event 'The Million Volt Light and Sound Rave' at the Roundhouse Theatre, along with the Beatles' 'Carnival of Light', an experimental piece of which only Paul McCartney is reputed to own a recording. It was while she and Hodgson were co-lecturing on electronic music that they met David Vorhaus, with whom they went on to form the group White Noise. With its quaint pop cadences and thematic naivety, their debut album, *An Electric Storm*, is a touch date-stamped; however, on opening track 'Love Without Sound' in particular, Derbyshire co-creates a bombardment of abstract, figurative effects, rearing like ghost-train apparitions from the mix at utterly unexpected angles and in 3D form: sinister bursts of laughter, cone-like percussive clusters, exclamations of unfathomable provenance, all products of the Delia psyche – a handmade sonic simulation of an LSD trip.

Derbyshire did not follow through with White Noise, though, which in time became a David Vorhaus solo project. She produced little work beyond the mid-1970s, taking up other lines of work, including a stint at the gas board, while sinking slowly into a red mire of alcoholism. One of the last photos of her was taken as she sipped a glass of the wine of which she had become overly fond, at a party commemorating the twenty-fifth anniversary of the Radiophonic Workshop. She is in conversation with Daphne Oram, with whom she remained on very friendly terms. She seems to be waving the camera away irritably, showing no desire to be rediscovered. She did, however, accept the friendship of Spaceman 3 frontman Pete Kember in the late 1990s, acting as a consultant on his Experimental Audio Research project, specifically the albums *Vibrations* and *Continuum*, released in 2000 and 2001 respectively. She died of renal failure in 2001, not living to see her rehabilitation.

Her best work was fitful and closer to the soundworlds of Eno and dark ambient than Stockhausen or Schaeffer. Academically speaking, it's not 'major', but at its best it's beautiful and prescient. 'Blue Veils and Golden Sands', composed as incidental music for the *Doctor Who* series, is a vivid event horizon of desert storms and dancing mirages, conveying in its exquisitely processed sound a sense of shifting colour. *Circle of Light*, meanwhile, co-composed with Elsa Stansfield for a 1972 film featuring the stills of photographer Pamela Bone, is at thirty-two minutes her longest known work. It's like a temporally extended panoramic photograph in its own right: featuring field recordings of nature, including cawing birdsong, it uses tape loops and transformative concrète methods to create a palpable yet enigmatic sound mood, disquieting evocations of a coastal dusk, tranquil yet ominous.

Perhaps most worthy of rediscovery, however, is the series of *Inventions for Radio* she produced with composer and 'sound inventor' Barry Bermange. I was alerted to these by Felix Kubin, creator of the wishful Ursula Bogner, who has a special interest in *Hörspiel*, a German radio form in which storytelling is enhanced by various sound techniques, and of which there is no real equivalent in the UK. That said, these works, produced between 1964 and 1965, exist in a twilight zone between music and drama, examples of 'pure radio' at a time when TV production was still a pretty crude and infantile affair, without much of a visual language at its disposal.

Bermange presented Derbyshire with a series of spoken-word collages in which British interviewees discuss, in various programmes, the onset of age, dreams and their belief in God. Phrases from various subjects are juxtaposed, sometimes repeated – 'I was running

a-way'; 'He cre-ayted me' – as if for the sake of their odd into-
nations. Derbyshire's Radiophonic backdrop – mostly extended,
grainy, arcing, intertwining pulses and drones – is subtly prompted
and triggered by the phrases uttered, from which it derives its tone
and direction. The overall effect is by turns sinister and sympathetic,
casting the voices into a swirling sonic miasma, giant quandaries in
which human beings struggle for certainties and footholds. They are
a reminder of the experimental possibilities that are sealed off and
left behind when technologies – in this case TV – insist on becoming too developed and proficient. Certainly, in 1964, the aural
depictions created by Derbyshire had no visual equal in the world of
television; this is painfully evident from the risible *Doctor Who* sets
at the time. Even today, the abstract scenarios, the vivid yet indistinct images Derbyshire was able to create with her limited technical
means far exceed anything TV or even cinema could concoct, for
all their digital advances. Her legacy, some of it over half a century
old, reminds us that today we could do with a twenty-first-century
Hörspiel of our own. Hers truly was a mind elsewhere.

> Do you think it is the role of music always to reflect the life of the day?
> Personally I think it is much more than that – we have already men-
> tioned its role of inducing resonance, its greatest role to my mind – but,
> as well as that, I think it should not only reflect the life of the day but
> show the possibilities for the future. It should show all the possibilities
> . . . the grim ones as well as the pleasant. We should not ask it to wear
> pink spectacles.
> *Daphne Oram, 1972*

Although Delia Derbyshire fully deserves her cult status as an early
British innovator for her work in the Radiophonic Workshop, still
more attention is due to Daphne Oram, among the great *femmes
seules* of electronic music. Inventor of the Oramics system, based
on an epiphany she had at seven years of age, when she wondered
if it were possible to convert drawings into musical sound, she

strove to kindle the imaginations of her own and future generations, challenging them to leap beyond their assumptions of what
music could constitute and how it could be made in the modern,
science-driven age.

With her horn-rimmed spectacles, penetrative, schoolmarmish
stare, just-so diction and twinset air, Oram looked every inch the
stereotypical British spinster, as if about to cycle down to her local
Women's Institute to deliver a lecture on the dos and don'ts of
pruning rhododendrons. This trifling image problem, however,
should not deflect from either her music or her ideas, as presented
in her 1972 volume *An Individual Note: Of Music, Sound and
Electronics*. She began her working life at the BBC, working as a
'balancing engineer', but before long developed an interest in the
new medium of tape-recording and its potentials, acquainted herself with the work of Pierre Schaeffer et al. and witnessed at first
hand the broadcast of Edgard Varèse's *Poème électronique*. She was
given commissions to create electronically sourced soundtracks for
radio plays such as *Private Dreams and Public Nightmares* and, in
1958, was appointed the first manager of the BBC Radiophonic
Workshop. However, for all its enlightened provision, the BBC
was also stuffed with reactionaries who took a rather dimmer view
of the sonic horizons beyond which she sought to push. 'In my
work I am not concerned with synthesizing orchestral sounds –
we have excellent orchestras for making those sounds: my interest
is in making new sounds which are musical,' Oram would later
declare. But when she expressed this proposal to a BBC executive,
she was loftily rebuffed: 'Miss Oram, the BBC employs 100 musicians to make all the sounds they require, thank you.' She was also
exposed to the ire of members of the BBC Symphony Orchestra,
who sensed that the new world proposed by Oram was one in
which they would be out of a job, and had to contend with an official sense that what she and her fellow Workshop colleagues was
producing wasn't music at all but mere 'sound effects', akin to the

rattle of sheet metal to convey a high wind in a radio drama. The final straw, however, according to her colleague Dick Mills, came in 1958, as he explained in an interview with the New Zealand branch of the *Doctor Who* fan club:

> We're all very health and safety conscious nowadays, but back in 1958 they were equally worried – especially with people working in an experimental department, doing things where they didn't really know what they could or couldn't do – with strange noises. Would that affect their health? So the BBC told Daphne that she could only work there for three months. Daphne said, 'This department is my life's ambition, and if you say I can only work here for three months, I shall have to resign.' They insisted; so she resigned.

This, coupled with a realisation that the BBC wasn't truly serious about exploring the potential of electronic music, saw Oram cast herself out alone. She cashed in her pension and built her own elaborate studio at a converted oast house in Kent, which she filled with her equipment. Thanks to grants from the Gulbenkian Foundation, this would include a 'photo-electric digital/analogue compositional machine', in which she transcribed by hand shapes representing sound components such as pitch, vibrato and rhythm onto parallel 35 mm strips of clear, sprocketed film, which would then pass through a sound system to generate the intended musical 'shapes'.

A Pathé-style news item of the day invites us to tour the premises, from which the 'oddest sounds' emerge. We see 'Miss Oram' stationed behind banks of equipment, conducting 'scientific investigations' into the 'sound of the future'. We see how loops are methodically processed into a fully-fledged electronic work. Later, in 1990, Oram would write of computer technology, 'How exciting for women to be present at its birth pangs, ready to help it evolve to maturity in the world of the arts. To evolve as a true and practical instrument for conveying women's inner thoughts, just as the novel did nearly two centuries ago.'

For all the stilted, monochrome quaintness of the item, they've at least taken the trouble to investigate. It's ironic that when the item is introduced on the British Movietone channel by modern-day presenters, they're considerably more inane, making comedy 'spooky' and 'bleep-bleep' noises when introducing the item, a gross deficit of hindsight, as if the intimations of the future present in the air in the late 1950s have evaporated completely in the twenty-first century, supplanted by feeble, postmodern snickering.

There was a duality to Daphne Oram's work. On the one hand, she saw the instruments of electronic music and musique concrète as a means not just of exceeding the staid vocabulary of traditional music but also of exploring hidden potentialities, both in music and in the human mind. The nuances and multiple effects now available thanks to new sound-making techniques might have all manner of unconsidered healing properties, she held. The medium of electricity wasn't merely a natural force to be harnessed. It could be calibrated and manipulated in all manner of exciting new ways; vibrational phenomena, for example, was an untapped area well worth exploring. This coincided with a rise in New Age thinking – wildly optimistic and untested ideas about the 'inner realms of tone', as posited by George Arnsby-Jones, or 'phono-therapy', as long advocated by the feminist and theosophist Maud MacCarthy. What excited Oram, unduly perhaps, was the idea that electronic music wasn't just an aesthetic medium but the means whereby the arts and the sciences would merge. As she wrote in *An Individual Note*:

> Now, in the 20th century, when science is so prominent, can it link more closely with imagination? Can science bend sufficiently to present scientific facts in such a way that they excite artists? Can artistic creations equally excite the scientists?

Do both the scientist and the artist need a new range of metaphor, verging on mythology: a new set of analogies which will provide a common meeting ground, giving each a stimulating and enriching glimpse of the other's world?

More of this later. For the time being, however, Oram was obliged to put these investigations on the back burner and produce a range of commercial sound work. Much of this must have seemed like a chore, her role restricted to a peripheral one of creating effects for radio, TV, theatre and so on. Nonetheless, her input into some of these productions is absolutely fascinating. She had already shown this in her work for a 1957 production of the Samuel Beckett play *All That Fall*, written specifically for radio (and which you can hear on the website openculture.com). Her sparing interventions in this tale of the peregrinations of an obese Irish housewife appropriately exceed the traditional whispers and exclamations of traditional orchestral incidental music. They are sound-shots of psychological moments of drama, using the tools of the studio to create synaptic events.

More widely broadcast, though uncredited, was her work on Jack Clayton's 1961 film *The Innocents*, an adaptation of the Henry James novel *The Turn of the Screw*, co-scripted by Truman Capote. It stars Deborah Kerr as a governess, Miss Giddens, who is given full charge of two children at a country estate by a wealthy but distant uncle, the previous governess, a Miss Jessel, having died a year earlier. After a series of apparitions, she gradually becomes convinced that the children have been possessed by two ghosts, one of them the late Miss Jessel.

The soundtrack for *The Innocents* is credited to Georges Auric, by now a veteran composer for British movies, with a filmography that includes such Ealing comedy classics as *The Lavender Hill Mob* and *Passport to Pimlico*. However, he had started musical life as a member of Les Six, a diverse group assembled under the wing of Jean

Cocteau that also included Francis Poulenc and Darius Milhaud. It was Auric who co-wrote the haunting faux-traditional ballad 'O Willow Waly' (later brassily reworked by Matty Lincoln as a piece of EDM), which opens the movie, emerging from a darkness that precedes the credits and hummed insouciantly throughout the film, quite often preceding moments of high horror.

Auric's overall soundtrack, though capably impressionistic and cut from the reliable cloth he was wont to provide, was not considered adequate to soundtrack the film's eeriest moments, however; the language isn't up to it. For that reason, Clayton turned to Oram to provide music that gets past the usual orchestral prompts and clichés, gets inside the viewer's ear and spreads anxious reverberations like ripples. *The Innocents* is among the most frightening horror movies ever made because its horrors are not externalised; they lurk ambiguously within the psyche of the main character, in whose subjective experience we are immersed, assisted also by the monochromatic cinematography, its use of deep focus and stylised lighting suggesting that we are in the corridors, bedchambers and stairwells of the mind.

Oram's contributions emerge when Miss Giddens catches a glimpse of a mysterious young man loitering on a tower top: hovering, tremulous sine tones, a disturbance in the fabric of reality, exacerbated as the flapping wings of rocketing birds take on a subtly processed, concrète air. They emerge again in one of the film's most disquieting moments, when Miss Giddens catches sight of an apparition of Miss Jessel across the water; pallid and Gothic, the apparition looks inadvertently like a creature of 1980s goth, staring with ghastly reproach at the very prim but flappable Giddens. Later, around the film's hour mark, in a sequence involving a ballerina music box and a terrifying pursuit through the mansion by candlelight, Oram's soundtrack meshes echoed childish laughter, a shrieking, analogue motif and a door that slams with a blackly resonant, repeated echo the like of which was hitherto unheard-of in mainstream cinema. It's a music which hints that the trauma experienced by Miss Giddens is mental and psychological, rather than objectively real. Oram once compared madness to the effect of feedback, and that suggestion is strongly advanced in this terrifying crescendo, whose unprecedented nuances and uniquely effective splicing were beyond the reach of even a Bernard Herrmann. It would be a stretch to say that mainstream film soundtracking would never be the same again because it would very much be the same again, and today it is arguably more the same than ever. However, Oram's work on *The Innocents* created a wormhole of other possibilities for realising cinematic psychodrama in sound.

Oram would continue to carry out her research and make her own private recordings, which were eventually made available on the collection *Oramics*, issued in 2007. These vary in quality from the sketchy, quaint and even literal to quite unearthly stretches of brilliance. To expose oneself in Oramics is to float and swim in a veritable dead sea of unrealised possibilities, a sort of liquid, timbral neurology, a vast vortex of magnificent solitude. It's a huge bequest of music, dateless, timeless – indeed, it feels untapped altogether. It means everything that it was made when it was, when the future we now live in was still unwritten. It's consoling to think that the even more distant future Oram posited might yet come to pass and sound something like this.

In their time, Derbyshire and Oram undoubtedly had to suffer sexist condescension at the hands of their male colleagues and 'superiors'. It says something about the nature of electronic music practice, however, that they were at least able to work, that it was more than thinkable for them to create in this medium. Electronic music's history of significant female contributors compares extremely well with that of rock music, especially its instrumental side, where problems of objectification, the inherently phallic nature of the genre and antediluvian attitudes in both the industry and among fans have always proven inhibiting. With electronic music, a more open and abstract medium, as well as an obscure one, composers like Éliane Radigue, assistant to Pierre Henry, who produced an elasticated, meditative take on musique concrète through her use of long tape loops on works like *Trilogie de la mort*; Laurie Spiegel, who, working out of Bell Laboratories, took early advantage of computer technology and made inquisitive, non-commercial music (and with whom Radigue shared a studio); Suzanne Ciani, whose most-heard work might be the signature supersonic 'whoosh' that strafes across the chorus of the Starland Vocal Band's guiltiest of guiltily pleasurable singles 'Afternoon Delight' (1976), but whose longer-form works are now celebrated in their own right; Pauline Oliveros, champion of 'deep listening' music, and many others, have been able to contribute tellingly, with less fuss and fixation on their female-ness. Which is not to say that they are the beneficiaries of male enlightenment; one suspects that Derbyshire and Oram were permitted to operate as they did in the 1960s because electronics was somehow considered 'woman's work', like hand-stitching or macramé, background work that did not apparently threaten male hierarchies.

In the twenty-first century, the number of non-male artists, transgender as well as female, has mushroomed. Whatever future the music has, it is the latter who are increasingly driving, colouring and shaping its narrative.

9

STEVIE WONDER AND THE
ELECTRIFICATION OF SOUL

You know, Homer was blind. Milton, Bach, Monet, Wonder.
Rasmussen, 'A Matter of Time', Star Trek: The Next Generation

If Delia Derbyshire's *Doctor Who* theme floated through the 1960s
and early 1970s as a weekly lunar reminder of the alien realm of
electronic music, it would be followed up from a wholly different
angle, transmitted via American soul music and one of the world's
most popular entertainers. Soul had exploded in a riot of colour
in the late 1960s, with Sly Stone, the Isley Brothers, James Brown
and George Clinton's Parliament among those who had raised their
game and groove to meet the psychedelic challenge of the turn of
the decade. Stevie Wonder had made an initially more awkward
transition from the black and white Motown machine. By the early
1970s, however, he was the greatest solo artist in the world and, in
his choice of instrumentation, among the most radical.

It was the blindness of Stevie Wonder that first opened my eyes
to the notion of musical discernment. In February 1978, I spotted
a paperback, a routine hack biography about the singer, whose
work I had distantly admired. I bought it and read it as avidly
as the *Rubaiyat*. A couple of months earlier, my attitude to pop
music was so unthinking that I would jig merrily in my room to a
cassette of Paul Nicholas's greatest hits, including his 1975 effort
'Reggae Like It Used to Be'. Now, a new dawn broke as I realised that certain popular music existed on a Higher Ground; that

this music was didactic and morally purposeful, as well as intrin-
sically superior. Stevie Wonder, like Bob Dylan, I understood, was
one of those artists who made music of quality and distinction.
Hitherto, I had wasted my teens grazing on troglodyte banality.
Paul Nicholas!

Painful as it is to reflect upon such adolescent epiphanies subsequently, and painful as it was for those who had to endure my
company at the time, I know I will never experience music with
the same keenness and devoted fascination as I did when I was
fifteen years old, my taste buds still quivering with curiosity, my
palate unjaded. I saved up for four weeks at a time to buy albums
over late winter into early summer 1978, beginning with Wonder's
unrivalled series of early-1970s albums – *Music of My Mind*,
Innervisions, *Talking Book*, *Fulfillingness' First Finale* and *Songs in the
Key of Life*. The connection I made with those albums is like none
I have made since. Whatever I liked to tell myself and others, in
truth it wasn't the socially conscious lyrical edge of songs like 'Big
Brother', 'Living for the City' and 'You Haven't Done Nothing', or
the religious sentiments of the likes of 'Heaven Is Ten Zillion Light
Years Away' (for as well as being deeply desirous of social change, I
was still an ardent Catholic), it was the groove, the tremulous, velvet ache of Wonder's vocals and, above all, the sheer liquid, metallic
emotion of the Arp and Moog synthesizers with which I connected.

The idea of Wonder's blindness fascinated me. I read up mor-
bidly on the subject. Stevland Judkins (later Morris) was born six
weeks prematurely in 1950 in Saginaw, Michigan. He had been
placed in an incubator whose necessary oxygen had the unfortunate
effect in baby Stevland's case of causing retinopathy of prematurity. At the time, I angrily believed that his condition was due to
the poor medical facilities afforded to African American children.
However, only a year after Wonder was born, it was suggested that
in fact there was a strong correlation between the incidence of
retinopathy of prematurity and well-funded welfare systems. Only

later was the issue of an excess of oxygen in the treatment of babies recognised as a factor. Since the early 1940s, there had been an epidemic of the disease, some 12,000 cases in all, including the American actor and author Tom Sullivan, born in 1947 and also blind from birth.

Wonder has known nothing but blindness. In an effort to help them understand how the world felt to a sightless person, journalists on a promotional junket for his album *Innervisions* were blindfolded for a trip around New York. But to be blind is more than merely to be deprived of sight. Close your eyes, and you'll experience a blackness, criss-crossed with vapour trails of colour and afterglows of dulled light. For a blind person, there is not even that, just a nothingness.

Wonder was always positive about his blindness. He said that it enabled him to judge people differently, rather than judging books by their covers. No superficialities for him. He was a denizen of the realms of depth, the way I now reckoned myself to be. However, as a child, there had been more than one attempt to seek out a way to mend his terminally detached retinae, with 1950s faith in scientific progress high. None was found. In later life, he was said to have secretly spent a fortune on operations in an effort to acquire vision. These were unsuccessful, but suppose they had worked? I had read stories of people who had been cured of blindness in adulthood but couldn't cope with the extra visual dimension they had done without all their lives, unable to reorientate and even begging to be returned to their former sightless state.

There was an ambivalence about Wonder's blindness. In tandem with the disadvantage that came with being born black in the mid-twentieth century, it seemed doubly cruel. However, much as black people in general had a perception of the world I could never hope to share, so Wonder was perversely advantaged, as indeed he claimed, by his lack of sight. From Homer onwards, the trope of the blind person whose deeper vision makes a mockery of his apparently dead-eyed stare, and of his students, who see but require guidance, is commonplace. Though Wonder's own visions might have seemed tritely expressed – 'To find a job is like the haystack needle / 'cos where he lives they don't use coloured people,' he sang on 'Living for the City' – they were delivered with a forthrightness and growling ferocity that dissolved all qualms. On 'Living for the City', moreover, the synths conveyed the ambience of crosstown traffic flashing slowly by, every blast of the horn an expression of a collective sigh.

By 1970, and soon to turn twenty-one, Stevie Wonder was understandably tiring of being a frontman for the 1960s Motown house sound. He even toyed with ditching his 'Wonder' moniker, though savvier counsel persuaded him of the importance of brand recognition. Stevland Morris would have a tougher time than Stevie Wonder. Other Motown acts such as the Temptations had taken on psychedelic tinges around their edges but otherwise retained the tried and tested Motown protocols. Berry Gordy saw the growing individualism of the late 1960s as a threat to his overall business strategy but was not so unwise as to try to stamp it out altogether.

In 1971, Marvin Gaye made his own mature statement of intent with the much-acclaimed *What's Goin' On*, an album that has been somewhat overpraised ever since its release, with its somewhat bland, subdued and unvarying groove. Its political sentiments may have been bold but they're also suffocated by religious piety and banally vague prescriptions. One suspects that many critics were overcome by the condescension implicit in the sentiment expressed by the writer Geoff Brown in another review, when he wrote of the 'creeping suspicion which must afflict us all from time to time, that black artists can only write convincingly these days about the topics of love and dancing'.

Nonetheless, the album was considered a success and saw Gaye make an effective transition to become a self-determining solo artist in the 1970s. Stevie Wonder tried to strike his own blow for artistic liberty with the album *Where I'm Coming From*, but it was a more fitful, incoherent and often lyrically convoluted affair.

It was around this time, however, that he heard the album *Tonto's Expanding Head Band*, by a British–American duo, Robert Margouleff and Malcolm Cecil. Margouleff was an early associate of synth inventor Robert Moog, while Cecil, despite his electrical engineering background, had spent most of the 1960s playing trad jazz and blues with Ronnie Scott and Alexis Korner, among others. Playing as a sideman, however, got him thinking. 'Many a time I have stood in the back of the stage in a jazz club after twenty-seven choruses of the blues, thinking I might as well be a machine,' he later said.

He and Margouleff would together construct a hugely ambitious synth system, of which TONTO was the acronym. Building up from an original modular synthesizer, it would also comprise four Oberheim SEMs, two ARP 2600s, as well as several custom modules designed by Serge Tcherepnin and Cecil himself. Later additions would include early versions of the sequencer. All of this was housed in a semi-circle of imposing curved wooden cabinets. These were the days when studios dedicated to electronic music felt like mission control centre.

The duo released their first album, *Zero Time*, in 1971. It's limited only by Margouleff and Cecil's limits as composers: the changes can be a little predictable, and its lengthy instrumental passages can feel more demonstrative than seriously thematic. The ideas contained in its pieces amount to little more than the regular hippy jetsam of late-1960s preoccupations. Texturally, however, it is revelatory, and one can only imagine the paint-gun effect it must have had on the heads of those who heard it first time around. It presents a multi-timbral palette of synth sounds that belie cold, metal, stiff, monochromatic, cubic expectations. The sounds generated here are warm, fluid, variegated, a sensitive, sensuous synthetic weave. Undercut by intricate lattices of rhythm (something Stevie Wonder would engage with less), *Zero Time* ebbs, sustains, colourises and, in sum, suggests the possibility of using Arp and Moog machinery for tonal, exquisitely emotional effect, rather than for the robotic simulation of, say, *Switched-On Bach*. The follow-up album, the similarly momentously titled *It's About Time*, added still further to the TONTO lexicon. Notes glowed in the air like fireflies or created laser, muezzin patterns, while the addition of a vocoder suggested something both unearthly yet strangely intimate.

Stevie Wonder found entire cities and plains of possibility in these albums. He met the duo on 20 May 1971, just seven days after his twenty-first birthday. Unable to believe that the sounds created on *Zero Time* could have been made on a single instrument, he demanded that they 'show' it to him, whereupon, as Cecil later recalled, he dragged Wonder's hand across the monstrous, nine-foot-long hybrid synthesizer.

Other musicians, from Pete Townshend to Keith Richards, had dabbled with synthesizers but quickly become exasperated with their cumbersome size, their volatility and what they felt was the relatively small sonic yield with which they were rewarded for their grappling. Being sightless, however, Wonder approached the new Arp and Moog worlds in a much more immersive manner. Oblivious to the cues of daytime and night-time, he would work with his engineers for many hours at a stretch, exploring the myriad options. It was appropriate that they worked at Electric Ladyland Studios in New York, which opened its doors in 1970, just a week before the death of Jimi Hendrix, for Wonder was involved in a similar exercise in expansion as Hendrix had been in 1968, when he and engineer Eddie Kramer had concocted tracks like '1983 . . . (A Merman I Should Turn to Be)'. Sound was no longer Motown, formulaic; it was now a vast malleable realm, as limitless as the imagination. Wonder could create his own imprints on virgin virtual soil. 'The synthesizer has allowed me to do a lot of things I've wanted to do for a long time but which were not possible till it came along,' he enthused. 'It's added a whole new dimension to music. After programming the sound you're able to write or process the melody line immediately and in as many different manners as you want.'

The results were immediately evident on *Music of My Mind*, whose title suggested that he had found a way of mainlining, unmediated, the world that roiled in his fertile yet non-visual imagination onto recording-studio tape. These were sounds enhanced not just by the Arp and Moog but by Wonder's own neural, sonic sense, heightened by way of compensation for his blindness. *Music of My Mind* painted electric pictures, limpid, hankering and tremulous with too-human feeling, but pictures created without any access to knowledge of what colour and figurative imagery even meant. (In one touching interview, Wonder tried to explain what colours meant to him. He had a vague idea, he said, that the colour purple had a strong association with weddings, perhaps, but he could never, would never know.)

From the tumbling clavichords of 'Happier than the Morning Sun' to the rippling Moog tearscape of 'Superwoman' and 'I Love Every Little Thing about You' in particular, Wonder had taken the Margouleff and Cecil toolbox and created a transformative new instrumental language for soul music, in which the jangle of rhythm guitars and deftly fingered bass suddenly sounded antique and inadequate. He would add further to this with *Talking Book*, released later the same year. Advantaged by his blindness, Wonder used Arp and Moog to convey a sensuous, aurally tactile range of experiences: the bruises that lingered from romantic disappointment; the adrenalin jolt of unbridled joy; the sweet, abiding, luminous and long-lasting sensation of true love; the tumescent rotate and grind of physical lust; the seething, slick, black tar pools of political anger. All of these were part of the fabric and deep soul

weft of *Talking Book*, *Innervisions* and *Fulfillingness' First Finale* –
all produced in tandem with Margouleff and Cecil – across tracks
like 'You and I', 'Superstition', 'Living for the City', 'Creepin'' and
'Boogie on Reggae Woman'. Each album brought new technical
refinements and innovations, such as sound-filtering device the
Mu-Tron III, which created the distinctive and unprecedented
wah-wah effect on 'Higher Ground'.

Herbie Hancock, who would build on Miles Davis's electric forays on *Bitches Brew* with the galactic spree of 1973's *Sextant* and,
later that year, the breakthrough funk fusion of *Head Hunters*,
noted of Stevie Wonder that he never used electronics in a merely
imitative way, for pseudo-acoustic effect. Rather, he embraced the
plastic, artificial, non-natural aspects of synthesizers, moulding
them to create representations of soul sensation that no other artist would even have thought to try to achieve. Still, his supreme
instrument was his voice, what the writer Barney Hoskyns has
described as a 'strange, consonant-less drone', slithering and
slinking across the lyrics, caressing the mic with sweet nothings,
every intake of breath offering an intimacy with his tonsils. Other
times, it is declamatory, its sustained, magisterial vibratos bringing
flakes of plaster fluttering from the ceiling. Wonder is probably
the greatest soul vocalist of all time; a tremendous mimic, he is
once again advantaged, having a heightened awareness of the
vocal inflexions that betray and identify human characters. He
ranges glissando-like from the playful to the declamatory, the
sassy to the reverent.

And yet Wonder made a virtue of gilding his vocal lily with
the vocoder on tracks like 'Girl Blue', the device hanging from
his mouth like a piece of emergency tubing. Roger Troutman of
Zapp later built an entire career on the same principle, enhancing
a perfectly beautiful voice in no need of enhancement to brilliantly
enhanced effect. Whereas Kraftwerk used it as a way of supplanting their meaningfully small voices in a sort of prosthetic manner,

Wonder and Troutman create a vocal style that is superhuman, that demonstrates how machinery multiplies rather than destroys soul. It's a demonstration, indeed, of soul supremacy, tweaky, playful and masterful; self-indulgent, playing with oneself, but in a way that triggers rapturous delight rather than boredom. Prince would take this principle to another level again, the vocoder another electric device on his Cupid's bow of polymorphous perversity.

Most famously employed, perhaps, by Peter Frampton on his massive mid-1970s hit 'Show Me the Way', the vocoder has a remarkable history, one documented by Dave Tompkins in his splendid volume *How to Wreck a Nice Beach*. He describes vocoder technology as the only one 'to have served both the Pentagon and the roller rink'. The original vocoder was designed in 1928 by Bell Labs, invented by one Homer J. Dudley, who would later become a fervent supporter of the anti-communist witch-hunts led by Senator Joe McCarthy in the 1950s. A cumbersome piece of equipment standing seven feet tall, it divided up the voice into its constituent frequencies, which were then spread across channels and transmitted via band-pass filters, before being resynthesized into an impression of human speech as 'described' by the machinery. The vocoder was purposed during wartime to enable Churchill, Roosevelt and US generals to discuss Allied invasion plans between 1943 and 1945 in 'scrambled' voices that would evade the attentions of German codebreakers.

This 'dehumanising' piece of equipment would soon find its way into popular culture, however. It had fleetingly featured in the 1941 Disney film *Dumbo* – remember the scene in which the steam engine whistles the phrase, 'All aboard! Let's go!'? It was even proposed as a precursor to today's Auto-Tune, as a device which might enable stars whose careers foundered with the advent of talkies to revive their careers, using the vocoders as voice-enhancing equipment. Robert Moog developed a vocoder in 1968, establishing it as part of the future armoury of pop technology. Meanwhile,

Bruce Haack, the Canadian musician who tried to bring electronic music to the masses through TV appearances on *The Tonight Show Starring Johnny Carson*, among others, developed his own version of a vocoder, which features on his 1970 album *The Electric Lucifer*. It would go on to be used by Kraftwerk on *Autobahn* and *Trans-Europe Express*, as well as, fleetingly, by the likes of ELO and even Phil Collins.

However, its use as a filter and enhancer in soul music, as well as electro-funk, is where the vocoder achieves its greatest poignancy. Machinery of this sort was somehow an apt appropriation for African Americans, whose tradition was one of dehumanisation, drudgery, alienation. When Michael Jackson, Roger Troutman, Stevie Wonder, Herbie Hancock and Afrika Bambaataa resorted to this particular means of vocal production, it felt less of a gimmick, more deeply resonant, the ironic affirmation of a long-suppressed humanity rather than mere robo-jinks.

By the time of *Songs in the Key of Life*, Stevie Wonder was at the top of the world indeed. Just turned twenty-six, he was the highest-paid recording artist in the business, and among the highest regarded – so much so that at the Grammy Awards, Paul Simon, on receiving his, had thanked Wonder for not releasing an album that year. *Songs in the Key of Life* was long awaited by 1970s standards, released a full two years after its predecessor, *Fulfillingness' First Finale*. A double album, its selection of tracks had been whittled down from some two hundred and fifty options, it was rumoured, with the final cut skewed towards mid-tempo MOR.

For all of this caution, the album was nonetheless greeted as a major artistic statement, and is stacked with immortal Wonder standards, such as 'Sir Duke', 'I Wish', 'As' and 'Ordinary Pain'. It was, however, made without the services of Margouleff and Cecil, who found it increasingly difficult to get past Wonder's inner circle and decided to part company with him (though they would return to work on the Spike Lee soundtrack *Jungle Fever*). Overall, the album shows signs that Wonder had expanded as far as he was ever going to, with tracks like 'Summer Soft' taking an age to fade out, climbing and climbing with each chorus to ever more pointless heights. 'Black Man' features some brilliant sequencing, but again falls victim to its own mawkish preachiness, culminating in a toe-curling call-and-response session. Having a child had an immense spiritual effect on Wonder, but a less positive one on his inner editor, as 'Isn't She Lovely' demonstrated.

It would have been hard to believe at the time but, a few fitful returns such as 1980's *Hotter than July* apart, *Songs in the Key of Life* would turn out to be Wonder's last hurrah. Having produced some of the best material of the 1970s, he would produce, later down the line, some of the worst of the 1980s (all together now – 'I just called . . .').

One of the ironies of Wonder's decline from relevance is that despite his own genuinely visionary embrace of electronics, his was a revolution of texture rather than rhythm. Tracks like 'Superstition', 'I Wish' and 'Higher Ground' are underpinned by conventional drumming, despite all the electricity popping and fizzing and twisting up top. Then, in 1977, along came Giorgio Moroder and Donna Summer and 'I Feel Love', and all of a sudden Wonder's drum kit felt as BC as the acoustic 1960s soul textures he had overshadowed in the early 1970s. Other artists, even the anti-disco George Clinton, adapted to the new 4/4 mode and thrived, but post-1977 Stevie Wonder was no longer the force he once was. He would follow *Songs in the Key of Life* with the soundtrack to *The Secret Life of Plants* in 1979, and suddenly he felt out of touch, behind the groove.

Nevertheless, thanks to Wonder, soul music became truly electric. He altered its surfaces for ever, colourised and expanded its fabric for all time. After Wonder, electric soul was a fact. The Isley Brothers were among the first to recognise the new element: with

1973's *3 + 3* they truly marked their evolution from the joyful stompers of 'Shout' and 'This Old Heart of Mine'. While the younger Isley incorporated the shrieking wah-wah of Hendrix (who had got his first break playing with the Isleys) on 'That Lady', brother-in-law Chris Jasper followed Wonder's footsteps, enlisting Margouleff and Cecil's assistance as he brought the ARP synthesizer to bear, to memorable firefly effect, on 'The Highways of My Life'. The album was huge, a second front for the indirect influence of Wonder's electronic mentors.

As the late 1970s turned into the early '80s, funk and disco proliferated on both the east and west coasts, with orchestras, brass and saxes gradually being accompanied, or even replaced, by signature synth squiggles, distinctive, ejaculatory phrases that told you the funk was coming: D-Train, with 'You're the One for Me', Sharon Redd, with 'Beat the Street', Odyssey, Kleeer and Brass Construction were among a slew of artists who rained down twelve-inches on urban dancefloors on both sides of the Atlantic. Kashif, whom Evelyn 'Champagne' King hired for her 1981 hit 'I'm in Love', was among the innovators of the day. Although he took his influences from the broad, jazzier realms of early Earth, Wind & Fire and Weather Report, he effectively reduced his electronics to capsule phrases. He admitted ruefully that his pioneering work might have over-democratised dance-music production: 'By using synthesizers, the strong get stronger and the weak get stronger, but that's the way of the world.' And for a while in the early 1980s, American R&B music did feel a little codified, with artists like the Trammps, Aretha Franklin and Gladys Knight & the Pips keeping pace with the times by the simple expedient of using the increasingly familiar ingredients and devices of early-1980s R&B: a broody bass intro, some funk-guitar clippings thrown in over the top, a glitter-ball explosion of keyboard or orchestra, a synth shimmy.

A young artist named Prince was one of those who, from 1980 onwards, released singles and albums in this idiom. Singles like 'I

Wanna Be Your Lover' were brilliant examples of the dancefloor genre – naughtily lewd ('I wanna be the only one who makes you come running'), taut, stiff and clipped funk backbeats offset by the bodily fluid-like squelch and release of saucy synth phrases. Prince was great, but like Madonna when she started out, he was just one name among many turning out R&B twelve-inches. For avid soulboys and girls, it would feel like months before these familiar names emerged as superstars.

Still, there was something distinctive about Prince. For R&B, the late 1970s and early '80s were much less heteronormative than today, it should be remembered, but even by the relatively tolerant standards of 1980, the way the little guy presented himself as a 'feminised' sex object on the cover of *Dirty Mind*, in underwear and open trench coat, was eye-catchingly outré. And then there were the lyrics, all of which were suggestive of a one-man melting pot on an electric stove of synth funk, professing faux shock at the attention it attracts. 'Am I black or white / am I straight or gay?' he sang on 'Controversy'. And then, in a weary monotone, 'People call me rude / I wish we all were nude / I wish there was no black and white / I wish there were no rules . . . Life is just a game / we're all just the same . . . do you wanna play?' Play Prince would, in the deepest, baddest, Frenchest deconstructive meaning of the word. Gender was bent and teased out of joint; race was a hang-up you left at the nightclub door – 'Black, white, Puerto Rican / everybody just a-freakin' . . .' Again, with Hi-NRG only a few feet below the surface of pop and Boy George practically a grandmother's choice on *Top of the Pops*, none of this seemed quite such a startling proposition as it might have in more reactionary centuries such as the twenty-first.

From 1983 onwards, Prince began to blossom and mutate and truly take over the decade, the way Bowie had taken over the 1970s. He made a creation of himself, a postmodern soul-pop aristocrat whose gorgeous, preening glam-boyance was unrivalled, unemulated, drawing on a host of sources, from Sly to Hendrix to the dandies of bygone centuries. He ran a gamut between egotistical machismo and sheer falsetto liquid submission, between grinding rock and airy grand-piano balladeering. Musically, he was everything, ranging from the new-wavey hop of 'Let's Go Crazy', to the heavy-rock-soloing frenzy of 'Purple Rain', to the elegant, string-adorned psychedelia of 'Raspberry Beret'. Sometimes he'd lose it, and some of his audience, in overlong free funk-jazz workouts, in which saxophonist Eric Leeds was allowed a touch too much soloing. However, studding his discography like vital bolts are a minimal, ingenious and unmatched series of robo-pop masterpieces, including 'When Doves Cry' and 'Kiss', all of which feature a certain signature LinnDrum motif, a familiar scraping like the revelation of metal beneath skin; as if Prince were, essentially, cybernetic, programmable, more than human, able to readjust and evolve at will. 'New Power Generation', Prince would call his backing band, in terms almost too reminiscent of an electricity grid, but a unique potency resided in him, and he knew it.

'If I Was Your Girlfriend', from the 1987 album *Sign o' the Times*, is among the tiny, elite cluster of Prince's greatest moments. For short stretches it subsists on the mere hum, the mere drone of a synth. Over and around it, Prince slithers and pole-dances vocally, his voice subjected to vocoderisation, varispeed, as if to suggest that he has no fixed place on the sexual spectrum, that he will come at you from all angles. A black superman, pretty and stinging as Ali, a pleasure machine. A black superman whose super-strength was his refusal to be bound by the diktats of race, category, gender. (Ironically, Prince's artistic determination in this respect may have been fatal: it has been suggested that his addiction to painkillers arose as a result of the damage he inflicted on his hips attempting dance moves that the male body is simply physiologically ill-equipped to perform.)

Like Stevie Wonder, Prince was utterly absorbed in his own world: the lavender-scented compound of Paisley Park. Like Stevie Wonder, Prince also went into a sudden and steep decline in mid-career. His vital years were between 1979 and 1990; he never sat quite as well with any subsequent decade, becoming more notorious for the record-company dispute which saw him cast himself as a slave or rebrand himself as The Artist Formerly Known as Prince. Maybe he had simply run his course, reduced to recycling the dazzling series of permutations he had pursued in the 1980s; certainly, each new album he produced between 1990 and the end of his life, though hopefully heralded as a 'return to form', turned out to be anything but. Maybe he suffered in the context of a decade, the 1990s, in which race and gender divisions were all of a sudden re-established, often with separatist militancy. No more melting pot. Or maybe there was a subtle electric shift in the pattern of the dance times, of the sort that had done for Stevie Wonder. Still, as with Wonder, Prince's bequest is so massive as to make the lack of any further addition to it in his lifetime seem churlish.

It was telling that Prince was a product of neither the east nor the west coast but hailed, like Charlie Parker of Kansas City, from the middle of American nowhere – Minneapolis, to be precise. Among the musicians he employed in his early days were James Harris III and Terry Lewis, better known as Jam & Lewis. Interviewing them can be almost, but not quite, like talking to Penn & Teller, especially by conference call. Lewis is happy to let Jam do most of the talking, as part of the division of their labours. But Jam confirms that working in the relatively stone-cold wilderness of Minneapolis, working according to their own instincts, was a boon. 'Our albums worked because we recorded them in Minneapolis, and that meant very little record-company interference. Not that record companies necessarily interfere that much, but we like creating stuff on our own, in a vacuum.

'We were never afraid of technology. We embraced it. I still have the first-ever synthesizer I bought, which I'm currently having refurbished. Our first experience with a drum machine was in the Time. We always liked the idea of that, but we would always add live percussion, live cymbals, to make it more "human". When I had a drum programme I wouldn't set a sequence; I would manually switch them back and forth and add my things in real time. There was no sequencing; everything is played live. These days, everything is looped, everything sounds exactly the same, and I don't like that.

'I was still DJing in clubs before Terry pulled me out and said, "You're a musician" – that was influential as a synth player. Terry was born with the P-Funk spoon in his mouth, but for me Prince was really influential, the way he used synthesizers. Early on, everyone had synths, but me and Terry always joked that they were like "simplersizers" – people just made noises on them [here, Jam goes through a vocal panoply of typical analogue presets]. We liked the idea of playing notes of horn lines, etc., and the Oberheim synth, which for us was better than the Moog and Arp.'

Despite their wish to move on from Wonder's choice of synths, Jam & Lewis shared his desire to use machines to lend an enhanced sense of humanity to their production, rather than use them as lazy labour-saving devices. They preferred to work with what they have referred to as 'underdogs' rather than with established stars. I recount to them the way the famed German producer and Krautrock midwife Conny Plank used to work with artists – sitting down, getting to know them, eating and taking walks with them, not merely to break the ice but to determine the ultimate shape and colour of the recordings he would make with them. 'It's funny, because that's something we try to do with all the artists we work for,' says Jam.

Their earliest success was with Janet Jackson, on the 1986 album *Control*. Around the time of its release, I interviewed her in a five-star hotel in London. She had barely made any serious impact on pop prior to this point, and was best known for accompanying her brother Michael in press interviews and repeating questions put to him by journalists by whispering them in his ear. She had also made a couple of fairly nondescript albums, one of which included a duet with Cliff Richard. Nevertheless, she was accompanied by two armed bodyguards, who sat in an adjoining room as I talked to her. ('When they're not looking, I sneak out,' she snickered, confidentially.)

Before I put a question to her, she put one to me: 'Are you from the sky?' I gibbered uncertainly, not quite certain how best to handle an apparently overwhelmingly spiritual inquiry of this kind, especially from a Jackson with an armed entourage. She repeated the question. Finally, she elucidated. '*Sky* magazine. Are you from *Sky* magazine?' The publication existed at the time. Somewhat relieved, I told her I was from *Melody Maker*, and things proceeded professionally from there. *Control* was a breakout album for Janet, who had rebelled against the patriarchal hegemony of the Jackson family by eloping with James DeBarge, in an ultimately short-lived marriage. *Control* was an album about female empowerment, a concept yet to become hackneyed. This could not be expressed in acoustic musical language; it required the stiff, cybernaut armoury of the Prince-influenced, minimalist 'What Have You Done for Me Lately'.

'The sound was very aggressive, which we intended, because one of the things we always saw in Janet, from seeing her on TV, was that she always had a lot of attitude, and we wanted to make tracks that matched that attitude,' says Jam. 'We had a meeting with Janet and her dad, and we played her the project we had done before *Control*, which was with Patti Austin, which was very sophisticated, swirling strings, big, plush drums. I remember Janet going, "I don't know if I want my album to sound like that," but we reassured her, "No, no, we'll create a whole new sonic for you."'

Prior to this, however, Jam & Lewis had crash-landed on the dancefloor like a funk spaceship with the SOS Band's 'Just Be Good to Me'. It was one of many splashdowns back in 1984. At the time, I ran a night in a gay nightclub on the periphery of Oxford, and a typical set list would include Frankie Goes to Hollywood's 'Relax', the megaton Hi-NRG of Shirley Lites's 'Heat You Up (Melt You Down)' (from which the name of the club, Meltdown, was taken), Shannon's 'Let the Music Play', the Peech Boys' dub-soaked detonation 'On a Journey', Herbie Hancock's 'Rockit', Scritti Politti's 'Absolute' and an Art of Noise megamix. Each of these dropped like a veritable bouncing bomb, and yet all were exceeded by 'Just Be Good to Me'. This track, and their production of Change's 'Change of Heart', were 3D, glowing, stupendously overgenerous funk monsters, the product of intensive mechanical funk excavation and a massive human spirit. This was beyond D-Train, beyond even Prince, beyond Chaka Khan. This was everything but the kitchen sink – and wait, here comes the kitchen sink, too. This was sheer concussion, invited blissful submission. And on it went, thrusting and layering for chorus after chorus, synths and regular instrumentation in a big-band tandem, a marriage of the organic and the synthetic in a shameless process of consummation. All it was lacking was a convincing feminist dimension ('I don't care about your other girls / just be good to me').

Jam & Lewis sailed on and on, adding gratuitously to the lush but finely wrought electric surfaces of R&B, working with acts including the Human League, Cherrelle and the Force MDs. Prince described what they did as 'chocolate music', perhaps dismissively, but this was guilt-free chocolate, a massive joy truly not to be quibbled with.

Janet Jackson was a constant in Jam & Lewis's trajectory. *Rhythm Nation 1814*, released in 1989, was perhaps their most formidable and ambitious release, a demonstration of metal, synthetic strength, its ore drawn from the same soul mines as those worked by Prince, a strength that was more effectively conveyed in the monochrome, industrial trappings of its videos and Jam & Lewis's turbo-charged production than it was in the vagueness of the lyrics ('It's time to give a damn / let's work together . . .'; 'Ignorance . . . no. Prejudice . . . no'). Nonetheless, this was as hard and funky and aggressive and as R&B feminist as it came in 1989, setting a high metal bar, and it rocks you back decades later.

Jam & Lewis were, at the very least, a blueprint; and more, in that you can luxuriate in their immense productions. As with Stevie Wonder and Prince before them, their ubiquity, consistency and success altered the R&B landscape irrevocably. All that proceeded after them was contextualised by the sunlight of their success. Electrification was complete.

In the 1990s and beyond, through such fresh mutations as new jack swing and production auteurs like Timbaland, American R&B was as contemporary as Lycra, at the absolute leading edge in terms of style, fashion and available technologies. But despite Prince's valiant, brilliant attempts at rock fusion, an apartheid developed between rock and soul: the latter audaciously slick, unabashedly commercial, all about today and tomorrow, whereas white guitar music, even at its best, seemed caught in a morose mood of neo-psychedelia, trying to dream lost 1960s and '70s dreams.

The 1990s hip-hop hegemony altered the R&B landscape, and feminist progress arguably regressed. There were sad stories, such as Aaliyah, the lost queen of urban pop, who married R. Kelly aged just fourteen and died aged just twenty-two, killed in a plane crash in the Bahamas, the pilot later discovered to have falsified his records in order to obtain his licence and to have had cocaine in his system while flying the plane. Her legacy was stifled for years when her uncle, the music-business executive Barry Hankerson, refused to release her back catalogue on streaming sites, owing to a complex and messy series of disputes involving him and his label, Blackground Records. TLC had a series of hits, including

'No Scrubs', a brilliant riposte to the sort of everyday sexism and objectification that was becoming enshrined in hip-hop video. But TLC went bankrupt and the group's most combustible member, Lisa 'Left Eye' Lopes – who in 1994 had set fire to the mansion she shared with American footballer Andre Rison, claiming he had beaten her following a night out – was killed in a car crash in 2002.

Still, from Missy Elliott onwards, there were formidable success stories. In 2016, Beyoncé Knowles released *Lemonade*, ostensibly a concept album themed around a difficult patch she was enduring with her partner, Jay-Z, which some suspected she was mining for material (if life hands you a lemon . . .). The album marked more than that, however. It was a monumental achievement, preceded by a half-time Super Bowl appearance that was a powerfully choreographed homage to the Black Panthers. She was connecting to a tradition established by the likes of Janet Jackson but upgrading it, and with more explicit militancy. By 2016, if *Forbes*'s rich list is any guide, most of the superstars in Beyoncé's league were in a post-recording age, making most of their money from commercial endorsements and fragrances they'd launched, as well as mega-tours, rather than from that least lucrative of pursuits, making new records. Beyoncé mega-toured and endorsed, but she did at least make *Lemonade*, in which she requisitioned a wealth of contemporary production talent, as well as outside collaborators and samples from the realms of non-R&B (Jack White, the Yeah Yeah Yeahs). More than just a solipsistic reflection on a failing relationship, the album is a salute to the historical struggles of black women, but also to the successes they have achieved, embodied by her own. The album is monumental, making proper use of her star power by drawing on all of the human and up-to-date technical resources it can command. It's the correct use of music celebrity, the anti-fragrance line. It far exceeds, rather than tries to live off, the early music that made her famous in the first place.

It's also steeped in electro, from the opening Laurie Anderson-style breathed vowels of 'Pray You Catch Me' to the simulated aqueous suspension of 'Hold Up' to the shards that fly supernaturally about the echo chamber of 'Sorry'. It's an album on which, fired by the rival examples of Björk, FKA Twigs, Janelle Monáe and even her own sister, Solange, among others, Beyoncé uses visual and audio technology to remake and enhance herself, pixel by pixel, as a pop icon – the great electro-existential project – to become rather than passively, acceptingly to be.

While Jay-Z, whose productions seemed to signify a maleness slowly falling apart, went low for Trump, Beyoncé went high, endorsing Hillary Clinton in the 2016 US presidential election. It must have seemed a safe bet as Clinton dominated in poll after poll, as well as historically inevitable, as the tide turned against an ageing white Republican demographic. The soaring rhetoric of Michelle Obama, who struck the most resonant moral chord of an often tawdry campaign blighted by the at times unbelievable boorishness of an elderly incompetent, suggested an impending triumph for modernity, for African American parity. Even Stevie Wonder himself weighed in, comparing a Trump presidency to asking himself to drive a car.

Instead, to widespread horror and astonishment, the vote went the way of Trump. The nasty white rump – Ted Nugent, not Beyoncé – would play at the White House. The future was deferred. But only deferred. As Stevie Wonder told Barney Hoskyns, 'The whole thing about music for me is that I've always felt futuristic – the mood of tomorrow rather than today. I see winning the fight against apartheid rather than saying, "Hey, we've gotta go out there and kick their asses."

'Even when I did "You Haven't Done Nothin'", though I wasn't talking about Nixon when we were doing it, that was around the time Watergate was about to break. I get a feel of things kind of before they happen, so the mood of the place is because we have succeeded rather than we're still fighting to win.'

PART THREE

10

FROM SUICIDE TO THE PET SHOP BOYS: THE ART OF THE DUO

The day I met Suicide, molten electronic rock/anti-rock extremists, the twentieth century was nicely dead and embalmed, the twenty-first century showing every sign of refusing to be born. It was 1998, and we were at the Columbia Hotel in London, the famous rock'n'roll stopover. Alan Vega was in his sixtieth year and had lost his iconic contours, but as older rock musicians sometimes do, he cut a still stranger, more fiercely incongruous figure than in his youth, in beret and thick glasses, staring at the younger indie-kid traffic passing through the lobby with a quiet despair. For him, the 1960s and '70s were a vivid, thick but distant memory, times from which you were supposed to catapult into the future. These callow kids, with their guitar cases and faded post-Britpop retro cords, seemed bent on somehow wormholing back to those decades.

'It's really strange,' he said, with a fixed thousand-yard stare. 'As we enter the next millennium, computers and electronics are changing everyone's lives, and still they have problems buying into this new music thing. It's like a fear of going into the next phase. Fear of the next century.

'I did a panel thing recently. I was with Philip Glass, Laurie Anderson, some rap guy, and the questions at the seminar were . . . unbelievable. This is the twentieth fucking century, man. And this guy was accusing us of being "keyboard-minded". I mean, what does he want us to do, play fucking ukuleles or what?'

It's a mixed blessing that Alan Vega would live long enough to see the rise of Mumford & Sons.

One man on vocals, one man on electronics, Suicide were a crucible in which so much of America, rock'n'roll, pre-rock'n'roll and way beyond, was burned down to a black, dense essence. Jack Kerouac. Albert Ayler. Elvis and doo-wop. Eric Dolphy. Industrial America, its chimneys gradually burning down to obsolescence as the century wore on. The New York art scene. The post-war consumer boom. Vietnam. Stockhausen and Varèse. Raymond Scott and disco. Bubblegum and black tar. Suicide were a logical extreme.

Considering the minimal, filthy, electric nature of Suicide's music, it's all the more extraordinary that keyboardist Martin Rev was a highly trained jazz player who had worked with the great Lennie Tristano. Like Can's classically trained Irmin Schmidt, he understood that virtuosity wasn't an end in itself; sometimes, hitting a single sustained note was the correct and relevant thing to do. He also loved doo-wop and understood how the brilliance of twentieth-century African American music ran in tandem with a desperate, appalling struggle for civil rights, feeling the tension every time he passed a black person in the street. This violence, and the violent hatred of that violence, was yet more grist.

Alan Vega, meanwhile, was a young boy being coerced into studying the sciences by aspirational parents who expected their child to aim and achieve high academically, but who rejected the best-laid schemes of his family in favour of the chaos of abstract expressionist art, the uncertain, open thrill represented by Kerouac's *On the Road*. When he was seventeen, rock'n'roll was birthed, and so was Vega. He threw aside his textbooks and headed underground.

It wasn't just Suicide. From the Velvet Underground to La Monte Young, the Stooges, Phil Niblock and Silver Apples, new American music was burning down to a new minimalism, an elementary pulse, as if America was in the process of flatlining in order to begin again, shedding the putrid flesh of the old. However, even Silver Apples would sound musically overdressed, psychedelic and florid by comparison with Suicide, while for all their raw-as-bloody-meat impact, especially live, the Stooges were still holdovers from the old guitar world.

Suicide sought to ratchet things down still further. By 1969, Vega was experiencing further epiphanies, including German electronic music, as well as Iggy Pop. His working life had been divided between taking factory jobs and trying to gain a foothold in the New York art scene. In 1969, he was appointed janitor-director at the Project of Living Artists, situated in a loft on Broadway. There he oversaw the activities of a variety of renegades, a vortex of poets, film-makers, musicians and political activists whose cross-fertilisation echoed that of the Factory, new art mutations in which everything poured into everything else. As for Vega himself, he paid homage to the twentieth-century avant-garde by doing violence to it, messing with basic electronic implements and scratching records by Bartók and Stravinsky as they played on his turntable, frantically trying to dig out new noise.

Martin Rev met Vega at the Project after a maximally chaotic night of political slideshows and free-form multi-instrumental music with his band Reverend B. 'You and I will make music together,' he pledged to Vega.

In November 1970, following a lengthy period of gestation during which the pair plotted a mode of music-making that would have the maximum impact on audiences, Suicide made their debut, with flyers advertising 'Punk Music from Suicide' whose ink looked like gunshot wounds. The name Suicide was a clear indictment of those black and sour times, a comedown from the brief moment of hippy optimism of 1967, before the new dawn faded and the skies darkened once more. Rock music was on the point of enduring several years of leaden corpulence and lethargy, and Suicide were attempting to apply emergency shock remedy several years early. Memories are hazy of those early 1970–1 gigs, in which Vega was on acid and crowds were sparse, uncomprehending and/or hostile, with Suicide themselves playing the roles of anti-tainers, dispensing sonic flamethrowers from the stage. In 1971, they played at the two-hundred-capacity venue Ungano's, armed with only a voice, feedback, keyboard, amp and snare drum. 'We thought we were going to get signed that night,' sighed Rev, recalling the gig to me. For all of their tactical repellence, Suicide always craved acceptance and must have realised how distant a prospect that was that night, as distant as a red revolution in America. The only people in the room were stragglers from a bachelor party, who fled, pursued by Vega's taunts.

Ironically, it was at a wedding that a lightbulb lit above Rev's head as a band played an obligatory cheesy set of covers, accompanied by a cheap drum machine. These had been on the market for a while and can be heard in the music of Raymond Scott in the early 1970s, on Timmy Thomas's 'Why Can't We Live Together', even on an early demo of Jimi Hendrix's 'Angel', but whose small, regular, woodblock, toy-town phut-phuts were rejected as banal by other electronic innovators. Vega, however, found something he could use in them, once messed with, distorted and amplified a little. The drum machine would supply the quickening, regular, frantic pulse that would drive Suicide, reaching the intensity of an Edgar Allan Poe novel, tell-tale heartbeats from under their floorboards.

Considered anathema by New York bookers, Suicide spent further years in the wilderness, Vega honing his vocal version of Elvis's dead twin imagined into rock'n'roll, Rev paring and messing with the electronic side of things. Their earliest rehearsal tapes, which only surfaced on later reissues, are items of sheer archaeological fascination, pre-echoes of a music whose time may never truly come, missives from a dank nowhere tossed like messages in bottles. 'Creature Feature', for example, with its flatline organ drones, scrunching machine rhythm and crumpled, industrial buzz, Vega prowling round the mix inhaling pure reverb; or 'New City', a lo-fi box of possibilities still to be unpacked, in which, like Alvin Lucier's 'I Am Sitting in a Room', the resonant frequencies of the space in which it was recorded are the dominant factor in the sound.

Suicide were more alive than most to their cultural and political environment: the feeling that America was on the point of crashing and burning, fast approaching bankruptcy, stranded a long, long way down the road from its past ideals and hurtling towards a black hole of oblivion. As Rev told me, 'New York was strapped for cash and Detroit was on the verge of collapse. The 1960s seemed a frighteningly long way back in the past, and there was a sense of having to face the future without the security blanket of illusions.'

As Vega approached his late thirties, he must have assumed that Suicide were themselves heading for total oblivion, never to be recognised in any way at all. Yet he and Rev remained honed, battle-ready. Finally, they were taken under the wing of Marty Thau, who had managed that other lost and derided cause of proto-punk, the New York Dolls. Thau it was who would see to it that Suicide would finally visit the inside of a studio in 1977, a year which, more than four decades on, still has a fatefully futuristic ring about it.

Suicide's eponymous debut album is a black milestone in rock history. It depicts the American rock'n'roll landscape as scarred and torched, a world in which it seems unlikely blue skies will ever be witnessed again. Rev had become fascinated with the new technology that boomed after World War II, materially blessed years for America that saw a consumer boom in domestic hardware and chromium-plated automobiles produced with loving care on busy factory production lines. On *Suicide*, however, Rev's sound machines are shorn of all trimmings, leaving just a bare, bleak essence of hiss, drone-like lingering radioactive emissions after the bomb has dropped, rhythms undulating and keyboard melodies ghost-like in their repetitive motions. Vega stalks this landscape like the last man alive, a battered witness spared to tell the story. 'Gonna crash . . . . gonna die,' he intones, as if from a black box, on 'Rocket USA'. 'America, America is killing its youth,' he breathes on 'Ghost Rider'.

The album's centrepiece is 'Frankie Teardrop', a tale of industrial woe as American industry hits the skids and crushes its lowliest drones, such as Frankie, unable to pay the bills, meet the rent, feed his family. Once, in American rock'n'roll land, Frankie might have had a steady job, a detached house, a fridge freezer, burgers, milk-shakes, a down payment on a T-Bird. Now, the black walls of the post-war American dream are collapsing around him, represented by the temple-thudding, building, migraine drones of Rev's mul-tiple, crashing, asbestos sheet waves of distortion and feedback, a sculpted studio feat for which Marty Thau was co-responsible. This is pure burn; rock music as sheer hell, yet cruelly gripping. Vega shrieks amid the indifferently pneumatic, vertiginous columns of charcoal noise, 'We're all Frankies . . . we're all lying in hell.'

As well as a psychic re-enactment of the trauma of America's seemingly irreversible economic decline, 'Frankie Teardrop' is also the sound of rock music as practised hitherto being ritually cast onto the pyre. With 'Third Stone from the Sun', Hendrix doused the early Beach Boy-dominated rock'n'roll 1960s in lighter fluid – 'You'll never hear surf music again'. On 'Frankie Teardrop', it's implied, may you never hear the sunshine jingle-jangle of guitar music again. That halcyon moment has passed. It is nineteen hun-dred and seventy-seven. The Suicide mission was clear: as they put it, they sought to 'widen rock's vocabulary by getting rid of the guitar and getting rid of the drums'.

This was a message Suicide fully intended to bring home live, with Vega in particular, seasoned and versed in performance art, showing particular physical courage, willing to bloody and batter and prostrate himself and face hostile missile fire onstage, willing to act as a conduit for all the seditious and reactionary violence of the punk era.

Kraftwerk, Gilbert & George-like, invested their selves in their art: their images up front and central, their beaming, leering faces prominent in the photography, their physical outlines used as measurements for their robotic replicas. The band members, however, absented themselves physically from the disagreeable processes of celebrity: photo sessions and, later, interviews. Alan Vega in particular was quite the opposite. He hurled himself bodily into the fray. He left nothing behind. He harangued audience members, lay prostrate onstage, allowed himself to become as possessed as a dervish by the drones and intensifying repetitions of the music. He shed blood. Marty Thau testified, after a gig at New York's Kitchen Room, that 'When Vega started cutting himself with a razor, some brave souls tried to leave the room but quickly realised they had been purposely locked in the dimly lit Kitchen and were at the mercy of his seemingly crazed hostility. Decked out in black leather, with motorcycle chains draped around his upper body, Vega thrust himself into the appalled faces of the most conventional, hapless souls he could find, most of whom were now undergoing a brutal sensory assault unlike anything they had ever experienced.'

Supporting the Ramones at CBGBs, Vega would wield a knife and chain and dare a hostile audience to violence, implying that there was nothing they could do to him that he would not do to himself. When Suicide supported the Clash in the UK, however, the antipathy of the crowds reached truly fearsome crests, particularly in Glasgow. The Clash, in their decency, wanted their fans to know that there was much more to unpack in the three-chord, incendiary moment of punk than guitars and gobbing, from reggae to New York electronic minimalism. And, having described themselves as making 'punk music' as early as 1970, Suicide surely had to be respected as an original article. Clearly, though, sections of the Clash's audience saw punk's back-to-basics ethos in more conservative terms, in which guitars, wielded in the traditional phallic manner, remained sacrosanct. Machines? Fuck off. That Vega himself, steeped in the traditions of art-house provocation that were almost as old as the century itself, made a point of goading these reactionaries made friction a certainty. However, even he flinched when, in Glasgow, an axe came flying in his direction. Presumably, it had been introduced into the venue in a spirit of extreme prejudice: who, you wonder, would attend a gig in the high hope of being entertained but bring an axe along just in case the occasion proved to be a disappointment? But part of Vega's onstage art was to draw rage.

Suicide were determined to make their music an occasion to let the bad blood coursing through the veins of the times spill. Confrontation wasn't a dismaying impediment to getting their music across; it was integral to the experience. Which is why they chose to release in flexi-disc form a bootleg recording of a concert in Brussels, in which they were billed as support to Elvis Costello. The title *23 Minutes Over Brussels* seems to echo the film *Thirty Seconds Over Tokyo*, implying a tense incursion into enemy territory. The duo generate highlights from their debut album. The impact of Rev's machinery feels like a generator, juddering the entire room like an unattended tractor with a crowbar on the pedal. They're greeted mostly with boos from a restive audience impatient for the main event; chants of 'Elvis, Elvis' punctuate the set. Then, some nineteen minutes in, a huge cheer goes up: someone has got up from the crowd and confiscated Vega's mic. Rev pleads for its return, 'otherwise there'll be no show', which only has the effect of encouraging the more ribald sections of the audience. Vega unleashes a 'Fuck you!', then bellows the opening lines of 'Frankie Teardrop' into a spare mic anyway.

Suicide seemed to draw both satisfaction and deep depression from these incidents. 'We're just a bunch of poor musicians,' Vega pleaded to the Brussels crowd, and so they were. For all that Suicide have a crucial place in the timeline not just of electropop but of rock as a whole, they were never able to afford the formidable stacks of equipment with which they might face an audience down, the way Tangerine Dream did in the 1970s, or Kraftwerk afterwards, with their onstage spectacle, coupled with formidable back projections. Whether in 1978 or 1986 or later, Suicide were like desperate, isolated soldiers in the culture wars, armed with small machine guns and grenades in the face of a vastly superior army of overwhelming hostility and indifference. There's Rev in his visors, partly to establish an air of concentration and impersonality, but also as if to protect his eyes from sparks flying upwards. And there's Vega, prowling around recklessly in no-man's-land, as if taking a permanent last stand, haranguing, pleading, facing impossible odds. Such was the doomed drama of Suicide.

Were Suicide beginning to have repercussions, however? Elsewhere in the late 1970s, another, more established group decided to shed their conventional band element and slim down to a yin-and-yang duo. The American group Sparks had first had an impact in the UK in 1974 with 'This Town Ain't Big Enough for Both of Us'. Apart from its whip-crack-away pop brilliance, it was most notable for the contrast between fashionable, effeminate Russell on vocals, falsetto-ing away in a big-flared trouser suit and floppy hair, and his brother Ron, short hair slicked back, hammering mechanically away on his piano, looking like a disgruntled hybrid of Adolf Hitler, Inspector Blakey from *On the Buses* and Basil Fawlty, slumped under sufferance at his typewriter in the reception area. This was perhaps the first example of the man–machine contrast between vocalist and keyboardist, a staple of such duos – one determinedly emotionless, exaggeratedly impersonal, the other deeply personal. On *Top of the Pops* Russell was quite the animated vocalist, while what the piano player was doing there was something we wondered wildly about in the playground the next morning. Had he been kidnapped? Overruled in a band meeting when he had proposed they perform a 1930s Bavarian drinking song instead? We were flummoxed.

Following a series of hits at the tail end of the glam era, Sparks appeared to run out of ideas, especially working within what felt like the mandatory confines of the rock-band format. They tried various conventional musical means to maintain their career but, by 1977, struck by the enormous success of Giorgio Moroder with Donna Summer's 'I Feel Love', they decided to reinvent themselves as a slimmed-down electronic outfit, working under the auspices of Moroder himself. The result was a series of hits, including 'Number One Song in Heaven' and 'Beat the Clock', in which they created vertical tornadoes from the Moroder sound that coursed and twisted gloriously across an otherwise arid and parched rockscape.

In an interview with *Melody Maker*'s Harry Doherty, the duo explained themselves in a way that showed just how far ahead of the times they were, while in other ways being very much of their time.

'We're sick of the whole thing. Guitarists are jokes. They're just so old-fashioned and passé that any band that has got a guitarist is just a joke. We've found a way to work that's kind of sprung us from the guitarist mentality – which is a pretty low mentality,' Ron Mael, the senior and driving creative force behind Sparks, explained. 'The weakest part of Sparks has always been the guitar-playing, because it was imposed on what we were doing. Now we're finally a more pure version of what we've always been. We want to completely strip away the whole idea of bands and the hipness of rock music, because that area is now just like a caricature of itself.'

When the *Melody Maker* interviewer lodged a predictable objection about the un-rock-like 'uniformity' of disco, Ron Mael retorted swiftly. 'I really like that uniformity,' he said. 'To me, individuality is a thing of the past. There are really very few personalities in disco music. It's all these manipulators behind the scenes, and that's really exciting for me; where there are just puppet groups and session people singing . . . I think that sort of cloning of the whole thing is really incredible and modern, whereas the whole thing of a band identity and a folk singer putting over a personal point of view just seems so old-fashioned to me now.'

And then, in a moment of somewhat airy, unreconstructed condescension, Mael asserts of working with Moroder, 'I would say that we were the first thing with a personality that he's ever worked with that has come across on record. As much as I like the Donna Summer things, it is still a black female singer on a disco background. I think the combination of his technological exper-tise plus our personality is what makes the record so strong. It's given him a new dimension, too, you know.'

Setting aside the dubious implication that black female singers weren't capable of 'personality' in the way that intelligent white males from a rock scene he now affected to disdain were, Mael had the germ of a point. In being quick to embrace the transplanted, sequencer-driven heart that would drive pop through the 1980s and beyond, Ron and Russell Mael extended their lease of life to the present day, and they remain an international pop treasure. I met them in 2017. Dapper and courteous, they had abandoned full-on electronics around the turn of the century in favour of a more elegant, all-round high-pop style in which strings were more to the fore. They chuckled as they recalled their controversial Moroder days.

'We don't really have a very long vision of things into the future, so we couldn't really be that certain about something like that,' said Ron. 'Sometimes in interviews you say things you don't 100 per cent mean. Also, maybe we were being a little defensive, because that album wasn't received favourably by the British press.'

'We got a lot of flak at the time, that in reducing to a two-piece we were traitors to the rock cause and going disco,' said Russell.

'Ironically, the critics were far behind the public on this – we had three hit songs in the UK. And there were a lot of folks in bands who watched and appreciated what was happening.'

'We gave an interview at the time and said, "Guitars are dead,"' remembered Ron. 'Paul McCartney obviously read it and said, "I see Sparks said guitars are dead. Well, just wait!"'

Russell was still flattered by McCartney's attention. 'The idea of him reading that and retaining that point . . .'

Meanwhile, in Switzerland, quite by chance, another synth duo was in the making. Yello were originally a trio featuring Carlos Perón, but when he left the group in 1981 they were reduced to just man and machine: Dieter Meier, a one-time performance artist, poker player and golfer from a wealthy family; and Boris Blank, the son of a truck driver whose introduction to music followed the acquisition of a tape recorder as a child, which he used to create basic samples and echo effects.

Despite their common interest in performance art and pure electronics, Yello were on the other side of the world from Suicide in many respects. They came from Zurich, cradle of the Dada movement, and their very choice of name, a cross between a yell and 'hello', was indicative of their absurdist, affirmative gusto. No shabby sofa in the corner of the Columbia Hotel for Meier. When I interviewed him, it was at the Savoy Hotel (or, twice, at his magnificent home high in the hills of Zurich), where he would hold forth grandly, extolling the virtues of the Egyptian vocalist Om Kalsoum, of the great peaks of twentieth-century art, of bullfighting. With his distinctive moustache, which bristled magnificently above and beyond petty youth cultural trends in facial hair, and his gimlet but twinkling eye, he felt like someone fashioned along the lines of a Francis Picabia, a Dalí or even a Marinetti, rather than Elvis.

Unlike Suicide, who threw themselves into the live fray with full-on masochistic willingness, hungry for slaughter, Yello rarely performed live, and when they did, they made extensive use of pre-recorded material. For all the extrovert tomfoolery which he displayed in Yello photo sessions, Blank hated playing live.

'It was never my way,' Blank told me. 'It always felt a bit cheap to be shaking your ass onstage and pretending to play live – because the music I make, and the way I make it, can't be reproduced onstage. I never care to see people like the Pet Shop Boys pretending that the music they play "live" is actually live. I prefer to see a real band play. Also, I'm not the sort of person who likes to be exposed in the middle. I prefer the studio. Dieter is different, of course. He is a natural entertainer, he enjoys the attention of a crowd. I'm an entertainer, too, but only really with people I know.'

Suicide pulsated with rage; Yello had nothing whatsoever to be angry about. Whereas Suicide were minimalist provocateurs, Yello were maximalists and attacked grey rockist taboos from the other side. They evoked Monte Carlo, or Cuba on the night before the revolution, as depicted in *The Godfather II*, North African dervishes, midnight feasts on the Algarve, fast cars sweeping down the coastline of the South of France. They dared pop to be luxurious, but not in the naff manner of Duran Duran's banally plimsolled yacht-pop. Rather, they wanted to show how electronic music could expand the pop palette, enlarge its canvas, expand its possibilities as a dream-maker. Meier functioned as a master of ceremonies, a scene-setter, with Blank rising to the challenge of creating an electronic music that was magisterial, wide-screen, cinematic; that told stories, created atmospheres, glistened like chandeliers. Album titles like *Solid Pleasure* and *You Gotta Say Yes to Another Excess* told their own story.

Yello still divide opinion. Some regard them as quirky Euro-popsters with a puerile fascination with belching into microphones; others as immaculate visionaries channelling the art and cinematic treasures of twentieth-century culture into perfectly curved, immaculately suggestive, chromium-plated electronica.

Meanwhile, Suicide, rather than sinking into obscurity with what could easily have been their first and last album, its contents an apparent play for commercial destruction, took an improbable leap popwards following a support slot with the Cars, who had scored a big hit with the new-wavey 'My Best Friend's Girl'. Cars vocalist Ric Ocasek offered to produce them, and the second album, *Suicide: Alan Vega and Martin Rev*, released in 1980 on Ze, was a prime example of that label's colourful attempts to subvert 1980s pop, a signal that, triggered by the successes of Blondie and Grandmaster Flash, Talking Heads and Kid Creole and the Coconuts, New York had popped back to life.

Did I say that Suicide were antithetical to Yello? Check out 'Diamonds, Fur Coat, Champagne', the second album's opener, whose electronics exude the dashboard odour of a just-bought car. This isn't a celebration of the high life, rather the high life framed like a Warhol Monroe portrait, both luxurious and conceptual. This is followed by 'Mr Ray', a vicious, sputtering yet still gleaming gobbet of Suicide, which fades out on a rasping, anguished, screaming 'EEEEEEE', from the word 'GOODBYE', sustained for fully ten seconds longer than you would have thought the human throat was capable of.

'Sweetheart' follows, mawkish and mushy, a poor example of the sentimentalism that always lurked in Vega's ultimately soft heart, the best manifestation of which was the immortal 'Dream Baby Dream', the sort of sentiment that saved Suicide from dissolving into absolute nihilism. But then comes 'Touch Me', one of the most sensual pieces of electropop ever made and proof of the medium's soft power to simulate the erotic, as evoked by Rev in a simple repeated keyboard phrase of velvet lushness.

From suggesting the death of rock, the death of the America depicted in rock, Suicide had somehow flipped and suggested the birth of a new pop. From black to checkered black and yellow. The album wasn't a commercial success, but Suicide had already provided a template for a Leeds-based duo who'd been scratching around since 1977, making low-rent cheap electropop recorded onto two-track tape recorders. They were enamoured of Suicide and made no secret of it. 'It's performance art!' enthused vocalist Marc Almond.

About a year after the release of Suicide's second album, Soft Cell made their move. A brilliant act of reduction: 'Tainted Love', a forgotten, frantic, northern soul classic, written by Ed Cobb and recorded by Gloria Jones in 1964, reborn as a two-note synth signal. Doop-doop. 'Puttin' Leeds on the map, Soft Cell,' intoned a DJ grimly as he introduced the single in a Leeds nightclub where I was sitting out another in a series of lonely and depressing eighteenth birthday parties. A few months later, it was number one.

Even seventeen years later, Alan Vega couldn't hide his bitterness at the success Soft Cell enjoyed. 'Suicide finally get to go to Britain, in 1978. And sure enough, a year or so later, you've got this big techno-pop explosion. Soft Cell, who admit to being influenced by Suicide – one guy on vocals, one guy on keyboards. And what happens? Soft Cell go on to sell millions of records, Suicide sell squat. Soft Cell come to America, they're huge, we come back, *nada*. To this day.'

Soft Cell, however, brought a beautiful scum to the surface of pop's liquid caldron. On the likes of *Non-Stop Erotic Cabaret*, Almond sang of the tacky, drab, gaudy, thrilling, dangerous, full of uppers and downers of pop and club life in the early 1980s, a scary act of 'escapism' indeed, one that could bring either ecstasy or the agony of a split lip. The scampering, linear pace of 'Memorabilia' felt at once like the frantic thrill of the pursuit of furtive and illicit pleasures, and the similarly pulse-racing horror of being chased down alleyways by queer-bashers. Dave Ball's electropop was elegant but also subtly stained, tainted indeed, not just by association with Almond's lyrics but by the public places in which it was played, from *Top of the Pops* to happy hours in Yorkshire cocktail bars, the silvery, seedy sound of tinselled backdrops and sticky carpets.

Pretty soon, the synth duo was becoming a familiar pop trope. As well as Blancmange, later came Yazoo and, later still, Bronski Beat. A further dazzling addition to its corps came with Deutsch-Amerikanische Freundschaft, aka D.A.F., originally a five-piece who had shed their rock elements like so much body fat and were now a duo consisting of Gabi Delgado and Robert Görl on drums and synth. Produced by Conny Plank, midwife to the Krautrock generation, D.A.F. made three albums between 1980 and 1982 that bounced and Mooged and arpeggiated at you from cubist angles with deliberately mixed messages; they queered everything, not least the pitch. To dance to 'Der Mussolini' was like trying to negotiate a moving and listing dancefloor. With their sleeveless leather and intent stares to camera, D.A.F. felt like creatures of pure physicality, dedicated to what they called 'Absolute Body Control', achieving a 'muscular' sound thanks to Plank's idea of recording their synths through Marshall amps. Not for them the tinny diffidence of the cheap Korg, its keys prodded at by fey young boys.

These men of iron, however, were also supreme ironists, purveyors of a mordant, cerebrally honed wit apparently unique to Düsseldorf. Nonetheless, they went unrecognised in their home town and country. They made for England, for London, which they regarded as the epicentre of all that was vital in the early 1980s, the city of *NME*, *i-D*, *The Face*, Heaven nightclub. They embraced the intellectual climate of the music press, fostered by Ian Penman, Paul Morley and Chris Bohn, invited deconstruction. They carried out a programme of works, and when that was complete in 1982, and to evade the crude codification of the Neue Deutsche Welle (New German Wave), ceased working together. A deeply conscious uncoupling.

As I sit with them in a hotel in Hannover in 2017, following a reunion gig at a festival, Gabi and Robert, eating a late-night salad, look decently preserved for boys around the sixty mark. The gig was a stormer, played to a fully appreciative throng who were mostly unborn when they first split up. They and the group are one. Gabi and Robert reminisce and chat eloquently across a range of subjects, from the German language to sacred iconography to Daniel Miller. I tell them of reading an interview with Foucault, in which he described the essence of his philosophy, his perception of things, in three words: 'All against all'. D.A.F. have a song called 'Alle Gegen Alle'. Gabi laps it up. D.A.F. are the last group in the world to affect disdain at any association of their work with the intellectual. 'That was my background,' he says. 'Philosophy, Foucault, Deleuze.' But it's another twist. During the gig, Gabi douses himself generously in bottles of water, strides up and down the stage, gesticulates like a mock Mussolini, invites, laps up and reciprocates the energy of the crowd. '*Du bist D.A.F.!*' he tells them at the conclusion – a single collective. D.A.F. are All for All.

For all the teasing, homoerotic implications of a D.A.F., the general rule of the synthpop duo was to offer a promise of the platonic. Despite the (often homo-) sexuality of the players, who in nearly all cases comprised two men, there was to be no sort of sexual charge between them. Their body language would suggest an entire separation, almost an obliviousness to one another. Dave Ball, Vince Clarke et al. would attend to their business with passionless, clerical attentiveness, eyes down, while the vocalists would throw deliberately contrasting contortions of pop emotion, as if existentially fraught at being caught up in the modern, indifferent world represented by the metal surfaces, both reflective and non-reflective, of the synthscape. And yet, paradoxically, there was also a hand-in-glove syncing going on, as if a perfect understanding had been reached between vocals and instrumentation in a post-rock world.

By 1983, however, pop was beginning to curdle somewhat. Artists like Howard Jones and Nik Kershaw, clearly not creatures sprung from a punk aesthetic the way, say, ABC or Depeche Mode had been, slunk into the fray, hair spiked and highlighted à la mode, but restoring pop to its default setting of mediocre MOR. Adaptable, virtuoso hacks.

It was at this point that the Pet Shop Boys made their appearance. At the time, to dedicated style-watchers alive to the dialectical twists and turns of the post-punk era via close reading of the *NME*, they seemed to have arrived late to the party. They were a little superannuated: Chris Lowe an elderly twenty-three, Neil Tennant a grandfatherly twenty-nine. Tennant had monitored the new pop of the early 1980s from the journalistic sidelines, in the employment of *Smash Hits* magazine. It felt significant that they appeared at the same time as the Smiths, a group who also felt initially like a needless addition to a well-developed indie guitar tradition. Both were a reaction against the frantically hedonistic gaudiness of early-1980s pop, as reflected on *Top of the Pops* in particular, which had revamped itself as if to keep pace with the ambience of city-nightclub life. In the 1970s, for all its glam and larger-than-life pop icons, when watching *Top of the Pops* the eye was always drawn to the darkness of the upper rafters, where the studio lights failed to reach, but which were still visible around the periphery of the TV screen. These were a reminder of how briefly the 1970s TV landscape glittered: a half-hour, and only about a third of that half-hour, was all that heaven allowed. Then it was back to the grim reality of *Waggoners' Walk*, *Sing Something Simple*, powdered custard and bedtime long before the *John Peel Show*, whatever that was.

By the 1980s, however, the *Top of the Pops* set was fully lit: glitterballs spun and strobe lights cast wide mauve beams, while the DJs were surrounded by extroverts in deely-boppers and ra-ra skirts, or boys in white trousers and sailor's caps, all rictus grins and attention-hungry mugging. By 1983, pop and its attendant culture – in some ways a defiant response to the miseries imposed by Thatcherism, in other respects a symptom of its greedy, individualist, deregulated feeding frenzy – felt overbearing.

In part, the Pet Shop Boys were a response to that, much as Morrissey's first appearances on *Top of the Pops*, despite his own eye-catching queerness, represented a wistfulness for a certain very English monochrome dampness, redolent of *Coronation Street* and kitchen-sink movies. The Pet Shop Boys didn't seek to be larger than life but about the same size as life. They were deadpan. They yawned. They stood side by side like two Men from the Ministry having arrived at the doorstep with grim news. However, whereas the Smiths, somewhat worryingly, hankered for the restoration of guitar-driven whiteness to post-punk and a cessation of its dialogue with funk, soul, reggae and disco, the Pet Shop Boys felt quite the opposite. As Chris Lowe said in 1986, in words that would become a sort of extended motto for the duo, 'I don't like country and western. I don't like rock music, I don't like rockabilly or rock and roll particularly. I don't like much, really, do I? But what I do like, I love passionately.'

The impetus for the Pet Shop Boys had come from a work trip Neil Tennant took to New York to interview the Police. There, he was determined to meet Bobby O, also known as Bobby Orlando, the writer–producer of a great many of the Hi-NRG hits that were the staple of gay nightclubs in the early 1980s: fast, hard, out-and-out unabashed floor-filling, synth-driven twelve-inches, fronted by the likes of Divine or Man 2 Man or divas like Hazell Dean ('Searching'), which had occasionally trickled into the charts. Bobby O would record versions of early Pet Shop Boys tracks, including 'It's a Sin' and 'Opportunities (Let's Make Lots of Money)'. Throughout the mid-1980s, an inert Chris Lowe would rain down beams and shafts of nightclub-style electropop, amid which a deliberately enervated Neil Tennant would sigh his very English vignettes, his fey but declarative vocals a sort of sardonic response to his sonic surroundings but also, more meaningfully, to the locked-in Thatcherism of the 1980s, with its nauseous mix of economic libertarianism and oppressive social conservatism, whose callousness was especially pronounced in the continued scapegoating and institutional discrimination against the gay community hit by the AIDS crisis.

I should confess that I never especially cared for the Pet Shop Boys. For all their worthy sentiments, I found them musically thin, their big, arcing hooks lacking the deviant squelch of a Soft Cell or a Frankie Goes to Hollywood, Tennant's lyrics a touch grating and arch. They didn't fire up or chill my bone marrow the way Suicide did; for me they weren't immersive but arch, at a remove. I canvassed those who felt differently, including lifelong fan Richard Augood and *Quietus* co-editor Luke Turner.

'The Pet Shop Boys speak to me of my own personal idealised Englishness,' says Augood. 'The Englishness that is quite happy we don't make a big deal out of St George's day. Other people talk about their archness or their irony, but what I think really sets them apart is that unlike Elvis, PSB's upper lip was always stiff. Emotions are aired, but it's never in a way that would frighten the horses. And it's done with the quiet precision of a well-managed sneeze. Their very best songs are dripping with emotional urgency. These are words that have to be said aloud for the sake of the one expressing them. But it's never done in a vulgar fashion. Yes, there's house and Hi-NRG and disco and so much more in there. It's English soul music.'

'To my mind they were the brilliant endpoint of post-punk and the desire to mix high art with politics and hugely accessible music,' says Turner. 'They even encapsulated this perfectly themselves with a one-line manifesto – "Che Guevara and Debussy to a disco beat" – in "Left to My Own Devices". They always pushed themselves incredibly hard, collaborated with Derek Jarman and so on, while at the same time writing songs that the proverbial milkman could whistle to. I don't think they're Smithsian at all – the melancholy is a lot more heartfelt and has to be seen through the prism of gay oppression and the AIDS crisis, "It Couldn't Happen Here" in particular. That track comes from *Actually*, which I think is one of pop's finest counterblasts to Thatcherism from the era. "Shopping" dissects privatisation, "It's a Sin" is about religious conservatism and sexual shame, "Rent" about dubious financial power dynamics. Sonically, it's very S&M, too. A very saucy record. I love them more than nearly any other group. They're always incredible live and have pretty much the best crowd of any arena-sized groups.'

For all their affectation of inertia and lethargy, the Pet Shop Boys have endured industriously for over thirty years, standing shoulder to shoulder at the centre of, and yet in reproach towards, an ever louder, ever more desperate and declining pop-music scene. They could hardly be described as electropop pioneers; they're about third generation. They represent a response to a pop world that has become terminally and ubiquitously electrified, in tandem with that perma-Thatcherism that has only set harder since their formation back in 1981. With each passing year they feel not merely on the side of the angels but like set-in-stone guardian angels of values that were fast disappearing even when they began.

Eddie and Sunshine, Erasure, the Communards, Hard Corps, Chris & Cosey, Blancmange . . . whether mixed or all-male, the synth duo was obviously a product of the reduced amount of human labour required in electronic music. These duos also scotched the often hierarchical nature of the old rock-band format, with its clear sense of charismatic leaders, creative mainstays and lesser backline members. With the synth duo, there is a more egalitarian sense, a binary division of labour that achieves a common purpose, frequently through sheer contrast.

Often overlooked when discussing such duos are former 10cc members Godley & Creme. They traversed a range of styles but some of their key works were synth-driven. They perhaps lacked a pop aura – Kevin Godley's beard never helped – and their inventions, such as the 'gizmo', an attachment designed to expand an electric guitar's range of effects when pressed against the strings, or their use of devices that anticipate Auto-Tune possibly mark them in the eyes of some as a pair who simply made records to try out their self-made toys.

They deserve reappraisal; even their 1977 triple album, *Consequences* (featuring both Sarah Vaughan and Peter Cook), which they bunkered down to record, only to realise when they emerged from the studio that punk had arrived to drive out such conceits. They adapted, however, and by 1981's *Ismism* they were back in sync with the times, albeit with idiosyncratic knobs on. 'Under Your Thumb', taken from that album, reached number three in the UK charts in late 1981, but unlike tracks by the Human Leagues, Duran Durans, Soft Cells and OMDs of the time, it has somehow failed to enjoy a lengthy afterlife of wedding disco/late-night minicab FM radio familiarity. As such, it has retained its pristine, silvery strangeness. It's a perfect piece of compressed pop film noir, a ghost story about a woman who chooses suicide rather than further endure an oppressive relationship, throwing herself from the carriage of a train. It's propelled by the fast locomotive thrum of a finely tuned sequencer, reminiscent, if anything, of Steve Reich's *Different Trains*, the vocals striking a midpoint between the decayed opulence of Marc Almond and the dry, straight delivery of the yet-to-be-famous Neil Tennant. Godley & Creme seemed so like-minded as to represent a single entity. By 1988, however, they could no longer endure working together.

The dusk was fast falling and my interview time with Suicide was drawing to a close. Alan Vega reflected drily on how his band seemed to be revived roughly once every ten years, enabling these ever-straitened artists to re-emerge once more. 'Every now and then, they scrape the bottom of the barrel,' said Vega, 'and that's where they find Suicide.' The duo triggered a synthpop timeline that fetched up a long, long way from the American heartland. But they were also a touchstone for groups like the Jesus and Mary Chain and Spiritualized, rock groups who understood that Suicide represent a permanent hotspot along the long, thin electric wire that connects contemporary rock with its base element. Even Springsteen saluted Suicide's very American rock'n'roll essential-ism, the landscape of Frankies and Cherees that they drew. Any time you need to get back to first principles, you need to get back to Suicide.

At their final London Barbican concerts in 2015, shortly before Vega's death, the singer participated in what was billed as a 'Punk Mass', with Henry Rollins on hand to deliver what felt like a heart-felt eulogy to the group, with the seventy-seven-year-old Vega incapacitated by a stroke. Vega rallied, movingly; one thought of all the physical pain he had willingly endured for his art, now finally taking its toll. Far more hurtful to him was the fact that Suicide had never enjoyed what he felt should have been their just commercial reward. In the early 1980s, following their second album, he had enjoyed significant commercial success – in France in particular – with the solo neo-rockabilly hit 'Jukebox Babe'. Yet, he told me, he had been unable to enjoy it. 'I wanted that success for Suicide.'

Suicide did have reach, though. I mentioned to him that Boy George was a big fan of the track 'Touch Me' and had included it on an *NME* top-ten playlist. This was news to Vega. He seemed visibly moved, turning to Martin Rev and saying, 'I told you. I told you . . .'

Back to the Barbican, this time in 1998. Suicide had been invited to play a ten-minute set in a lobby adjacent to an exhibi-tion of Harley-Davidson motorbikes. It was a bit of a bash, with members of Pulp, the Jesus and Mary Chain and Martin Gore of Depeche Mode among those in attendance. Vega wasn't even sixty at this point and was still, it seemed, in his growling prime, practically eating the microphone alive, passing among an occasionally nervous crowd like a preacher seeking out a sinner to make an example of, while an impassive, visored Rev generated black, belching, remorseless volleys of power-drill electronica. It could have been 1977 or 2077.

11

THEY WERE THE ROBOTS: KRAFTWERK AND POP AUTOMATA

If Suicide's 1977 debut album was a masterpiece streaked in black and red, Kraftwerk would deploy the same colours, albeit in a far tidier geometrical manner. 1978's *The Man-Machine* was actually their seventh album, although Ralf Hütter and Florian Schneider succeeded in creating the impression that 1974's *Autobahn* was the moment their robo-pop had been created, trundling immaculately off their conveyor belt; all the messy, organic, developmental stuff prior to that point had been 'archaeology'. Once, Schneider's flute had been a central feature. In the new mechanical order of things, it had disappeared, like the loom.

The Man-Machine glistens impeccably and vividly. Above and beyond the neat, deadpan perfection of their machine-driven sound, a dry, tapered response to the phlegm- and sweat-soaked histrionics of the Anglo-American rock considered by many to be the only real deal in the 1970s, it has about it a sheer pop acumen, not only melodically but in the pictures it paints with such minimal finesse. 'Neon Lights' is a perfect example, conveying in the briefest but most telling of synth strokes the shimmer of lamplit city avenues by night. This isn't the city of *Taxi Driver*, of the seedy, unpunished scum whose body fluids Travis Bickle must hose from his cab every night, but the city viewed aerially, like jewellery on a black velvet backdrop, with Hütter and co.'s choral harmonies reminding of gods looking on in satisfaction.

Other sections undulate a little more routinely. 'Metropolis' and 'Spacelab' follow the sequencer tracks laid down by Giorgio Moroder the previous year with Donna Summer's 'I Feel Love', a foundational individual track that sits adjacent to Kraftwerk's overall achievement in the founding of electropop.

If anything, however, the most memorable and defining aspect of this formidable album is not the music but the artwork. It feels like a provocation, anti-rock right down to the knot of their black ties, calculated to set the teeth of the denim-clad and the hairy on edge. Posing, almost pouting in red lipstick, wearing matching red shirts and with their short hair lacquered to lend their appearance an artificial action-man air, the cover screams artifice, mechanisation, effeminacy, conformity, all carried off with the calculated arrogance that was typically, exaggeratedly German, the sort you'd expect from a thin-lipped young *Kommandant* just asking to be riddled with lead by a machine-gun-toting, square-jawed Brit.

As well as raising the hackles of the agoraphobic, synthophobic rock herd, the cover has deeper connotations. Some considered its combination of reds and blacks to allude to the colour scheme of the swastika, but it is, of course, a homage to the constructivist artist El Lissitzky, whose most famous work was the propaganda piece *Beat the Whites with the Red Wedge*. This was Kraftwerk, already gaining the sort of traction with African American audiences that would later see them reshape black dance music, beating the whites in their own way. They are staring backwards, looking not to the west – the American dream supposedly dangled in front of the world by rock'n'roll – but east, much as Bowie had done, in his dialectically shrewd abandonment of America in the mid-1970s for Berlin and the 'new Europa'. Despite their futurist reputation, they are also facing backwards, quite explicitly, to the Bauhaus movement, which (like Kraftwerk) went through an initially messy, hippy-ish period before settling into an aesthetic pattern which sought to unify art, function and design, bringing art into the everyday and the everyday into art. They were fans

of the architect Hermann Finsterlin in particular, who was most
famous for leaving no actual legacy of realised projects. He was a
visionary, however, whose dreams of houses made from fluid forms
moulded from transparent plastic feel like an architectural equivalent of Kraftwerk's music. Finsterlin was also a toymaker and a
composer, but there had been no Bauhaus music, as such, music
going unconsidered by the art movements of the 1920s and '30s.
Kraftwerk were seeking to redress that, some forty-five years after
Bauhaus was so brutally terminated by the Nazis.

Kraftwerk saw themselves as workers, their albums as product;
specifically, as stated on the sleeve of *The Man-Machine*, a product of West Germany. This accorded with the neo-Bauhaus ethos,
although as was sometimes the case with Kraftwerk, interview-
ers somehow found a way of finding associations with the Third
Reich. 'We work on sounds, on our instruments, on our videos, on
the studio. It's very basic and so very honest. You can't call it anything else but work,' said Ralf Hütter in 1982, only to find himself
paraphrased by the journalist in the follow-up question: 'Work,
says Kraftwerk, is freedom.' One rather doubts they would have
used those words, reminiscent as they are of the words engraved
above the entrance to Auschwitz: '*Arbeit macht frei*'. But this was
only in the tradition of appending some Nazi reference to every
early Kraftwerk piece.

Get past the Kraftwerk = German = Nazi equation so commonplace in their heyday and their insistence on industrial terminology
to describe their output has far more interesting connotations.
Even as late as 1977, when *Autobahn* and *Trans-Europe Express* had
earned the group international acclaim, Hütter told the American
journalist Glenn O'Brien that his and Schneider's parents 'would
like to prevent us from doing what we do. We are doing business,
but we should be doing office business.'

Hütter had once spoken of Kraftwerk as having 'no fathers',
and the generational tension that came from growing up during

the late 1960s, an era of dawning consciousness for young West
Germans, was palpable within the group, as they emerged from
the fog of secretiveness in which their parents and grandparents
had voluntarily hidden themselves. Both Hütter and Schneider
came from well-to-do families who expected their children to
follow in their high-achieving footsteps. Hütter had temporarily left Kraftwerk shortly after their formation to devote himself
to his architectural studies. One imagines his family looking on
stiffly and aghast as Kraftwerk went through their formative years,
when, despite their early adoption of drum machines and minimal
synths, they dressed very much as bohemian longhairs, who an
older generation regarded not merely as scruffy layabouts but as
potential terrorists.

One driving factor in their later faux-bourgeois appearance and
'work' aesthetic may genuinely have been to prove a point to their
parents: that what they did was as worthwhile and as substantial
as, say, the legal profession or town planning. Or it may have
been part of the deep, sardonic, comic sensibility that always lurks
beneath the surface of Kraftwerk, a group much laughed at but
who, of course, had the last laugh themselves. Yes, they employed
machines, in the manner of good German industrialists, but, as
they always insisted, 'Our machines have soul' – the soul, perhaps,
missing from post-war West Germany.

Kraftwerk knew the cultural history of post-war West Germany,
in which they would ultimately play a starring, pivotal role. How
their parents worked off the trauma of defeat and disillusion
by toiling to bring their country back up to speed industrially
and commercially, with the assistance of the Americans and the
Marshall Plan. How, in so doing, they averted their eyes from
the criminal stain on their collective consciousness by refusing to
discuss the war or make any serious gesture of remembrance and
atonement that would redeem them. How it was young post-war
artists, including the Krautrock generation with which Kraftwerk

were bracketed, took it upon themselves to redeem Germany, artistically at least, by reconnecting with the country's great but broken traditions of innovation, creating new sonic, often electronic configurations on the *tabula rasa* that was their bequest. Hütter put all of this more succinctly in 1982: 'Our parents were bombed out of their homes. Their main interest was to reconstruct a life for themselves. They became obsessed with material things and went over the top. In the sixties our generation reintroduced consciousness and a social conscience into Germany. Music didn't exist and we had to make it up.'

For all that they reintroduced consciousness, however, Hütter and Schneider seem to have inherited a habit of censorious secretiveness that was a collective condition among their countrymen after the war. Maybe that was simply to preserve the conceptual conceit of Kraftwerk as a work of art(ifice), or maybe it was a horror of impending celebrity, of which they spoke like tribespeople afraid that the lens would steal their soul. 'We don't do photo sessions now because of experiences we've had of people coming at us and trying to kill us with their cameras. They don't realise what they're doing. Now the dummies do the photo sessions and as a result we have almost an overflow of energy for our own lives.' For them, the creation of robot doppelgängers was a means of presenting a 'self' that would do all the celebrity work in the hope that their own private lives (the details of which, as biographers would discover, they guarded fiercely) would remain unprobed. It may well have been that they didn't have anything to hide in particular, but that they came from a high-born background in which it was deeply frowned upon to expose oneself gratuitously to the public gaze.

Kraftwerk had first explored the ideas of the celebrity gaze and the artificial human substitute on *Trans-Europe Express*, another album that seemed to lay railroads to the past as well as to the future, in the serene pre-war picture-postcard group poses for the artwork and on 'Franz Schubert', whose sequencer and orchestron treatments were both state-of-the-art and obliquely nostalgic for a greater Germany.

Previously, on *Autobahn* and *Radio-Activity*, they had not so much celebrated new technology (the autobahn was a creation of the Weimar Republic, the radio sets in the artwork reminiscent of those over which Goebbels would have broadcast his propaganda) as the possibility of a harmonious working relationship with technologies regarded with a Luddite mistrust, not least in the hippy communities that still determined much of the sensibility of rock music.

With *The Man-Machine*, however, they put their selves on the production line as never before. 'We are the robots,' they declared on the opening track, with vocodered but unmistakable insouciance. The soundtrack felt like a transcription of a Fernand Léger picture, with its clockwork whirrs and shamelessly visible circuitry. 'We're charging our battery / and now we're full of energy,' sang Hütter, echoing uncannily the sentiment he had expressed to American journalists on the freedom afforded by devolving all publicity duties to their dummies. 'We're functioning automatic / and we are dancing mechanik.'

'*Ja tvoi sluga, ja tvoi rabotnik*' ('I'm your slave, I'm your worker'), they follow up, tellingly, creating an element of doubt as to whether this is simply Kraftwerk's dummies somehow celebrating their own role as subjugated human substitutes, or Kraftwerk the humans, wont to describe themselves as 'workers', asserting their own functional role within the Kraftwerk machine.

At the time, and despite Bowie's patronage, Kraftwerk had yet to acquire the gravitas and retrospective adulation that they currently enjoy, over thirty years since they last created any new significant body of music. They were comedic, of course, which frivolous commentators mistakenly saw as a reason not to take them seriously. Only retrospectively can we see how, in 1978, Kraftwerk

stood four-square at a threshold that would determine the course
of both black and white cultural identity, pop and art, soul and
artifice, the impending structures of pop, as well as broader considerations about work and leisure in an increasingly automated
age whose volatile anxieties were in stark contrast to the studied,
bland serenity affected by Ralf Hütter's vocals.

In her 1978 study *Robots: Fact, Fiction and Prediction*, Jasia
Reichardt speaks of the history of mankind and machine-kind,
and of the age in which she writes, as lying 'somewhere between
the creation of protomachines and sentient machines, at a stage
when man is building the machines themselves'.

In many respects, Kraftwerk found themselves at a nicely poised
midpoint in the man–machine relationship in music-making. It
was a new frontier. Cheap synths were coming onto the market; the machines were no longer as forbiddingly cumbersome
and expensive. The more ambitious musicians who emerged in
the post-punk era to fill (or delineate) the void left by punk were
resorting to arpeggiators, Prophet-5s, as a mode of expression that
felt more accessible to non-players than even the three-chord min-
imum requirement of punk, or its continued, retrograde resort
to guitars. Thomas Leer, Robert Rental and Daniel Miller were
among the musicians welding a prototype electropop that was
inspired by Kraftwerk, but which was more urgent, stroppy and
rough-edged, a product of punked-up, pumped-up Britain.

As for Kraftwerk themselves, perfectly reduced to metal essentials, it was increasingly clear that they weren't in the 1970s
tradition of novelty synth acts like Hot Butter or Space, but instead
were fundamentalist advocates of an emergent techno-pop that
was becoming increasingly familiar to pop audiences, but which
was yet to reach its saturation point of dreary ubiquity and was still
shimmering with immanence.

1978 was a time of hope and fear on the part of humankind
and machines. In West Germany, Kraftwerk were still disdained

by a public who barely appreciated the Krautrock revolution that had happened under their noses, and who were still in thrall to the Anglo-American rock it had been Krautrock's mission to depart from. It had, but it hadn't taken very many West German rock fans with it. Kraftwerk were far more appreciated in France, the UK and the US than in their homeland. There were reasons for this. First of all, their 'Teutonic other' shtick cut little ice in their home country; Germans found nothing amusing or exotic about being German. There were other factors, too. Their apparent homage to the Soviet Union – in the Russian script across the cover of *The Man-Machine* and red-heavy, neo-constructivist artwork – smacked unmistakably of communism, at a time when fear and loathing of the Red Army Faction was at its height and the West German government was mobilising against suspected hard-leftists, with the Communist Party of Germany (KPD) banned.

Furthermore, Kraftwerk's benign celebration of automation would not have sat well with large sectors of the public whose jobs were increasingly under threat from the increased use of robot machinery from the late 1960s onwards. Not every factory would have seen the need to employ four men to do the amount of work Kraftwerk did. Why not two, or one? Or none at all?

However, in the immediate period prior to the coming ravages of Thatcherism, there was optimism that the rise of the silicon chip would drastically reduce the number of hours workers were required to put in and usher in a new era of leisure. After all, had not the history of machines, from automobiles to washing machines, been one of liberation from the drudgery and toil of our ancestors, freeing up such previously unknown concepts as the weekend? A spate of BBC documentaries assuaged us with this benign promise, in the teeth of more pessimistic prognostications by, for example, trade unionist Clive Jenkins, whose book, *The Collapse of Work*, warned of imminent mass unemployment, unseen since the 1930s.

If this represented a muddle-headed take on the nature of capital, labour and economic growth, then so did *Metropolis*, the 1927 Fritz Lang film to which Kraftwerk paid homage on *The Man-Machine* with a track of the same name. They saw themselves as providing an imaginary soundtrack to the film. 'We are the band of *Metropolis*,' Hütter once said – and they were not the only ones. Giorgio Moroder and Jeff Mills would later be among a raft of contemporary electronic musicians who stepped up to offer a more up-to-date alternative to Gottfried Huppertz's original, somewhat passéist orchestral soundtrack.

However, the scenes for which *Metropolis* is best known – including a futuristic twenty-first-century, Manhattan-inspired cityscape with aerial railways and automobiles, as well as the robot that will take on the guise of Maria – are relatively fleeting. The overall look of the film is in the vein of *The Cabinet of Dr Caligari*, a matter of static set pieces and dream-like expressionist theatre, with the actors emoting wordlessly in slow-motion melodrama. Lang later disowned the film, which he, like most modern viewers, enjoyed mainly for the futuristic elements.

Overwhelmingly, the film is given over to a somewhat dubious saga scripted by Lang's then wife, Thea von Harbou, concerning a two-tier society in which an industrialist elite runs society for its own pleasure and convenience, exploiting the labour of a roboticised, downcast, uniformed mass of workers carrying out dreary, soul-destroying machine operations. One of them, Maria, seeks to quell their restive stirrings, but instead of preaching communistic revolt she promises them the arrival of a 'mediator' to unify the classes. Freder, the louche son of the industrialist Fredersen, falls in love with Maria and comes to understand that he is destined to be that mediator. However, a jealous, jilted inventor, Rotwang (also an employee of Fredersen), is constructing a robot which he ultimately plans to use to wreak revenge on the industrialist and his son. Meanwhile, Fredersen orders Rotwang to transfer Maria's likeness to his own robot so that it can ruin her reputation among the workers. However, the robot Maria wreaks havoc, fomenting an uprising before being captured and burned at the stake, its metal interior revealed. Freder prevails in a subsequent life-and-death tussle with Rotwang and proves himself as the mediator foretold by the real Maria.

H. G. Wells was among the film's most pertinent critics, arguing that in a closed society of mass production, the workers would be consumers as well as producers, and the quality of their lives, therefore, much improved. Who, he asked, was actually buying all this stuff produced round the clock by the workers in order to make its manufacture worthwhile, if not the great mass of workers? Furthermore, among those who did admire the film were Goebbels and Hitler, who recognised all too well the film's potential as a parable for the coming National Socialism, with the Führer as the destined 'mediator'.

Metropolis did, however, contain echoes of a recurring theme in the science-fictional treatment of robots and other such uncanny, not-quite-human, man-made creatures, these not-at-all-privileged 'persons': the possibility that they would rise up against humanity. This had been the theme of Czech playwright Karel Čapek's 1920 philosophical melodrama *R.U.R.* (Rossum's Universal Robots). This was the first time the word 'robot' had been coined, though, as Kraftwerk noted, it bore a close relationship to the Russian word for 'worker', '*rabotnik*'.

The preoccupations of *R.U.R.* would recur in more benign creations such as *Star Trek*'s Commander Data, who is capable of vastly complicated computations but, until he eventually receives an emotion implant, is unable to compute what it is to be human; or the more sinister *A.I.*, a future scenario reflecting present-day anxieties; or, prior to that, *The Terminator*, with its vision of Skynet, whose human replicas will take on self-awareness in the year 1997 and immediately turn on and annihilate humanity rather than coexist with them.

Historical examples of human automata include the 'Turk', created in 1769 by Baron Wolfgang von Kempelen and set inside a large cabinet atop which was laid a chessboard. Audience members would be invited to challenge the Turk to games of chess, which the man-machine would invariably win, his mechanical workings grinding audibly as he worked his pieces remorselessly to checkmate. It was an illusion, of course, most likely the work of diminutive chess masters secreted in the cabinet, but it remains a landmark in the history of the public's imagination of machine-men in our midst.

The development of doll-craft led to a number of uncanny creations, including George Moore's 'steam man', an armour-clad, man-shaped locomotive created in 1893 which was powered by a gas-fired boiler and could walk at speeds of up to nine miles per hour, sporting a 'cigar' that was actually a steam vent.

Today, robots perform vital industrial functions with great efficiency and for long hours, though the makers of those working in the creation of automobiles don't trouble to endow them with the quasi-human forms of our childhood toyboxes and dystopian nightmares. But predictions regarding robot capabilities have, thus far, exceeded reality by some distance. In 1970, one Marvin Minsky had written that, by 1978, 'We will have a machine with the general intelligence of an adult human being. I mean, a machine that will be able to read Shakespeare, grease a car, play office politics, tell a joke, have a fight.' Kraftwerk's robots, themselves almost comically jerky and rudimentary, certainly didn't seem imminently capable of appreciating *The Merry Wives of Windsor*.

From the myth of Prometheus to the present day, robots and automata have played on the imagination of mankind, exciting every emotion from curiosity and wonder to fear and loathing. Kraftwerk's *Man-Machine* coincided with a particularly high tide of anxiety. However, despite the extreme affront the group represented – their 'queering' tactics, pouting unabashedly, and their obvious opposition to every sacred 1970s rock tenet – Kraftwerk did not suffer critical brickbats, at least not from the more sophisticated rock press, for they were under the protection of David Bowie. He had deemed them cool, and his say-so counted for a great deal. He endorsed the *froideur* of the great East Wind blowing through popular culture, as filtered through his own Berlin albums and by the likes of Kraftwerk, as well as lesser known West Germans such as Neu! spin-off La Düsseldorf. Those in the know knew better than to risk being made fools of by attacking Kraftwerk or, indeed, Bowie himself. There was another emergent electropop presence, though, who did not enjoy Bowie's protection, and consequently found himself bearing the brunt of the hackles raised by pop's new synth wave. That pale young man was Gary Numan.

Having both interviewed and met Numan informally, I can attest that he is well up there among the kindlier, friendlier superstar interviewees. He's forthcoming in his responses, with none of the passive-arrogant, self-absorbed laconicism to be found among some of his peers. He has been acknowledged as a primary influence by such subsequent electronic-industrial behemoths as Nine Inch Nails. He has made a very tidy living indeed, even in the years when he was out of the spotlight, and comes across as humble and happy with the hand life has dealt him.

In late 1979, he rose precipitously to fame, having adopted the clearly expedient strategy of presenting himself as a pasty pop mannequin. He clearly wasn't an existentially driven creature, reinventing himself out of sheer, authentic necessity; he just reckoned it would go over well. He instructed his band, when first appearing on *Top of the Pops*, 'Just stand there. Don't smile or nothing. Look at the camera and stare at it . . . it went down a storm.'

As much as he was adored, though, Gary Numan was detested. David Bowie was not the only one to believe he was stealing the monochrome thunder of his Berlin period – a straight rip-off. The level of resentment he faced suggested he was the new whipping boy for pop's impending age of automation.

'I'm sure I got more abuse than the average rapist,' he told a sympathetic Phil Sutcliffe of *Sounds*. 'I just don't know why I annoyed people. There were death threats: I'm on about number 12 now. A petrol bomb put under my dad's car. Two kidnap threats against my mother which the police took very seriously. I mean, I went to New Zealand once, got off the plane and the first thing I saw, written on the side of a building, was "Numan, Fuck Off". I thought, 12,000 miles for this! I didn't take to that sort of thing very well at all, actually.'

Extracts from a 1994 interview with Simon Price in the *Melody Maker* section 'Rebellious Jukebox', in which artists discussed some of their favourite records, capture some of the almost Pooteresque pathos of Numan:

I went into a really cheap studio in 1977, and found a mini-Moog someone had left behind, hooked up to a bass amp. I'd never seen a synth before. So I started playing, and I thought 'Monster! More power than 10 heavy metal guitars!' I tried to find out if anyone else was doing electronic music, and I found two records: Kraftwerk, and Ultravox's *Systems of Romance* album. Suddenly, everything started to explode, and luckily I became the focal point. The Musicians' Union tried to ban me, and ban synthesizers, which is a bit like trying to stop a bulldozer with your hand.

The thing I admired about Bowie, like a lot of stars from that period, was that he was larger than life. I'd have been scared shitless to meet him. What do you say? The man's from outer space! Later, I actually met him, but we didn't get on. Which is a great disappointment. I did a show for Kenny Everett years ago, and Bowie was on the same show. I was there, Geldof was there, it was a bit of a fan club convention, all watching. And Bowie spotted me, stopped everything, and made the guards come and throw me out. I was gutted.

Further stories only confirmed the disparity between the monster he was perceived as and the bathos of his true self: how the group Japan took to a high-speed car in Tokyo in order to shake off Numan, who had understood that he was to play with them in a guest slot, as well as another tale in which he hurtfully recalls a critic writing that his mother and father should have been doctored so as not to give birth to him ('That's going too far. My mum is the loveliest person you could ever hope to meet').

As a schoolboy, however, I detested Gary Numan with the heat of a thousand neon bulbs. I railed in the school magazine against what I perceived as his pudgy and punchable countenance, describing one of his Moog-based synths as no more than 'a sequence of organised electronic farts'. It further annoyed me that a small claque of fellow sixth-formers, generally suspected of being gay, colonised the common-room record player, removing their school ties and, in buttoned-up grey shirts, embarking solemnly on a series of jerky, robotic moves to 'Are "Friends" Electric'. I couldn't quite admit it but I resented this out-and-out queering. Despite my deep intellectual commitment to equal rights, including for Gary Numan fans, homosexuality had, so far as I was concerned, only been introduced to the British Isles in 1975 with the broadcast of *The Naked Civil Servant*, in which John Hurt played Quentin Crisp, and was still taking some getting used to.

The inestimable Charles Shaar Murray spoke so eloquently for me in his 1980 review of *Telekon* that I punched the air in triumph:

All non-musical considerations temporarily to one side, I'd say that it was a woefully dull and monotonous album, pompous in the extreme and exceptionally limited in its range of tempi and tonalities (how a man who owns so many different synthesisers can be satisfied with so few noises is utterly inexplicable). His mannered whine drives me completely up the wall, and titles like 'I Dream of Wires' and 'Remember I Was Vapour' seem almost risible. Moreover, Numan's work seems almost entirely untainted by anything even faintly resembling wit or passion.

He concluded with a pun about the 'synths of the fathers', which I didn't understand but would spit cryptically in the faces of the Numanoids when jostling for turntable time.

Today, it's clear that Numan, considered an obnoxiously plastic and derivative mannequin by his detractors in his day, was, if not an outright innovator, a shrewd early adopter in the Bowie vein, with a sure grasp of pop drama and dynamics. 'Cars', his masterpiece, ranks alongside Kraftwerk's best work, working in Moog zigzags and dripping with the paranoia and deliberate, hermetic self-alienation of the modern automobile driver. For that alone, he deserves enormous respect.

Murray did make other points in his review, however, which applied to the brief period of 'reactionary futurism' that occurred in the era in which he was writing: that artists like Numan, even in dystopian mode, alluded to a future that was unlikely to resemble the one in store for most people in the Thatcher-dominated 1980s. 'It prefers to extrapolate from the vision of SF writers of the '30s to the accompaniment of large slabs of third or fourth-hand Kraftwerk (via Bowie, Eno and Ultravox).'

Nonetheless, Numan glowed brightly but briefly. He actually announced his retirement after *Telekon*, which he followed up with a massive tour. He immediately rescinded the decision, releasing a series of albums that saw him diversify his musical range but which were entirely eclipsed by the 1980s synthpop that actually came in his wake.

Perhaps what Numan represented – and which enraged so many, albeit unfairly – was the prospect of robot-as-clone, with

synth music, with its already familiar tropes and presets, representing a new era of homogeneity. An odd example of the sort of
quaintly speculative sci-fi fantasies of ultra-conformity came from,
of all people, Mike Batt, creator of the Wombles. Having made
his pile with a series of Wombles-related material (astoundingly,
comprising six albums), Batt created a customised synthpop on
his 1982 solo album *Zero Zero*, a concept created in conjunction
with Australian TV that envisaged a future society lived amid the
checkered blacks and whites which spoke of a binary digital age,
in which emotions were banned and falling in love could earn you
a lobotomy.

In fairness, this was not synthophobia on Batt's part; he had
actually been making Moog music since the early 1970s, including an album called *Ye Olde Moog* (1974), a strange collection of
sketches of pastoral England rendered in 'synthesonic' colours,
years ahead of 'folktronica'. However, *Zero Zero* did vividly capture
the horrors conjured up on the horizons of the public imagination
about what mankind might be reduced to if culture were rewired
and electrified as a whole along the Numan lines. The pang of this
fear was felt widely, not least in Australia.

This was a wild projection. What happened next as Numan
was supplanted was a pop movement inspired by the deliberately mechanical gestures of *'Heroes'* Bowie and post-*Autobahn*
Kraftwerk, as well as the King's Road, dressing-up end of punk.
New Romanticism jerked and swayed portentously about the
dancefloor to a soundtrack by DJ Rusty Egan. The New Romantics
swarmed like the breakaway mannequins from Kraftwerk's
'Showroom Dummies', bursting through the glass across Soho,
postmodern gilded poseurs, narcissistic, queered to the hilt,
decked out in outlandish combinations that drew on every gracious, glamorous manifestation of the twentieth century, with
even some eighteenth- and nineteenth-century throwbacks and
sartorial figments of an imagined twenty-first century. They subtly

invited accusations of po-faced pretentiousness, of implying rather than possessing depth. That was the point. Spandau Ballet was meant to sound like it meant a great deal while meaning nothing at all. All was surface play, a mockery of punkish old-school ideas of 'content'.

And yet, tinfoil-deep as they were, the New Romantics were as serious as new jazz and walked through the world with the same emancipated intensity as punks. Conversely, for all their dead-eyed, determined, Teutonic, synthetic hauteur, their love of artifice, of *Vogue* covers of yesteryear, of mannerism and of Garbo, these weren't human flunkies but gregarious, regular, fun-loving, generous, sometimes political, sometimes dim, sometimes pugnacious people (New Romantic denizens like Boy George and Chris Sullivan knew how to look after themselves), all pursuing an aesthetic that wasn't whimsical, sci-fi or cyber-futurist but very much rooted in the very real and very present cultural circumstances of their time.

Their dressing up was in direct defiance of the economic downturn of the era. The New Romantics began in London but gained real traction in some of the most depressed areas of the UK – the north and Wales, to name but two. Despite the dubious, faintly fascistic posturing of Spandau Ballet's 'Musclebound', the New Romantics were partly a counter-cultural celebration of free play in a post-industrial world in which there was no work to be done, one in which you defined yourself not by the job you had but what you decided, stylistically, to become. They refused to abide by the normal signifiers of the 'human' in pop – the matey, the chirpy, the passionate, the sincere, the lovey-dovey, the lonesome – because these were abnormal times. These were the 'robots' of the early post-industrial 1980s, Kraftwerk and Bowie's bastard brood of plastic children, dancing mechanically to 'Fade to Grey' yet refusing to do just that.

The history of robots, factual or fictional, can traditionally seem like an all-white, all-European affair, racially speaking, sprung from the imagination and ingenuity of Czechs, Teutons and white-haired boffins, the product of some assumed greater disposition towards the mechanical on the part of the northern Europeans. However, as the writer Louis Chude-Sokei points out in his excellent *The Sound of Culture: Diaspora and Black Technopoetics*, the fear and fascination surrounding robots in their uncanny not-quite-human-ness and the recurring horror that they might rise up against us has a coded racial component that has long been overlooked yet, when touched upon, seems starkly obvious. The sense that robots, ostensibly our slave workers, were not human as yet but perhaps on the way to becoming so, and the anxiety about what they might do once they achieved emancipation, runs parallel with concerns about African and Caribbean slaves, whose freedom and gradual empowerment prompted fears that 'they' might someday take over and make victims of us. As we have seen in the Obama and post-Obama era, these 'concerns' are still very active in American political life.

Slaves were not thought of as human from a legal perspective when first shipped from Africa to the 'civilised' world from 1800 onwards, while the sense that they had human capabilities but lacked human sensibilities was generally internalised. Hence, one hears stories of southern belles who had no qualms about undressing in front of even male slaves, any more than they would in front of their pet dogs.

From the early nineteenth century onwards, however, there was a lurking, troubling sense that this natural order of things would not hold and that the future might bring terrifying developments. In this context, Mary Shelley's *Frankenstein*, commonly considered to be the first science-fiction novel, can be seen as springing from a fevered sense that the colonial enterprise might unleash uncontrollable human forces as creatures considered under the ownership of their white masters acquired power, consciousness and self-realisation. Shelley herself was a forward-thinking liberal, an abolitionist who even boycotted sugar because of its connection to the slave trade. She was also deeply conscious that the Haitian revolution between 1791 and 1804, in which slaves successfully rose up in the French colony of Saint Domingue and established the Haitian state, was a harbinger of things to come. From this perspective, the story of *Frankenstein* speaks not merely to lurking anxieties about the potential to be unleashed by the new technological age but to the doom of the colonial enterprise. The violence Victor Frankenstein, the 'slave owner' (if this metaphor holds), would seek to wreak on his creation once it had exceeded his civilising control and recoiled back to its base, 'bestial' self is salutary also.

Although Shelley's novel contains references to the slave trade, the connection is not made explicit. However, there are more conspicuous examples of how black people and automata were connected in the collective consciousness, not least that exploited by the nineteenth-century showman P. T. Barnum, who would make a career out of acquiring and touring various 'freaks', most famously the dwarf Charles Stratton, aka General Tom Thumb, whom he trained up from the age of four years old but maintained till he was much older; by the age of five, with much training, Barnum had him drinking wine and smoking cigars for the entertainment of the public.

Barnum launched his career in 1835, when he purchased from another showman one Joice Heth, a blind and partially paralysed slave woman whom he claimed was 161 years old and the supposed 'mammy' to George Washington. Her paralysis meant that she was only able to lift one arm, while her lower legs remained straightened. Her status as an owned being, coupled with her physical condition, left her entirely vulnerable to Barnum's manipulation and the public gaze. Superhuman due to her supposed great age yet not quite human, she acquired nicknames such as 'Egyptian mummy', 'living skeleton' and 'venerable nigger'. She would become the founding acquisition in his eventual empire.

Barnum wasn't content to leave it there, however, especially when public interest in his exhibit began to fade. In a further twist of deceitful showmanship, he inserted into a newspaper an item supposedly by 'a visitor' – almost certainly Barnum himself – in which it was asserted that far from being an extremely old woman, Heth was in fact a mechanical creation, a 'curiously constructed automaton' made up of whalebone, rubber and various springs that enabled her to be operated by her controller. And so, with deep cunning, Barnum was now passing her off not as a human curiosity but a mechanical one; and such was the lack of agency on Heth's part that, of course, she was in no position to protest, much as black people in America in general had little or no means of protesting their lot, depending even for their suffrage on their white benefactors. Ironically, these included Barnum himself. As a senator, he campaigned vigorously against the slave trade, if not his own particular dubious trade. Meanwhile, the fiction that Heth was not human but machine was quite an easy one for the public to take, since it accorded with their view of blacks as only physically and mechanically resembling humans in any case.

Barnum also traded in minstrelsy, the most popular phenomenon of the nineteenth century, which reflected whites' fascination with blackness or their crude notions thereof, in all its uncanny otherness, while, of course, the rights of African Americans, even post-emancipation, were cruelly suppressed with the vengeance of the Jim Crow laws. Blacks continued to toil unremittingly in cotton fields, labour-saving devices for whites, while enduring the further indignity of being parodied in blackface as happy-go-lucky and lazy, as if to stave off fear of what they might truly become if allowed. Even blacks in the entertainment industry were obliged to take part in this farcically complex and charged artifice, performing as their darkie 'selves' but passing themselves off as white entertainers blacking up.

The most obvious example of robot-as-subjugated-African-American cited by Chude-Sokei is 'Mr Rastus Robot', the 'Mechanical Negro' designed by the Westinghouse Research Laboratory and first exhibited in 1930. Here, for Americans of a certain twistedly nostalgic bent, was the dream of the robot, and of the 'Negro', as a possible labour-saving device of the future. Rastus was one of a series of robots created by the laboratory, which also included Herbert Televox, a similarly reassuring and non-threatening creation. Made of rubber, and bearing the quietly devotional expression which white Americans found so becoming in African Americans, Rastus was capable of uttering six words, when prompted by his controller, as well as rising and sitting and moving his hands. To further put him in his yes-suh place, Rastus wore the blue overalls and coloured bandana typical of a manual labourer from the Deep South.

Conversely, Chude-Sokei also notes the anxiety tapped into in *Metropolis*, when Maria's doppelgänger is created by the inventor Rotwang, her features transferred to the machine. Upon acquiring mobility and consciousness, the machine breaks into a dance unmistakably reminiscent of Josephine Baker, whose frantic, exotic and erotic flapping dance style represented for many the worst and most dangerous manifestation of African American liberation: the jazz age, which was perverting the nation's white youth and undermining white, Christian morals. This was a clear signal of the mayhem and insurrection that Maria's doppelgänger was about to wreak, inflaming the restive masses before order was restored.

Once introduced into the public consciousness, robots became the subject of popular hysteria. The fear was that these uncanny metal beings would quickly exceed their station. Fevered and speculative illustrated tales appeared in newspapers and magazines. In 1933, the *San Antonio Light*, a Texas journal, featured a cautionary cartoon in which a cyberman attempts to have his way with a pretty young domestic servant. The 'robot' is unmistakably black in hue, its lips conspicuously reminiscent of minstrel caricature. Once again, science fiction became a coded means of expressing real-life fears, in this case the virility and supposed predatory nature of the lower-class black male.

All of these were the projections of whites upon black people, who, as the industrial age wore on, slowly, very slowly began to assert their civil rights, their sense of identity, equality and humanity, wordlessly articulated in jazz or codified in the blues, and amplified via new technologies like the gramophone and radio, on which African American-sourced musical styles now dominated the airwaves.

That black artists themselves should be the agents of new technologies was barely considered until well after the end of World War II. The musique concrète studios were the almost exclusive province of white Europeans, and it was unthinkable that black musicians, considered to be repositories of raw, authentic, acoustic spontaneity and soulful earthiness, should wish to partake of these cerebral, schematic and frankly rather complicated devices. And so it was that Sun Ra ploughed a lonely furrow with his clavichord explorations of the 1950s. Electronic instruments were considered antithetical to jazz, and his use of them was seen as of a piece with his outlying eccentricity.

As the decades progressed, however, Afro-futurism rose up, its mission not to rage against the machine but to lay claim to it. James Brown wrote 'Sex Machine' and insisted that his musicians labour to achieve industrial standards of accuracy, and they would suffer fines if they should be so human as to err or miss a note or arrive a second late for rehearsals. Tracks like 'Give It Up or Turnit a Loose' are so tight, so elaborate in their drilled, pneumatic, pinpoint riffing (more sewing machine than sex machine) as to qualify as 'honorary electronica', a music that in its execution betrays none of the weaknesses of the flesh.

By the mid-1970s, among the most enthusiastic fans of Kraftwerk's *Autobahn* were DJs in Detroit, the Motor City. From the early 1980s onwards, it became abundantly clear that young black musicians were the new Futurists, just as white rock and its audiences were about to enter into a long, postmodern period of conservative retrospection. This made sense, of course. Whereas white audiences could hark back wistfully to the earlier decades of the twentieth century, perceived through a halcyon gauze – more innocent, purer times – black people had no reason to feel any fondness for those decades, the experiences of their immediate ancestors scarred by Jim Crow, segregation and every kind of indignity and injustice. The present wasn't so great either. But the future? Maybe.

This perhaps explains why, since the electro-funk of the early 1980s (and preceded by dub), black artists have been responsible for so many of the rewirings of pop, from hip hop through to drum 'n' bass, grime and a host of subsidiary developments. Roboticism was parodied and, in a sense, reclaimed from its slave implications in the stiff, improbable motions of body-popping and the moonwalk.

In 1986, it was techno, led in Detroit by artists like Juan Atkins, Kevin Saunderson and Derrick May, who asserted to the writer Kris Needs in 1990 that 'It comes from the theory and the theme of advancement, from the technological revolution which is known in Alvin Toffler's book as the "third wave" of technology.' He openly acknowledged that Kraftwerk were the progenitors of techno, but also said, 'The biggest joke is to see an Italian or Belgian or English record and they're called techno.' To him, for white Europeans to lay claim to this music was as absurd as Kenny Ball or Stéphane Grappelli claiming to have invented jazz. The black primacy of techno was now a given. This was music reduced to its metal essentials, like the robot Maria's flesh burned away in *Metropolis* to reveal the workings of her machine nature.

That said, when I interviewed the Detroit-born, though later Chicago-based, Jeff Mills, he did not follow the conventional wisdom that Kraftwerk were the prime inspiration for him musically.

A little, he agreed, but he was more anxious to talk about the likes of the B-52s, whose bouffant bop was underpinned by a stiff-gesturing, new-wave-derived deliberate gaucheness, a riposte to the smooth and the fluid. He was also a fan of the halting robo-pop of Visage. They made a particular connection with Mills as a young DJ.

With an event he was due to play later that night having been cancelled, Mills had more time on his hands than he had antici-pated the evening I turned up at a hotel near Trafalgar Square to talk to him. Slight, dapper and well preserved, it was hard to believe that he had been a player for so many decades. However, he was also looking decades hence.

A one-time member of Underground Resistance, Mills's techno, as evidenced on tracks like 'Alarms' or 'Outsiders', eschews the lush melodic adornments of Derrick May or the pop hooks of Kevin Saunderson's Inner City in favour of a punitive, propulsive quality; drilling hard and drilling fast forward into the future. He makes no apologies for the lack of concessions or sweeteners in his music. He regards it as a sort of rigorous conditioning.

'I was never convinced that all music should be pleasant. I tend to believe that it's more of an extension of one's voice and some-times what one has to say is not pleasant. I know that a lot of music I make doesn't make sense now because the world is different now. But the future will be a very different situation. It's our nature to think about preparing for tomorrow. And a large part of that is trying to find another place for us to exist – for us to have water, a liveable atmosphere. This isn't science fiction, it's science. We may come to a point where life on this earth is unliveable and we have to find new ways. Just the idea of surviving may well be the largest part of a human's life in the future. Not shopping, working – just surviving. So a lot of the drama, the suspense, the aggressiveness in the music is conditioning the listener for this. And learning how to listen is a part of that.

'We need to think further and further ahead to prepare ourselves more. I think something's going to happen that's going to
make us put all our priorities in place. I have no idea what it could
be but I sense something will happen that will bring us back down
to earth again, think about what's the most important thing. And
I just want to help people to be mentally prepared for that.'

Mills estimated that mankind would reach a new key evolutionary stage in 'about 2067', a hundred years after the first flower
power revolution. When I told him that I had never in my life
especially given much thought to future times – the year 2017, for
example, never entered my head prior to the chimes of Big Ben
that heralded it in – he rocked back in his chair. 'Wow! Seriously?'
Mills's head is already well into tomorrow, past the here and now
and our present divisions, above and beyond unresolved racial tensions, in a higher place.

'I dropped most of my impressions of the differences between
black and white some time ago. People are people. There are good
people and bad people, good people who do bad things and vice
versa, and that's about it. There isn't particularly one way to be.
Looking beyond race, I think we'll have a situation where the difference will be between keeping people back or allowing them to
expand. And this will have nothing to do with economics or where
they live but their capacity to overcome fear. I think race is not as
important as we make it out to be.

'And it's going to be even more different in the future. We've
become more able to communicate with people completely off the
radar. And that's the reality of where we are. So the idea of being
proud of being from a certain place or ethnic group will become
part of the past, a ball and chain, if anything. But then, some people
feel more comfortable with that, saying that they're from Detroit
and feeling that they're part of the Detroit techno legacy . . .'

Today, there is such a thing as a Museum of Techno in Detroit.
Just a block or so away from the Motown Museum, it's situated in

a former union hall acquired by Underground Resistance back in 2002. Among its exhibits are images of Leonard Nimoy (Spock in *Star Trek*), George Clinton's P-Funk project, with whom Clinton dared to invite the public to 'conceive of a nigga in a spaceship', and the cover to Kraftwerk's *The Man-Machine*, as well as a room full of the electronic hardware that launched Detroit techno, an engine room of keyboards, synths and 808 and 909 drum machines. There is also a larger item: a lathe used to master those early vinyl recordings, built back in 1939 and resembling, according to one newspaper article, 'a giant Art Deco sewing machine'.

Ironically, just as Detroit techno was being birthed in 1986, Kraftwerk were about to wind themselves up as a recording force. No one was to know it at the time, but *Electric Café*, released that year, would be their final album proper. They have spent the last thirty years or so issuing vague promises of new material, the odd remix album and, in December 1999, the single 'Expo 2000'. The twenty-first-century tour circuit is choked with superannuated megasaurs filling the O2 night after night and plying audiences with the hits of yesteryear; it's easier to list who isn't at it (Abba, the Smiths) than who is (everyone else). And yet even if only in the form of solo releases, at least these acts have made token appearances in the studio to add to their catalogue, despite the cries of their audience to party like it's 1972. Kraftwerk, however, have left their futurism long behind them. From a creative viewpoint, this band, just a few years short of celebrating its half-century, was only operative for twelve years – 1974–86.

There was a reason they deprogrammed that year; in fact, *Electric Café*, for all its graphic brilliance and impeccable assembly, may even have been an album too soon. For, by 1986, their man-machine project was done. They were victorious. Their use of synthesizer no longer marked them out as novel, inhuman, effeminate, inauthentic, Teutonic, fleshless, deadpan provocateurs. Synthesizers were ubiquitous in 1980s rock. Their warm sheet waves acted as an FM lubricant for everyone from Van Halen to Bruce Springsteen ('Dancing in the Dark'). Yes, even Springsteen, rock's very own woodsman and impassioned yearner for the human touch, the anti-Hütter, was freely using synths. From funk to jazz fusion, light pop to heavy metal, synths were as quotidian as computers in the workplace. So, when Kraftwerk ominously vocoderised the words 'industrial electronic sounds' on 'Musique Non-Stop', far from being confounded or making bad Hitler jokes, the world simply said, 'Yes, we know.'

Like Rotwang creating the doppelgänger of Maria in *Metropolis*, pop had added flesh and blood and warmth and obvious soul signifiers to synth-based pop. Only this wasn't an attempt to subvert or create insurrection – the 1980s popsters were synth-cere. It was no longer a Meccano affair, all its workings exposed. A prime example was the Eurythmics, with their debut single, 'Sweet Dreams Are Made of This'. In the manner of Alison Moyet of Yazoo and others, Annie Lennox emoted in waves over Dave Stewart's bed of synth. They could cultivate an air of *froideur*, immobility and androgyny in the video, but this melted the moment Lennox unleashed one of her trademark sub-Aretha wails. This would become a formula for 1980s pop, one that was reminiscent of Derek Smalls in *Spinal Tap* describing his guitar colleagues like 'fire and ice' and himself as the mediator between them, 'like lukewarm water'. With its envious fixation on Real Black Music, mid- to late-1980s electropop, from Bronski Beat to George Michael, would flood the airwaves with so much lukewarm water as it hastened towards the passion revue that was Live Aid.

1986 was also the year in which analogue was at its lowest ebb; all was now digital. So much so that Bob Moog discovered that the rights to his name, which he had sold some years earlier, had expired due to lack of use. Who needed Moog? Who needed analogue?

It would fall to a newer generation – not just May, Saunderson, Atkins and co. but also A Guy Called Gerald and the first British acid wave – to strip back electronic music to its Kraftwerkian bare metal essence.

Today, then, Kraftwerk are the most supremely nostalgic of all bands, dedicated solely to their legacy, their creative additions all in the stage presentation, which is now a truly state-of-the-art visual bombardment of retro-futurist kitsch, from the 1980s-style green glow of their graphics and fonts, to sweeping, digitally colourised cycling footage projected on previously unavailable wide screens, to reproductions of the *Autobahn* artwork; it's one long futurist flashback which only now do they have the technical visual wherewithal to put on. This has been required to realise Kraftwerk ultimately as a pop *Gesamtkunstwerk*. Footage from the group in their heyday shows the contexts in which they were forced to play as leaving much to be desired, despite their own best sartorial efforts and onstage arrangements – glum, brown-panelled, all-purpose concert halls, as well as abysmally dated pop videos. The music they barely tamper with, but the visuals are now what they might have hoped for or come up with forty years ago, as they contemplate their small, perfectly formed body of material over and over.

What is it that draws music-lovers to Kraftwerk's live shows, though, beyond the consoling and enhanced spectacle of the twentieth-century familiar? Perhaps it's because despite all that has developed as a result of them, and the fact that they have long lost their tag as the only electronic players in town, they remain, in a deeper sense, the most electronic pop group who ever lived – an ideal, a pinnacle, an extreme. No one has outdone them in this respect. Everyone else is just a bit too humanly deviant. They exceed everybody and everything else. Conceptually, their very bodies, their very selves, are wired up and into the Kraftwerk entity. Of the four original members, only one remained in 2017. They are generous employers – not for them the utilitarian glumness of a single sallow player hunched over an Apple Mac – though their employment policy could be criticised for being non-inclusive. However, who is to say that one day, when its members go the way of all flesh, Hütter included, Kraftwerk will take on new members – women, ethnic minority, transgender or even man–machine hybrids as yet unconceived?

And could it be that when Kraftwerk intoned, 'We are the robots,' the shock they created, and forced rock critics to absorb, lay in their declaration of an oblique solidarity with the hitherto put-upon not-quite-humans who had endured so much for so long? Hence the natural connection with African American music and culture, from body-popping to electro-funk and techno, as well as compliments such as Carl Craig declaring that Kraftwerk were 'so stiff, they're funky'. As white and male as they come, Kraftwerk were anti-white and anti-male in ways that mattered. For years, I misheard the opening lyric of 'Robots', 'We're charging up our batteries,' as, 'We're charging on to victory.' Kraftwerk did charge on to victory. It's a victory we still have to deal with.

12

SUBSTANCE: FROM JOY DIVISION TO NEW ORDER, THE HUMAN LEAGUE TO THE HUMAN LEAGUE, DEPECHE MODE TO DEPECHE MODE

Around 1981, in a calculatedly offhand aside while writing about some other group altogether, the *NME*'s Paul Morley referred to 'hard' groups like Depeche Mode. It was a provocation, uttered as though it were a given that Depeche Mode were hard. They were generally regarded as nothing of the kind, of course. The 'hard' groups of the day were part of the New Wave of British Heavy Metal, the likes of Tygers of Pan Tang or Saxon or Iron Maiden, denim-clad, poodle-haired bastions of defiantly unreconstructed roaring and Viking maleness, hard and heavy rockers who would nut you if you so much as suggested that Freddie Mercury was a puff. Come and have a go at playing like them, if you thought you were hard enough. In your air-guitar dreams, mate. Their hardness lay in their power chords, wrought and smelted with visible effort, unleashed at 750cc engine volume. Contrast them with a new, emergent, doily-thin wave of synthpop bands, dressed in Fauntleroy-esque garb like they were on their way to Bertie Blenkinsop's birthday party, prancing nimbly on *Top of the Pops* and dabbing softly at keyboards as if licking their fingers to turn the page of a clothes catalogue. It would take a particularly perverse and ironic mindset to describe these pouting, mimsy, ostentatious little bantamweights as 'hard', and, as we knew, they didn't come more perverse and ironic than Paul Morley.

Morley was having an acute dig at the spuriousness of ascribing densities to particular musics based on whether they were rock- or pop-based, guitar- or keyboard-orientated. He was arguing that what constitutes substance was something more subtly, deceptively durable and meaningful, whose durability might even consist in its supposed flimsiness. He was more right than he might even have anticipated, however. Today, Tygers of Pan Tang are part of the soft, dead mulch of rock history, while Depeche Mode's own history is an epic one of American conquest, stadia and debauchery on an appalling scale.

Depeche Mode's durability has been astonishing – as has that of New Order or, in their different way, the Human League – while their German forefathers, Kraftwerk, far from being blown away by gales of Zeppelin in the 1970s, continue to overarch all. Not that substance or hardness are contingent on long-lasting success. As Morley understood, it is a more elusive, metaphysical quality, one which even those in possession of it are loath to discuss.

Depeche Mode emerged in 1981. There is a possibly apocryphal story that a newspaper from their native Basildon, covering the band just as they were on the cusp of chart success, led with the headline 'Posh Clobber Could Clinch It for Mode'. It did, along with substances even less material than clobber.

Before that, however, there was a shadow zone, as the 1970s were petering out prematurely, a world of Wimpys and Tescos, of supersonic vapour trails, of the last generation of working horses treading the cobbles, of transistor radios and ominous, paternalistic public-information films, of poison and violence and endless summers, of a nation in flight from itself and from its own post-war construction, of the decaying old and the already decaying new. A handful of boys, working in the fading new dawn of Krautrock, scratching out a tentative new music on the black sheet of the future that was the 1980s, unknowable in 1979.

2017. I'm in the back room of the Bar & Kitchen in Hoxton

Street, adjacent to a noisy room of lagery carousers. Daniel Miller, founder of Mute Records, is giving a talk and slideshow of his street photography, a passion of his in which he exercises the principle established by the French photographer Henri Cartier-Bresson of the 'decisive moment'. The scenes he captures aren't particularly interesting for their subjects or for the inconsequential incidents they represent. He's more interested in the fleeting, inadvertent symmetries you can capture with a single snapshot if you happen to be in the right place at the right time, ready to anticipate the possibility of the spontaneous. Accompanying him is an ongoing bubbling of modular synthesizer. Miller makes the point that there are such things as 'decisive moments' in music-making. 'I just get very sick of the thousands of presets you get in modern synths. It's got worse and worse. For me, if you're making electronic music, the idea of using presets is a very boring, non-creative way of making music. When I worked as a producer, one of the rules I set was no presets.'

I suggest to Miller that one aspect of the synthpop emergence circa 1978 was its imagistic nature. Despite the scratchy, monochromatic feel of the cheap, basic synths that were emerging from Japan onto the market at that time, you could paint pictures, suggest atmospheres, rather than merely drive the narrative lines of three-chord punk. Had that aspect of the new instruments appealed to him?

'In a way, yes. I think a lot of people making music back then had a visual arts background. I studied film – my first job was as an assistant film editor, making commercials. The content wasn't very inspiring but the process was fascinating. I learned a lot about structure and about compressing ideas into a very short space of time. Peter Christopherson from Throbbing Gristle was part of the Hipgnosis design team who created album covers for Pink Floyd, among others.'

Miller was among a handful of rarified, isolated and dispersed souls who had taken inspiration from the experimental West German music scene of the 1970s, which in terms of its form and ambitions was antithetical to the dominant Anglo-American prog rock and its classical pretensions and ascension into the clouds of Tolkien-esque whimsy. Sensing the exhaustion and coming extinction of the 1970s behemoths – just what was the point of Led Zeppelin come 1978? – they took the opportunity to seize a new means of production, on a less epic and heroic but more accessible and meaningful scale.

The new technology also encouraged the phenomenon of bedroom recording. The extroversion necessary to form a band and knock heads with fellow members in a rehearsal space was no longer an absolute requirement. Glasgow-born Thomas Wishart, aka Leer, had moved to London and joined a punk band called Pressure with, among others, Robert Rental. He understood the importance of punk in recharging music in the UK, dispelling the whiff of staleness that was almost palpable when you surveyed the pages of *Melody Maker* in particular, and the ageing, hirsute music it reported on in a dully ruminative manner. But within months he found the limited room for musical manoeuvre within the three-chord format stifling. He retreated to the bedroom of his tiny Finsbury Park flat and recorded his debut single, 'Private Plane'. The equipment at his disposal was a four-track recorder and a little mixing board, a tape-echo unit, a DrQ filter, a preset drum machine and a Stylophone. Wobbly and aerial, trailing wispy clouds of synth, its vocals sound whispered, as if not to disturb other sleepers in the house while recording. It's antithetical to punk's public and soon-to-be-predictable holler. It's a product of introversion, discretion, yet it's exploratory; a private plain, indeed. With its Germanic suggestiveness, Leer was the perfect moniker. It's the German for 'empty', and the terrain Leer and his contemporaries were alighting on felt empty indeed, like a grey yet fertile pop planet awaiting discovery and development.

As for Miller, he enjoyed modest success as the Normal with 'Warm Leatherette'/'T.V.O.D.', the former's irresistible pneumatic inhalation/exhalation a very obvious tribute to J. G. Ballard, which suggested that the newly minted synthpop had peculiarly erotic possibilities that made it ideal for chart consumption; Grace Jones would recognise this in covering the song herself. The lessons in terseness and compression he'd learned from the advertising world came in useful and would become the founding stone of Mute Records.

'1978 saw debut releases by Throbbing Gristle, Cabaret Voltaire, as well as the Normal and Thomas Leer, among others,' says Miller. 'And there's a historical reason for that. It came out of punk in a way, but wasn't punk. A lot of punks hated electronic music because for them it represented Emerson, Lake and Palmer.'

Miller discovered this when he toured with Robert Rental. They toured with Stiff Little Fingers and, as with Suicide supporting the Clash, found themselves facing the wrath of punk fans who viewed synthesizers with Luddite disdain, seeing them as mysterious black boxes of alienation and a betrayal of everything they were pogoing for.

'It went down very badly,' recalls Miller. 'We played with Stiff Little Fingers from Belfast, who'd just released their first album on RT, which was a success. The venues were much bigger and it was a punk audience. We often left the stage with burns from lighted cigarettes that had been thrown at us, covered in alcohol from bottles hurled onstage . . . However, we made a pact that we would never allow ourselves to be bottled off stage. We would complete the gig. And always there'd be one or two people who came backstage who said that they'd been inspired by what we'd done. And that made it worth it for us.'

The most potent document of their work together is the one-sided 1979 disc *Live at West Runton Pavilion*. The very name West Runton Pavilion sticks out with rustic soreness in the annals of early electronica. Closed in 1986, it was situated on the North Norfolk coast, Alan Partridge country, a venue whose excellent acoustics made it a preferred drop-in for pop and rock acts looking to try out new material before going out on tour proper. According to the blue plaque that now sits outside the former venue, in its heyday it saw Chuck Berry, T. Rex, Black Sabbath and the Sex Pistols, among others, pass through its doors. Unmentioned are Robert Rental and the Normal, who played there on 6 March 1979.

Live at West Runton Pavilion is a milestone recording, one which I purchased with school dinner money shortly after it came out, and whose surfaces – machine-generated crags and rough contours – I came to know intimately, like a climber his favourite rock. It begins with a random, haywire scatter of analogue, as if the newly activated machines are spraying ideas everywhere to see what might stick, before giving way to a kitschy extended section of mid-twentieth-century dance-band music, as if channelling the sort of brassy, MOR tea-dance fare in which the venue had specialised before the advent of rock'n'roll. Decades later, Leyland James Kirby, the ambient artist also known as the Caretaker (an allusion to Jack Nicholson's role in *The Shining*), would poignantly frame this sort of music in his sympathetic explorations of the symptoms of Alzheimer's. In 1979, however, it still provided the dismally patterned aural carpeting of Radio 2's daily output, a part of the frustrating soundtrack to young people's lives.

From there, however, an analogue signal strikes up, like the first flashing lighthouse signal of an electrified music to come. What follows is a churning, looping deluge, reminiscent of Faust, like a ruthless agricultural process, as if machinery is tilling the dull earth to lay cable for the impending decade. Onwards and upwards pours the noise billowing from Miller's and Rental's wires and boxes, flooding out the venue, as if purging it of all its previous musical connotations, from the dance bands to Chuck, even the Pistols, until, around the fifteen-minute mark, in what feels like a Decisive Moment indeed, a silvery eruption, a three-note signal and a shuffle of drum machine burst up like a spinning top from the morass, and the immediate future – from OMD to Ultravox, Numan to Depeche Mode – is up and online. 1980 is months away.

From Thomas Leer to Martin Zero. In 1978, a producer going by that name went down to Salford Tech to catch one of the many bands who had taken up guitars in the wake of the Sex Pistols' appearance in Manchester. The producer had already carved his first historical mark by producing the Buzzcocks' indelible *Spiral Scratch* EP, and even had a hit, producing Graham Fellows's Jilted John single. It was a disastrous gig – the PA had broken down and the guitarist and bassist had to compensate as best they could – but the producer was impressed by the drummer, Stephen, and his industry and application. He also divined, amid the muddy push of fretboards and the distracted intensity of the vocals, a sense of space. A space in which he could work. 'It was a very big room, they were badly equipped, and they were still working into this space, making sure they got into the corners,' he later told Jon Savage.

The group had been known as Warsaw, a worthy post-punk moniker, suggestive of the cold war's permanent grey clouds, the twentieth-century promise of the world becoming a socialist utopia long since faded into a dreary oppression from which the only likely release was thermonuclear annihilation. They'd dumped that, however, in favour of the rather more dubious Joy Division. It was as Joy Division that they made their first recordings with Martin Zero, aka Martin Hannett: 'Digital' and 'Glass', their contributions to 1978's *A Factory Sample*, alongside the Durutti Column and Cabaret Voltaire.

Hannett had been a bassist himself but he wasn't especially musicianly in the conventional sense. He enjoyed the distance and contrast between treble and bass, the effect you could get on a snare drum if you isolated it, the way you could use echo, delay and reverb in ways that made the spaces between the playing as electric and as meaningful as the playing itself.

Although Hannett never claimed to be a creative element within Joy Division or co-author of their spirit – he had no hand in writing the songs – he can be credited with crucially enhancing their sound, adding vital details, teasing out the very best of them sonically. This he did in various strange ways: injunctions to play faster but more slowly at the same time; mild methods of psychological abuse, such as turning up the air conditioning to freezing in the studio. 'Martin did not like musicians,' Peter Hook later remarked. 'It was a constant battle with him. He was a genius but also a lunatic. He'd do things like go record the silence on the moors and listen back to it in the studio.' His curly hair and shades, meanwhile, gave him the air of that other martinet of the mixing desk, Phil Spector.

Among the ways Hannett helped seal and glaze the permanence of Joy Division, however, was through electronics. Ironically, the band had been signed to RCA but demanded to be released from their contract when the label insisted they add synthesizers for the purpose of softening their edge. With Hannett, though, Joy Division would use synths not just to add an icicle sharpness to their sound but to make metaphysical piercings.

The first synthesizers Hannett and guitarist Bernard Sumner owned were Transcendent 2000s and ARP Omnis. Hannett also owned and used several Jen SX1000s and an ETI 4600 modular synth. Images show Hannett himself at the controls, looking more au fait with their workings than the onlooking Sumner. Hannett, you might say, was the machine in the ghost of Joy Division.

On their debut, *Unknown Pleasures*, keyboards are less in evidence; there are, however, ingenious ambient features, such as the lift-shaft effect on 'Insight' – a spatial sleight that only adds to the overall feel of the album as sucking you into its charismatic, echo-laden black hole – and, on the same track, an ambush of *Space*

Invader-style munchkins. Then there is the strobe-lit drone and broken glass that strew the closing track, 'I Remember Nothing'.

By the time of 1980's *Closer*, electronics are like an artificial limb added to the Joy Division body, or maybe the means of dispersing their spiritual ectoplasm. All of this had as much to do with the sonics of the recording space as the instruments – drawing energy from architecture. 'We used a half-completed construction project as an echo room,' explained Hannett. 'A huge shell with plaster walls. I invented all these little tricks to do with generating sound images, like a holographic principle. Light and shade . . . I like deserted public spaces, empty office blocks. They give me a rush.'

On 'Atrocity Exhibition', Ian Curtis's homage to the J. G. Ballard collection of 'condensed novels', a machine-like clatter snakes remorselessly and impersonally through the track, subjects its lumps of guitar to a sort of evisceration. The effect reminds one of a Francis Bacon painting, in which flesh is ripped and tugged by invisible psychotic forces.

Track two, 'Isolation', is synthpop as pure ice, dispensed in sub-zero waves as if actively to repel human warmth. Borne by the wisp and slap of Stephen Morris's electronic drum pattern and under-pinned by Peter Hook's typically low-slung, high-register bass, it seems to sleigh and skitter impossibly, as if at the mercy of an imminent thaw, yet so precisely is it customised by Hannett that it has been preserved through the ages, and will be through ages to come.

And then the album's final two tracks, advancing like a sol-emn procession, as if in advance knowledge of Curtis's fate. The gothic cricket drones of 'Eternal' threaten to tropically overwhelm a track otherwise dominated by a sense of sad, sepulchral *froideur*; it's a paradox that elevates the track from ponderous despondency. Finally, 'Decades' continues in the same sombre, black-hooded vein: 'Here are the young men, the weight on their shoulders . . . we knocked on the doors of hell's darker chambers.' Precocious, but it's a precocity that is deserved. Its concluding grainy synth layers are drawn over the song like a shroud. Curtis's death was a pitiful one: a washing machine, a Macclesfield kitchen, the guilt of an everyday act of infidelity. It was a private tragedy. The production, however, of *Closer* is one of the key factors in lending Curtis's demise an inadvertent symbolism, the marble entombment of a myth and another paradox: the utterly perished and the imperishable.

Joy Division occur in that dark moment between the death of the modern and the birth of the postmodern (or the beginning of the post-space age). Slum clearances had taken place, to be replaced by nothing; the crater-like evocations of Joy Division's sound evoke this emptiness. Manchester and the environs from which the band's members were drawn seemed to be in a state of terminal decay. During the group's tenure, there was a breakdown of the city's sewerage system, which emitted a stench symbolic of the collapse of civic infrastructure. Joy Division represented a sense of collapse at personal, existential, local and global levels: from Curtis's private traumas as worked out through the lyrics of '24 Hours' or 'Shadowplay', to the imminent disaster about to be wrought by the incoming Conservative government, to the paralysing terror of nuclear war that saw CND's membership jump tenfold around 1980. All of this, however, is my reading. Joy Division themselves put up a northern bitterman's carapace in interviews, their comments essentially reducible to 'fuck off', saying as little as possible, as if journalistic inquiry might disturb the mystery of what they were drawn to do live and in the studio, or maybe force them to reflect on a music they preferred to channel instinctively.

As anyone who lived through the 1970s in the north knows, it was not as monochrome as represented in the photos of Anton Corbijn and Kevin Cummins – not that these brilliant images were deceitful, but they were super-real, not unlike the synths that shimmer round the edge of Joy Division. It was a place of hideous oranges and browns, garish flare-and-tanktop combinations, plastic signs in bad orange fonts outside cheap cafes, and patterned carpets. Monochrome felt like an escape from all of this; the silvery releases of synth in Joy Division's music feel like temporary escapes from the oppressive, cyclical grind of their traditional instrumentation, in the midst of which Curtis writhed like a trapped butterfly. The emissions of the aptly named Transcendent 2000 hint at other dimensions, perhaps only imaginable rather than within grasp – vaguely European dreams of Belgium, Kraftwerk, Herzog, Bowie's Euro-melancholia. Curtis was to be denied all of these things. Joy Division remained, alluringly frozen on the very edge of the 1980s.

I never saw Joy Division live, knew very little about them until the first edition of the *NME* appeared after several weeks off the shelves due to industrial action, the issue dated 14 June 1980 announcing Curtis's death a month earlier. My first exposure to them was 'Love Will Tear Us Apart': my ear's eye was drawn to the synth lines that drew diagonally across the track, like a solemn semaphore. Then there was 'Atmosphere'/'She's Lost Control', a pairing of absolute perfection.

The decades to follow did not pan out in the way Ian Curtis's frightened gaze appeared to foretell. There was no ice age, no apocalypse. Warsaw was liberated. The times became increasingly hedonistic and frivolous. Happy Mondays, happy pills. The European dreams were of Ibiza. And yet nothing has dimmed the immaculacy of 'Atmosphere'/'She's Lost Control'. The latter was an upgraded version of a track that had originally appeared on *Unknown Pleasures*. This new take was rid of the earlier version's dank reverb. Built around a taut, amplified snare drum, it impacts violently, like a flashlight. It's whiplash, urgent, on stalks, so brutally minimal that when the synths cascade sparsely in the fadeout, it feels like the stars are dancing in sympathy. Others used the same synthpop machinery, the same tunings, but, crucially, never in the same context.

Finally, 'Atmosphere'. For all the desperate sadness of Curtis's demise, it's like a pre-recorded message from beyond the grave. For all that the world changed in ways Curtis would never get to recognise, there is a strange, moving, even triumphant sense of consolation, a cheating of death, that occurs in these verses. All of this is signified by the fountain of synths that is the song's centrepiece, as magnificently inappropriate as confetti at a funeral. Despite his personal extinction, despite the way the world eventually walked away, this track sealed Joy Division's permanence.

Today, Sheffield is a postmodern, heritage version of itself, the area surrounding the station brightly scrubbed and boasting a water feature as a symbol of perpetual self-cleansing, as well as a ghastly piece of doggerel carved in stone paying tribute to the city's charms. Rather than a centre of the steel industry, it nowadays seems to have put itself at the service of the much-expanded university. The city is still flanked by hills, a reminder of the raw beauty of the Peak District that lies just twenty minutes away, but it is a far cry from its grim heyday. Destitute fossils of pubs and vestigial blocks of grand nineteenth-century architecture nestle with depressing neatness alongside various civic heritage and commercial initiatives dating from the Blair years. It's like *Threads* never happened.

Back in the 1970s, the air was still grimy and toxic, the cultural landscape featureless apart from Tony Christie. The Sheffield scene that emerged revolved around Cabaret Voltaire, at a pub, the Beehive, near their Western Works studio in West Street. Among the assorted would-be Futurists and overcoated post-punksters, such as Clock DVA, were a group of floppy-haired young men who had started life as the Future but would switch their moniker to the Human League.

The substance of the Human League originally lay in its two founders, Ian Craig Marsh and Martyn Ware, a pair of computer operators who decided to acquire a Korg 700S. Deciding that they

needed a visual focus for their instrumental musings, they brought
in a vocalist, a hospital porter called Philip Oakey. Having released
the portentous 'Being Boiled', in which Oakey intoned nonsense
lyrics with utter conviction, they decided that they needed to
enhance their visuals still more and brought in Adrian Wright,
whose collection of sci-fi and vintage memorabilia – including
3,500 bubblegum cards, 1960s *Observer* magazines and horror
and sci-fi paraphernalia – would provide a sort of mulch for the
Human League as they approached the threshold of the 1980s.

Weaponised with the past to face the future, their early sets were
highlighted by a version of the Delia Derbyshire-created theme
to *Doctor Who*. In 1979, they released the Eisensteinian EP *The
Dignity of Labour*, a salute to Yuri Gagarin, told in vaulting electronic strokes using the Roland System 100 as their toolkit. They
further covered Gary Glitter's 'Rock'n'Roll Part II', in a manner
which sounded a death knell for rock'n'roll. Their debut album,
Reproduction, featured 'Empire State Human', in which Oakey
imagined growing 'tall, tall, tall, as big as a wall, wall, wall', through
sheer 'concentration'. While Marsh and Ware were immersed in
the adventures of board and wire afforded by the new generation
of affordable electronics, Oakey saw no reason why he, his hair and
the Human League could not become pop, as big as a wall. Why
not? Everyone else was doing it. Oakey quarrelled with Ware, and
Ware and Marsh left the group, agreeing that Oakey and Wright
could keep the name Human League but also deal with the debts
they had accrued.

The Human League now consisted of a haircut and a collection
of slides. Realising the need to add substance to the group, Oakey
went to a nightclub in Sheffield city centre and spotted two teenage girls, Joanne Catherall and Susanne Sulley, 'dancing differently
to anyone else in the building'. Their defiantly ill-co-ordinated
efforts would remain core to the Human League throughout their
years of success. Oh, and then they hired some musicians.

The new Human League released a single, 'Boys and Girls', on 21 February 1981, minus the girls. It was inauspicious in every way, looking in briefly at number forty-eight in the charts. Just a month later, Marsh and Ware made their own altogether more substantive chart smackdown with '(We Don't Need This) Fascist Groove Thang', immediately hailed by Paul Morley as one of the greatest singles of all time. Impetuous, but maybe not wrong. Heaven 17 were now a trio featuring Glenn Gregory – their original first choice of frontman for the Human League, but who had been unavailable at the time – his deadpan, chin-in-chest vocals perfect for skating across the slick chromium surfaces of Marsh and Ware's synth generations.

Tongue-in-cheek but deadly earnest and lethally brilliant, '(We Don't Need This) Fascist Groove Thang' was a protest song against the march of the right on both sides of the Atlantic, expressed in a parody of the funk vernacular. At a time when politically minded pop commentators, like the *NME* cartoonist Ray Lowry, were lamenting the post-punk drive towards the hedonism of the dancefloor it was an inspired soldering. The multi-layering of the drum programming gave it a near-impossibly accelerated feel, like a rapid, urgent mobilisation brought on by the prospect of a Ronald Reagan presidency. At the same time, it was a demonstration of synthpop's potency and ability to marshal new powers for new, more complex times. The likes of the Clash suddenly felt like stragglers, still toting their guitars like spaghetti-western rifles in a machine-gun age. With this single Heaven 17 were moving faster than Pacman, harder and smarter, too. Keep up if you dare.

Heaven 17 would follow up 'Fascist Groove Thang' with *Penthouse and Pavement*, a melange of white funk and polemical lyrics delivered from within the framework of electronics buffed to a high shine. The cover featured animations of the group members looking uncannily like the yuppies who would be ubiquitous in 1987, several years hence. Sporting ponytails and pinstripe suits,

against a backdrop of glass-fronted office blocks, and working on
keyboards, telephones and tape machines, they were not ragged
outlaws looking on helplessly in torn jeans but a group who would
engage with the system by using its own technologies, subverting
from within. Was this the group of the 1980s?

Phil Oakey, meanwhile, planned a new album with the Human
League. He had initially considered calling it 'Jihad', perhaps still a
little in thrall to the spirit of Cabaret Voltaire, whose latest album,
designed to conjure geopolitical nightmares, was called *Red Mecca*.
Oakey decided against the idea, since he anticipated having repeatedly to explain its meaning to journalists.

In 1982, Oakey made a vow to the *NME*'s Charles Shaar
Murray: 'I always said that there would only be two albums with
Martyn, and I've said to a few people that there'll only be one more
Human League album after *Dare* because I don't want it to run
forever. There is something trashy about the Human League that
ought to be stopped at some stage.'

With ex-Material drummer Fred Maher now making up the Scritti
Politti trio, Green Gartside, the founder member of the erstwhile
DIY post-punksters, approached Arif Mardin, best known for
his production work with Chaka Khan, particularly on her 1981
album *What Cha' Gonna Do for Me*, which featured the splash-funk
of 'I Know You, I Live You' and the dappled 'Any Old Sunday'.
At a time when white hipsters were turning to black music for the
earthy, worthy antiquity of old 1960s grooves, Green was steeped
in its most recent modernistic manifestations. (I first learned of
the existence of Run-DMC from reading a Green interview.) He
wasn't interested in grit – all that 'soulfulness, honesty, earnestness'
– he was interested in the gloss, contemporary black gloss, and the
exquisite twist a Mardin could bring to his material.

Cupid & Psyche 85 sat alongside the black boombox brilliance of
Trevor Horn's production work with Frankie Goes to Hollywood,

Propaganda and the Art of Noise. Both shared a predilection for the Orch5, for example, whose single symphonic stabbing effect was said to have been used on Rockers Revenge's 'Walking on Sunshine', Afrika Bambaataa's 'Planet Rock' and, most recently, the Art of Noise's 'Close (to the Edit)'. Perhaps its origin as an idea, however, is in Chic's 'Good Times', that sound of the strings snapping back as if to simulate a snort of cocaine.

If Trevor Horn's productions sometimes overwhelm their subjects with a black box of tricks, on *Cupid & Psyche 85* there's a perfect balance between material and medium. Yes, Maher's LinnDrum made for a huge scaffolding, the biggest and best of the 1980s. Granted, American keyboardist David Gamson can take great credit for this album (as co-writer of some songs also), adding layer upon layer of PPG Wave 2.3, Minimoog, Yamaha DX7, Oberheim OB-X, Fairlight CMI and Roland's MSQ-700, Jupiter 8 and JX-8P, all of this jewellery perfectly arranged and presented on a black velvet backdrop – mass music of quality and distinction. However, it's Green's dialectical mastery that raises *Cupid & Psyche 85* to its pinnacle status.

The very title of the album is indicative of Green's philosophical take: that all is 'provisional'. Pop is full of ideals – the sweetest this, the perfect that – and Green's songs reflect this ironically because he believes such ideals are open to interrogation, are shifting and illusory. Hence titles like 'Perfect Way' and 'Absolute', while 'Wood Beez (Pray Like Aretha Franklin)' alludes to a singer regarded wistfully by white soul crooners like George Michael as representing some unmatchable state of holy pop grace. Green's lyrics see him peel away these layers of certainty, at which point the pop song and its traditionally romantic subject matter are revealed as a metaphor for broader ideals and conditions, political, social, philosophical.

These agonies, however, are hard-candy-coated, in a music that seems to ascend to states of glittering immaculacy, whose validity is questioned in the lyrics, the searchlights somehow all the brighter because the search is futile. The cod-reggae gait of 'The Word Girl' is showered in sporadic bursts of diamond manna, its perfect curves stressed by a heavenly upward arc in the bridge. No pop star was more studious than Green, yet there's absolutely nothing studied about his ability to turn a melody. 'Wood Beez', simulated by the pirouettes of contemporary dancer Michael Clark in the video, features a swooning, starlit chorus and synths that descend in chunks like white plaster from the ceiling as if Franklin herself were shrieking gospel. 'Absolute' is cavernous, the keyboards shimmering galactic, soaring and plunging in tandem with Green's vocals.

Cupid & Psyche 85 is an album absolutely of its time, a showcase for the latest in high-budget mid-1980s state-of-the-art studio technology, as bold as it is commercial. It is at once date-stamped and timeless. Its machinery of sampling and sequencing would soon become more developed and widespread, and yet this is not a record that 'anticipates' anything further down the line as such; rather it is a supreme pop expression, to be ranked alongside ABC's *The Lexicon of Love*. It uses samples, but not in the referential manner of early sampling, full of nods and winks, quotes and references. *Cupid & Psyche 85* refers to itself only, its exquisitely twisted sheet layers of synth acting as corridors of mirrors; it's an album in the distinctive depths of whose surfaces the listener can, perversely, admire themselves. It's exquisite, but with a built-in critique of its own exquisiteness. It's an album that has its cake and deconstructs it.

Perhaps Green himself reflected that paradox. In interviews, while expanding with post-structuralist meticulousness on the uncertainty that underlies all things, he could come across as absolutely assured of his own rightness and superior analysis. In this case, it was utterly correct to go pop, to eschew the sort of 'importance' vaguely hankered after by the likes of Talk Talk's Mark

Hollis which lay somewhere beyond the margins. For Green, the progressions of the white avant-garde were deluded, invalid, irrelevant. The great Now, the splashback of the moment, was contemporary African American music, soul × machinery, the subject of Green's contemplation from afar. 1985 – the perfect moment. However, come 1988, the wheel had rotated 180 degrees. White rock was enjoying a ghostly resurgence and white pop stars mediating black American music had become a cliché. That didn't stop Green making what was effectively *Cupid & Psyche* part 2, as if he had settled on a Great Permanence in 1985 rather than something provisional. All the more ironic, then, that the 1988 album should have been titled *Provisional*.

1985 saw peak Scritti – pretty much matchless, with the exception of Kate Bush's *Hounds of Love* and Prefab Sprout's *Steve McQueen*. On both of those albums, synths waft and shadow subtly, in a manner that would soon be considered obsolete as the technology moved on. Consequently, all three albums feel magnificently preserved, even as 1985 has melted into air.

In 1993, Depeche Mode were on top of the world. By this point, they had outlasted just about everything there was to outlast. Industrial, rave, techno, metal, grunge, all were coalescing into a swirl of sludge as trends and narratives began to slow down and slop over into one another. That collective tide was the one that the Mode sailed. Initially regarded as the sort of paper-thin flunkies who would be blown back to Basildon the moment the flimsy trend that had blown them onto *Top of the Pops* in the first place abated, Depeche Mode had proven both resilient and absorbent. Moreover, unlike even the mistrusted Duran Duran, they had made the transition to American success. Theirs was an unexpected hardness. In the US, however, their lead singer, Dave Gahan, suffered the ravages of that success. Isolated, gaunt, scarred and tattooed to within an inch of his pampered, pitiful life, as blackened as Johnny Cash, living in apartments with blacked-out windows, he was about to suffer backstage in New Orleans the sort of near-death experience, the Act Two hitherto unassociated with synth bands: total collapse brought on by a surfeit of booze and hard drugs, because when you reach the top and there's nothing there, that's what you do.

Basildon. As with Neasden, there's an inherent comedy in the name, its shallow history as a 'new town' created after World War II to take on London's overspill adding to its sense of provincial banality. How very Basildon that in 2010 they erected a miniature version of the white Hollywood sign boasting the town's name in a bid to attract tourists. Having played host to a number of heavy industrial firms, such as Ford, from the 1960s onwards, it is mainly memorable for its construction of an enormous shopping mall and for voting in larger numbers than expected for John Major, an early indication on election night 1992 of yet another Conservative victory. And for spawning Depeche Mode.

There is, though, a strangeness about the essential depths of England, obscure forces lurking in its backwaters, which give a place like Basildon its unique abnormality. As with Joy Division and Greater Manchester, Depeche Mode were in some ways typical specimens of the place, broad of accent and blokeish rather than foppish. 'We're *Sun* readers, basically,' Martin Gore once said. However, Depeche Mode's various band members were of somewhat intense provenance. Vince Clarke and Martin Fletcher were born-again Christians right through their teen years. Gore, whose own sense of moral introspection saw him oscillate between the virtues of devout vegetarianism and assorted rock'n'roll vices, had been somewhat fazed to learn that his real father was an African American GI, while Dave Gahan was busy accumulating a modest rap sheet for petty criminality.

It was not Kraftwerk but punk that fired up Depeche Mode. In later years, when punk appeared to have been banished to a handful of scowling, Mohican-haired beer-swillers on a bench on the King's Road and new pop was king, Gahan surprised an interviewer by chanting the words to Sham 69's 'Borstal Breakout', before adding, 'Those were the days of proper music.'

Further fired up by the dark pop clouds being generated by Orchestral Manoeuvres in the Dark, the Human League, Gary Numan and the Cure, the various Mode members in their preincarnations began to eschew conventional instruments in favour of electronic keyboards like the Minimoog and the Yamaha CS-5. Gore described synths as 'punk instruments, a do-it-yourself kind of tool', a still easier means of access to music for those who couldn't even afford vans or amps, who had to walk to gigs.

All in all, the Mode felt unremarkable. When they arrived on the scene, they were hardly trailblazers; indeed, they seemed somewhat guileless – when they were interviewed about the subject matter of their debut single, 'Dreaming of Me', Gahan piped up with the question, 'What's a narcissist?' Daniel Miller, head of Mute Records, where they were eventually to find their home, found them so nondescript the first time he was exposed to them that he overlooked them completely (but not the second time). They felt like the sort of group that if they did not exist, it would not be necessary to invent them. Miller had, however, invented a group, the Silicon Teens, a fictional teen synthpop outfit, a marvel of inauthenticity which had pulled the wool over many pairs of eyes. 'They could only play one note at a time,' noted Miller of their minimal compactness. Clean, no chords, no messing.

Still, with songwriter Vince Clarke taking up all songwriting duties, Depeche Mode had a knack of hitting the sweet spot every time on their keyboards. 'New Life' shuffled and sashayed across the dancefloor tiles with nifty, machinic gloss. 'I Just Can't Get Enough' was a sparkling affair, deceptively slight, the sort of pop item that would be discarded like a glittered glove come the next fashion season. Even by 2006, however, the Mode were playing it live, accompanied by a veritable Luftwaffe of electronics, its riff delivered with imposing, Front 242-style density.

Clarke was a strange one. He sat out high-profile interviews. It was as if he felt the machinery of pop he had set in train was overtaking him, and the group. A schedule, a programme of media obligations and appearances had kicked in, which to him was far more insidious than the machinery of machines, the toys he wanted to play with. He could bear it no more, and Clarke, the creative mainstay of the group, abruptly quit following the first album. He'd grown apart from the rest of the group, grown contemptuous of their mannequin willingness to do whatever their commercial handlers asked of them. He would pack up and go on to play the deadpan keyboard foil first to Alison Moyet in Yazoo, and then to Andy Bell in Erasure, pegging down their ballooning flamboyance and soulfulness with his tautly memorable keyboard lines, a lone figure in the back row.

Surely that was the Mode clobbered. 'I think we should have been slightly more worried than we were,' Gore would later comment.

'Our biggest singles have been the ones on which Joanne and I have made the biggest vocal contribution. It's not to slag off Philip, it's just the truth. Look at the sales figures for "Fascination", "Don't You Want Me" and "Human",' Susanne Sulley told me when I interviewed the Human League in 2001, at which point I was interviewing them, this long-standing institution, at the regular rate of once a decade, each time just a stone's throw from Sheffield railway station, each time treated to a tour around a mini-museum of their vintage keyboard units, enclosed in glass cases.

Phil Oakey doesn't take offence. He agrees.

'The musos who more or less control the music business underestimate the communications aspect of what we do,' he says. 'Pop music is about communication between like-minded people. It's

D.A.F. The Düsseldorf duo whose music was still more minimal than their seventies precursors Kraftwerk, with a physicality all their own.

Suicide. More punk than punk, they were bottled off stage by enraged fans when they supported The Clash.

Scritti Politti. Scratchy, ideological post-punksters who consciously turned pop with a dazzlingly wrought sheen.

Cabaret Voltaire. Inspired by Krautrock, James Brown and Williams Burroughs, the Sheffield trio added multiple dimensions to post-punk.

Jeff Mills: the most gruelling and futuristic of the techno pioneers.

Derrick May: the architect of techno, the modernistic sound born in the ruins of Detroit.

The Aphex Twin: a hugely prolific Warp artist and always a disquieting pop presence.

William Basinski, who incorporated physical decay as a musical factor in his poignant masterpiece *The Disintegration Loops*.

Fatboy Slim. Everybody is happy.

Janelle Monáe: one of the stars of the cyberworld of twenty-first-century R&B.

Deadmau5: the high priest of EDM, in which dance music took on the scale of stadium rock.

not about great singers. The people who succeed are the ones that are so good that they don't sound too much like Michael Jackson, or the ones that you know what they're talking about, just from their voices. Like John Lydon or Neil Tennant. Ordinary people. We're ordinary people.'

The latest musicians hired by the group to perform the necessary and not-to-be-sniffed-at keyboard chores, Russell Dennett and Neil Sutton, do not give their opinions. They are absent from the interview.

Ordinariness was the factor plastered over the alien strangeness in which the Human League had initially traded. Around 1981, I remember going to the Leeds Warehouse, the only club in that city that played the truly emergent electronic and new pop sounds of the early part of the decade, rather than the more mainstream fare of Duran Duran and the Jam, which was more the staple of the junior common room and mobile discos. Around that time *The Face* had put out their 'hard times' cover, an exercise in sartorial rebranding which saw torn denim supplant the more flamboyant garb of the New Romantic era. Still, the Human League were a part of the overall defiantly glam response to the first great recession to hit the north. The big, shiny, sequenced sounds of a synthpop hit were part of the same sonic continuum as the rattle of a bucket of coins on a street corner. 'Hard Times' was also the title of a Human League release, its big synth theme resounding like a siren's wail as Sulley, Catherall and Oakey chanted the title over and over like a terse bullet point. I remember Sulley- and Catherall-alikes moving uncoordinatedly up and down the dancefloor, together but incapable and unwilling to sway precisely in sync. They were similarly frocked in outfits doubtless picked up from second-hand shops, reclaimed and modified rather than bought off the peg from Top Shop or H&M.

Before that came 'The Sound of the Crowd', and the Human League's first appearance on *Top of the Pops*. Large tape reels signified the wheels of electronic industry, while Phil Oakey still hadn't cropped the fringe that curtained half his face (a look I shamelessly copied during my sixth-form years, along with a little Midge Ure moustache – all facial bases covered). Most striking, however, were Sulley and Catherall, attacking the song with their determined non-choreography, Sulley brandishing an imaginary lasso, Catherall in high heels stamping on the beats as if trying to squash snails on the dancefloor. This was ordinariness *in excelsis*, dancing as you saw out in clubs, dancing not just to the actual song but to the song as it played in your imagination, acting out its attitude rather than conforming exactly to its rhythm. 'Everyone would absolutely agree with me: I can't keep time,' Catherall would tell the *Guardian*'s Paul Lester. 'I can't do step class or anything like that at the gym, because I've got no rhythm.'

Moreover, this was dancing in the true analogue spirit – spontaneous, independent, imprecise, non-preset. Phil Oakey once said that the Human League were making music as all music would be made in the future (i.e. in a mechanical, post-guitar age). In fact, it did not pan out like that. Guitars made their comeback, in a corollary to perma-conservative cultural and political times, while a digital era of electronic pop brought with it a more digitalised, disciplined choreography that in its faintly joyless bump'n'grind felt regressive, post-feminist (which, in effect, is to say, pre-feminist). The League themselves had to militate against this when they were invited onto the American show *Solid Gold*, whose producers tried to impose their own professional choreographed go-go dancers on them. An act of sheer, more uncomprehending pop sacrilege it is hard to imagine. 'We don't have dancers – that's a rule,' insisted Oakey.

With *Dare*, the Human League captured the spirit of the pop age like an electric eel by the tail. This was the future, for the time being, and this was now. Electric typewriters, shiny lipgloss, reflections in shop windows, hard stares. 'Love Action (I Believe in

Love)' struck up with a mewling, underlying pulse, then an elaborate dial-up synthtone and then 'Phil talking', expounding his typically home-baked philosophy over an electropop that was at once a silver lining of escapism and a representation of the times, their pulse and the pathways we walked to and from work. Glad time it was to dance away the day's frustrations, economic, social, political and sexual, in northern clubs, with Soft Cell cued to come up next. Much of the credit for the Human League's sound has to go to Martin Rushent, who, like Martin Hannett with Joy Division, helped conceive, frame and realise their electric dreams. Basically, they would bash something out, waywardly, on a keyboard, with added syndrums, and take it to Rushent, who would run it through the computer to make it presentable for mass consumption. But for all that, he was never close to being the essence of the group, neither superficially nor spiritually.

The Human League sealed their dominance with 'Don't You Want Me', which, even more than 'Love Action', would, over the decade as well as the decades to come, become embedded in the sonic warp of British life, its drama reflecting to a degree the drama that existed romantically in the Oakey–Catherall–Sulley axis. Oakey dated Catherall; they split up, but the trio would remain together as everything and everyone else around them fell away and fell apart.

Following the departure of Vince Clarke, Depeche Mode might easily have disbanded and melted back into their old jobs as bank clerks or non-occupations such as petty crime. That this didn't happen was down to a variety of factors: the care they were afforded by being on Mute, a small indie label with a small roster, which they might not have enjoyed had they been signed to a major, along with the personal attention of Daniel Miller; the fact that in Martin Gore they had an able stand-in who'd already proved his songwriting skills; their desire to retain their foothold in the pop world, of which Clarke had been disdainful; but, crucially, they were about something, tapped into deeper undercurrents – depravity and political indignation, the virtues and vices of the early-1980s experimental underground – all of which were coming up electric.

Granted, there was a moroseness, almost valedictory, about their immediate follow-up album, *A Broken Frame*, penned entirely by Gore and leading off with the single 'Leave in Silence', which was about the quiet termination of a tempestuous relationship ('This will be the last time / I think I said that last time'). Yet while such gloom might have seemed out of kilter with the garishly overlit early-1980s new-pop ethic of mandatory brassy upfulness, with songs like this Depeche Mode were sowing black seeds. An unlikely, disaffected swell of people were listening.

However, the third album, 1983's *Construction Time Again*, signalled an explicit determination to clamber out of their slough of despond. Depeche Mode were tracking the methods of outfits like Einstürzende Neubauten and Test Dept, 'metal bashers' who supplemented their electronic music with the physical field-recorded sounds of metal detritus and discarded parts of a disintegrating post-industrial society, taking up broken metal pipes like cudgels and, in the process, deconstructing/reconstructing popular music. It was a fairly short-lived trope, which too easily become codified as a sort of modern skiffle, with cheerfully improvisational theatre groups leaping around in dungarees to the rhythmic accompaniment of dustbin lids. However, in the moment the idea was at its white-hottest, Depeche Mode converted it into pop ore, with hits like 'Everything Counts', a direct attack on corporate greed whose backdrop of sampled noise simulated the havoc such bodies wrought on the social structure.

(Co-running a club night in the early 1980s, we once had ranting poet Attila the Stockbroker in as a guest, who had often railed in somewhat unreconstructed terms against the likes of Depeche

Mode, whom he saw as deserters of the true agitpop spirit of punk, foppish and apolitical. On being played 'Everything Counts' he offered a qualified onstage mea culpa, though he did insist on doing a mincing, tinkly parody of the Mode sound.)

Despite the often clumsy descents into handwringing angst of some of Gore's lyrics, as on 'People Are People' ('So why should it be / that you and I should get along so awfully'), they seemed impervious to failure, drawing ever-bigger crowds from the shadows. 'People Are People' would be their biggest international hit to date.

The more Depeche Mode descended as people, the higher they ascended commercially and the wider their influence spread. 1986's *Black Celebration* was the creative upshot of Martin Gore following Bowie's footsteps and relocating to Berlin, with a view to acting out his own dark cabaret, reading Camus and Brecht and dressing in women's clothing and rubber S&M garb. Dave Gahan looked on disdainfully – he was going through a sober patch in the mid-1980s – before later his own absorption in his role as frontman and spinning dervish saw him gradually cut himself off and anaesthetise himself with booze and drugs. But his deterioration contrasted with the ever-ruder health the band were enjoying. Americans in particular found something authentic in their dark matter and atmospherics, their objections to invading 1980s English haircut bands waived in the case of the Mode. By 1990, with *Violator*, they were, in the eyes of millions, leather-clad, stadium-filling symbols of the triumphant ubiquity of synths as valid rock instruments, channels of male authenticity rather than disposable pop toys for girls. It was, however, an evolutionary process that would be achieved at great personal cost to their lead singer. Substance at the expense of substance abuse.

Despite mostly exceeding its own expectations with regard to the extent to which it would occupy the future – in 1980, it felt optimistic to dream that there would be a 1985, let alone a 2018 – electropop had its share of Missing Boys, to co-opt the title of the Durutti Column's paean to Ian Curtis. Robert Rental dropped away from the front line of synthpop almost the moment it was established – he died of lung cancer in 2000. Thomas Leer, his old *compadre*, made the brilliant *4 Movements* EP, an exquisite colourisation of the ideas he had sketched in synth charcoal on his earliest releases, followed by the album *Contradictions*, and yet he found few takers in the aggressive pop marketplace.

John Foxx left Ultravox to be replaced by journeyman of journeymen Midge Ure, only to return when electronic dance music dissolved into the abstracts of ambient and rave. Figures like Thomas ('He Blinded Me with Science') Dolby and Landscape ('Einstein a Go-Go'), who perhaps overplayed the boffin-ish aspects of synthpop, gave way too as the music became quotidian in pop, though Dolby was a discreet influence as a producer on Prefab Sprout's 1985 masterpiece *Steve McQueen* – the banjos on opening track 'Faron Young' were actually programmed by Dolby. There were enigmatic, electronic pop pearls that were washed utterly away by public indifference – Video Aventures' 1981 EP *Musique pour garçons et filles*, a series of Satie-esque miniature electronic sketches of irresistible cartoon panache, remains pristine through sheer underexposure.

Most tragic was the case of Düsseldorf's Wolfgang Riechmann. He had started musical life in the 1960s in the proto-Krautrock group Spirits of Sound, alongside Kraftwerk's Wolfgang Flür. His career faltered in the 1970s, but he resurfaced in 1978 with the electropop album *Wunderbar* – a corollary to Kraftwerk's *Man-Machine*, released the same year – his hair dyed blue and with matching lipstick, as if to invite further contrast/comparison with Hütter and co. An album of compact, futuristic, icicle warmth, the title track in particular is a spectral, melodic instrumental, spangled with the effects of the day, reminiscent of Cluster but projecting forward into the imagined 1980s. Riechmann never reached the '80s. In January 1979, he was unlucky enough to be in a bar in Düsseldorf's Altstadt, where he was confronted by a pair of drunks who took exception to his appearance. They set upon him and stabbed him; he later died of his wounds. Synthpop's first martyr, perhaps.

Ian Curtis had hanged himself on the eve of Joy Division's planned first tour of America. There was an inadvertent symbolism here, as Joy Division did not share what Simon Frith once called rock'n'roll's essential 'fascination with America'. Curtis's gaze was set towards Europe. The remaining members of the group, however, now travelling under the moniker of New Order, did travel to the States and were fatefully taken by the emerging 'electro-funk' club scene there, in which Arthur Baker was a lead player. They would shed their more gothic electronic trappings and become increasingly dance-orientated and sequencer-driven, albeit as a counterpoint to the deadpan solemnity of Bernard Sumner's vocals and Peter Hook's lugubrious driving basslines. This dance noir would reach its apotheosis with 'Blue Monday', prefaced by a legendary live *Top of the Pops* appearance in 1983 that revealed all of their musical fragility when exposed in real time. No matter. As a synthesis of Joy Division's magisterial shadowplay and the radical electronic dance ethos of the early 1980s, the song would become so successful as to be a cliché. I recall being there the night it was rolled out at the Leeds Warehouse, played four times within an hour, and dancing to it time and again in a state of total absorption, drink- and drug-free, oblivious to the young things in physical proximity to me.

Thereafter, New Order developed a synth groove that saw them ride the 1980s like a quad bike: 'Confusion', 'True Faith', barely breaking stride, the surviving, thriving link between the gothic despair of the late 1970s and the Madchester delirium of the late '80s, whose acid squelch they mimicked on 1988's 'Fine Time', recorded in Ibiza. Sumner began to sing the praises of the Prozac with which he had cured himself of a fifteen-month creative block and, by the late 1990s, true to themselves and yet somehow the opposite of their old selves, they were playing to Britpop-crazed audiences bobbing en masse. With 'World in Motion' they even managed to cheerlead England's 1990 World Cup team without upsetting too many people – the logically evolved, increasingly electronic New Order sound was that mainstream.

New Order and Depeche Mode occasionally sounded in tandem. Take 1990's 'Enjoy the Silence' by the Mode (what was it with Depeche Mode and silence? Is to speak and to spell to suffer? Was the taciturn ring-fencing it implied part of the secret to their durability?). It loped with the same stoically elegant gait of any New Order hit from around the same time.

Still, despite the fact that they were never outright originators, and often faced accusations of triteness from British music critics, subsequent beatmakers found an inspiration in Depeche Mode that they did not find elsewhere. DJ Shadow, who in 1996 created the sample-based trip-hop masterpiece that was *Endtroducing*, said that it was Depeche Mode who had introduced him to synth music proper, that they were the only group he listened to outside of hip hop. Something about the way they plotted their music appealed to him. House innovators claimed Depeche Mode as precursors, even to the bemusement of the band themselves. 'It was clean and progressive and you could dance to it,' said Inner City's Kevin Saunderson.

Ricardo Villalobos, perhaps the foremost auteur of minimal techno, started musical life as an ardent Depeche Mode fan and imitator; all of the ultra-offbeat excursions and strangely filtered, looping mixes that have snaked from his rhythm boxes over the years find their origin in his Mode appreciation. Jacques Lu Cont's remix of 'A Pain that I'm Used To', building and grinding and reviving, not only captures the sheer gnarl and persistence of

Depeche Mode's career, built on a pleasure/pain principle, but also demonstrates how today's innovators may have extracted more from Depeche Mode's music than the Basildon boys themselves consciously intended to put in in the first place.

As for the Human League, they honestly attempted a variety of metamorphoses throughout their intermittent career, while bloody-mindedly remaining true to their fiercely, extraordinarily ordinary selves. They tried political handwringing with 'Lebanon', 1980s Motown pastiche with 'Mirror Man', went to Minneapolis and attempted to partake of the silken lusciousness of Jimmy Jam and Terry Lewis, yielding the wonderful 'Human', though they were best when they hewed closest to the *Dare* principle, with the wonderfully wobbly 'Keep Feeling Fascination', in particular, a masterpiece of knowing pop naivety, perfectly turned; watch the video and see the fleeting, sardonically polite smile Joanne Catherall delivers as the camera closes in on her dancing midway through the song. It quietly, subtly epitomises why she is one of the great siren keepers of the spirit of electropop. Maybe it's a northern thing. In 1990, when I met them, they were nervously optimistic about the studio they had just invested in, promising an album every year to maintain its upkeep. When I interviewed them again just over ten years later, they were reminiscing on the financial destitution and nervous breakdowns this business decision had visited on them.

They survive. Come the twenty-first century, and every few years they play the Royal Albert Hall, maybe, or the Royal Festival Hall, essentially a vocal threesome, belting out 'Don't You Want Me' and 'Love Action' to ever better, ever more upgraded light shows that put the basic filters of their *Top of the Pops* days to shame, while looking like immaculately preserved versions of themselves; it's not unlike Kraftwerk's permanently touring re-presentation of their 1970s and '80s canon. They're extending their fifteen minutes of fame into eternity, flying through the decades in a 1980

Tardis, and everyone with an opinion on them surely wishes them well.

There is, after all, a sense that despite electronics being permanently wired into pop today and forever, 'electropop' is an extinct species now that the otherness of electro has been lost. Later incarnations like Ladytron, who tried to re-establish that distance between (wo)man and machine with 'Playgirl', could not dispute that despite the wonderful 1980s manqué contours of their single, they were dealing in retro pastiche. Has all that was once substantial vanished into mp3 air?

To describe the likes of Depeche Mode as hard or substantial might well raise eyebrows, for during the late 1970s began to pump a new electronic music whose density was arguably even greater – ambient.

PART FOUR

13

BRIAN ENO, THE APHEX TWIN AND AMBIENT'S LATE ARRIVAL

'I've always felt that subtraction was as important a process in music as addition. The bias in our culture is towards being additive – do more, get more, eat more, play more, spend more,' Brian Eno told me when I asked him what prompted him to (re)inaugurate the concept of ambient music at a time when it was utterly alien to rock and pop culture. 'In the 1970s, the impulse was overdub more! I preferred the other direction. I started making up cassettes of quieter, slower music. I valued music that was about creating space, not just filling it.'

Eno is the sort of outsider, the anti-force that popular music depends upon for its eventual shape. Like many kids my age, I first became aware of him during the glam-rock era, on *Top of the Pops*, the show on which a sensation-starved younger generation depended for their weekly morsel of tinsel. I bracketed him then alongside Steve Priest of Sweet: shockingly effeminate, pouting, spangly, a provocateur of short-back-and-sided elderly Britain whose purpose seemed to be to out-glam the leader of the group, who represented moderation by comparison. I remember his VCS3 synth diallings zigzagging across my young mind, blazing electric scorch marks that outdid even those laid by Giorgio Moroder on Chicory Tip's 'Son of My Father'. Then he was gone – extinct like a burned-out bulb in the pop scheme of things, I assumed, fallen away to make way for the Bay City Rollers, or whatever was coming next.

I had no idea then that he had been edged out by bandleader Bryan Ferry, who sensed that Eno was taking up too much of Roxy Music's limelight and duly reasserted his top-dog status. I only renewed acquaintance with him in my late teens, through a library copy of *Here Come the Warm Jets*, and then seeing him staring out in a dry, scholarly, penetrative manner from the pages of *NME*, in a feature about his album *Music for Films*. So that's where he ended up.

Brian Eno was described admiringly by Damon Albarn as having 'not a rock'n'roll bone in his body'. Like Kraftwerk, he seemed to represent a calculated offence against the earthy, instinctive, male-driven spirit of 1970s rock. He was arch, effete, cerebral. He drew diagrams on the backs of his albums. He hung out with Germans. In time, he would take a considered interest in perfumes rather than drinking in the honest cocktail of armpit, beer and cigarette smells of the rock moshpit. He would have taken the description 'pretentious' as a compliment, because pretentious, in the best, non-pejorative sense of the word, he was.

However, unlike colleagues and contemporaries such as Michael Nyman and Gavin Bryars, he wasn't someone whose career would be confined to academe or the fringes of contemporary classical music. His attitude towards pop is reticent at times; when I asked him if he considered himself a pop musician, he gave a typically Eno-esque, round-the-houses, self-deprecating response: 'It's funny, when people ask me what I do, I certainly don't say that, but when pressed, I have to say I make pop records! I don't know what else there is to say – there's no other word for what I do. If I'm on a plane now, and people ask, I say I'm a patents attorney. Unfortunately, one time the man who asked was a patents attorney himself, which was awkward . . .'

Yet there was always a touch of the attention-seeker about Eno that drew him to pop's flame. He was, briefly though he dallied with the genre, pop *in extremis*; even Bowie seemed sober and

MOR next to him. Furthermore, he was, somewhat improbably, always highly, unabashedly sexed, profoundly heterosexual by inclination. He seemed to sit somewhere between John Cage and Kiss's Gene Simmons. It was necessary that he be all of these things, that he impacted the way he did, for him and his ideas to gain the traction they did.

He's paradoxical, someone who is literally 'eccentric' in his aversion to centrism and orthodoxy, yet someone who as a producer has always been at the popular heart of things, producing Bowie, U2, Coldplay, Travis. While giving me a tour of his home studio in Camden, David Vorhaus of White Noise reminisced about the time Eno paid a visit to work with him. He recalled him as agitated, flitting about the consoles, a dynamic, fretful bundle of energy, before eventually settling on a keyboard and producing a series of slow, pacific drones. Although for a long time Eno was synonymous with ambient, it seems antithetical to his character and his creative nature – a polymath, flitting between media, a non-instrumentalist who duly feels freed up to have a go at anything, a livewire, a garrulous cultural gadabout who's never happy in one fixed place. Contrast this with his sometime collaborator Harold Budd, a veritable creature of the vast stretches of the Mojave desert, where he was raised, whose ultra-minimal music (he refutes the term 'ambient') reflects his own steady, self-effacing temperament.

Eno's character is probably more reflected in his non-ambient material – the agitated, latticed rhythms of 'St Elmo's Fire' on *Another Green World*, perhaps. For Eno, despite the emotions it instils and contains within its rich waters, ambient was more of a strategy than a frame of mind: something that would work, something that was right for the overloaded, overstressed times. It was time, he felt, to recede, to 'create space', as he says. It was also an approach that chimed with his first discipline as a painter. In his ambient works, Eno was creating sound canvasses: not front-and-centre, declarative, balls-to-the-wall rock songs but wispy, deceptively inconsequential pieces which conjured up a variety of nuanced moods, created ripples in the memory pool.

In an effective spot of myth-making, Eno tells the story of how, in 1975, he was forced to take a prolonged break from his hectic schedule of multiple projects and collaborations when he was knocked down by a taxi. He claims that while laid up at home, his friend Judy Nylon came to visit, bearing the gift of an album of eighteenth-century harp music. She put on the record before leaving, only for Eno to realise his stereo was turned right down and one of his speakers was not working. Unable to get up to adjust the knob, he allowed the harp music to wash over him at reduced volume, mingled with the gentle spray of steady rainfall coming from outside, creating a hazy aural effect that would inspire him to create a sort of 'discreet music'.

According to Eno biographer David Sheppard, however, when he interviewed Judy Nylon she told a slightly different story: that Eno and Nylon consciously collaborated in balancing the sound system to create the melded effect of the low-level music and the outside rain. This was doubtless an idea already on his mind and already in the culture. The idea that he made a Livingstonian 'discovery' of the phenomenon of ambient is bunk.

The concept of 'ambient' as a conscious practice was first coined by Erik Satie, who proposed to:

> bring about a music which is like furniture – a music, that
> is, which will be part of the noises of the environment, will
> take them into consideration. I think of it as melodious,
> softening the noises of the knives and forks, not dominating
> them, not imposing itself. It would fill up those heavy
> silences that sometimes fall between friends dining together.
> It would spare them the trouble of paying attention to their
> own banal remarks. And at the same time it would neutralise

the street noises which so indiscreetly enter into the play of conversation. To make such a music would be to respond to a need. Don't listen! Keep talking!

The antecedents of these remarks lie in Satie's own experiences of playing popular tunes at cabarets and cafes, his purpose to be both heard and ignored. For all their modesty, though, they bristle with mischief and subversion; not only was Satie the author of such wonderfully mischievous tracts as *Memoirs of an Amnesiac*, he was also closely connected with radical early-twentieth-century art movements such as Dada, whose aim was to lay low the grandiose assumptions and over-elaborate structures of a still overbearing nineteenth-century culture. Satie's music, spare, limpid, unassuming, playful, was an implicit riposte to Wagner, who still enjoyed cult status at the turn of the century.

The concept of a music whose purpose was not to impose was not taken further as a serious artistic venture for decades. However, the 1950s did see the establishment of muzak, based on 1920s technology developed by one Major General George Owen Squier to transmit music to listeners without the use of radio. Entrepreneurs saw how muzak could be piped into environments such as workplaces in particular, its purpose to maintain productivity through variations in pace and style. This was an 'industrial music' of sorts, produced by skilled musicians, with all artistic pretensions completely eschewed in favour of quietly manipulating those people who were subjected to it. This eventually led to protests and lawsuits, but muzak in various forms was still maintained – in hotel elevators and supermarkets, for example – its swirling, synthetic, strategically inoffensive tones taking on a certain attractive kitsch quality for some. A more recent purpose for the genre has seen it blasted at higher volume in shopping precincts so as to deter groups of youths from loitering in them after hours.

Other artists like John Cage saw the extremist potential in so-called 'background' music. Cage helped rescue Satie's reputation, staging a performance of his *Vexations* in 1953. Written in around 1894 by Satie, though, to the best of anyone's knowledge, never performed by him, its strangely skewed theme is designed to be played 840 times and, despite Satie's bland assurances about ambient music, is intended as an endurance test. As Cage discovered, it took eighteen hours to play in full. Astonishingly, all of six people stayed to the end of the piece, which was played by a piano relay team at the Pocket Theatre in Manhattan. One of them is said to have shouted 'Encore!' at the conclusion.

Brian Eno ultimately fell somewhere between muzak and the more challenging questions posed by Cage about the relationship between music and environment. His music was certainly never intended as a sonic lubricant to oil the wheels of human industry, but unlike Cage's pieces, which were designed conceptually to confound and confront, you could at least eat your dinner through Eno's works. As he told Mike Barnes:

> You often hear great music that is very rich, but it's also
> very demanding – it doesn't want to be in the background.
> Most rock is like that, because it's designed to assault you.
> On the other hand, there is also music that is designed to
> remain in the background, and which cannot withstand close
> investigation. So I thought, 'Why not try to make music that
> can occupy all of these possibilities, where the listener can
> choose his position in relation to it?' Then, of course, this idea
> got translated as 'Eno is making background music.'

As a child, filled with sensory curiosity, he had appreciated doo-wop and artists like Buddy Holly, not least because of how they used the studio, how they suggested a sense of interior space and reverberation, in a way that primitive early pop records are more capable of doing than today's compressed, in-yer-face productions.

He was especially smitten by an early Holly effort entitled 'Wait Till the Sun Shines, Nellie'. Holly had recorded this song at the behest of his mother and perhaps swaddled it in exaggerated, swaggering layers of reverb to compensate for his embarrassment at this unhip concession. Eno would also fall for the sounds of the Ray Conniff singers, enamoured by the sheer physical fabric of their vocal lushness.

During the 1960s, Eno's art-school education took in the Who's 'My Generation' and their shocking, auto-destructive antics, as well as minimalists such as Terry Riley and Steve Reich. His first instrument proper was a tape recorder; two of these had everything required for Reich to compose his pieces 'Come Out' and 'It's Gonna Rain'. Eno was developing an interest in the form and framing and texture of music, as opposed to the somewhat oblivious rock'n'soul drive towards spirit and content, which reflected a not typically British avant-garde sensibility. By the late 1960s, he was beginning to stage 'happenings', in homage to the Fluxus movement, which danced the line between music and artistic gesture.

Before his supposed epiphany in 1975, Eno had already created an album of 'systems' music with Robert Fripp – 1973's *No Pussyfooting*. Its cover is dated by Fripp's massive flares and stacked platform soles but in every other respect it is timeless. Richly amorphous and beatless, with Eno's looped synth patterns throbbing like sonic striplighting and Fripp's soloing snaking in and out of the mix, the album consisted of two lengthy tracks, 'The Heavenly Music Corporation' and 'Swastika Girls', and while they were preceded in principle by the work of La Monte Young and Terry Riley, they had absolutely no resemblance to anything going on in the Anglo-American rock milieu of which Eno was a member in 1973. The album was greeted at once with mute incomprehension and sales that would be the envy of any twenty-first-century common-or-garden soundscaper – around 100,000, such was the traction of the duo.

Fripp and Eno followed up with 1975's *Evening Star*, which featured 'An Index of Metals', a slow, burgeoning piece that seems to
move in lava phases across the periodic table. There was one other
piece released that year that had an architectural kinship with 'An
Index of Metals': 'Unfinished' by Can, which had the same feel of
tentative metallic construction, of vast new build.

This was apposite. By 1975, the spontaneous, disparate West
German cultural undertaking that was Krautrock was passing
some of its peaks and reaching various others. Krautrock had been
greeted, if at all, with enthusiasm by a minority that included
John Peel, journalists Richard Williams and Ian MacDonald, and,
it must be said, the Virgin label head Richard Branson. It was,
however, greeted with mass indifference by the general public, for
whom World War II still remained a sore point, and by the more
hard-bitten rock establishment.

Eno grasped the innovations of Krautrock very early on, which
were a matter of cultural, historical and national necessity, much
as they had been for Stockhausen. These musicians were among
the children who had come of age in 1968, having grown up amid
a prosperity that in many ways, from Coca-Cola to the Beatles,
felt somewhat imported, as well as a domestic culture of Schlager
and *Heimatfilm* that felt like chocolate-box kitsch, nostalgia for
a German time and place that had not actually existed, its songs
designed to get drunk and forget to. By the late 1960s, the youth of
Germany were coming to understand the full enormity of the Third
Reich – the crimes against humanity never mentioned at the family
dining table, the sense of the dreadful gaping schism the Nazis had
created in the sense of German national identity and esteem.

For a small, disparate but subsequently colossally influential
handful of German musicians – Tangerine Dream, Amon Düül 2,
Can, Faust, Neu!, Cluster, Kraftwerk, Ash Ra Tempel among them
– it become a matter of urgency to create a music that was German
in origin but antithetical to the folkish banality of Schlager, yet one

that also avoided the imitative, faintly humiliating dependency on Anglo-American beat music, the sort that many had earned their musical spurs by playing at dances for British and American troops stationed in West Germany.

What Eno grasped about the practitioners of Krautrock was their need to stake out a space: inner, topographical, notional, cosmic space. Their task was also to reconfigure the rock song, create a more open-ended version of the music that eschewed verse and chorus, the old hierarchy of singer up front, drummer in the back seat, opening up new terrains of possibility, fresh, untilled, virgin territory, across unexplored horizons. This was the direction in which the linear motorik music of Neu! was heading, driven by the Apache beat of drummer Klaus Dinger, whom Eno hailed as providing one of the three most important rhythms of the decade, alongside James Brown and Fela Kuti.

The tools required to make this new music were not always electronic; quite often, as with Can, it simply involved playing conventional instruments in novel ways, or treating the editing process as part of the compositional method. In other cases, as with early Tangerine Dream and Faust, electronic effects were achieved by modifying or processing regular instruments through little add-on gadgets or customised boxes. Sometimes the varied, idiosyncratic effects achieved this way were preferable to the familiar presets of the unfeasibly expensive synthesizers then available on the market. The independently wealthy Florian Fricke of Popul Vuh did own one but got bored with it fairly quickly, bequeathing it to former Tangerine Dream member Klaus Schulze and returning to his piano.

The formalism of Krautrock appealed to Eno, as well as its general refusal to pay obeisance to the ancient conventions of the blues, which by the early 1970s seemed to be dragging British rock still further into the mud, if anything. He travelled to Germany and met and recorded with Dieter Moebius and Hans-Joachim

Roedelius of Cluster and Michael Rother, temporarily estranged from Neu!, who performed and recorded together as the 'supergroup' Harmonia. Both learned from each other. Eno the musician drew on their sense of sound-as-watercolour, their spontaneity and their absolute lack of recourse to the tropes and clichés that kept early-1970s British rock so hidebound and earthbound, so horizonless and mired in boogie fatigue.

It wasn't just Cluster and Harmonia among the West German experimentalists whose ideas ran parallel to, even anticipating, Eno's work. Ash Ra Tempel's celestial, *kosmische* explorations, like Pink Floyd's late-1960s space rock, billowed and ascended luxuriantly into outer space; druggy, perhaps, rather than schematic, but up and out there nevertheless. Not that space was the sole province of the acid-head, however; since the televising of the Apollo missions in the late 1960s, it represented a vast backcloth for the popular consciousness. The straight-edged Edgar Froese and Tangerine Dream, meanwhile, used electronics to convey a sense of space that was looming and impressive but far more impersonal than Eno's later ventures on his album *Apollo*. Froese explicitly sought, on albums like *Atem*, to instil feelings of smallness and insignificance in the listener, to whom the wider universe, conveyed in the gigantic stasis of his music, was utterly indifferent. Yet audiences were in somewhat masochistic thrall to this gloomy and hostile spectacle, despite its lack of trippy consolation. Its largeness, as represented by their dwarfing stacks of equipment and speakers, made Tangerine Dream one of the few Krautrock bands to draw large audiences in their own time.

Even Faust and Kraftwerk, in their more vividly pastoral earlier periods, prefigured some of Eno's watercolour tendencies, while Can's 'Ethnological Forgery Series' was a precursor of Eno's adventures in tandem with David Byrne on *My Life in the Bush of Ghosts*.

It was Eno's influence that drew David Bowie to Berlin, his relocation to Europe driven by a desire to clean up following a dreadfully drugs-sodden period in his life while beached in LA, and a romantic Germanophilia that ranged from recasting himself as a latter-day Christopher Isherwood on the stranded island of cold war decadence that was modern West Berlin, to an unhealthy obsession with Hitler and his associated paraphernalia, to a deeper, dialectical understanding that the Titans of Anglo-American 1960s rock, from the Who to Lennon, Elvis to Zeppelin, were all washed up and spent, bloated and creatively exhausted. The future was eastwards, in Europe.

Hence the Berlin trilogy, and *Low* in particular, whose icy, metallic, European-tinged instrumentals featured contributions from Eno (who co-wrote 'Warszawa') and would have a profound effect on the post-punk movement, introducing a New Teutonic Cool hailed in a famous Jon Savage article for the late magazine *Sounds* entitled 'The New Musick'. Suddenly, Teutonic music was greeted not with condescending laughter but a respectful reverence. Bowie's influence may not have entirely created the Europhilia evident in Joy Division, Simple Minds ('I Travel'), Bauhaus and the New Romantic movement and its icy use of electronics, but it certainly acted as a blessing on the tendency. This mature mood of Europhilia would recede somewhat, all but obliterated by the retro-wave of Britpop. For a while, however, a chic frost settled across 1980s pop, an imperious *froideur* that had a number of antecedents, one of whom was certainly Eno.

During the late 1970s and early '80s, Eno made a series of records on his Ambient and Obscure labels. They seemed as calculated in their own way to infuriate hairy, guitar-addled guardians of rock authenticity as had his glam period the armchair moral guardians of the early 1970s. His erudition seemed pointed. As he told Mike Barnes in *Mojo* in 2009:

> I can remember very strongly how powerful the resistance
> was to that in the '70s. It was like people were terribly

disappointed if you could articulate a sentence because it
meant you weren't really a proper passion-driven, lust-driven,
rock'n'roller. Because you have to remember that the archetype
then was Keith Richards – a very powerful archetype.

And so it was considered, especially by music critics – who,
of course, are much more rock'n'roll than any rock'n'roll
artists ever are, in their minds at least – to be really bourgeois,
a real letdown. You had to be working-class, which I am,
actually: much more than most of them, as it happens. But it
was like you (*adopts slightly moronic voice*) had to really fuckin'
show it!

Eno was a tease. The series included *Music for Airports*, featuring
guest musicians such as Robert Wyatt, whose simple suspended
chords (reminiscent of some of John Cage's early piano sketches) and
gentle, deodorised, synthetic choral passages felt like a Hockney-
esque effort to wreak art from the luxurious blandness of modern
airports. In keeping with its ostensible functionality, *Music for
Airports* was played at actual airports: at New York's LaGuardia for
a month in 1980, and later at Minneapolis/St Paul's, among others. Its transmission seems to have gone mostly unnoticed, which
is just as well because the piece was not muzak; it depends for
its quality on a certain lurking existential truthfulness, prompting
reflection, like a mirror, rather than a porthole to a fictional blue
sky. There were supposedly complaints from one or two passengers
of a certain queasiness on being exposed to its strains; my own
anecdotal evidence, from playing the album at college to fellow
students, was that rather than choosing to immerse themselves in
its total balm, they were put out by its amorphousness, its absences
– of tune, of vocal, of 'direction' or structure.

Others followed, including *On Land*, perhaps the greatest
in his 'Ambient' series, each of whose tracks is an evocation of
a childhood rural memory. Listening to this album 'blind' lends

it a strangely nocturnal air, the feeling of a nature that is more active when the humans have gone to sleep. Each track bristles and thrums with thickets of electronically simulated bucolic activity, a palpable undergrowth, a lurking, even threatening abstraction of animal life: voles, grasshoppers, drones, the topography of memories, revived in a way that still lifes hanging on a wall cannot manage. The album culminated in 'Dunwich Beach, Autumn 1960', my favourite single Brian Eno piece, which evokes such cawing longing for a place I never visited at a time when I was never alive. What's striking here isn't just Eno's artistic strategy or his unabashed use of the studio technology available to him at the time; it's a reminder that for all his intellectual abilities and systems applications, his willingness to explain himself, the piece works supremely because of Eno's ability to drop notes in the pool of sound in exactly the right places. That's what happens in this piece – a series of plumb, dead-on keyboard strikes that send perfect patterns of ripples across the dark waters of the listening mind, his aim so true that you could almost believe it was your own submerged memories that were being jolted, not Eno's.

With Eno considered a peer of the rock realm alongside figures such as John Cale, David Bowie, Robert Wyatt, Kevin Ayers, David Byrne and many others, his 'Ambient' series received an increasingly appreciative reception from critics who had initially thought his drift into instrumentalism inconsequential and banal. However, it was also notable how few, if any, musicians in the late 1970s and early '80s sought to go ambient themselves. It was as if the music were Eno's own private domain, where he was joined by a select group of associates like Harold Budd and his younger brother, Roger. The atmosphere of the post-punk era was too fevered, the anger and urgency of its counter-cultural element too great and, conversely, the need to party too frantic for more than a small minority of artists and listeners to hear the relevance of the repose of the 'Ambient' series.

There were exceptions. Wire, and Colin Newman in particular, had always been fans of Eno, and this was reflected in their own work, which always felt like a brilliantly angled assault on the song form rather than expressive emissions from the rock'n'roll heart. In their solo work, in particular, they explored more abstract options. Newman's *Provisionally Entitled the Singing Fish* contained instrumental pieces that felt like Eno-esque studies in miniature, while as Dome, or under their own names, Bruce Gilbert and Graham Lewis created long-form electronic pieces that sought new aerial and architectural possibilities beyond the over-ploughed, muddied bounds of the rock format.

Wire had picked up a punk following with their debut album, *Pink Flag*, who would cram into the moshpit at their every gig and bellow for their favourite anthem, '12XU'. The band would then spend the remainder of the decade moving in an ostentatiously art-rock direction, as if only to bait their lumpen following, culminating in the live performances recorded for the album *Document and Eyewitness*. (Decades later, at a gig by the now veteran Wire at the Royal Festival Hall, the same moshpit brigade, now in middle age, was still turning out, still braying raucously and in vain for '12XU'.)

However, *NME* critic Ian Penman, reviewing Eno/Budd's *The Plateaux of Mirror*, panned the album as mere ambient fiddling while Rome burned. Penman was one of the more playful and cerebral writers on the *NME* at this point, but so left-field was the magazine in 1980 that even he was not prepared to run contrary to the paper's agit-pop leanings. So serious was the *NME* that year that it ran an obituary for Jean-Paul Sartre when he died, as well as a frightening series by the late Ian MacDonald entitled '1984', in which he predicted totalitarianism and nuclear exchanges by the end of the decade. The *NME*'s anti-Thatcher line was a given, with interviews largely given over to the struggle against Toryism, Reaganism, fascism and the general lurch to the right. To opt out of this discussion marked you as a shallow, oblivious fop or trog-lodyte. Eno and his ambient music stood accused of luxuriating rather than agitating.

Even in the less militant pop and rock circles of the early to mid-1980s, the mood of the times was too kinetic, too caught up in the myriad bundles of energy released by punk to have much truck with ambient. There was no place for it, no space for it. But by the mid-1980s, youth culture was beginning to feel crammed, overlit, overloaded with mediocre opportunists who made one regret the punk dictum that 'anyone can do it'. Too many people were; too much middling activity. Crowded House just about summed it up. Too many pop shows. Too few highlights, too many highlighted hairdos. Too many strobe lights. Too much jostling for attention. Too much consciousness, but of the wrong sort. Too many faces. Too much.

This was the tendency Eno had noted years earlier when he first began to take an interest in ambient music and the value of quiet: the importance of 'subtraction' in a culture that was excessively additive, especially in the 1980s, when the postmodern and mod-ern combined led to a general overload, of the pop present and the still-lingering pop past. It was the first time there had been cause to feel this way. In the 1950s, '60s and '70s, rock and pop were desperately scarce commodities, afforded very little mainstream airtime beyond the small weekly doses of *Top of the Pops* and, for night owls, *The Old Grey Whistle Test*. Arriving at *Melody Maker* in the relative downtime of 1985/6, Simon Reynolds and I dreamt not so much of a 'new big thing' – the mythical 'new punk' that so many commentators were still confident would happen – but more of a wipeout, a dub explosion . . . a great silence, maybe. This we found in the neo-psychedelic, punk-inflected resurgence of gui-tar bands, from the Jesus and Mary Chain to A. R. Kane and My Bloody Valentine, Big Black, Sonic Youth and the Butthole Surfers. Groups like black holes, come notionally to swallow up the dross.

However, the way things played out in the wider culture was different. In their alternative ways, Live Aid in 1985 and the acid-house scene that rose into being in 1988 represented two different forms of retreat from the 1980s, two different forms of 'self-loss' (to add to the sense of immolation and wipeout implied in the concussive tremolo waves of My Bloody Valentine). Live Aid as an event presented for what seemed like the first time in a while in the culture the 1960s phenomenon of vast numbers gathering in a field to worship rock. The event's cause lent it an air of a vast collective striving towards a common idealistic purpose, while the rock veterans Queen, who had been around since the early 1970s, unselfconsciously grabbed the opportunity to be objects of adoration once more. (Just a few years later, the Stone Roses would be offered the same opportunity, but fumbled it.) For those there it wasn't about the punk/post-punk impulse to have your shout, to have a go and be someone, but simply about being part of a larger human organism, a multitude.

Rave offered a similar ecstasy, both experientially and in pill form. Except in rave there were no stars. Wolfgang Voigt of Gas, who would go on to fill the air with a range of musics, from ambient to microhouse, in the late twentieth and early twenty-first centuries, explained to Rob Young in *The Wire* what rave meant to him. 'There was total anonymity,' he said. 'Networks were created by using a non-verbal, almost secret musical language.'

No more faces – this aspect of rave alone hampered and subverted the music and rock-media industries' efforts to feed off and mediate acid. No familiar faces, whose familiarity depended on them making familiar music – despite its obviously recognisable tropes, rave would allow for a suddenly vast and expanded slew of textural sound to flow across the 4/4 beat.

It was at this point, some twelve or thirteen years after Eno, that ambient at last gained popular traction. Raves were nocturnal affairs far from home, with a lengthy comedown appended to their sustained peak of euphoria. Bleary punters greeted the sunrise, and as they made their slow descent back to earth they were assisted by the beatless but patterned, mesmeric flow of ambient music. Hence the KLF's *Chill Out*, a long, flowing and deliberately allusive piece. With its cover art alluding to Pink Floyd's proto-ambient 1970 album *Atom Heart Mother*, *Chill Out* felt like a slow return journey through pop time on a notional last train, one that clanged mournfully like the snippet of locomotive that concludes the Beach Boys' 'Caroline, No'. Fitful, strafing bursts of sequencer rear in and out of its mix, which feels like a deep, luxurious, wistful sigh, a postmodern river of time along which floated echo-drenched snippets ranging from Can to Acker Bilk's 'Stranger on the Shore', Fleetwood Mac's *Rumours*, Elvis Presley's 'In the Ghetto', American radio bulletins, slide guitar, the tinkle of herded animals and bleating of sheep, throat singers, submarine signals and the occasional fading refrain of their hit '3 a.m. Eternal'. In this case, it felt like an eternal past rather than an eternal future. The recurring chant of 'After the love has gone' that runs through *Chill Out* hinted strongly at the melancholy of comedown, but there's a real bliss about the overall piece, a feeling of submerged ancient troves.

Jimmy Cauty of the KLF also worked with Alex Patterson, co-founder of the Orb, whose 'A Huge Ever Growing Pulsating Brain That Rules from the Centre of the Ultraworld' was similar in its loaded drift to *Chill Out*, but pumping outwards into the cosmos rather than into the interior waters of nostalgia and memory. Borne on a rotating, airborne sequencer riff emerging spacebound from lapping, watery beginnings, it's a gloriously picaresque journey onwards and upwards, with a heavenly host of sampled choral voices looking on. There's a real feeling of Apollo mission about this musical venture (though in interviews, including with me, Patterson has expressed scepticism that the moon landings actually took place). We pass the dead soul of Minnie Riperton, still soaring through the registers in deep space, evade percussive meteor storms, come surreally face to face with a rooster, float on through gravity-free zones in which ancient snippets of church bells revolve freely, duck to avoid progressive waves of jet fighters. We're taunted as the piece threatens briefly to touch down into 4/4 rhythm (indeed, live Patterson has been wont to play 'Pulsating . . .' with a stomping four-to-the-floor underpinning), before finally touching down on the unknown shores of the back side of the moon.

Despite the sheer immensity of the Orb and all their works, there was always a puncturing sense of mischief and cackling earthiness about Alex Patterson, Chelsea fan and former roadie with Killing Joke; which is not to say that his work was intended as a parodic spoof of prog-rock excess, but it was one of the ways in which it was consciously framed. The cover of the Orb's *Adventures Beyond the Ultraworld* features the backdrop of Battersea Power Station, an allusion to the cover of Pink Floyd's 1977 album *Animals*, whose inflatable pig symbolised the abiding conceited hubris of prog, even as punk was raging down below in London. Patterson was strongly implying that with acid, the deliberate smallness and narrow horizons of punk had run their course. It was time once more for shameless inflation and expansion and the re-embrace of all that hippy bollocks punk had supposedly come to drive out; new, old room to roam.

While ambient was reborn as a post-rave comedown, Patterson wasn't above using his music as a tease to those who still hadn't done with dancing. Richard James, aka the Aphex Twin, recalled to me an early-1990s Glastonbury appearance the Orb made: 'All the E-heads and ravers turned out to see them en masse. And the Orb played this totally ambient set – you know, the sound of the whales and the sea – and it drove them mad. There was one bloke stamping up and down, absolutely screaming and gurning with rage. And, of course, the Orb knew exactly what they were doing.'

Meanwhile, there was gracious acceptance of the Orb's new worlds from Mr Johnny Rotten himself. 'Johnny Rotten came and saw us play one night,' Patterson told me. 'I'd had some history with him, our paths had crossed during my Killing Joke days. He came up to me and said, "Alex, I think the Orb are beautifully boring." And that about sums it up! So's most minimal music, that's the idea. The idea is to give you the time and space to unclutter your mind.'

The Aphex Twin was another of the stars of the anti-stellar movement that was early-1990s ambient who seemed bent on subverting any of the solemnity or seriousness his music might seem to exude. When I first interviewed him at the tiny flat he then occupied, he took a delight in assuring me that he had never heard of the highfalutin artists such as Stockhausen and Steve Reich who had been suggested as antecedents for his growing body of work, which included *Selected Ambient Works 85–92*. Still, given that he had been brought up in Cornwell and recording since his early teens, initially as a refuge from the 'bloody awful' Jesus and Mary Chain records his sister insisted on playing, his explanation that his main inspiration had come from the blip and boost of video and arcade games was plausible. He remained a computer games fan.

'When I'm tripping, usually,' he told me. 'I can't play them straight. I like God games, where you have a bird's-eye view of a city. Computer games when you're tripping are like virtual reality, but about a hundred times better.'

He delighted in striking anti-poses. In 1994, he was living in Stoke Newington, an area he assured me was 'well scary' after dark and from which I'd be best off scarpering as soon as possible before night fell, if I valued my tape recorder. We met in a greasy spoon, where he was perusing a copy of *Loot* and wondering aloud whether he should buy a Dalek, a cast-off from BBC props, which led to some daft, knockabout waste of interview time.

Eventually, however, it became clear that his intention in making music, whether ambient or jackhammer frantic, was to create a sort of hermetic sonic system in which he had complete, conscious control. He posited the idea of a portable backpack-style studio you could 'literally walk around with. I don't think I'd ever listen to anything ever again, I'd just be creating the whole time. You'd be sorted. You could just go up a mountain and write loads of tracks, go anywhere you wanted. It's my fantasy, just to be locked away somewhere for ever. I do enjoy other things, but whatever I'm doing, at the climax of it, however good it is, if I ask myself would I rather be in my studio, the answer's always "Yes", I'm afraid. I try to persuade myself I'd rather do other things, but it's not really true.'

Even unconsciousness was, for Richard James, a time to exercise creative consciousness. He had, he reckoned, perfected the art of lucid dreaming. 'You don't need much time. Dreams don't take place in actual time. A twenty-minute kip'll do. I've always had sounds in my dreams, and that's where stuff from the album came from. I couldn't do it at first. I'd sleep for twenty minutes, dream a track, wake up and then forget it. Be pissed off. Do it again. And finally get it right. It's something I've just started doing. My most successful thing is to go to sleep in the studio, then dream I'm in the studio along with real or imaginary bits of gear, do the track in my dream, then wake up and recreate the whole thing. I was so amazed when it actually worked. In about two years' time I reckon I'll have the whole thing completely sorted.'

For James, 'ambient' meant a closed, sealed environment, whose organic output we in the rest of the world were welcome to hear and purchase, but which had little or no time for the products of others. Like Brian Eno, he felt a sense of crisis at an over-additive culture, as he told me when we met again in 1993, in an interview for *The Wire*. By this time, he was living in what had once been a bank branch, just off the Old Kent Road. We met in an even greasier spoon than before at the top of that south London thoroughfare.

'To be honest, I'd be quite happy never to hear anything new again,' he told me. 'There's an overemphasis on the new, especially on the part of the media, who need this continuing diet of new things to write about. But if you're really serious about listening to music, there's so much great stuff already that's out there – you're not bothered about scenes. It's bad enough when you're running a label and you run into those moments when you make decisions you shouldn't be making in order to pay the staff and keep them in work. But with a magazine, this need to have new things all the time is just a fiction. To my mind it's completely wrong. It's not reflecting reality, but a need to fill space.'

By this point, James was in a powerful enough position to turn down doing a Madonna remix. He offered the deliberately unacceptable suggestion of having her 'bark like a dog'. For someone who a few years earlier professed to be a restless, relentless music-maker, whether asleep or awake, he seemed to have become rather less prolific of late. Why was that? 'The Internet!' he laughed. 'For a while computers were very liberating, but now the big problem with computers, apart from the fact that they keep going wrong, is that you've got so many distractions – email, looking at downloads. Once all you could do was make music, but now you really have to be disciplined . . .'

Today, ambient is ubiquitous, both as a private, hermetic experience, a retreat from the world, and as aural filler in the public domain, seeping everywhere. I'm working right now to the sound beam of an installation at the Barbican, Zarah Hussain's *Numina*, which draws on designs from Islamic art and architecture, as well as contemporary digital art, and is accompanied by an 'infinitely looping electronic soundscape' designed by Mike Roberts. It's an irony, albeit a sustainable one, that a music that is essentially a response to what Eno called the 'additional' nature of modern culture is itself now so abundant.

Ambient is the space, the afterglow left when the centre has collapsed. It's in the amorphous, beatless oscillations of post-rock, the multiple releases of abstract electronica which criss-cross the twenty-first-century skies like fading vapour trails. It implies an absence of subject. Bill Laswell's drifting sound-weave of classic Bob Marley tracks, minus the great man's vocals, is a case in point. Another is US shoegazer group lovesliescrushing's *CRWTH*, a take on their album *Chorus*, an attempt to do without guitars and other instrumentation altogether and simply create a miasma of sounds from Melissa Arpin-Duimstra's voice. *CRWTH* carries the process of subtraction still further, working off mere fragments of her voice to create cirrus-like electronic ambient effects. And then there is a remarkable piece by PhD student Ryan Maguire, which purports to be a version of Suzanne Vega's 'Tom's Diner' consisting of nothing but the sounds 'clipped' from the original recording when it was compressed for mp3. The maker has cheated slightly, adding a little reverb, but the inversion still has a ghostly, reproachful resonance, in an age of echo-less pop in which every last pixel is filled, blaring louder and fuller than ever, ignored more than ever.

In its drift away from the centre, ambient encourages a quiet attentiveness to other worlds, other cultures, other options, the expanse of the past as well as notional futures. David Toop's 1995 volume *Ocean of Sound: Aether Talk, Ambient Sound and Imaginary Worlds*, was helpful in defining ambient as A Thing in the 1990s. However, in its deliberately non-centric, circumlocutory way, it was talking about musics and sound sources emanating from places and cultures that long preceded our own, from gagaku to Terry Riley. Only when the din of egocentric Western white rock was turned down, its imperial dominance reduced, could these be heard more distinctly. In the immediate future, Toop envisaged a non-hierarchical music, 'fluid, quick, ethereal, outreaching, time-based, erotic, immersive and intangible', that reflected a broader sonic environmental awareness. 'There's been a breakdown in the notion of what is "important",' Toop told me at the time, 'meaning that all these marginal things – TV incidental music, bar-code flickers, car alarms, soundtracks . . . the entire sound-scape has risen to take its place alongside Phil Collins.'

As we have seen, a common theme among ambient music-makers, from Eno onwards, is that of clutter – either mental clutter or the clutter of overproduction. This was not the case when Erik Satie first proposed ambient music. He intended to compose and perform pieces that would humbly take their place in the back-ground, amid the clink and clatter of diners' cutlery and crockery. However, when he played these pieces, he found people disap-pointingly attentive. Music was a scarce resource in the early twentieth century; no such problem in the twenty-first.

The empty plains and open skies of ambient imply an imag-inary solace from the hectic traffic of extraneous pop and rock. Brian Eno had first felt this impending cultural crisis in the late 1970s, although at that point many of us were still experiencing the pangs of famine and felt a long way from being sated. There were too few outlets for new music, too little money to buy it. I had to wait three years, for example, between first reading about the abstract synth-driven Cleveland group Pere Ubu and actually hearing them. When I did, I cherished the experience more than I possibly could today, in the age of YouTube, Spotify and other means of instant access.

By the late 1980s, however, more and more people were begin-ning to feel Eno's sense of surplus. The minimalism of ambient, with its deserts of drone and distant horizons, chimed with a feel-ing of crisis in materially cluttered lives. In my experience, one of the signs of the generation gap between today's elderly – those past their mid-sixties – and the eternal children of post-rock'n'roll youth culture like myself (born 1962) relates to stuff. Older people, which is to say the generation prior to mine, have side-boards, mantelpieces and other surfaces laden with trinkets, bowls, souvenirs, all of which offer comfort and assurance and stave off emptiness. Carpets and wallpapers are patterned, furniture skews towards the dark brown. The younger person, on visiting such a house, is inclined to make a sweep of all these knick-knacks, men-tally bundling them into boxes and carting them off to a car-boot sale or even just a skip. For them, space is more valuable than stuff, and comes at a higher premium. Colours should be light, furniture spare and minimal. It's as if John Lennon, sitting at his white piano in his empty mansion in 1971, singing, 'Imagine no possessions,' has established a lifestyle creed.

For others, there is a higher dimension to this aversion to stuff, a riposte to the vulgar, wealthy hoarders of old, the Citizen Kanes or the *fin de siècle* millionaires with their crowded chambers of spoils, tiger rugs and mounted stags' heads. A minimalist, declut-tered ethos implies an anti-materialist outlook, creating an airy flow for mind, body and spirit, for musing and reflecting – not least reflecting in self-congratulation on what a terribly spiritual person you are.

Of course, this 'minimalism' is a conceit. Wealthy Westerners still squander obscene amounts of the world's resources, but have found stylish, discreet ways of doing so: storage solutions that free up pri-vate space in which a pretence of anti-materialism can be indulged. Apple computers, meanwhile, unveiled with quasi-religious cere-mony, stress the minimal: clean, silver surfaces, feather-light and circuitry hidden, but whose gigabytes of storage space allow for an unfeasibly vast glut of music, films, social media and apps of every description, of the sort which the Aphex Twin complained were slowing up the organic flow of his creative activity.

Poverty, by contrast, is a visibly maximal experience. It is shop-ping trolleys crammed with wretched but vital belongings which you have no place to park. It is sitting on the streets of Delhi, your possessions fanned out all around you, which must go with you wherever you go.

Is there, perhaps, an echo of this conceit in pieces like Brian Eno's *Discreet Music*? Do they offer a mirage of spiritualism, an illusion that they have some ennobling, mind-cleansing effect? Like many people, one of the uses to which I put ambient music is when writing. *Discreet Music* brings back memories of all-night essay-writing stints at university, laborious, handwritten attempts to feign an understanding and enjoyment of the works of Sir Philip Sidney that were greeted with ill-concealed boredom by my tutors when read out the next morning. When writing today, I am still inclined to reach for Eno, or William Basinski, or David Tagg, on the assumption that their throb and ebb will encourage and lubricate my cerebral motions.

It may well be that they do. However, working in the Barbican Library recently, I found myself turfed out of the place as it was closing early that day. I was forced to find a seat in the cafe area, which was crowded out by a children's bash featuring raucous musical events and an amplified set by a percussion trio, as well as the general rambunctiousness to be expected when kids get to run amok in a large public space. To my surprise, though, this didn't especially affect my literary output, either in terms of quality or quantity. I worked no better or worse than I would have done had I been submerged in the repetitive oceanic wash of some expansive piece of quiet electronica.

R. Murray Schafer has spoken of 'keynotes' – the sounds that define the character of an area's acoustic environment. These are more evident in 'hi-fi' areas such as the countryside, where one is more easily able to attend to and pick out the myriad sounds of nature, as well as the distant drones of human civilisation. In a piece entitled *The Soundscape*, he sets out his thoughts in a way

that parallels Luigi Russolo's *Art of Noises* manifesto, while also
pitting himself against the Futurist:

> Modern man is beginning to inhabit a world with an acoustic
> environment radically different from any he has hitherto
> known. These new sounds, which differ in quality and
> intensity from those of the past, have alerted many researchers
> to the dangers of an indiscriminate and imperialistic spread
> of more and larger sounds into every corner of man's life.
> Noise pollution is now a world problem. It would seem that
> the world's soundscape has reached an apex of vulgarity in
> our time, and many experts have predicted universal deafness
> unless the problem can be brought quickly under control.

There is a touch of hysteria about the prediction of 'universal
deafness', while the word 'vulgarity' triggers grave suspicions about
the author's sensibilities and raises one or two hassles, as does the
faintly agrarian undercurrent of Schafer's diagnosis. One finds
oneself sticking up for noise pollution as an occasional artistic
necessity, as an electric broadside against Schafer's mooted deli-
cate ideas of squeamish harmony, enforced, one assumes, by an
appointed army of 'shushers'. Music should reserve the right to
be violent, invasive, disruptive, and certainly vulgar. Ironically,
the piece I immediately think of is not by Throbbing Gristle or
Merzbow or some similar noisenik but by the late San Franciscan
composer Pauline Oliveros, who in her later years devoted herself to the accordion and the 'deep listening' movement, which
certainly encourages the sort of attentiveness Schafer regards as
under threat. In 1965, however, she also composed the piece 'Bye
Bye Butterfly' for two-channel tape, turntable with record, two
Hewlett-Packard oscillators and line amplifiers, and two tape
recorders in a delay setup. The piece is intended as a dismissal of
nineteenth-century ideas of modesty and decorum, a social and
aesthetic system that itself regarded vulgarity with abhorrence but

also, as Oliveros noted, repressed women like a whalebone corset. The piece incorporates Puccini's *Madame Butterfly*, a disc of which she had to hand, but which she douses with a caustic emission of oscillator that is effective to the point of making me feel physically nauseous on the rare occasions I can bring myself to listen to this excellent piece.

An indisputably valid ecological application of ambient, however, comes from Bernie Krause, who began life as a Motown session man before becoming a pioneer in electronic pop (he played on the Monkees' 'Star Collector', one of the first pop recordings to use a synthesizer, released in 1967). He himself deplores the 'human din', but sees it as a metaphor for the destruction by mankind of countless habitats and species, not just as an aesthetic offence.

Krause subdivides the 'acoustic signals' that make up our soundscape into three main categories: firstly, 'geophony', which are non-biological sounds, such as the wind as it blows through trees and grass, the sounds of storms, waves crashing in the ocean; these are the most ancient noises, the first, and most likely the last, that will emanate from this planet. The second category is 'biophony', the signatures made by all sound-generating organisms. The third category is 'anthrophony' – i.e. all the sounds generated by human beings – to which Krause adds a subdivision: the 'technophony', which he categorises as irritating, man-made noise, though it's interesting to note that on his 1967 album *The Nonesuch Guide to Electronic Music* he anticipated the polyrhythmic, cerebral frenzy of the sort of 1990s IDM (intelligent dance music) produced by Autechre and their ilk.

That was then, however. When I interviewed Krause in late 2015, he was eager to tell me about a soundscape installation at the Fondation Cartier pour l'Art Contemporain in Paris. 'It will feature over half a dozen rare habitats whose biophonies are spectacular and critically impacted by human endeavour. It will also demonstrate how biophonies are a narrative of place, an eloquent voice telling us how we're doing in relation to our surrounding habitats; for example, how healthy they are. It will be the first sound-art exhibit of its type, bringing natural sound art into the realm of fine arts in ways never expressed before.'

In a sense, Krause's current archive contains some of the most disturbing ambient music ever recorded: the sounds of species that no longer exist, preserved for posterity.

Today, ambient proliferates like a thousand mushroom clouds on the horizon, a music of gentle devastation. Just to pick a few practitioners at random: Taylor Deupree, Richard Chartier, Grouper, Stars of the Lid, Fennesz, Arve Henriksen, Magnetik North, Tim Hecker, Deathprod, Oubys, Loscil, Kevin Drumm, Terre Thaemlitz. Between them, the tonal whispers of their music evoke, inter alia, a host of nebulous emotions and evocations: hypnagogia, the transitional phase between consciousness and unconsciousness; the sepia grain of memory; the sense of drifting sands that will someday reclaim the plains on which cities currently sit, of the benign motions of the atmosphere, untroubled by human strife, and which we use to soothe our own troubles in turn; of seismic collapses and dissolutions, the subtle lullaby of Mother Earth; nostalgia for the infinite; a quiet sandstorm with a universe in every grain; imaginary nuclear winters or warm breezes from distant continents; the sound of natural forces millions of years older than us, which will in turn survive us and our machinery by millions of years; a truly post-industrial time, when the beat, the hammer of industry has long since ceased – all of which tend to come under the catch-all tag of 'soundscapes'.

And yet recently, after years of supersaturation, of listening to and over-intensively consuming music, there are days when even the discreet wisps of ambient feel like an aural imposition, a human attempt to create a grid of sense on the environment. Increasingly, I find myself taking off my headphones and letting whatever is happening wash over my eardrums: a distant barking, the collective drone of distant traffic, the doleful thrum of a strip-light, the rising intonation of a passing vehicle, the punctuating chatter of birdsong, the clatter of debris falling into a skip, the enigmatic scrabbling noises coming from an upstairs apartment; life as a permanent, Cageian '4' 33"'. The feeling passes, however, and I return to ambient for its attempted approximation of the impossible condition of silence, or true peace in this world.

14

CUTTING UP THE WORLD:
FROM CABARET VOLTAIRE TO J DILLA

Although it didn't lead to any ideological set-tos, from the 1970s onwards there was a division between industrial music and electropop similar to that between the Pierre Schaeffer school of musique concrète and the pure electronics proposed by Herbert Eimert. There were some artists who used modern technology, be it arpeggiators or synths, to create abstract electronic sounds which gloried in their non-representational artifice; and there were others who used cut-up tape – or, later, samplers – to integrate elements from outside of their own self-generated musical content, in some cases making music that consisted entirely of pre-existing sound.

Cabaret Voltaire, formed in Sheffield in 1973, were pioneers in the cut-up approach, existing for several years before they could be critically comprehended. And yet, as their name implied, they themselves were standing on the shoulders of previous giants. It alluded to the avant-cabaret night founded in 1916 by Hugo Ball and the Dadaists at a Zurich cafe, inaugurating a new (anti-)art movement that mimicked the chaos and despair and senselessness of World War I but with moral disgust and high purpose. It was Tristan Tzara of the Dadaist movement who devised a new form of 'poetry' by tearing up newspapers and brochures, putting the pieces in a hat and strewing them randomly, their juxtapositions constituting the verse. This form of association had already been anticipated by Isidore-Lucien Ducasse, the French-Uruguayan poet who before his death aged just twenty-four had proudly declared that 'plagiarism is necessary' to justify his openly stealing and refashioning of the work of other writers in his *Poésies*. In his most famous work, *Les Chants de Maldoror*, published between 1868 and 1869, he described a young boy as being 'as beautiful as the chance meeting on a dissecting-table of a sewing-machine and an umbrella', a phrase that would become a motto and cornerstone for the surrealist movement.

Picasso had already taken to attaching sections of *Le Figaro* to his artworks, interventions from the new 'real world' of the print media impinging on the traditionally oiled plains of the canvas and its *natures mortes*. T. S. Eliot incorporated newspaper head-lines into *The Waste Land* to add to the near-impossible challenge of its modernistic, multidimensional complexity, while the more ur-inclined Kurt Schwitters also incorporated street-advertising slogans into the simultaneist rush of his spoken-word pieces.

The purpose of these techniques was multifold: to create port-holes between the hermetic constructions of art and the actual dynamic environment in which they sat; to undermine old hierar-chical notions of developed subject matter in art; and to beat new creative pathways and make fresh connections by spontaneous/ intuitive methods rather than schooled or preset ones.

For William Burroughs, the cut-up method, which he first practised in 1959 with Brion Gysin, was similar to that employed by Tzara, but more focused and radical in its intent, a means of scrambling the 'order' imposed by mainstream texts and official discourse. Burroughs believed that language itself was a 'virus' whose controlling mechanism could only be subverted by seizing it, cutting it up and reordering it. He and Gysin did this by snip-ping pages of text into vertical columns and then rearranging the columns at random, creating new and unintended narratives, with bizarre new meanings and juxtapositions that at once disempow-ered the traditional authority of the author and created a 'third mind', the product of which no individual was responsible for, but which spoke with a potency of its own.

Cabaret Voltaire were excited by this idea of recontextualisation as a political weapon, and embraced it. Tape would be a key weapon in their arsenal, a means of capturing excerpts of, say, American clansmen or TV evangelists, which could help 'recondition' the listener, make them more conscious of the media environment. It was a form of counter-subversion. 'There was definitely an anti-Establishment vibe to Cabaret Voltaire,' group co-founder Richard Kirk tells me. 'The idea of control, of the machine of surveillance – taking the piss out of the bourgeois. We were still hung up on the counter-culture of the 1960s, which we factored into the music. It was instinctual, inevitable, and we were cool with that.'

The three members of Cabaret Voltaire were at once energised and alienated by the early 1970s in which they grew up. Today, Stephen Mallinder is a member of Wrangler, whose mixture of antique electronics and sleek-as-tomorrow synth riffs takes up where Cabaret Voltaire left off years ago. Despite the seething hiss of his vocal style, Mal is as friendly a fellow as you will meet in the left-field music scene, his good humour and lack of intensity almost undermining the radical intentions of his music; but he is fully conscious of those intentions and, as one who now works as a lecturer in Brighton, is vivid when explaining them. 'Brian Eno using the VCS3 [with Roxy Music on *Top of the Pops*] and the Velvet Underground – and the Radiophonic Workshop, but only stuff like the *Doctor Who* and *Quatermass* soundtracks – and that was about it really, in 1972. That was the kick-start for us,' he says, when I ask him what initiated his interest in electronic music. But there were other elements, too, which drove him and the two founder members of the group – Richard H. Kirk, the son of a communist steelworker in Sheffield, and Chris Watson, the tape genius who would leave the group to work in TV with the likes of David Attenborough. James Brown, Fela Kuti, John Cage, ska, northern soul, amphetamine sulphate – all of these lurked subculturally in the early 1970s, repressed in an environment still determined by those whose values and tastes were forged in the 1930s and '40s. The younger generation were barely pandered to, their preferences ignored in the media schedules.

As for Sheffield, it was not, Kirk tells me, the vital crucible whose romantic, satanic mills forged the 'industrial' sound for which Cabaret Voltaire would be credited. He grew up on the east side of the city, amid the clank and belch of the factories, but while he concedes it may have 'sunk in a bit psychologically', he protests, to the disappointment of geographical determinists, that the only inspiration it provided was as something to react against. 'I think there's a myth about Sheffield that we were try-ing to replicate the sound of factories. I lived in the East End of Sheffield, and from where I was you could see right down into the valley, which was full of all these big fucking black buildings churning out Christ knows what. You could hear the stuff going on at night – but there was never any notion in Cabaret Voltaire of trying to make the noise of the factory. Why would you want to do that? You want to move away from that, escape into some alternative reality. It was grim, Sheffield, but it was the boredom it created that prompted us to start the band. There were very few clubs, very little music apart from Tony Christie or whatever, so we decided to invent some.'

Cabaret Voltaire's sense of soldering things together from scratch, musical and non-musical alike, arose from a fertile void: a lack of musical ability, which lent an unconditioned, outsider edge to their bashing and scrawling; and a lack of anything beyond basic equipment, which accounted for the sinister, under-the-floorboards feel of their early work. Tracks like 'Headkick (Do the Mussolini)', inspired by the violent and public death of the Italian, his corpse suspended upside down by its ankles, feel like the Lascaux cave paintings of modern electropop – primitive yet, as Kirk himself tartly notes, shot through with a politics that has largely drained away from twenty-first-century music.

Before even that, however, Cabaret Voltaire had a prehistory of live events which bore all the hallmarks of chaos and not-unexpected confrontation of Dadaist happenings.

'In 1976, we did a performance at a school in Bury,' recalls Kirk. 'It lasted four minutes. We were playing to a load of schoolkids in the assembly. It was nine thirty in the morning and we were blind drunk. Someone set off the fire alarm, then they pulled the power.'

Meanwhile, Chris Watson recalled an event he managed to pull off via his university connections. 'We conned our way onto the bill. It was an organisation called Science for the People, who had a disco every week at Sheffield University, and they were looking for something to liven it up, and I happened to be working with one of the organisers, and he said, "Hey, you're in a group, can you play rock music?" So I said, "Yeah, sure, anything you like." And he said, "Great, we'll get you on halfway through the disco." We were advertised as rock and electronic music. It's hard to give you an idea of what was going on. We had like a tape loop of a record-ing of a steam hammer as percussion, and Richard was playing a clarinet with a rubberised jacket on it covered with flashing fairy lights, and it just ended with the audience invading the stage and beating us up.'

The band fought back, though, Kirk using his clarinet as a weapon and launching his guitar like an axe into the crowd, while Mal fell from the stage and broke a bone in his back, forcing him to be hospitalised. He received little sympathy from the event's organisers, who were banned by the university from putting on any more discos.

Cabaret Voltaire, however, did have a future, one they fashioned themselves using a tape recorder, a basic oscillator, synths and a handful of conventional instruments. Like the key groups of the Krautrock generation who were such an inspiration to them in their reconfiguration of the relationship between form and content in rock, in their use of electronics and building of intensity via loops and repetition, the Cabs understood the importance of establishing their own studio space in which they could create their own modus operandi, rather than following the conventional production channels of the regular music industry. They set up at Western Works, located in a dilapidated part of town, in premises formerly used by the Federation of Young Socialists. ('Warhol's Factory on a thirty-bob budget,' remembers Kirk. 'They still had all the old posters from that time – which was a nice backdrop.') It was a space for work and play, and also for other groups to come and record; a genuine zone of independence, when such premises were affordable in the city; a marginal area for a cultural opposition that is no longer feasible now that Sheffield has been all but swallowed up by its university and given a postmodern makeover to impress incoming tourists and students.

Back in the late 1970s and early '80s, though, Sheffield, like all the major northern towns, had a ravaged Gothic air, casting reproachful shadows and throwing up brilliantly misshapen artefacts that were the product of first-hand experience. Cabaret Voltaire were as misshapen as anyone in their warped, filtered, elongated and starkly electric emissions, Mallinder's bass loops churning with funk noir intent, Kirk's scabrous guitars wailing like dental drills, his sax and clarinet hoving mournfully in the mix. And then there were the outside elements, be it ominous Islamic chants on the tauntingly titled *Red Mecca* or, on the opening title track of 1980's *The Voice of America*, an old-school southern police chief issuing instructions to his officers on how to cope with fans during a Beatles concert ('We will not allow any dancing, running up and down the aisles . . . is that clear with everyone?'), which, taken out of its original context, sounds like the wary, baleful eye of authority ensuring that rock'n'roll mayhem shall only take place within strictly circumscribed and policed borders.

Cabaret Voltaire had far more in common with Europe and the art world than with Duran Duran or the Specials, and yet, with the excited patronage of journalists such as Paul Morley and *NME* front covers, there always seemed to dance the prospect that, much as the Conservative government might be toppled by a popular uprising, Cabaret Voltaire might get on *Top of the Pops*. It was a subject to which they repeatedly returned in interviews. They wished to burst through, albeit absolutely on their near-impossible terms. As they slimmed to a duo and joined the Some Bizarre label, it seemed even closer as their dance element came more to the fore.

Funk was integral to Cabaret Voltaire, as well as to contemporaries such as the Pop Group and A Certain Ratio, all of whom were steeped respectfully in black music but deployed an inverted, Gothic, morbid version of it, turning its hedonistic imperative inside out to ironic effect. It was at once a riposte to those who felt protest music needed to have the grey stamp of authenticity about it, the sort of cloth-cap, stripped-down authority that would later characterise Billy Bragg. Cabaret Voltaire used funk to create a pulse, a dynamic urgency that was just one component of their overall intensely colourised sound, its mix of serrated guitars, sheet-metal electronics and found tapes creating a mood of heightened, paranoiac awareness in the listener. These were times shot through with terror, whose adrenalin at least broke up the gloom; the Thatcher/Reagan years, when global apocalypse felt like a real possibility, while in the north of England towns and cities were experiencing the actual trauma of being uprooted by Thatcherism and its naked determination to lay waste to traditional industries and cut away the ties that bound working-class communities. As Mallinder himself wrote in the introduction to S. Alexander Reed's *Assimilate: A Critical History of Industrial Music*: 'Everyone was collaterally implicated. The city's sounds during the 1980s were both a considered response and a practical resolution to the industrial atrophy that was well under way by this time.'

Cabaret Voltaire made riotous and notionally danceable music; it was escapist, not intended to alienate, entertaining even. But it was a reflexive and necessary response to frightening times, an attempt to jam the signals of geopolitical authority and surveillance, not least the Tories' much-repeated mantra of 'There is no alternative.' Cabaret Voltaire were 'alternative' in the most meaningful sense of that often meaninglessly used word.

Their southern corollary was 23 Skidoo, whose 1982 album *Seven Songs* explored similar themes to Cabaret Voltaire, mapped out a similar neurology, constructed a dance music that was more of a grim physical imperative in hard times than a flight of fantasy. 'Kundalini' was a violently electronic churning loop that applied itself to the head like a clamp; 'Vegas El Bandito' was typical of the clipped white funk of the era, except that its brass sections were mournful blasts, as if portending the arrival of the Four Horsemen, while overall 23 Skidoo's percussive frenzy felt like the sort of distant, jungle tom-toms that might assail a river traveller into the Heart of Darkness, derived from a rigorous study of Burundi and Kodō.

As with Throbbing Gristle, their gigs were a form of deconditioning, intended to purge rather than please the audience. 'We were so aggressive because we really wanted to antagonise people who came to see us, to make them think about what they were doing,' Skidoo's Johnny Turnbull said. 'We'd try and unhinge them by the performance we did.' When I saw them play in Oxford in 1982, the set ended with a gigantic churning loop that sounded like it had been created with an anvil, whose purpose seemed to be to try to scrape clean the craniums of everyone in the room. It was a reminder that savagery and turmoil weren't the stuff of history and faraway places but were located deep in our own cities, our own heads, burned deep into our DNA. Their music was a forceful means of implicating us in the excesses and predicament of our species, making us feel, in some way, rather than merely spectating from a comfortable distance.

To further that end, they made extensive use of tape loops: the ringing scream of 'Fuck you, GI' from *Apocalypse Now*; a found interview with Diana Mosley, née Mitford, the wife of a fascist, in which she denounces the degeneracy of pop music. Most effective of all, however, was 'Just Like Everybody', a collage spliced beneath a swirling, self-perpetuating black cloud of looping ambient noise that depicts with bone-chilling vividness the sinister, anti-democratic amorality of US foreign policy more effectively than any tract or hackneyed polemical lyric ever could. 'It's not abnormal at all . . .' intones an anonymous voice of America. 'We were taught to obey . . .' 'It's how I was brought up.' 'Go back to your seat and sit down.' 'I regard myself as basically neutral and commercial.' Its centrepiece is a hideously jovial conversation between renegade CIA agent and supplier of torture equipment Frank Terpil and Idi Amin.

Throbbing Gristle, who unselfconsciously employed the phrase 'industrial music', were also very much about deconditioning. When I interviewed them around the time of their comeback in 2007, Cosey Fanni Tutti recalled a gig at the Lyceum in 1981, just as post-punk's slate greys were being supplanted by the plumage of new pop. 'The first half an hour was noise, just to drive away all the liggers and Spandau Ballet clones,' she remembered. 'See how committed are you, can you get through this for ten minutes?'

Like Cabaret Voltaire, Throbbing Gristle, while being a product of their time and geographical place, weren't merely about conveying some Lowry-esque artistic impression of the factory conditions of a certain age. They were interested in creative industriousness, as the antidote to the inertia that keeps the vast majority of people down and in their place, easy prey for programming by religion, education, political propaganda, advertising. They too were influenced by William Burroughs and the cut-up method, cut-up as a strategy to achieve the disorder necessary to jam and break the circuits of presets and narratives imposed from above. Genesis P-Orridge recalled a meeting with Burroughs in the early 1970s in which Burroughs had sat the young man down and, as they spoke, overlaid their conversation with the interspersions of a cassette recorder and hopping through the TV channels on a remote control. It was an act of sabotage against the routine, everyday, constant machinations of the media environment.

Formed in 1975, Throbbing Gristle arose from the COUM Transmissions art collective. However, despite participating in avant-garde happenings that involved maggots, injected genitalia, dildos and soiled tampons, the group's members realised that contemporary galleries, in their tolerance and respectability, only served to confine and limit their ability to make a societal impact; the galleries were too-safe spaces. They therefore took recourse to the Death Factory in Martello Street, adjacent to London Fields, and, making the decision that their instruments would be 'sound generators' rather than conventionally musical, they began to play, laying down sounds that combined regular instruments and electronic gear. One key decision they made early on was to dispense with drums, not be held down in that rock way. Their music, therefore, had the feeling of seepage, of effluent, of unlocked emissions. There was a sense that their music was intended to drift into the world like a toxic cloud, and that the outside world was in turn drifting into their music, mutually accepting, mutually resistant.

Although their music has never dated – indeed, it feels more impressive with age – it is very much of its time – a vanished time. I interviewed them in the lobby of a smart hotel in long-since-gentrified Shoreditch, an area now rife with bearded hipsters and a surplus of 'creatives'. In the late 1970s, when they lived in the area, it was razed and apparently futureless. 'What a Day', with its electric riff like an eel in a churn, features P-Orridge barking the song title over and over in a cockney accent – a 'sample' of one of the stallholders at Broadway Market. Today, Broadway Market is very upmarket and cupcake, in postmodern Britain. These were the 1970s, however – modern Britain – in which the stallholder's cries struck a defiant note of cheeriness in a part of London that felt terminally ruined. Similarly, when Throbbing Gristle performed 'Tesco Disco' in 1977, its strafed electronics feeling like anti-aircraft fire, 'Tesco' did not signify what it would later become, a retail corporation, but rather a desperately everyday feature of a high-street Britain that felt impoverished in its dismal consumer options, a Britain ready to explode like a boil.

Albeit filtered through aggressive machine-gun assaults of noise, oblique layers of tape, synth loops and the disquieting hollers of P-Orridge, Throbbing Gristle convey a taste of Britain in the 1970s – the dirt, the black-and-white grain, the rubble, the dilapidation, the stench of corruption, decay and immobility, the boredom, the terror, all absorbed, rearranged and flung like filth at the pop kids in order to galvanise them. It's a music that is redolent of the Flixborough chemical disaster, of Baader Meinhof and the IRA on the news, of atrocity and atrophy. But despite titles like 'We Hate You Little Girls', 'Zyklon B Zombie' and 'Hamburger Lady', in which Chris Carter's glowing red synths convey the miserable agonies of a multiple burns victim, Throbbing Gristle themselves weren't lazy decadents merely indulging sadistically in shock tactics, the 'wreckers of civilisation' they were condemned as by Tory MP Nicholas Fairbairn. They were active in the post-punk days, parodying the business culture of initiative so espoused by Margaret Thatcher in the way they secured funding and put together their own record label, issuing albums in the form of 'Annual Reports'. However, Throbbing Gristle pre-dated punk; for all the shades of grey, TG were born out of the hippy era, considered their music 'psychedelic' and hoped and believed they could help create a world better than the one reflected in the dank waters of their music. 'We were very idealistic about what we were doing,' P-Orridge insisted in 2007. 'And we still are.'

One of Throbbing Gristle's key tracks is 'Discipline', built around a bullwhip of an electronic riff that was born out of urgent improvisation when they were about to take to the stage with nothing but Carter's rhythm to play. '"Discipline" was born out of one of those moments when I didn't know what to sing about,' recalled P-Orridge. 'That's what happened in Berlin. I turned and said to them, "Give me a word, give me a phrase." And Peter [Christopherson] said, "Why don't you sing about discipline?" And that was all we knew. And Chris had a rhythm which went with the word "discipline". But it was that casual, just five minutes before we went onstage.'

'Discipline' is another example of P-Orridge as spontaneous generator, throwing into the works a piece of hastily dredged-up mental detritus that suddenly takes on multiple new meanings in a different context. The way he screeches the phrase 'We need some discipline in here!' sounds like the half-remembered yelp of a cane-wielding teacher trying to impose order on a class of unruly kids; at its most banal, it could be heard as mocking the imaginary authority figures who try to stand in the way of rock'n'roll riotousness. Given TG's penchant for perverse subject matter, it has about it the distinctly possible smack of S&M. However, it is most likely a genuine call for discipline, the sort of rigour and application that was at the heart of the TG project. As P-Orridge himself put it to me, 'You need discipline to apply yourself to being liberated.'

'I think we were all brought up with very strong moral backgrounds from our parents,' said Cosey. 'We, the post-war children. We had this strong moral grounding yet also this great sense of liberation – a sense of freedom and aspiration and that desire to go out and change the world for the better. The other thing is that, coming from the time that we do, there was a point at which we all chose to be outsiders. We had a freedom either to be like our mum and dads or to become hippies or whatever. So we were outsiders and we commented from the outside looking in. And that's what a lot of people have difficulty doing nowadays. There is no longer an "outside". They have no idea what the outside is. Some people think the Gap is the outside.'

'The world has gone full circle, it's become as corrupt as when we first started,' said P-Orridge. 'We didn't believe that would happen, we believed the world would become a more altruistic place.'

In such a world, it was harder for the wreckers of civilisation to make an impact the way they had hoped to when the electropop machinery was in its infancy, and the corollary of a society whose post-war consensus was coming unstuck was physical, affordable space to be a cultural worker – when anarchism had a foothold and felt like an option on the sociopolitical spectrum. All they could hope for in the more complex, built-up, marginless conditions in place in 2007 was for someone to take up their baton, somehow.

Throbbing Gristle showed great discipline in winding up early on, once they felt their programme had been carried out, disbanding in 1981, following the recording of their last album, *Journey Through a Body*, an art piece for Italian radio. 'Industrial' lingered as a subcategory, however, coming to include a corps of artists – Front 242, Skinny Puppy, Nine Inch Nails, Die Krupps, among others – whose work accrued in volume and sonic strength. This was a music that set itself dramatically and apocalyptically against the forces of societal evil. In the case of Canadian group Skinny Puppy, this involved an electronic assemblage whose multiple angles, prods and blades at times felt like a simulation of the animal torture which they vigorously protested against on the album *VIVIsectVI*. However, as the music accrued a larger following, it began to merge with goth and metal, and, while highly popular with raging male adolescents in search of visceral catharsis, felt codified and unthreatening. Gone was the terrifying sense of abjection conveyed by Throbbing Gristle on 'Weeping', from the album *DOA*, in which P-Orridge narrates as the victim of a drug overdose, a physical, shivering wreck. Instead, there were pile-driving rhythms and leather-clad self-aggrandisement. Gone, too, was the genuine pang of terror inspired by the cut-up, taped voices of America that spooled through Cabaret Voltaire and 23 Skidoo. As the equipment got bigger and better, the audiences enlarged, the equipment more sophisticated (and the geopolitical times safer), something in the basic wiring of the late-1970s innovators was smothered.

When the sampler became an affordable and ubiquitous piece of kit in the mid-1980s, it proved to be as enslaving as it was liberating. Machines with previously unheard-of digital capacity enabled users not only to store snatches of old instrumental recordings or already existing works but to tweak them in such a way that they could play them back on keyboards at different pitch values or shifted up or down a semitone. Equipment like the E-mu SP-1200 percussion sampler was a boon to hip hop, which, as David Bowie pointed out at the time, 'reconfigured' the pop song. Hip hop was a sort of African American revenge, a form of plundering and looting after years, decades of black musicians being routinely ripped off. Now it was their turn to 'steal'. There was an insurrectionary insolence about the way groups like Public Enemy lifted from pop history via sampling, forming part of a movement that was unmoored from the old soul notions of musicianship, authenticity, craft and the tightness that wasn't just at the behest of bandleaders but also part of a broader demonstration that black people were, indeed, capable of discipline.

The Beastie Boys parodied this in 1986 in the video for 'No Sleep Till Brooklyn', in which they turn up at a venue and announce themselves as the band. 'The band?' splutters the manager. 'Where's your instruments?' To which they hold up a piece of twelve-inch vinyl. And yet, at the same time, the work of DJs like Eric B or the Shocklee brothers was brilliant, judicious, revolutionary. The sample of Bob James's cosmo-jazz piece 'Nautilus' that courses through Eric B and Rakim's 'Follow the Leader' was as masterful a piece of decision-making as could be achieved on any instrument. And then there was Public Enemy's 'Rebel Without a Pause', which, using the digital capabilities of the new technology, twined together a vocal sample from James Brown and a snatch of Miles Davis's horn to create a wholly original shrieking siren effect that ascends repeatedly through the track. This was a music that was about breakthrough, not just in the rhetoric of Chuck D's rapping but also in its sources and composition. This was a music that didn't follow the gradual evolutions of the past but broke through into another dimension, leaping free from the shoulders of historical African American giants. This was liberation music, crashing through the glass, showing just what live black American culture was about in relationship to the dead past. Everything was now up in the air, up for grabs.

Conversely, De La Soul, at the forefront of hip hop's supposed 'Daisy Age', offered a less incendiary yet equally creative use of sampling on their debut album, *3 Feet High and Rising*. In their own way, they were also a marker for African American advancement. When I interviewed them in New York in 1989, I wasn't confronted with sullen, keepin'-it-real boys from the 'hood telling tales of gangsta desperation and ghetto-to-bling success stories. All that came later. They had just played a gig at the Jacob Javits Center, attended mostly by young African American students from various sororities. They were nice, easy-going, middle-class boys. Their rhymes and tunes, as fresh as spring breezes on a campus, were backed with samples not just from George Clinton, on 'Me, Myself and I', but also Hall & Oates and Steely Dan's 'Peg', whose undulating electric-keyboard riff they sampled on 'Eye Know', interwoven with a few notes of Otis Redding's whistling solo on 'Dock of the Bay'. They were so young at the time. What had prompted them to raid these particular sounds? They were culled from their parents' record collections, they told me. Wow. It was 1989, and rock and pop music was no longer a matter of confounding your parents. That sort of generation gap was becoming history.

The Beastie Boys, with the assistance of the Dust Brothers, paid hip hop due homage on their second, somewhat overlooked 1989 album *Paul's Boutique*, put together when the reputation they had gained with 1986's *Licensed to Ill* was fading and they were in danger of turning into serious artists. The assemblage of *Paul's Boutique* felt like a homage to vinyl crate-digging. It juxtaposed with gusto the Isley Brothers, Johnny Cash, Alphonse Mouzon, Ronnie Laws, Funky 4 + 1, Curtis Mayfield, Bernard Herrmann, Tower of Power, solo Paul McCartney, John Williams, the Eagles, Public Enemy, Sweet and the Fatback Band. It suggested multiple possibilities; it affirmed that we were in postmodern times, as if to suggest (as did the Orb) that, reapplying Jacques Derrida's dictum that there were no books, only other books, there were no records, only other records. *Paul's Boutique* was other records. It wasn't about instrumental dexterity, which suddenly felt as relevant a contemporary craft as hand-sewing. What mattered now were the DJing skills of selection and programming, throwing out what was needed in the moment. Although there had never before been a record like *Paul's Boutique* (and, really, not one entirely like it since), it was a record that seemed to say, *The old ways of making music, the instrumental ways, the ones we were using only just a few years ago, are now the stuff of a dead age of technological innocence. The end of history has arrived. We are postmodern.* Granted, you could play the old way if you wished, much as you could take up your accordion and play schottisches and waltzes if you wanted, but you would only come across as wilfully antiquated.

None of which, however, was to imply a Futurist-style, anti-passéist contempt for pre-mid-1980s mid-sampler music. On the contrary. Through reference via sampling, such music, though treated as a source to be picked at like a carcass, suddenly acquired the sort of reverential sheen applied to the classics. Despite the gleefully inauthentic method of sampling, it somehow engendered a newfound respect for the old recordings. These were not mere oldies but now authentic relics of simpler, better times, when the soils of creativity were fresh and virgin and the best work was done. As sampling spread through pop in the mid-1980s, falling into lesser hands than the Beasties, rather than opening up multiple textural potentialities it degenerated into a box of tropes and tics and habits. The same stuttering effects, the same incredibly narrow pool of source material (pop, then and now, was very much about achieving similarity to other records; unique selling points were usually more trivial). James Brown's 'Funky Drummer' was ripped off ad nauseam, while the late John Bonham's physical labours were digitally revived to offer an easy, artificial boost to many an insipid platter.

The mid- to late 1980s, flooded with samplers, was, in some ways, a depressing time. Every 'Oh YEAH!' poking out of the middle of a workaday radio song or Max Headroom-style stutter-ing voice lift felt like a testament to laziness and the resigned sense that there was nothing new under the sun. Far from being the con-temporary device that would launch a thousand chance encounters between sewing machines and dissecting tables, the sampler felt like the resort of retrograde scoundrels, the anti-serious, for whom pop music was no longer an innocent effusion but a postmod-ern lark, meta- and neo-, something hung up by inverted commas in too-knowing times. It was nothing that mattered any more; indeed, it was composed of dead matter.

In Switzerland, however, a group called the Young Gods were using samplers in a wholly different manner. Unlike their coun-trymen Yello, for whom the sampler was a means of filling out their cinematic creations, the Young Gods were not a dancefloor proposition. Their leader, Franz Treichler, bore a faint resemblance to U2's Bono and had about him a similarly dramatic way of pro-jecting himself onstage and through his French-spoken vocals.

Both had an elemental air about their lyrical subject matter, too. But whereas Bono and U2, with their aerial, cirrus-cloud-like guitar stylings, pined for the empty, pre-postmodern terrain of the Mojave desert, where a man could wear a ten-gallon hat and stare into the unspoiled distance as he breathed in the clean air of authenticity, the Young Gods were post-postmodern. They created a truly unforgettable fire, a heat source derived from a highly original cull of samples, taken mostly from classical and rock sources – everything from Shostakovich to Gary Glitter. On the cover of their 1987 debut album, their name was scratched onto a grey stone backdrop, as if they were making the first mark of something wholly new. Their lyrics felt like homages to an earth being reborn. All this was achieved with vocals, drum kit and a sampling machine, which, in lieu of rock guitars, billowed out charred, reshaped, processed rock noise, a veritable fossil fuel in which the stuff of the past heated the present and the future. On tracks like 'Jusqu'au bout' and 'Jimmy' from their debut album, they commanded all of the power of Beethoven, punk and Zeppelin combined, but in palpably keyboard-derived blasts; you could hear the joins where the virtual editing scissors had been applied, lending these tracks a certain prosthetic, hi-tech power, a new lease of rock life. That they were from Zurich felt immensely exciting in 1987, a riposte to the wry, self-deprecating, retrograde smallness that had overcome British music sensibilities in the post-Smiths era, as if worn down to pebbles by the relentless wash of the Thatcher era and the futile counter-cultural efforts to resist it. The Young Gods felt like a gaping, galvanising force from abroad, but despite the best lyrical efforts of a vanguard of writers at *Melody Maker* – I recall an interview with the band in which I repaired to a Zurich cafe and, like a good Futurist, blackened many reams of notepaper with an inky burst of adjectival frenzy that would form the basis of a two-page spread – their immense sound and our immense enthusiasm were met only with immense apathy from our UK readership.

The Young Gods did enjoy some success when the physical mechanical force of their music coincided with a penchant for nu-industrial in the early 1990s, but ultimately what maddened about the sampling craze was that far from opening up infinite possibilities, or at least a more expansive range than a mere fistful of tropes, it was commandeered as a tool to enforce pop and rock's increasingly nervous, conservative will-to-similarity as the twenty-first century approached. It was a mere postmodern tic machine, designed to provide a quirky, referential soundtrack to the increasingly retro mood of the late 1980s, as well as to signal another tendency of the era – a craven sense of Caucasian inferiority to the great black music of the 1960s and '70s, excerpts of which were now stored, looped and recycled by hipsters, to increasingly tedious effect, in new movements like rare groove.

Not that there weren't exceptional examples of sampling virtuosity, as pop indeed began to eat and regurgitate itself. There were John Oswald's late-1980s Plunderphonics adventures, culminating in 1989's 'Dab', which tore Michael Jackson's 'Bad' molecule from molecule in an advanced act of sonic cubism, rearranging its constituent parts into a rising tornado of fragments, as if the true multiple energies of the song had been repressed rather than released in the original. Coldcut were more mainstream but nonetheless spliced together rollicking, virtuoso, fast-cut amalgams of rhythm, vintage TV dialogue and kidnapped grooves, all of which belied their association with too typically 1980s soul divas Yazz and Lisa Stansfield.

Come the 1990s, and sampling in dance and hip hop became a matter for litigation as the obvious issue of copyright reared its head. Oswald himself was forbidden from releasing the fruits of his Plunderphonics project following upset over his violent rearrangement of 'Bad'. One significant test case was brought against the rapper Biz Markie, who in 1991 faced prosecution for lifting from Gilbert O'Sullivan's 'Alone Again (Naturally)'. It was an open-and-shut case as far as the judge was concerned: referring the case for criminal prosecution he appended the remark, 'Thou shalt not steal.' Black Box's 'Ride on Time' had clearly sampled Loleatta Holloway's 1980 hit 'Love Sensation', and while the Italian production team responsible for the song had cleared the samples with Salsoul, Holloway's record label, the singer was able to secure an undisclosed settlement in recompense (which she was forced to hand over to Salsoul to pay off arrears on her advance). Meanwhile, De La Soul found themselves being sued by Mark Volman and Howard Kaylan of the Turtles for having used a brief snippet of an obscure song on which they had performed, entitled 'You Showed Me', on the track 'Transmitting Live from Mars', from *3 Feet High and Rising*. Again, a settlement was made out of court, with De La Soul forced to pay out $141,666.67 for each of the twelve seconds they had used of the track, the money, curiously, going to Kaylan and Volman the artists rather than the songwriters.

All of which raised a debate, angry at times, as to what truly constituted theft and whether De La Soul's actions really were the equivalent of, say, George Harrison clearly lifting the central melody from the Chiffons' 'He's So Fine' for his own 'My Sweet Lord' or, later, Robin Thicke flagrantly grave-robbing Marvin Gaye's 'Got to Give It Up' for his own 'Blurred Lines'. De La Soul had clearly reshaped and reworked a piece of pretty much extinct and obscure pop matter into something else altogether. When, after all, was there such a thing as absolute originality? Aren't all records, to paraphrase Derrida, merely other records? To this day, it remains a matter of indignant contention. One high-profile post-rave artist told me that pretty much as a matter of principle, he composes his music almost entirely from samples of other people's work, but in tiny snippets that are undetectable to those in the legal profession. On the other hand, to older-school musicians and those of a straightforward frame of mind, stealing is stealing, and countless hits have indeed been lazily constructed on the foundations of breakbeats and solos – such as the Winstons' 'Amen' break – with impunity. However, the threat of a flood of litigation put the mockers on hip hop's golden age of sampling in the 1990s, as the genre went global and increasingly commercial. Sample libraries were set up, the equivalent, in a sense, of presets; alternatively, the likes of Dr Dre grew their own serviceably minimal plastic beats. Mainstream hip hop, as DJ Shadow complained, became 'tighter and tighter, more inbred'.

Not that there wasn't the occasional wholesale act of 'sampling' at the bling-addled, dominant end of hip hop. Puff Daddy's 'I'll Be Missing You' (1997) mawkishly and witlessly wrapped itself in the borrowed overcoat of the Police's 'Every Breath You Take' as it paid tribute to the Notorious B.I.G., the victim of the ugly turf wars that were playing out in gangsta rap, to the distant enthralment of a now 70 per cent white audience. Whereas previous hip-hop samplers had enhanced the work they lifted by recontextualising it, adding inadvertent meaning through juxtaposition and reuse, Daddy's borrowing of 'Every Breath You Take' diminished the original, as if unaware of its menacing intent, which had been removed to leave the banal equivalent of a bouquet of flowers.

In 1996, I interviewed DJ Shadow. He began by lamenting the shift in emphasis in hip hop from sampling to rap, which he described as 'the bastard nephew that's shunned its family'.

'On a cultural level it felt like something was really going to happen, outside the music industry shit, and when it didn't, I felt totally let down. Me, I'm trying to articulate an aspect of hip-hop culture, the more instrumental side, that's been buried by rap-music dollars.' He had called one track 'Why Hip Hop Sucks in '96'; he briefly considered, mid-interview, whether it would have been better to have called it 'Why Rap Sucks in '96'.

By now, hip hop's mainstream cast was primarily composed of increasingly belligerent, apolitical, overwhelmingly male characters who inhabited a video world in which there was no white powers-that-be to fight, because white people were simply absent from the pictures they painted.

As for Shadow, his album *Endtroducing . . .* felt large and lonely, remote from the mainstream. It reverbs with the resonant, ghostly sounds of hip hop's long-abandoned chambers, their rapless interiors making for uneasy listening space. Made using a modest array of equipment (an Akai MPC60 sampler, a Technics SL-1200 turntable and an Alesis ADAT tape recorder), it was quilted together from a range of sources, including David Axelrod, Meredith Monk, Tangerine Dream and ''Pon a Hill' by Tyrannosaurus Rex.

DJ Shadow's music, though seductive enough to be considered fileable under trip hop, the heavy-eyelidded, luxuriant mode of the 1990s, also delineates a certain desolation, a vast quandary. The listener feels alone in the mix, as past musics seem to recede like ancient radio broadcasts further into space. Everything is unfamiliar, disorienting. So many styles in the galaxy, so much to get to grips with in an era in which the stuff of the past is now the bricks and mortar of the future. *Endtroducing . . .* endtroduces a new era in which the pop cultural clock is set at three minutes to midnight. Over twenty years on, it still is. Eclectic, fragmentary, wilfully unfamiliar, *Endtroducing . . .* represents everything mainstream audiences implicitly feared in the bright-blue, retro, guitar-driven 1990s, with their craving for big, central, familiar, yesteryear-style 1960s sensations, which willed first the Stone Roses and then Oasis into being.

Despite DJ Shadow's misgivings, hip hop and sampling were by no means done; indeed, in the early twenty-first century two records were dropped that can be considered masterpieces worthy of sitting alongside any sort of masterpiece.

2000 saw the release of *The Unseen*, by Quasimoto, aka Madlib, aka Otis Jackson Jr, who was born in the sleepy town of Oxnard,

California, to musician parents – his father even put out his son's
first record on his own label in 1995 – and whose uncle was Jon
Faddis, a jazz trumpeter and academic expert in the genre. He set
up his own Crate Diggas Palace in Oxnard and was associated
with a variety of acts over the years, including J Dilla and MF
Doom.

The Unseen was the product of a month's intake of weed by
Madlib and has about it a blunted, woozy, easy roll, bathed in the
crackle of vinyl, punctuated by coughing fits as clouds of smoke
seem to get into his lungs. Just to listen to it makes you feel a little
stoned. But for all its languor and the enervated drawl of Madlib's
raps – often tweaked the way Prince liked to finger his own vocal
on the likes of 'If I Was Your Girlfriend', as if to put him into character – this is a serious assemblage, its seductive, lo-fi indolence a
product of a lifetime's dedication, and an African American cultural lifetime before that. It's achieved on pretty basic equipment
– no computers or Pro Tools, just a basic sampler, a digital board
and a pile of records. 'I do my stuff the old-school way, the hard
way,' he once said.

Wily old African American voices course through *The Unseen*
– Madlib has an uncommon respect for his elders. Melvin Van
Peebles is all over the record, while there's a bit from Redd Foxx
berating the modern dietary habit of self-denial to preserve good
health: 'You're gonna feel like a damn fool at the hospital dying
from nothing.' Samples from Augustus Pablo and, on 'Astro
Black', Sun Ra course through the mix. Meanwhile, the portentous announcers sampled from sci-fi and public-information films
from long ago mock the stiffly unhip voice of white male American
authority. The record derives entirely from the culled beats and
instrumental fragrances of records that Madlib's family owned and
which he listened to from the age of three onwards (he acquired
his first sampler when he was eight), their electric keyboards, flutes
and cymbal brushes flitting like fireflies.

There's a halcyon, deeply nostalgic feel about his clear attachment to the jazz, funk and jazz-funk of yesteryear. One skit sees him in a record store with a pasty know-nothing clerk who has never heard of Stanley Clarke or Chick Corea. *The Unseen* casts its eye affectionately over the faded antique treasures of post-war America, its comedy, its TV, its great black music. It's utterly derivative but wholly original in its collage, the brilliance of its editing, the tiny, ambient details like the distant street chatter that courses through 'Good Morning Sunshine'. Its west coast warmth filters through like the sun through the nicotine-stained net curtains of a bedroom filled with vinyl, a single mattress, a TV and a remote. It's a record that could only be made in 2000, twentieth-century music stripped of its bad clothing, shorn of its dull stretches, yellowed with age, highlighted, clipped, remixed, revered and ruthlessly messed with, shaped and made good in ways we only know of now.

In February 2006, J Dilla released the perfectly programmed *Donuts*, his crowning work, at the age of thirty-two. It's a circular river of joy, ending on the sample with which it begins, Motherlode's 'When I Die' – time eating its own tail. Wholesale samples of 10cc's 'The Worst Band in the World', Lil Brown's 'Light My Fire', Raymond Scott's 'Lightworks', the Sylvers' 'Only One Can Win' and Motherlode's 'When I Die' are interspersed with snatches of the Beastie Boys, Stevie Wonder, the Jackson 5, the Three Degrees and the Undisputed Truth, among others. The liquid whole provides high after starburst high, a montage of sweet, subtly misshapen nuggets whose abrupt cuts jolt the listener impatiently, as if Dilla the artist is determined to drag the listener from frame to frame in this gallery of master works. The originals are very often recognisable and quoted at length, but Dilla's treatments – jumps, loops, scratches, Rizla-thin edits, touches of reverb, overdubs, subtle emphases – at once enhance the old 45s and subvert the easy, sequential flow of familiarity.

Three days after he released the album, J Dilla died. In 2002, he had been diagnosed with TTP, an incurable blood disease; he was already a victim of lupus. In February 2006, he was in hospital, receiving dialysis treatment. He'd been there since the previous summer, when his friends brought him a sampler and a small record player to enable him to work on *Donuts* between his doses of medication. Twenty-nine of *Donut's* thirty-one tracks were completed while he was undergoing hospital treatment.

Listening to the album, as I have done hundreds of times, I am reminded of Bob Dylan's 'A Hard Rain's Gonna Fall', written during the Cuban missile crisis in late 1962, when global nuclear annihilation appeared to be imminent. The song, downcast and urgent, is composed of a series of lines, each of which was intended to form the basis of songs the young Dylan feared he would never get to write. The moment of truth never transpired, and decades later Dylan lives on. *Donuts* is similarly frantic in its desire to lay down as many ideas – future templates for rappers – as possible before J Dilla's blood gave out. He just made it, and the album has a poignancy, an inevitable resonance as a result. More remarkably, however, for what is an epitaph it is as uplifting as a triple shot of endorphins, just the album you reach for if you're feeling low – a perfectly sculpted, meticulously wrought monument to sweet soul, to lateral thinking and to the fine art of hip-hop production. J Dilla is among the immortals. *Donuts* is a defiant reminder that even if the classical eras of pop, rock and soul are behind us, sampling has the potential to deliver an infinite aftermath of ingenious mutations.

In 2005, Matthew Herbert, known for creating house music under a variety of pseudonyms, including Doctor Rockit, Radio Boy, Mr Vertigo, Transformer and Wishmountain, and whose music ranged from customised musique concrète to swing, published the following:

PERSONAL CONTRACT FOR THE COMPOSITION OF MUSIC (INCORPORATING THE MANIFESTO OF MISTAKES)

Stressing that this wasn't intended as a formula by which he would insist others abided, just himself, he drew up a set of rules that included the following:

The use of sounds that exist already is not allowed.

No drum machines.

No synthesizers.

No presets.

Only sounds that are generated at the start of the compositional process or taken from the artist's own previously unused archive are available for sampling.

The sampling of other people's music is strictly forbidden.

No replication of traditional acoustic instruments is allowed where the financial and physical possibility of using the real ones exists.

The scrupulous rigour of this manifesto was of a piece with Herbert's political beliefs, which he unapologetically promoted in his work, not through lyrical tub-thumping but by making the very sound matter that constituted his music the stuff of politics, particularly the politics of consumption and globalisation. This was integrity of a literal sort, which had never been applied to pop music before and was only possible thanks to sampling. It was a modus operandi that resulted in works like *Plat du jour* (2005), which takes a forensic, highly caustic look at the excesses and cruel iniquities of the food industry. On tracks like 'The Truncated Life of a Modern Industrialised Chicken' and 'Nigella, George, Tony and Me', Herbert made connections between politics, the spectacle of celebrity chefs and the cruelty of battery farming, constructing an ironically pleasurable mode of music derived from sources appertaining to the subject matter. This was a method he took further on *One Pig* (2011), whose lush electronic tones are derived from, among other sources, the blood of a slaughtered pig dripping into a bucket. The sheer pleasure of the music is part of the point – however ill-gotten, the politics of consumption depends on the desirability of its products. Nor did Herbert wish to repel audiences by mirroring the ugliness of the processes he decried in his music, but rather draw them in. Nor is the listener meant somehow to glean independently where the music is coming from – all is explained in detail in the albums' sleevenotes, or even accompanying websites, where you could find supplementary explanations of, for example, the coffee trade's connections with Vietnam and the slave trade. All of which made it matter that, like a master chef himself, Herbert chose precisely the correct and apposite ingredients for his sound. So, in making a point about the fruit industry, and the ecologically dubious practice of making out-of-season produce available for all-year-round purchase, it was important that a specific apple, say, be used in the sampling process. 'If I just used any old apple without considering where I bought it or where it was grown, my point becomes invalid.'

Herbert's fastidiousness and environmental awareness were evident when I interviewed him in his home town of Whitstable, on a cool-ish day, at a pub table located on the beach. He would interrupt proceedings every few minutes to bound off in pursuit of a rogue Coke bottle or plastic glass that had blown free from a nearby rubbish bin, restoring it to the can, scrunching it down if necessary to prevent it from escaping again.

'When everything I read politically and watch and hear has been absorbed, there comes a point where you must feel it viscerally,' he told me. 'Otherwise you are closed to the horrors of it and, thus, closed to the possibility of action, closed to the idea that you could make a difference or could have prevented the outcome. This internalising of the struggle, the friction, the melancholy I feel, should be at the emotional core of the work. After all, I am making music and not writing a newspaper article. But with the invention of the sampler, I can now explicitly root my work in the literal, critical present. I can describe the real in the frame of the imaginary.'

Further works in this vein included 2006's *Scale*, whose sound sources included someone vomiting outside a trade arms fair, recordings made covertly inside the Houses of Parliament, the sounds of petrol pumps and RAF Tornados, and a recording, made from inside a coffin, of its lid being shut. Again, however, far from presenting a gruelling, naturalistic montage to represent the repulsiveness of the arms trade, the music is silvery, shimmering and seductive, with Herbert getting to 'have his artistic cake and eat it', indulging his sweet tooth and delicious turn of musical phrase, while also mimicking the blandishments of capitalism, from whose comforting clutches it is hard to extricate oneself.

In 2017, there is such a thing as the Sample Music Festival. Its founder, Alex Sonnenfeld, set it up as a way of acknowledging and assessing excellence in the fields of turntablism, controllerism and music production. Asked how he felt sampling had changed over thirty years, Sonnenfeld said, 'These days you can take a millisecond of a sample and modulate it via sound design to create a new synth tone from it. So the question about sampling now is where does it start and where does it end? In these days every sound can be an instrument!'

That truth has held since the days of Pierre Schaeffer but, as Sonnenfeld points out, today's precision-tool technology has long supplanted the old days of scissors and tape. Early sample-based records, which at the time felt so state-of-the-art they were almost depressing in their postmodernity, wistful reminders of a golden pop age that could only be referred to rather than exceeded, now themselves feel like quaint relics of pop's past. No one will ever make a record like *Paul's Boutique* again. It's locked in 1989.

Listening to a present-day practitioner like, say, Hudson Mohawke, what strikes one about his assemblages is that, towering and resourceful as they are, they make little or no discernible reference to the past, no nods and winks to the good old days; they are creations of the twenty-first-century moment.

This is of a piece with the millennial condition, and that of the pre-teens coming up after. Retromania, the cultural state so excellently diagnosed by Simon Reynolds, has given way somewhat to a newer culture in which, like smartphone upgrades, all that really counts is the last few months or so. When *The Simpsons* first started in 1990, it could take for granted that its audience would immediately catch all of its pop cultural references to, say, *The Twilight Zone*, Hitchcock and *It's a Wonderful Life*. Its mass audience collided with these programmes and films as a matter of course, during their childhood and beyond, in the days before the schedules became atomised by cable. We of a certain generation were not just steeped in our own times but in a televisual and filmic past that stretched right back to the 1920s. We 'lived' all the decades.

Nowadays, TV's mainstream schedules are crammed with the recently made. *Tom and Jerry*, *The Phil Silvers Show* and *Laurel and Hardy* have not been broadcast on terrestrial channels in the UK in years, having long since been farmed out to vintage-programming channels. And despite the disproportionate market share of oldies like Elton, the Stones and Led Zeppelin, they belong to a century – the twentieth – in which today's generation barely live at all. This is not a generation that is looking wistfully over its shoulder, as parents of a certain age will attest with horror when they ask their children the most elementary questions about the Beatles. They have entered a post-postmodernity of their own. They'll make of it what they will.

In the spirit of sampling's ability to make a nonsense of timelines, let's end with Steve Reich and go backwards and forwards.

Reich is another artist who has made 'honorary electronic music' – I refer to his *Music for 18 Musicians*, a piece for xylophones, bassoons, strings and vocals, among other acoustic instruments. By the ingenious expedient of having the players 'double up' on their instruments, Reich achieves an uncannily sequenced piece of pseudo-machine music whose motions resemble time-lapse footage of traffic in a faultlessly functioning city. It's a model for a perfect mode of modern, social, technical, community interaction.

Fast forward to 1994 and his piece *City Life*, a chamber piece that, in a homage of sorts to Edgard Varèse, incorporated samples of everyday New York life into its musical portrait of Manhattan. It felt a little similar, however, to *Different Trains* (1988), in which Reich bases his melodies on the speech patterns of taped interviewees discussing momentous railway journeys before, during and after the war in America and Europe – including the trains that transported Jews to the concentration camps. The huge emotional and thematic heft of *Different Trains* rather put *City Life* in the shade; in the mid-1990s, Reich decided he was done with sampling for a while.

Fast backward to 1966. A young Steve Reich had become fascinated with tape loops, particularly those of people speaking, and the strange, unintended effects of their meter, especially when repeated. For 'Come Out', he repeated the treatment he had applied a year earlier to a piece called 'It's Gonna Rain'. He used as his source a recording of Daniel Hamm, a snippet from seventy hours of tape presented to him by civil rights activist Truman Nelson. Hamm, a teenager, was one of the so-called 'Harlem Six', arrested for murder following a riot in Harlem which resulted in a fatality. Hamm was ultimately acquitted, but not before, by his own account, he had taken a beating at the hands of police while in custody. Reich uses the snippet of tape in which Hamm recalls, 'I had to, like, open the bruise up, and let some of the bruise blood come out to show them' – i.e. he had to demonstrate he was bleeding in order to be admitted to hospital. In the piece, Reich runs this excerpt in full, before repeating the words 'come out to show them' on two mono recorders just slightly out of sync. The intonation of Hamm's speech becomes musical: E flat, C, C, D, C, over and over, but increasingly out of time, so as to create a reverberant, trance-like effect in which the words have first been processed into music and then, finally, as they split into four and eight, into sonic bruisings in their own right, a barely intelligible, tonal, rhythmic blur. It's conceptually immaculate, converting a fleeting moment of political indignation into a processed and pre-served sound piece which has resounded down the decades; it's also sonically overwhelming, rebounding and echoing around the cranium like a latter-day piece of IDM. If you should feel the need to begin again, to be walked through an ideal example of the fruit-ful and necessary relationship between non-musical and musical matter, then you could do worse than end up here.

Decades later, musicians would return to the sort of techniques employed by Reich, so nascent and primitive and forward-looking in their time, and use them in a more obliquely retrospective way to create a poetry of decay and disintegration.

15

REVERBERATION AND DECAY

Cut back to the futures of long ago. Modernism was never really about avant-garde obscurantism and intellectual exclusivity, even if things eventually wound up that way. The twentieth-century modernists – the likes of Kandinsky and Boulez, for example – dreamt in *Gesamtkunstwerk* terms of great, overarching artistic unities, the like of which had never existed before. A movement like Dada, with its punkishly insolent collages and outrages, may have appeared to embrace the globe-shattering chaos that the new century had ushered in, whether in the carnage of World War I or on the canvasses, but at another level it lamented the tragedy of disunity and disharmony. Despite the negativity that was at its heart, Dada resounded with a desperate 'YES!' It was an attempt to whip up new totalities from the shards and fragments of the dead old, using the energy of the movement's manifestos and happenings.

It was interesting to interview Steve Savale, aka Chandrasonic, of Asian Dub Foundation in 2008. Since the late 1990s, ADF had made it a point of pride to align themselves with, and absorb into their sound, every new manifestation of black musical invention, from drum 'n' bass onwards. They saw this as a riposte to the retro tendencies of the Britpop era, which they suspected, almost certainly correctly, of signifying an unspoken desire for simpler, pre-multicultural pop times. Hence, ADF's sonic futurism was in tandem with their political thrust.

In 2008, however, Savale felt less inclined towards this continuum. He remarked that each successive great new underground movement went through a familiar pattern of eruption and absorption, and that to expect otherwise – that this time this new movement would succeed where others hadn't – was in itself retrograde.

The twenty-first century is not, thus far, the age of Big Things. This is the age of the aftermath, of afterglow, disintegration and breakdown into tiny constituents. Music aspires not to achieve some new alchemy of sound, fresh, youthful purpose and progress – the 'wake-up call' – but instead embraces fragmentation, decay, disintegration, breakdown, the submerged and dormant past.

The term 'hauntology' was first coined by Jacques Derrida but has more recently been co-opted by thinking luminaries of the blogosphere to describe forms of music whose relationship with the past is more profound, more visionary in its indistinctness than that of the nostalgia industrialists who brought us programmes like *I Love the 70s*. As the late Mark Fisher, among the most eloquent commentators on this phenomenon, put it:

> Hauntology is about attuning ourselves to the ways in which traces of events continue to perturb the present. What is important here is not the reiteration of the actual past, but the persistence of what never actually happened, but might have – the logic of events that failed to fully unfold but which can still be returned to.

Hauntology needs emphatically to be distinguished from the lazy, backwards gaze of a rock industry for which the present and the future are dead zones, and only the past remains alive. Instead, the operatives on the Ghostbox label, such as the Focus Group, or similar projects, such as the Advisory Circle, weave a boneless, at times faintly ectoplasmic tapestry of samples and cut-up juxtapositions that teases up unspecific memories of the themes to BBC schools programmes, library sound sources, naive synthesized signature tunes, mid-morning breakdowns in transmission, all couched in an authentic, wavering analogue fuzz. Its comedic corollary was the BBC comedy series *Look Around You*, in which surreal 'modules' are presented in a clever jumbled parody of the style of college educational programmes of the era. Further viewing is also recommended in the form of *Charley Says*, a collection of public information films dating from the late 1950s to the late 1970s, at which point they petered out, and which also provide a rich source of oblique references for the hauntologists. The likes of the Focus Group, however, are looking for effects that are more disquieting and evocative. In the assemblages of the Advisory Circle, there are intimated flashbacks not just to the programmes and analogue-synth incidental ambience of the late 1970s but to memories both halcyon and harrowing to those who grew up in those times – of harsh wintry landscapes, crows cawing and bare twigs scratching the dusky horizon, of the general, nameless, toxic gloom of that overcast, brown-oak-panelled era, as well as of days off school with a head cold, sitting by a two-bar fire, cheerfully staring at the test card through a rheumy haze.

But the resonance of this music, of the spirit it distils, extends beyond the merely personal and wistful. It's about lost futures. In 1978, despite the *Protect and Survive* short films, designed to tell the populace what to do in the event of a nuclear attack, fear of the apocalypse had yet to inflate into the full-blown dread of the early Thatcher/Reagan years. Deregulation was just around the corner; the clipped, authoritative tones of the British voiceover provided us with narrative guidance on how to live our lives, what to guard against and when not to panic. Figures like Raymond Baxter on *Tomorrow's World* patiently and lucidly explained to us that the future, heralded and underscored by the bass tones of the Moog synthesizer, would be an orderly affair, in which the microchip would do away with much of the drudgery of everyday life, leaving us more time to go for walks or listen to Johnny Dankworth. The

Soviet Union was here to stay, sadly, but at least in the West we would be free, albeit benevolently supervised, to live our lives on a gentle, upwards gradient of progression, labour-saving and general improvement.

Life could have been worse. Perhaps that is what it has become. One simple question posited by this particular brand of hauntology is: Suppose Thatcherism had never happened? Suppose punk had never happened? Suppose postmodernism had never occurred, and the old welfare-state frontiers had never been rolled back? Suppose we had travelled down one of the many other pathways towards the year 2000 that we had imagined? But hauntology's relationship with the past is more complex than that. It's about what abides, albeit blurry and dimly delineated, in our past, in our memory banks, and by reanimating the aspects of those times still alive to us, how the events they contained could indeed conceivably be 'returned to'.

If there is a problem with the Ghostbox school of hauntology, it's that its deliberately implanted 'memories' only resonate with those born in a certain time (1955–70, approximately) and a certain place (the UK). There are those, however, who apply hauntological principles in a less time-and-place-specific manner. One of them is the Liverpool-born turntablist Philip Jeck. His background is in the visual arts – he loved music, but as a child soon realised that he had no singing voice and wasn't much use wrapped around a guitar, and so concentrated on painting and drawing. But he swiftly tired of the static nature of visual art – 'paintings hanging on walls, sculptures in galleries' – and moved into more mobile media. One of his first epiphanies came in the New York disco scene in the late 1970s – not Grandmaster Flash, but mixers like Walter Gibbons and Larry Levan. 'I loved the way they used extended breaks, broke down the music – and the way they incorporated tape loops into their mixes. I started off trying to copy what they did.'

Jeck eventually dropped his budding aspirations of following in their dance footsteps and, involved as he was with the likes of the London Musicians' Collective, his work took on the contours of sound art. He started working with dance theatre groups, on pieces staged by the likes of Laurie Booth, and it was in doing this that he alighted on his signature style. His first major release was *Vinyl Requiem*, in 1993, for 180 turntables, nine slide projectors and two 16mm movie projectors. He has made frequent audio-visual collaborations since then, but the formidable body of solo work he has built up over the last fifteen years (generally, albums with single-word titles beginning with 's' – *Sand, Stoke, Surf, 7,* etc.) has become far more than a supplement to the visual, creating vivid, disquieting abstracts for the mind's eyes and ears.

Jeck's music is generally drawn from samples – 'I have the whole history of recorded music to work with.' However, he keeps two record collections: one of the music he enjoys recreationally and does not use as a sound source ('I normally shy away from the super-recognisable. I don't want to get my record company into trouble, for a start!'); the other a dusty, scratchy collection of dis-carded vinyl trifles and oddities – demonstration records, lullabies, cheesy old MOR, the light orchestral fodder of the Radio 2 of all our yesteryears, the sort of music that were it not dredged up, diced and reassembled by Jeck, would most likely never be played again by any other human being on the planet.

Jeck deliberately uses antique technology – Dansette record players, tape loops, obsolete samplers – to alter, isolate, repeat and generally decontextualise his samples. Occasionally, a frag-ment of something recognisable will bob to the surface of the mix – a spectral passage of early Suicide, played backwards, which runs through 'Spirits Up', or, on 'Fanfare', a recording of Aaron Copland's 'Fanfare for the Common Man', which Jeck arrived at erroneously while playing a festival in Holland. 'It's from a vinyl demonstration record for a Hammond organ. I put the needle onto track two by mistake but decided I liked it. It's fantastic when accidents like that happen.'

Indeterminacy plays a key role in Jeck's work, from the mere chance of these old records washing up in his possession in the first place, to the process by which things incite his artistic curiosity. 'Something will catch my ear and my imagination. Something appears, something emotionally strong. So I go into that sound, expand on it, add to it, tweak it, put things next to it, change its context. Sometimes I hardly know what I've done . . .'

Certainly, there is an emotional tug to Jeck that is absent from his fellow practitioners. Jeck picked up from fellow turntablist Christian Marclay the trick of creating loops by placing stickers on the vinyl to make the needle stick in a specific groove. However, whereas Marclay deals in witty and acute sound collages, in which the recognisability of the source material is part of the fun and part of the point, Jeck's music, with its gaseous, intermingled swirl of loops, delays and drones, stirs and overwhelms in a way that Marclay's does not. The use of crackle and the clicks of locked grooves on, say, 'Shining' are pointed reminders that these pieces are sourced from vinyl, but that only enhances their emotional appeal, as opposed to functioning as reminders that this is just all so much avant-garde trickery.

But in what does that emotional appeal consist? Is it the displacement of these sounds from their original unassuming and banal sources? Is it their musty redolence? Is it the distress they have incurred over the years of neglect, all those pops, scratches and clicks, which remind one of the passing of time and the history these artefacts have accrued? All of these things contribute. But it is the tapestry Jeck weaves together from his samples that somehow lends them an inadvertent nobility of purpose and abiding emotional weight which they could never have hoped to have achieved in their original incarnations. The ancient voice of a woman, double-tracked as she sings the 'Now I lay me down to sleep' lullaby, feels like a channelling, a raising of the dead – one of the reasons many find Jeck's music to be 'nightmarish'. Voices are slowed down to 16 rpm, like old speak-your-weight machines whose batteries have almost, but not quite, died. Muzak swirls and pans around these beatless, amorphous mixes, the sort that used to resound through the dismal dark-brown rafters of northern shopping malls in the 1970s. It should be depressing, and yet it isn't. A track like 'Fanfares', with its huge, billowing blasts of trumpet, distorted and sepia-tinted by age, galvanises the spirits like the wind lifting up the leaves in autumn. It's a profound, melancholic yet somehow affirmative surge of 'nostalgia for the infinite', rearing up ghost-like from the cellars of the subconscious.

'For a while I shied away from thinking it was about this sort of thing,' says Jeck, 'but now I realise it is. These super-influential moments and memories somewhere in your life – they tug at you, they mean something.'

If one piece of music can claim to be a hauntological milestone, it is Gavin Bryars's *The Sinking of the Titanic*. No home, frankly, should be without at least one of the three recordings made of it to date. Its date of composition is always listed as (1969–), to impress that it is an open-ended piece. Over the years, it has accrued various layers of new material as more comes to light about the 1912 tragedy, as well as various additions and extensions and reinterpretations. Despite its subject matter of perished souls, it is as near as a piece of music has come to being a 'living' thing, retaining the capacity to grow and develop.

The Sinking of the Titanic takes as its jumping-off point (to use a completely inappropriate phrase) the famous story of how the band played on as the boat sank. The *Titanic* story is generally regarded as the prime example of the hubris of modernity being laid low by an implacable force of nature – i.e. the iceberg. The fate of the musicians, in particular, lends the piece all the poignancy it needs, but what intrigued Bryars more was the technological speculation it excited in Guglielmo Marconi, the Italian pioneer of wireless telegraphy. The technology he had developed came into play during the course of the *Titanic* disaster, but sadly to no avail – one rescue ship, the *Birma*, received a radio distress signal from the liner, but only ninety minutes after it had finally sunk beneath the waves.

Towards the end of his life, Marconi became obsessed by the idea that sounds do not actually die but merely diminish, become fainter and fainter without ever expiring. He was convinced that extraordinarily sensitive equipment could be developed to trace these sounds, still fractionally alive, albeit many fathoms below the threshold of human audibility. Indeed, he dreamt that by such technological means it might one day be possible to hear the Sermon on the Mount.

The most recent version of Bryars's piece, recorded in 2005, begins with an extended collage of vinyl crackle, provided by Philip Jeck. What's being created is a living memory gauze, every tiny scratch a living flicker of the dead past. 'It's beyond the fact that these are recorded memories,' says Jeck of the scratched vinyl he uses. 'It's about what's happened to these things since they were recorded. All those pops and marks and scratches and crackle that they gather over the years – they are a history in themselves, translated into this sound. The more things get scratched, the more they are affected. Somehow or other you're introduced to the idea that this is a record of history.'

Eventually, the tolling clank of a buoy announces the introduction of the Italian chamber group Alter Ego, who strike up with the piece's central motif, a variation on the Episcopal hymn 'Autumn'. Gently seeing and sawing at their strings, the arrangement lists solemnly, as if at the mercy of the water itself, forever sinking, forever rising, decaying and renewing, fading and resurfacing over the course of an hour or so, constantly assailed by its own shadows (the delay effects of the wind instruments), as well as new sound sources attached like barnacles to the recording. The strings spread out laterally, as if imitating soundwaves sealed by the ocean's surface. This is more than just avant-garde schematics; the lingering push and pull on the heartstrings is soberly overwhelming, a sort of massage for the soul, inviting an implicit and profound meditation on the relationship between music and time, life and death and memory, the past and the future.

Through this infinite sea of sound drift elements old and new to the piece. The rise and fall of a bass clarinet serves to single out one victim of the tragedy, a Scottish piper, an individual lamentation. Reminiscences from survivors wax and wane throughout the mix. The piece is achronological: some sections reflect the decades-long deathly quiet of the rusting hulk on the seabed; woodblocks and marimbas reflect the stresses and groans of the great craft; while, thirty-eight minutes in, taped sounds of a crowd illustrate the probable mass panic on board as the ship began to sink, with no space left on the lifeboats. Marconi would doubtless have believed that those cries of terror are still 'alive' somewhere in the water. Jeck's turntablism spindles discreetly through the liquid mix, while the sound of crickets adds a surreal cinematic counterpoint. Finally, the piece fades, for the time being, giving way to some ancient vinyl jingle from Jeck, as if the piece is disappearing back into a closing music box. This is the third version of *The Sinking of the Titanic* (unless you count Aphex Twin's 1994 remix, *Raising the Titanic*). A fourth will follow later in the century.

The 2005 recording of *The Sinking of the Titanic* was made at the 49th International Festival of Contemporary Music at the Venice Biennale, at the Teatro Malibran. Although Venice is no rock'n'roll town by any stretch of the imagination, it is a beautifully apt location for this sort of 'decay' music – the bell towers wonky with subsidence, the architecture around St Mark's Square corroded with pigeon shit, the nauseous, sweet tang of the stagnant and toxified and darkly turquoise canal waters, the white bannisters of the bridges worn down to an almost frictionless shine by centuries of merchants, citizens and tourists. It symbolises the precariousness of civilisation, sinking under the prodigious weight of its legacy. I saw American sound artist William Basinski perform at the Venice Biennale in 2008, at the Teatro alle Tese. As a child, Basinski harboured impossible dreams of becoming a 'British rock star', then became a classically trained clarinettist, and was introduced to works by twentieth-century composers like John Cage and Iannis Xenakis. From there, he got into Steve Reich and Brian Eno, and in the early 1980s he built up an archive of tape loops based on found sounds, shortwave radio and the sort of delay systems Eno used in pieces like *Discreet Music*. Almost two decades later, these would form the chance basis for his 2001 *Disintegration Loops* series: wishing to transfer his tape archive from reel to reel to the less perishable hard-disk format, he realised that as they were playing, the tapes were flaking and breaking up on him through sheer age.

'Knowing the fragility of old magnetic tape, I wanted to transfer them to digital before they were destroyed,' recalls Basinski. 'After about ten or fifteen minutes, to my shock and amazement the first loop I put on the reel-to-reel deck began to disintegrate, the glue having lost its integrity. The iron oxide began to return to dust, gradually, over a period of about an hour, in a remarkable way.'

Basinski realised that he wasn't so much re-recording these loops as documenting their death throes. These recordings happened to coincide with the events of 11 September 2001, when disintegration of a far greater magnitude occurred, just a mile or so from where Basinski was living at the time.

'No one who wasn't there can imagine what it was like to see such a catastrophic, shocking spectacle as the World Trade Center disappearing from the skyline in two hours,' says Basinski. 'I know the world was shocked and saddened to see on television what happened in NY that day, but being there that day and the days and months that followed was truly terrifying. After making a videotape of the last hour of daylight, looking towards the smoke coming from the devastation of Lower Manhattan, I put "Disintegration Loop 1.1" on as a soundtrack the next morning. I added a postscript on the liner notes to *The Disintegration Loops* a few weeks after the tragedy, and decided to use four frames from the video for the covers of the four volumes and to dedicate the music to those who were lost and those who lost loved ones in the horrific atrocities of that day. The events gave grave new meaning to the musical pieces created by catastrophic decay in my studio a few weeks before.'

Basinski would dedicate *The Disintegration Loops* to the victims of that tragedy, and on one level they provide a moving tribute: despite material disintegration, the 'spirit', in the form of the repeated loops, abides. 'I immediately recognised and was profoundly moved by the redemptive analogy and was amazed at the way each of the loops retained its core "personality" to the end somehow.

'I want [*The Disintegration Loops*] to survive the coming apocalypse, if possible, and last into the age of no electricity. There will still be musicians.'

Just as powerful as the live experience is walking around the labyrinths of Venice, attempting to depart from the beaten track, with *Disintegration Loops* as an iPod soundtrack. This serves in part to zone out the actual soundtrack of Venice: a mixture of turgid Italian power ballads blaring from every other cafe, 1980s hits such as Survivor's 'Eye of the Tiger' – like stodgy, non-recyclable landfill still a stubborn feature of the soundscape – and the cafe orchestras in St Mark's Square, competing to outplay and out-cheese each other in their brash selection of popular classics. Zone out also the city's entire ground floor of designer and souvenir outlets and you experience a frightening synergy between soundtrack and architecture, as Basinski's loops move in their magisterial decaying circles.

The originals started out in the bloom of their (and their author's) youth as simple but epic, arching, pastoral motifs. However, the creases and fissures of age lend these tapes a cumulative character, as they roll, magnificently, remorselessly and catastrophically on (the loops can last for anything up to an hour, a 'lifetime' of sorts in recorded musical terms). When the tapes audibly physically dis-integrate, one is reminded of footage of great chunks of iceberg in the melting polar ice caps dropping elegantly and fatefully into the ocean. Basinski, incidentally, is aware of the 'destructive' nature of feedback loops: as applied in ecological terms, they are said to represent the greatest danger posed by global warming – the more the Arctic melts, for example, the less whiteness there is to reflect the heat of the sun back into space.

Other pieces, such as 'Particle Showers' (from *Shortwavemusic*), offer their own exhilarating, terrifying pleasures, the track's typi-cally recurring, unresolved motif crashing like a giant wave, over and over, as gigantic currents of dub and echo wash like water over the shelves as the waves recede – memories of future catastrophe in slow, reiterated motion, endlessly fixating. But it's to the loops that one returns, over and over. They are monumental, tragic in their implications, salutary and yet somehow defiantly affirmative, star-ing down mortality rather than retreating into 'live for ever' fantasy.

The most popular hauntological specimen is Burial, the (initially) anonymous figure who arose from the south London dubstep scene, refusing for a long time to divulge his identity, be photo-graphed or even play live. It was as if he felt that any trace of his corporeal presence in the dissemination of the music would some-how compromise it. His two albums – his eponymous 2006 debut and 2007's *Untrue* – are very similar in atmosphere and texture. They at once express past, present and future tension. Ingrained in them is the elegiac premise that the once great underground club and rave scene has vanished. This he conveys in his trademark rhythms, which rattle deathly and drily like the clacking bones of what was once flesh and beat, energy and squiggle. On a track like 'Ghost Hardware', the rhythm can be heard scrunching, as if across blackened, fragmented remains. All the funky tropes of yesterday are reduced to ethereal wisps in the Burial mix, fluttering about like the shadows of bats. Old soul vocals hang mournfully like holograms, faded and dissolving in their own echoes of dub.

There's a palpable sense of the present, both in time and geography, as titles such as 'Night Bus', 'South London Boroughs' and 'In McDonald's' directly convey. Burial conveys the dusky, looming, indifferent toxicity of the city, its undercurrent of menace and yet, somehow, its unlikely Gothic beauty. And then there is the future, as portended in the concept to the first album, which imagines a London decades hence fallen victim to some local environmental disaster. The luminous shafts of 'Distant Lights' are watery and bleak indeed, the general feel of a dystopia that is closer to science fact than fiction.

And yet for all the desolation, retrospection and anxiety, Burial broke through to a wider audience unmoved by much of the dubstep scene from which he sprang, an audience that has found something altogether exciting in his scorched, charcoaled beatscapes, something new. However, it isn't just this writer who finds something greater in the disintegrated, crumbled beats that blow and billow like soot about Burial's albums, more pleasing than the hale and hearty club scene they lament. Maybe it's morbidity – not unlike preferring a poem like Goldsmith's 'The Deserted Village' to some Merrie England-penned popular verse extolling the jollity of maypole dancing. Maybe also Burial shows how in 'disintegrating' dance music is actually evolving, transcending its past corporeal limitations.

In his 2001 book *Microsound*, electroacoustic composer Curtis Roads celebrates the emergence of 'sound particles', an entirely new realm of sonic matter that represents a riposte to those who believe that everything under the sun has already been discovered and mined to exhaustion. 'Microsonic techniques remained invisible for centuries,' he writes in the Introduction. 'Recent technological advances let us probe and explore the beauties of this formerly unseen world. Microsonic techniques dissolve the rigid bricks of music architecture – the notes – into a more fluid and supple medium. Sounds may coalesce, evaporate or mutate into other sounds.'

Nowhere have these ideas been more effectively practised and popularised than in the worlds of electronica and techno. Autechre, big fans of Roads, took the ideas he propounds to infinitesimal extremes on albums like *Draft 7.30*, using a combination of new technologies and those prematurely declared obsolete to achieve unearthly, year 3000 beatscapes that at times sound like the magnifications of millipedes scratching their kneecaps. So far ahead were they of conventional appetites for electronic music that they've had to rein in their experimentation on more recent albums like *Quaristice*. The sound labs of labels like Raster-Noton, in which 'glitch', the deliberate incorporation of the sort of tiny mechanical 'errors' into the very tapestry of the sound, are dealing in ever tinier molecular structures. The future of electronic music is very much about breakdown, fragmentation, finding new modes of expression in ever tinier fragments, rendering the big sound ideas of the past obsolete.

Listen back to early house or disco or hip hop or electropop and, for all the fond memories they trigger, it's hard not to suffer a twinge at their technological limitations. Even on an album like Kraftwerk's *Trans-Europe Express*, a twentieth-century masterpiece, you have to overlook the joins and retrospectively allow for what was available to them in the studio at the time. Sometimes it's the bits of jet-black silence that are unhidden between the laid-down grids of sound that seem conspicuous and awkward nowadays – on the Beastie Boys' *Licensed to Ill*, say, and the pauses lurking between the beats. This is the sort of 'nothingness' people used to imagine constituted space, before we learned about atoms and molecules, or imagined the sky to consist of, if their only experience of the night-time was in dull-weathered, low-lying countries like the UK. In the 1980s and '90s, people started breaking beats down, but this wasn't a halcyon era, nor the beginning of the end for the robustness and integrity of dance music; merely the beginning of a process which, in the era of Pro Tools and the like, has allowed for the sort of coalescence, evaporation and mutation celebrated by Curtis Roads.

One of the albums that helped initiate the diffusion of electronic music was Basic Channel's *BCD*, from 1996, which brought together the cuts Berlin-based duo Moritz von Oswald and Mark Ernestus had been working on since 1993. This is the album on which techno is launched into the outer realms of dub like a space probe, burnt up and reduced to shards, a showering area of micro-details and filings disporting among themselves outside the realms of gravity. On tracks like 'Mutism' and 'Quadrant Dub', the mind's eye is assailed by a notional outer space as revealed in all its incandescent, cloudy, pointillistic detail. The regular rhythm keeps pumping, like a necessary heartbeat or a distant connection back to base, but it's no longer the main event. Here the beats aren't merely broken, they're crumbled, reduced to a fine and fascinating new consistency. The exposure of techno to dub radiation had been a long-overdue event and the results were every bit as mindbending as you could imagine; indeed, listen to *BCD* nowadays and it still sounds unearthly, still tingles in the ear canal and excites the synapses, given that it has yet to make the headway into popular currency that is its due.

As with Kraftwerk, it's a wonder that these sorts of innovations come in disproportionate numbers from Germany or, in the case of Pole's Stefan Betke, Austria. Christian Fennesz is another Austrian, who began life as a guitarist but then realised he could yield more

if he processed his guitar via his laptop. In this respect, he was taking still further the extreme weather conditions emulated by My
Bloody Valentine on their album *Loveless*. Fennesz immerses the
listener using glitch and twisted, sculpted sheets of noise, as well as
unnaturally distorted fretboard emissions, but as with My Bloody
Valentine again, there is a tenuous, vital connection with pop, or
the memory of its outline. A track like 'Rivers of Sand', from his
2004 album *Venice*, is apposite. It's as liquidless as the title suggests, as if revisiting Planet Pop centuries after it has been scorched
to aridity, tracing the contours it has left behind, which are now
perverted by the shifting of the sands and harried by dry storms.
All of which sounds bleak and fanciful; however, the reality of this
fantasy soundscape is a granular deluge of new possibilities, more
malleable and versatile matter with which to make music – the
rigid bricks dissolved, indeed.

The innovations of microbeat have managed to pervade the
realms of more popular music – in the work of Matthew Dear,
for example, or minimal techno crowd-pullers like Richie Hawtin,
Luciano or Ricardo Villalobos. While these artists may play it
relatively straight in their DJ sets, their own productions are supple, shape-shifting investigations into just how far you can bend,
mutate and disintegrate the genre they work in, while maintain-
ing a notional relationship with the backbeat. The word 'minimal'
often feels like a misnomer – these tracks are minimal insofar as
they are repetitive and fixated. However, they are florally abundant
with micro-detail. Take a track like Villalobos's 'Duso', for example, in which, adjacent to a discreetly toiling backbeat, strange,
seahorse-like molecular chains rear up from the mix, before receding. Or his 'Sieso', borne by tiny, splintered and sub-splintering
rhythms, like a miniature array of pots and pans working to the
strict and detailed discipline of a computer program. Where
once there was nothing, now so much detail – not just detail but
fresh pathways, new (dis)solutions, which, slowly but surely, are

insinuating themselves into the orthodoxy of what constitutes acceptable popular music.

As well as enabling new artists to create new forms by breaking down what was once considered to be irreducible, new micro-sampling software means that a new crop of musicians can now freshly renegotiate the relationship between today's music and the mountainous pile of its own living-dead past.

As for present/future sounds, advances in technological record-ing continue to be an enabler. The great technological enemy today, however, is the insidious and all-pervasive studio practice of compression. This is the process whereby the usual level variations you get in a sound recording, the peaks and troughs you might see on a waveform, are ruthlessly excised and replaced with a flat-lining, illusory 'bigness'. This is the process whereby Coldplay, at the same volume setting on a hi-fi, and even at their jangliest and organic-woolly-hatted mimsiest, will sound louder than Led Zeppelin, even though they're not actually trying to play heavy metal. If there has been a vogue in recent years for those mak-ing experimental music (Raster-Noton, for example) to express themselves graphically in lower case only, then the tendency for mainstream pop has been to express itself sonically in UPPER CASE only. No dips, no use of space, no variance – instead of 'AaaaaAAaaAAAAAaaa', simply a brutal 'AAAAAAAAAAAAAA'.

This is the latest, though perhaps not the last, attempt to assert the supposedly desirable Big Thing. But bigness of this sort, unmerited and for its own sake, is the last thing that's currently required. It's like hoisting a cornerstone to the top of a spire in the closing stages of building a cathedral. The Big Thing seems healthy – resurgent, reunifying, galvanising – but in this day and age, it is false, irrelevant and enervating. Instead, perhaps, the interplay of smaller and smaller components: clusters rather than crowds, universes discovered in pinhead details rather than grand universal themes.

Things aren't what they used to be. Things are disintegrating and decaying. It's unsettling, exciting.

I'm sitting with John Foxx in a bar near Broadcasting House in London, which commands views across the capital. It's apposite: one of the main images that has haunted and sustained Foxx creatively over the decades is a painting he saw in the 1960s of the city. 'It looked like a woodland or jungle, but if you looked carefully you could see it was the view of Centrepoint over Soho. Beautifully painted, no explanation.'

This image wasn't without precedent: in 1873, the French artist Gustave Doré came to London and painted *The New Zealander*, which sees a young traveller from that country sitting on the broken arch of a bridge looking out towards St Paul's – only St Paul's is in ruins. So too is Cannon Street station, only recently built but here in a state of neglect and decay, the iron bridge that leads from it across the river rusted over.

In his 2001 book *In Ruins*, Christopher Woodward examines ruins of various kinds, including the Colosseum, which in the nineteenth century, prior to its abrupt refurbishment, was a neglected luxury of botany, some of it rare and exotic, deriving from seeds borne on animals from Persia or North Africa that had been brought over for gladiatorial games. For him, ruins are symbols of the future, reminders of impermanence but also of resilience and a fascinating richness that in some ways outdoes monuments during the span of their more active life. They are architectural equivalents of the long reverberation, or decay, so favoured by Foxx in his ambient recordings.

'When I was in the choir as a kid, I realised that when you sing, you unconsciously harmonise with your own delayed reflections from the walls,' recalls Foxx. 'The harmony bounces back at you from your own voice. I used to go to the church in St Mary's in Chorley. I didn't understand what was happening then but I did enjoy it. And then, when longer loops became available in the 1980s, I set them up to see what would happen – and what I did had that chant mode, that feel, that out-of-body experience you get with choirs.'

Ruins are not tragic sites for Foxx but fertile spaces. 'I grew up when the mills were emptying in Lancashire. These were huge towns in their own right but now they were overgrown, with nature reclaiming the territory. Lord Lever built a house on a hillside in Chorley, overlooking the moors – he imported exotic plants, diverted rivers to make waterfalls, built stone pagodas – but one day he destroyed the house and moved away, leaving the remains to the town. We played in that. It was a jungle, full of waterfalls, rhododendrons, tangled pathways . . .'

Later, he speaks of attending 'The 14 Hour Technicolor Dream' in 1967, at Alexandra Palace in London, a fund-raising concert for the journal *International Times*, which marked the beginnings of the UK counter-cultural movement and featured bands like John's Children and Tomorrow. 'The place was almost in ruins, covered in leaves – it felt like a Victorian estate.'

Later still, when looking to set up a workspace in London, Foxx came to Rivington Street in Shoreditch, east London. Today, Rivington Street is a painfully hip hive of galleries, book-shops, cafes and upscale hotels. Not then. 'You could have mown Rivington Street,' remembers Foxx. 'We bought an ex-department store for next to nothing, a birch tree growing out of the window. I used to imagine walking around London and speculating on the place being overgrown.'

Such are the scenarios Foxx recreates on albums like *Cathedral Oceans*. 'The whole process of echoes in *Cathedral Oceans* is like overgrowth – unpredictable organic gardening,' he says. 'Things blooming all over the place.'

Foxx's preoccupation with ruins, present and future, is not a polemical one, he says. 'I've been thinking, writing, drawing about it for years. I don't actually understand it, I don't want to understand it. It's not necessarily a political, ecological thing.' Contemplating pieces like 'The Beautiful Ghost', from *London Overgrown*, however, one feels not a sense of tragedy or dystopia but a comforting respite, a step away from the frantic, futile traffic of the everyday Now, the Now that is permanently dissolving. Decay is the future indeed, but as befell the Colosseum, even decay may only be temporary. Today, Detroit is a latter-day urban ruin, the spectacle of which would have alarmed the Motown kids of the 1960s the way Doré's painting would have alarmed viewers from London in the late nineteenth century: vast abandoned factories and suburbs reclaimed by rust and grass, a grim yet strangely beautiful monument to white flight and the lost hopes of the American post-war period. Yet Detroit, like Shoreditch, like Alexandra Palace, may yet be regenerated in our lifetime. Maybe ruin and decay should be something we savour while they last.

Describing the Caretaker, aka Leyland James Kirby, the late Mark Fisher spoke of his music suggesting a certain cultural condition, as well as a form of mental deterioration: 'Not so much a longing for the past as an inability to make new memories.' Certainly, with pieces like 'All You Are Going to Want to Do Is Get Back There', discreetly processed, echo- and crackle-laden tracks based on 1930s vinyl bought from an obscure record shop in Stockport specialising in 78 rpm gramophones, I'm reminded of conversations with my grandmother back in the early 1980s, shortly before she died of Alzheimer's. There we would sit in her flat, a grandfather clock ticking, surrounded by furniture originally bought in the inter-war years, or perhaps earlier, with her regaling me with anecdotes of her childhood in the Edwardian age, vivid in every detail, her voice rising to a cackle when she reached the punchline. These stories, rendered in her silky, genteel but fraying voice, were among the final, vestigial reminders that the people in these stories ever lived. She would then turn to me and ask, 'What was your name again, dear?'

Like Burial, Kirby is preoccupied with the melancholic aftermath of the post-rave era (he states as much in his V/Vm project *The Death of Rave*), the lengthy quandary following that temporary 1990s moment of coming together in the here and now in which we have become re-atomised by new technologies, a period that might better be known as the twenty-first century. For Fisher, 'inability to make new memories', the condition suffered by my grandmother in her dotage, has a broader application in a popular culture that has ceased to provide the collective markers of the passing of time. It is the music of the likes of Burial and the Caretaker which, in their very different ways, delineates and implies that absence.

Kirby took his moniker the Caretaker from the Stanley Kubrick film version of the Stephen King novel *The Shining*. In that film, Jack Nicholson plays the 'caretaker', a role, he is informed by a 1920s apparition, that he has always occupied. Kirby is not so much concerned with Nicholson's famously frenzied antics with an axe and the corridors of blood; nor is he responding in particular to Kubrick's typically audacious use of twentieth-century composers like Bartók, Ligeti and Penderecki on the soundtrack; rather, he is fixated by the eerie ballroom music that drifts through the soundtrack, the music of Jack Hylton, Ray Noble and others.

On a series of numbered pieces entitled 'Memory', on the 2005 collection *Theoretically Pure Anterograde Amnesia*, Kirby creates some of the most eerie, barely-there ambient ever recorded: creaks, enigmatic groans and abstract whispers that speak of a vast construction which may or may not be haunted, may or may not have some malevolent force of its own, as if the past is exercising a deeply held supernatural grudge against the present. They suggest the sort of troubling forces slowly unleashed when a decaying mind turns on itself. Kirby's work is informed by extensive study of brain disorder and memory loss, the symptoms they provoke, one of which is constant repetition, which provides the theme for 2008's *Persistent Repetition of Phrases*.

However, for albums such as 2011's *An Empty Bliss Beyond This World*, Kirby opted for pieces that were pretty much wholesale recreations of platters from the 1920s and '30s. The effect of these is at once more tonally pleasant, with their balmy renderings of the consoling standards that saw people through the inter-war years like musical cups of tea, but also tinged with a disquieting melancholy.

'I spent a lot of time searching out music from that era over a two- or three-year period,' he told Fisher, 'and started to play around with this source material. The interesting thing for me is the fact that most of that music is about ghosts and loss, as it was recorded between both the world wars. It's of a totally different era and had more or less been forgotten. Titles inspired new ideas, as did the audio itself.'

An Empty Bliss . . . works beautifully as an accompaniment to contemplation of the onset of mental decay. However, these songs would have been the defining memories of people who, had they lived, would by 2017 be anything up to 120 years old. What might be the equivalent memories of those just entering into decline and old people's homes now? How long is it before those memories consist of Elvis, Bill Haley, Tommy Steele and, later, the Beatles and the Stones? The Human League?

And then I come back to Fisher's phrase about the inability to make new memories. What are the pop memories of the twenty-first century, a century that has been more a communications revolution – the means whereby stuff is conveyed – than one of stuff itself?

16

LEGITIMACY: FROM CASTLEMORTON TO SKRILLEX

In late 1983, while at Oxford University, I began to DJ for money. Exceedingly small amounts of money, it has to be said; a haul of £20 on one unusually busy night was as high as my bounty ever ascended. I played at what was at weekends a gay nightclub on the outskirts of Oxford, which attracted a Saturday crowd drawn from as far away as Reading and Aylesbury, hungry for Hi-NRG, poppers and what was referred to as 'trade'. I learned a great deal about the undercurrent of gay influence on ostensibly hetero pop, how big, beaty hits by brassy figures such as Hazel Dean and the Weather Girls were often none-too-subtly coded gay anthems. And, despite the fact that men at the club were invariably referred to as 'she', there was an indisputable thirsty maleness about the Hi-NRG scene, a hardness about even the effete-looking Phil, who ran the decks, and as for the truck driver in voluminous pink drag, 'Don't even look at her, she's murderous!' warned Rod, the barman. These men danced hard and, in the booths, snogged hard. Any vestigial homophobic 'shut that door' notions I had about homosexuality were extinguished in those murky environs.

There was a thrusting girder directness about Hi-NRG, tracks like Lime's 'On the Grid', Man Parrish's 'Hip Hop Be Bop', Shirley Lites's 'Heat You Up (Melt You Down)' (after which I named my own Tuesday club night, for all-comers, straight and gay – Meltdown). I published a manifesto for the night, posted on every noticeboard and toilet wall in every college in Oxford, in which

I promised that Meltdown would be 'greater and more beautiful than SEX', though, pitifully, I wasn't actually in any great position to make such comparisons myself at that stage.

Initially, the club was moderately successful. The competition was the Era Club in central Oxford, where they played Duran Duran, Bonnie Tyler, Howard Jones, the compromised Simple Minds, etc., in a vapid apology for hipness. I, meanwhile, played an electric, eclectic selection that included Afrika Bambaataa, Liaisons Dangereuses, the Peech Boys, the aforementioned Shirley Lites and Man Parrish, D.A.F., Kraftwerk, Frankie Goes to Hollywood, Chaka Khan, Sharon Redd, the SOS Band, Cabaret Voltaire, as well as a selection of imported funk twelve-inches, bought for a student-grant-depleting £5 a disc, on labels like Tommy Boy and West End Records. If you didn't like these discs at first, you damned well learned to; and if you accidentally left them by your radiator to warp, you put them under a pair of baggy trousers and ironed them back into shape, hoping for the best.

Who wouldn't go to a nightclub with a playlist like that? In 1984, the answer, ultimately, was: almost everybody. Running that night was a rueful lesson in how even ostensibly hip punters are deeply attached to the very familiar. The risk-averse Era Club suffered no problems in this respect. Perhaps students and locals were wary of venturing into a gay nightclub, especially one that involved a mile-long walk. Or perhaps nothing fails like failure. As numbers dwindled, the club owner settled on a ruse. The sight line from the entrance led directly to the dancefloor. If he saw potential customers coming down the road, he would signal to me to pump the dry-ice machine up to maximum. They would look in, see the fog, the lights, hear the booming music, assume the joint was jumping and shell out their £3 . . . only to wander in and, as the dry ice lifted, realise they were the only people in the club. This worked, but just occasionally. Sometimes the only customers were a couple of plain-clothes police officers, wont to drop in for a late-night drink and chat at the bar, their interest in avant-funk from Sheffield pretty negligible, it seemed.

Merely to have a box of records and an ability to segue records without too many mishaps made one a DJ, however, and late in 1984, I was asked to do a DJing slot down in London, in a Soho basement, in what was, in retrospect, a forerunner of later rave events – a non-licensed, speakeasy-type club night, in which the only refreshments on offer were tap water and stacks and stacks of warm tinned lager. I was preceded by a couple of DJs playing slightly ball-aching, tasteful rare groove. I decided the joint needed to jump and dug in my box for the biggest, fattest grooves I could find. These culminated in Afrika Bambaataa's 'Looking for the Perfect Beat' and Trouble Funk's 'Trouble Funk Express'. The joint did jump, a mixed, crowded room, a change from the floorboards I'd been used to staring down upon in Oxford. Then, a signal to switch the music off – a visit from the police. Finally, a signal to crank up again. They'd been bunged £80 and were on their way.

The mid-1980s were very much an in-between time for DJing. The club scene remained urban, esoteric: pre-hip hop, pre-house, pre-acid; slightly over-ripe electro-funk, big, fruity, phat and soulful. Jimmy Jam and Terry Lewis and Prince represented the most advanced, voluptuous and successful take on the music – lush, velcro, landing on the dancefloor with a splashdown. Big voices, big synths.

What followed was a paring back, a retreat to basics, away from the sequins, cocktails and velvets to something more raw, unlicensed. Lofts in Chicago and basements in Detroit, where Derrick May, Juan Atkins and Kevin Saunderson lay down the rails for techno with their earliest recordings. The club scene that developed from this was racially eclectic – a core of African Americans, plus Latinos and adventurous young Caucasians – but this wasn't a case of returning to black roots. This was a music that shamelessly reversed the traditional borrowing by white artists from black sources. Techno was unabashed in citing everything from new-wave pop, like the B-52s, to Depeche Mode, to Kraftwerk and Tangerine Dream, to D.A.F. and Liaisons Dangereuses as influences. Its futurist mission involved jettisoning the trappings accrued by black popular music in the late 1970s and early '80s in favour of a more minimal, streamlined, spacebound sound. It was a music that represented 'black flight' in other ways also – on the part of affluent African Americans who wished to disassociate themselves from the inner city of Detroit and its hapless inhabitants trapped in the first great American urban ruin.

Back in the UK, in 1985, the same year as Live Aid, another gathering took place: the infamous Battle of the Beanfield, a less celebrated cultural moment in its own right, a symbolic attempt to reclaim the land of England by those dispossessed by Thatcherism. The Stonehenge Free Festival had taken place since 1974 and over the years featured a range of bands across a variety of genres, from Dexys Midnight Runners to the Clash, from the Thompson Twins to Jimmy Page and Roy Harper. By 1985, however, a High Court injunction had been put in place preventing the festival from going ahead. The New Age travellers represented an affront to a Conservative establishment that brooked 'no alternative' and shamelessly used the police as a political arm with which to combat the perceived 'enemy within', as the striking miners had discovered to their cost at Orgreave months earlier.

The Battle of the Beanfield generated horrific images of visored police moving against festival-goers, including women and children, of young men under arrest whose bloodied faces suggested they had been subject to disproportionate, vindictive force. There were anecdotes about police, their IDs covered, setting about the travellers indiscriminately, with one heavily pregnant woman clubbed as she attempted to exit a coach. There was the spectacle of a chief constable swooping over the site in a helicopter, bellowing through a megaphone that the travellers were all under arrest.

Of course, there were a few travellers who had responded violently, hurled missiles of their own; eight police were hospitalised. However, the subsequent comments of the driver of a police support vehicle, one David McMullin, that this was a battle between 'anarchy and law and order', suggested that the police response was political, existential even: *Live outside the boundaries we prescribe, however peacefully, and you will come under the cosh. You are not free-born. Get jobs, mortgages, suits and shares, or be hunted down.*

House was in its urban infancy, with techno and rave yet to emerge in 1985. Dance music belonged to the city, on licensed premises, behind velvet ropes, a lush, well-upholstered and urbane experience. Cocktails and lager. Suits, highlighted hair, frocks, heels and finery, and shades of androgny in between. Or there were the thumpingly loud but discreet gay bars. There were still vestiges of the tribal and the elitist about the urban club scene, with its rare grooves and door policies.

From the late 1980s onwards, however, dance music across the board began a process of paring back, as if conscious of having reached a baroque stage. Hip hop had abandoned the sequins and spangle of the early Sugar Hill era in favour of a more brutal, cropped, streetwise, minimal approach, starting with Run-DMC. House and garage were strikingly effective when reduced to basic clipped piano chords, the sort around which Derrick May, aka 1987's Rhythim Is Rhythim's 'Strings of Life' were born. Warp Records, born in Sheffield in 1989, would also bring dance music back to Meccano basics. The Sheffield avant-funk scene involving groups like Chakk, Hula and later Cabaret Voltaire felt laden with its own tropes, no longer quite right for the times; ditto the pop that had emerged from the city, ABC, Heaven 17 and the Human League, who, despite their eventual longevity, felt like they were making a statement about the year 1982.

And then there was acid house, in which the tribalism and occasional violent undercurrents of youth culture were dissolved in

Ecstasy and replaced by a general inclusiveness, albeit with hedonism rather than late-1960s idealism back to the fore. The rise of
rave dispelled a lot of the anger and despondency and pessimism
that had been a by-product of the punk years' culture of disaffec-
tion and mistrust of the Big Thing. Suddenly, there was a collective
desire to gather together again en masse, hinted at by Live Aid, but
in fields rather than in the city.

Rave was open, democratised, the velvet rope broken. An escape
from the city, in discreet convoys, to hangars and abandoned
spaces beyond the M25. It was an escape also from the licensed
strictures of alcohol, that ultimately depressive drug, in favour
of water, Lucozade and yellow pills that kept you up till dawn.
Initially, raves merely consisted of the sort of big, popular music
sneered at by metropolitan taste-makers – a typical mash-up of
the period sees Queen's 'Bohemian Rhapsody' and its 'Is this the
real life?' juxtaposed with Simple Minds' 'Theme for Great Cities'.
However, rave found its signature squiggle with 'Acid Tracks', a
freak noise yielded when DJ Pierre was messing with a Roland
303 and found among its presets the squelchy, neon-lit, plasticine
noise that, stretched hither and yon over a basic beat punctuated by a clap track, was irresistible – sheer cosmic bubblegum,
chomping, morphing, drilling and tweaking. It had precedents:
Liaisons Dangereuses had alighted on a similar sound a couple of
years earlier on their 'Neger Brauchen Keine Elektronik' (recorded
under the name CH-BB). An Indian composer named Charanjit
Singh, meanwhile, had issued an album called *Synthesizing: Ten
Ragas to a Disco Beat* in 1982, which uncannily prefigured acid
house. You could go back further. As Simon Reynolds observes
in *Energy Flash*, his study of the rave scene, the acid squiggle is
akin to the wah-wah that suddenly denoted a shift in the counter-
culture twenty years earlier in 1967. That sound felt like a squirt of
psychedelic liquidity, an excess; the acid squiggle felt like it was a
gremlin messing with your brain, scrambling your synapses. Or go

back further still, to the trumpet sound of very early jazz trumpeter Freddie Keppard, whose cachinnating, yee-hawing breaks were in their own way as mischievous and disruptive as the 303 squiggle.

For many, myself included, rave created a generation gap. I was just twenty-five, but I was a creature of the city club scene, more at home with the juxtaposition of Michael Jackson, Earth, Wind and Fire, D.A.F. and Kraftwerk than the beat continuum of rave. 1982 had been my year – everything from Lipps Inc.'s 'Funkytown' to 23 Skidoo's 'Kundalini'. I wanted to drink wine and dance stiffly. I didn't want to take drugs – be sold a bad batch and your statutory rights were very much affected. Rave felt like a threat to my own profession, a sheer stream of beats and vinyl, without faces or stories you could construct around those faces. If you worked in the music business, however, you had to admire the fact that here was an alternative industry – more egalitarian, more immersive, way less up itself – in which egos were submerged and a reconnection made with the euphoric collective for the first time in decades. The danger of obsolescence was palpable. In 1988, I'd asked Kurtis of Mantronix if he agreed that the future of funk lay in ideas generated by producers working in club caverns, trading in machinery and turnover as opposed to glamour.

'I'd agree. Somebody said to me, "It's the producer that controls the industry." And I think that's true. Who was it that said that to me . . .? Oh yes, my manager.'

Was this how it would be from now on? Nonetheless, I appreciated, from afar, the sheer proliferation of the scene's minimalism, the new world of the young that was superseding me. I appreciated its illegitimacy, its existence outside of the laws which I myself had not only abided by, but as a staff writer for a weekly music magazine, a desk sergeant in the taste police, had a small hand in helping make.

The rave scene, however, was a product of British cultural circumstances. It could seem, from footage of the time, to have comprised a sea of white faces, but black MCs played a pivotal role in its early days, names like Everson Allen, Robbie Dee and Shabba D, whose improvised streams of patter not only channelled the mentalist energy of the crowds as they lost themselves in the largely lyricless pools of acid but were distinctively British in flavour ('Oi, oi!') rather than invidious efforts to mimic US rap. In America, the club scene that arose from, and was served by, the techno emerging from Detroit and Chicago was very much about the cities and the youth, particularly young African Americans, whose very existence made them automatic suspects in the eyes of the police, whether in the city or beyond its outer edges. In *The Underground Is Massive*, Michaelangelo Matos quotes Derrick May, who from 1989 onwards was experiencing problems in setting up techno club nights, telling the story of trying to throw parties in his loft in the middle of nowhere and attracting 800 or so people plus overspill, only to be raided. 'I got citations,' said May, 'not from the neighbours because there are no neighbours where my building is situated, but from the police.' When, as the officer wrote out a ticket, May protested that no one was complaining, the policeman replied, 'I'm complaining.' Therein was revealed the racial animus, as well as moral panic, that directed operations against black clubbers in America, an experience sadly familiar to those in the UK as well.

All of which made Tony Wilson of Factory Records fetching up in New York at the New Music Seminar in July 1990 to host his own panel by the name of 'Wake Up America, You're Dead' more saddeningly ironic. Wilson was riding on the massive success not just of rave but of Madchester, in particular the success of the Happy Mondays, which unleashed a wave of uncouth, laddish, E-fuelled hedonistic energy. I went up to interview the Happy Mondays in late 1989 and was astonished at the extent to which Madchester was a palpable reality. Wilson drove me proudly around a city that appeared to be in the grip of a cultural insurrection, with flared jeans practically flapping from tenement windows like tricolour flags. The Mondays had been booked into a venue on the Saturday night that in every respect represented an underestimation of their appeal. For a start, it was all-seated ('I hope they fookin' tear those seats out,' Shaun Ryder told me), while hundreds who'd hoped to gain entrance on the night found themselves locked out, pressed en masse against the entrance doors. Wilson was a deeply patriotic Mancunian who once told the *NME* that it deserved to be shut down for not having put the dance act K-Klass on its front cover. This was a moment of blue-sky delirium to match the black sky of doom he had also presided over with Joy Division.

At the American conference, Wilson had in tow, for some reason, Keith Allen, who was putting himself about everywhere in 1990, like a more intrusive Zelig. He was involved in New Order's 'World in Motion', featuring the rapping of John Barnes, an early sign of football and rock music, once considered antithetical in the UK, merging as a popular force in a way they never had before. E was said to have had a transformative effect on fans across the terraces, providing a contrast to the notoriously violent 1980s, when the game had sunk to pariah status thanks to its subculture of organised, at times lethally violent hooliganism. The near-success of England at the 1990 World Cup, which had finished just nine days before the New Music Seminar, had had a transformative effect not just on perceptions of English football but on the culture as a whole. The untroubled, euphoric 1990s had been birthed, with a bawling Paul Gascoigne its physical representation.

There was a contrast between the hubris of Wilson and co., attempting to provoke the sort of transatlantic oneupmanship that occasionally erupts between America and the UK when Britain is feeling particularly cocky, and their more earnest US counterparts. Wilson said America had 'forgotten how to dance'. But who was he addressing exactly? The US in its entirety, whose tastes were still defined by mountainous ranges of rock, from Kiss to Bon Jovi and, pretty soon, the emergent grunge scene? Or the club scene initiated by the likes of Derrick May, which was being aggressively and enthusiastically stifled by police forces across the country?

Allen's role was as an accompanying jester. He bragged that he had arrived in America laden with thousands of Es, as if ready to strew them among America's enervated, danceless youth at a moment's bidding. Wilson, too, stressed that the re-emergence of the club scene in the UK was not down to the reconfiguration of the dance experience but instead was a result of the sheer amount of drugs suddenly being enjoyed by Britain's liberated, upbeat youth. While E led to an at times risible response in the UK, from the tabloids especially – a *Sun* cartoon showed two fresh-faced young clubbers being ushered into a club by a pill-touting doorman, only for him to be revealed as Satan as the clubbers fall through a trapdoor into the flames of hell – in America, drugs were understood to be at the heart of the tragedy of African American life in particular, as later laid bare in the TV drama *The Wire*. (Wilson himself would have rued his chipper provocations when the Haçienda later had to be closed down, after local drug dealers made life at the venue impossible.)

Derrick May eventually responded with exasperation to Allen's claims, exploding thus: 'We – and I say we, I mean blacks – we all do something and you'll come up behind us and turn it around, and add somebody singing to it or some sort of little funky-ass or weak-ass chord line or whatever, and get some stupid record company that doesn't know jack shit about shit to put £50,000 behind it, and you got a hit because you shoved it down mother-fuckers' throats,' only to find himself teased almost to the point of race-baiting by Allen. What ultimately emerged from the seminar is that while Britain, a small but pop-culturally hyperproductive country, could be swayed by a phenomenon like rave, in a larger, less fickle, more conservative country like America it would take a lot longer. The US was not ready to rave just yet.

In the early 1990s, fears were allayed that rave would replace the industry model in which both record companies and the music press had a stake. Characters and auteurs emerged from the scene, album makers also, such as the Aphex Twin and Orbital, alongside a resurgent guitar-music scene that had become a little neo-psychedelic and acid-fried in its own way, with groups like Curve (remixed by the Aphex Twin) and My Bloody Valentine, with their tremolo wipeouts. Still, traditional rock fans like those at Glastonbury were having difficulty taking the new music on board. Asked at a *Melody Maker* round-table discussion around that time whether Glastonbury was making any plans to cater for rave and dance fans, Michael Eavis explained that if loudspeakers played after midnight there would be fines; he would therefore arrange for an all-night radio station to broadcast rave music. 'We're asking people to bring headphones and transistor radios along.' This idea was met with widespread scepticism in the room.

And then, in 1992, came Castlemorton, a culmination of rave culture in many ways, but one whose tribal assembly and determination to reclaim Britain's green outdoors reminded one of the Battle of the Beanfield. Only the soundtrack to Castlemorton wasn't Luddite troubadours strumming wistful ballads about old Albion but massive techno sound systems that shook the hills, not always to universal appreciation from festival-goers. These included Bedlam, Circus Warp, Spiral Tribe, Circus Normal, DiY and L. S. Diezel, their eclecticism perhaps lost on angry locals as far as ten miles away, to whom the electronic, amplified sound of the 4/4 beat resounded like war drums.

The Castlemorton site nestled in the Malvern Hills, Edward Elgar territory, as it happened, a renowned site of natural beauty that was enshrined in that eminent English composer's tone poetry. To some, this would have only exacerbated the sense of defilement represented by the assortment of crusties, travellers and ravers whose decision to opt out of Conservative-run Britain represented a challenge and an affront to Middle England. However, the festival had only pitched up at Castlemorton after having been refused access to the site of the Avon Free Festival in Bristol by the local police force, who were determined to put a stop to an event that had taken place for several years, moving on the convoy of trucks and assorted rusty antique vehicles further north. The convoy settled on Castlemorton Common. There, they had the advantage of numbers and met relatively light resistance from the local force.

Gradually and spontaneously, the festival grew in size by word of mouth, with even Radio 1 giving it a shout-out. The sounds being pumped out ranged from classic early house to the more militant techno-drill of Underground Resistance, music that rolled like the giant occupying vehicles and juddered the marrow in a manner that was anti-bucolic, a reminder of the uneasy relationship between mechanical/industrial proliferation and production and the ecological ideal, between electronic modernity and its modern inconveniences – sanitation at the site ran to a sign instructing festival-goers to 'bury your shit'. Spiral Tribe tried to reconcile these opposites in their self-description as 'terra-technic': techno as a means of excavating the true spirit of the land.

Nonetheless, there was an air of pop-up utopia about Castlemorton: the sweltering weather; the heavy, heady scent of weed carried on the air; the wide availability of a range of hallucinogens; the exclusion of the sort of overbearing commercial and corporate presences and brand names that would soon enough become ubiquitous at large-scale events; the short shrift given to anyone who attempted to rip off festival-goers – anyone who tried to overcharge for cigarettes, beer, water would find themselves beaten up by festival enforcers in what was described by one festival-goer as a system of 'functional anarchy' – summary rough justice dispensed to enforce the ultra-liberal values underpinning the festival. One recalls Bob Dylan's line: 'to live outside the law you must be honest'. Why not live like this? Was respectable society with its discreet, faraway zones of violence and misery run so much better? Was it worth it for the toilets?

However, there was inevitable friction with local communities, for whom the festival-goers might as well have been invading zombies – disfigured, ex-human species, some of whose dogs ran amok, while others left drugs paraphernalia, including needles, dumped in gardens. The *Daily Mail* reported one local complaining that he had seen 'youngsters injecting heroin in a Renault 5'. The BBC covered the event, betraying its deep-lying middlebrow prejudices by stressing the Third World aspect of the assembled community on the ground with the sort of sombre gravitas used by Michael Buerk when reporting on Ethiopia: the ragged desperation, the police powerless, sheep lying dead, vets struggling, villagers under siege, fences torn up, windows boarded up. The emphasis is clear but the reporter tries to make amends with an exercise in ostensible BBC balance. First, three local women advance their grievances about loud noise, litter and drugs, offering stories of cars smashed to pieces and a policeman run over; there are also complaints from a local conservationist. And the noise, the noise. They'd had to wear earphones. They'd been driven into a frenzy by those repetitive beats. The reporter then turns to three far more mild-mannered, almost sheepish crusties who murmur promises that extensive clear-up operations are under way, that you always get a few bad people, to whose number they clearly don't belong.

After four days, the festival did eventually die down, but Spiral Tribe were deemed to have outstayed their welcome, pumping techno out to the last, and as the numbers they faced dwindled, police moved in and thirteen members of the Tribe collective were arrested. Their trial, during which they initially wore T-shirts bearing the slogan 'Make some fucking noise', lasted four months and cost £4 million. They were eventually acquitted of all charges, but the high profile of the trial and the stand-off it represented gave

rise to the Criminal Justice and Public Order Act of 1994, one of
social conservatism's last stands of the twentieth century.

The Act covered a great deal of ground. It actually legalised anal
sex between heterosexual couples, thereby relieving from their
position whoever had been responsible for checking up on devian-
cies from that law hitherto. Mostly, however, it introduced a broad
range of measures against perceived social deviants, from squat-
ters and unauthorised campers to protesters and free-festival-goers.
Its most notorious, most risible section, though, was 63 (1)(b),
which gave police officers the power to remove people from events
at which music 'wholly or predominantly characterised by the
emission of a succession of repetitive beats' was being played. This
was an extraordinary effort to legislate against music, one which
took specific exception to the mechanical mode of its production.
No one had ever attempted to legislate against amplified electric
guitars by specifying the raucous and irregular emissions of their
free-form digressions, or against brass instruments for their exuber-
ant tootling. Some deep-dyed phobia against electronic machinery
lurked in the drafting of this bill.

The phrase 'repetitive beats', with all of its nonsensical implications, was seized upon gleefully by electronica artists. In a sense it
was flattering for them to be thought of as generating a mode of
music that had the power to make governments quail and the walls
of cities shake. Simon Reynolds, who attended Castlemorton, certainly believes that the idea that techno had the power to 'disturb
"normals" and unlock the savage within' would have had tremendous romantic appeal to the Spiral Tribes of this world. Autechre
issued the three-track *Anti EP*, explaining in the notes that it had
been 'programmed in such a way that no bars contain identical
beats and can therefore be played under the proposed new law.
However, we advise DJs to have a lawyer and a musicologist present at all times to confirm the non repetitive nature of the music in
the event of police harassment.' Ironically, Autechre would become

paragons of virtue in the eyes of the new law, moving towards scrupulously irregular beats on albums like 2003's *Draft 7.30*. Orbital, meanwhile, released a 'Criminal Justice Bill?' remix of their track 'Are We Here?' which consisted of four minutes of law-abiding silence. The law was a piece of nonsense, rarely invoked save to break up the occasion, its only effect to bolster the renegade status of electronica artists who were in no danger of landing in court for their repetitive emissions, while making a mockery of what was increasingly looking like a dead government walking, about to be trampled in the impending onrush of Cool Britannia.

And yet that same sociopolitical drift towards a centrist prosperity was the undoing of the free-festival scene, of the crusty spirit of Castlemorton. The claims of trauma caused by the free festival turned out to be either exaggerated or unfounded. One local conservator who had complained to the press about the 'irreparable damage' caused by the site later admitted that the common had completely recovered in a short space of time. Nonetheless, there was no Castlemorton 1993, despite a cogent application from the Mean Fiddler organisation to stage it.

Meanwhile, the cultural mood shifted. The mood for togetherness in a field was transferred to indie rock, in particular Oasis, though UK dance was beginning to generate its own raft of superstars. Spiral Tribe moved on to continental Europe, taking with them their idealistic and somewhat hippy-dippy ideas, including a preoccupation with the number 23. Fellow travellers the Levellers bought up property in Brighton, turned it into a studio complex and, to their embarrassment, made a killing. A counter-cultural green margin, opened up during the 1960s, persisting through the 1970s and coming under siege through the 1980s, finally closed up almost entirely in the 1990s – in Britain, at any rate. There was, at last, no 'alternative', no opting out. Things, instead, could only get better. Fatboy Slim better. The spirit of Castlemorton – muddle-headed, ramshackle, medieval, idealistic, noisy, druggy, mud-caked

and ecstatic – fizzled out and something in Britain died, and everybody was happy, as Britain instead gave way under Blairism to an
extended programme of crusty-free postmodernisation.

In truth, however, reflects Simon Reynolds, 'That whole travel-
ler/squat/free-party subculture had the same contradictions as the
1960s counter-culture, insofar as it was at once a valid repudiation
of aspects of conventional life (soul-crushing routine, exploitation,
lack of joy, blinkered horizons) but still parasitic on the bounty of
capitalist society, organised around economic growth, exploitation
of nature, etc. So on the one hand there's that romance of the idea
of living on the outside of society, but actually in cold-eyed reality they were dependent on this well-organised, productive society
and economy – for everything from the roads they travelled along
to the petrol they put in their caravans or trucks.'

The energy of rave that had gathered up outside of the cities
gradually returned to them; megaclubs like Ministry of Sound
and Fabric became the established urban homes of modern dance;
events became more organised, licensed, safely in house rather
than in the wild outdoors. The industry breathed again.

Around 1995, while working at *Melody Maker*, I received a call
from a press officer. He had an idea. He wondered if I'd be interested in interviewing one of his acts 'in character' as 'Mr Agreeable',
a persona I had created for the paper, a dyspeptic columnist given to
hurling foul-mouthed abuse at famous acts of the day. It seemed a
pretty desperate and sorry proposition, a low moment of ignominy
akin to Spinal Tap being billed below the puppet show. Who would
be sad enough to subject themselves to such demeaning treatment?

The answer was, Moby. He had had a breakthrough hit in the
early 1990s with 'Go', a reworking of the theme to David Lynch's
Twin Peaks. In his wonderfully vivid and self-deprecating autobiography, *Porcelain*, he describes his first appearance on *Top of
the Pops*, living the dream, jumping frantically and whacking his

Octapad for a few minutes in sync with the single, before being
ushered off by a stagehand, his time up. Was that it? Afterwards,
he headed for the airport. He somehow imagined that having
been emblazoned across the Thursday-night pop stratosphere, he
would be mobbed by adoring fans. He was utterly ignored. He
felt low, and utterly unlike a bona fide pop star. Perhaps he was
just another of those white, funky-ass, weak-ass boys like Adamski
whom Derrick May held in such contempt, on and now off the
conveyor belt.

Moby struggled, predictably perhaps, to match the first flush of
'Go', and by 1995, he decided he would revert to a core of supposed authenticity, expounding on his militant veganism with the
album *Animal Rights*, accompanied by a serrated, 4-real soundtrack
of the hardcore punk that had been a formative influence in his
youth. The album tanked, media interest in this has-been sinking
to a low ebb. It was around this time that I received the call from
his press officer.

In *Porcelain*, in which he looks back on his exciting life as a DJ/
artist struggling to make it in New York in the late 1980s/early
1990s, Moby emphasises the seediness, the funkiness, the urban
grime – the filthy windscreens of a cab, broken bottles, battered
apartment futons, the old meat-packing plants with sloping floors
to drain the animal blood that were now cheap living spaces, the
steam heat from the radiators and the street gratings, the smell of
ethnic cooking, discarded flyers for club nights on rainy sidewalks
– all of which provided the thick urban ambience for a nascent NY
rave scene. Having had his hit, he then reflects on the squalid sense
of failure he endured as a support act for Soundgarden, playing to
a handful of indifferent, often hostile punters night after night – a
life that had descended into shit and mud. He considered rebuild-
ing his life. He considered a career in architecture.

Instead, he made *Play*, which belongs to a whole new world
of opulence and cleanliness. The sweeping, mechanically retrieved

strings of 'Porcelain' function like windscreen wipers, while keyboard droplets fall as pure as mineral water. All that mud and shit
and steam and stain was about to become a distant memory. *Play*
is an impeccable mix of shiny chromium techno and sensitively
sampled American roots music, plucked from the field recordings
of Alan Lomax, including the repeated use of verses from African
American gospel singer Bessie Jones's 'Honey'. It is hard to doubt
that Moby intended to signpost and showcase this music with
the utmost respect, but there were sceptics who suggested that he
was just another in a tradition of white boys exploiting American
roots music, transfusing it to compensate for their own anaemia,
à la Led Zeppelin. Certainly, there's an ironic stand-off in the
music between notions of soil-based authenticity and frictionless
modernity.

Play initially sold as disappointingly as had been expected.
Daniel Miller of Mute had agreed to release it in the UK, but
only because of Mute's long-standing policy of loyalty to acts they
signed. However, Moby had decided on an ingenious expedient
to ensure that the album did not die away for want of exposure:
he licensed every track for use in various films, TV shows and
adverts, including for Volkswagen, American Express and Baileys
Irish Cream. We were a very long way away indeed from the anti-
corporate spirit of Castlemorton, it seemed. Seven years down the
line, electronic dance music was marching towards the end of that
sort of combative history.

Furthermore, there wasn't the usual sense of sacrilege felt when,
say, a Jimi Hendrix track crops up to sell denim. Moby's music,
sleek and open-ended, with its vague, distant, borrowed sense of
the religious and its state-of-the-art technological assembly, was
perfect late-twentieth-century soundtracking, to which goods were
sold to the discreetly aspirational by appealing to both their sense
of the material and the spiritual. In purchasing high-quality products you were somehow helping to nourish the world, to make it

a more beautiful and refined place. Moby's music was no longer buffeted by the frantic forces of the urban/underground music scene but a Mazda cruising smoothly along a deserted road on a Highland landscape bathed with the amber sunset glow that dominates 1990s advertising. *Play* sold millions, while millions more consumer items were sold as a result of its aural blandishments. It said something about the state of electronic dance music in particular that it had supplanted cheesy rock or MOR as the preferred accompaniment to leading-edge on-air salesmanship, from drum 'n' bass's injection of super-fast hipness to trip hop's retro-elegant upholstery to Moby. Everyone was happy.

These were the late 1990s, in which the Anglo-American world was still surfing on a sustained crest of euphoria and prosperity following a series of collapses, from the Berlin Wall to apartheid, from Thatcher to eventually the seemingly interminable Tory administration. For all the reproachful efforts of the Manic Street Preachers and Tricky's talk of pre-millennial tension, there was never a less gloomy, less fretful time in pop history. Dance music was suddenly dominated by nerdy, white, often middle-class boys playing at being DJ/auteurs and getting away with it, and with nobody minding because we were past all that factionalist 1980s political stuff for the time being, pre-intersectional. From the Chemical Brothers to the brilliant Basement Jaxx to Fatboy Slim, glad time it was to be young, male, Caucasian, with a box full of vinyl, mixing, matching and stealing to the march of big beat, the thudding pulse of a pop time approaching the end of the century ass-backwards, retro but free from fear, doubt and alienation, happy to crowd together in perma-party mode.

Few, if anybody, worried about white boys ripping off black culture. After all, this wasn't like Led Zeppelin and the blues, or Vanilla Ice. Derrick May had every right to feel disgruntled, but techno itself was unabashed about borrowing from white European music – Kraftwerk, D.A.F and Tangerine Dream in

particular – while Jeff Mills even cited the B-52s as an inspiration. The technology and its innovations had their origin in the
experiments of white men: John Cage and Pierre Schaeffer. As for
minimal techno, and its principal genius, Ricardo Villalobos, he
had started out as a huge Depeche Mode fan. His music – looping
and isolated rhythms in mixes that were prevented only by their
repetitive beats from floating out into realms of sheer idiosyncratic
abstraction – was not traceable back to the blues but rather to the
dusty backroads and humid swamplands of Basildon.

Complaints about inauthenticity were also becoming drowned
out. An understanding had built that in pop's postmodern stage,
originality was impossible to attain – there was no more virgin soil
to till – and that ideas about real music played on real instruments
were the province of music criticism's equivalent of real-ale bores.
There was an understanding that the pop world in which we now
lived was actually a huge, compound mess of stuff from the classical dead past that was being perpetually remixed and reanimated.
This machinery had been around for a long time now, we knew
the score. No more earnest qualms; this was the time to party, hard
and clever, all of us together, above ground. Everybody was happy.

The greatest beneficiary of this was Norman Cook, aka Fatboy
Slim. No one would have picked him out of the line-up of the
Housemartins, for whom he played bass in the 1980s, and marked
him down as the man who would make millions cramming Brighton
beach with ravers who were more than happy to make a superstar
of him, a High Priest of Party fully deserving of his success.

He had actually been DJing since 1980, playing private parties
in Sussex on hired decks as a teenager. After his brief diversion
into hamster indie with Hull's 'Martins, he quit the group in
1988 and, by his own account, lay down his bass, never to touch
it again. He'd already released a version of the SOS Band's 1980s
dancefloor monster 'Just Be Good to Me' with Beats International,
in which he took all of the weight and layering of the original,

instead resetting it over a bantamweight cod-reggae beat and cleverly juxtaposing it with a desolate harmonica motif culled from a Sergio Leone spaghetti western soundtrack, lending his version a wittily mordant distance from the unmatchable Jam & Lewis version. Juxtapositions and resettings of old material would be key to Cook's (patch)work.

He was part of the same cultural flow as the Chemical Brothers; they'd met and bonded during a 1994 visit to London's Heavenly Social Club, to which he'd been introduced by Beats International singer Lindy Layton. It was here that he really began to meld with the times, mutate into Fatboy Slim and all that that entailed. He would eventually draw comparisons with Moby. (Like Moby, he had suffered a severe mid-career setback, lapsing into depression and near bankruptcy in the early 1990s and considering an alternative career – in his case, as a fireman.) These were prompted by his single 'Praise You', which sampled Camille Yarbrough's 'Take Yo' Praise'. There were mild concerns, as expressed by Barney Hoskyns when he interviewed Cook for his website *Rock's Backpages*. 'Do you ever stop and think the original music-makers are being overlooked in all this?' he asked Cook.

'Well, to be honest, James Brown was old until Eric B came out with "I Know You Got Soul",' Cook replied (alluding to Stetsasonic's 'All that Jazz'). 'As long as you credit people and pay them, at the very worst they've got some money. Imagine if, like Camille with "Praise You", you made a record in 1973, never had a hit, became a schoolteacher, and 20 years later someone goes, Here's a check. It's like winning the lottery. And then quite often the record gets re-released and people re-investigate it. I mean, Camille was great, she went on chat shows talking about it.' Everybody was happy.

After all, this wasn't the sort of 'blackface' you had with white soul imitators in futile search of authenticity in the 1980s. The sheer artifice of the DJing approach precluded that, for a start.

As with Moby, this was a presentation of the 'spiritual' in a way that was at once sacred and deconsecrating; sampling as a means of mechanically extracting gospel soulfulness for the benefit of a more secular, less obligated age, when the most appealing idea of religion was that we could all live really happily for ever. As Cook went on to say to Hoskyns, 'It's funny, I really like the spiritual, uplifting thing about gospel music or preaching or religion or whatever – everything apart from the God bit! It's a shame that religion had to get hi-jacked by God.'

'Praise You' was deeply reverent towards Yarbrough, who was presented as a creature of sheer soul the like of which a white late-twentieth-century boy like Cook could never hope to become by mimickry or osmosis, but only through the process of sampling; at the same time, and coupled with Spike Jonze's video of an enthusiastic but thoroughly amateurish dance troupe, it was part of a musical package that represented a propulsive upwards motion away from old-fashioned ideas of subterranean cool and tastefulness. 'Praise You' spoke to the sense, both frivolous and zen, that prevailed in the late 1990s: nothing 'mattered'. There was no need to agonise the way we used to. We were free. We could just be. Rock music was just about dead and nobody believed it had the capacity to transform the world. The counter-culture had long disappeared; the motorways were here to stay. The Great Battles had either been won or lost but, whatever, they had been fought. The time for fighting, the time for protest was over. What was left was a vast, democratised mass of people in the same large cultural (and physical) peacetime space who wanted nothing more than to live really happily for as long as possible, preferably for ever. It was a space once exclusively occupied by rock superstars and the spectacle of heroic agonising they presented.

Oasis had held that space during the Britpop years but, unlike the Beatles, Noel Gallagher was unable to evolve, to enter a *Sgt Pepper* phase. In 2015, Garry Cobain of the Future Sound of

London, aka Amorphous Androgynous, would express his frustration when he and Brian Dougans tried to entice the Oasis songwriter onto more colourful, neo-psychedelic, experimental and electronic terrain when working with him on a putative solo album. 'We tried to force him to write new material,' Cobain told the *Guardian*'s Paul Lester. 'But he dragged his heels and failed to stretch himself.' Their efforts to encourage 'a liberated, exploratory Noel Gallagher, cutting loose from Oasis, enjoying his freedom; the Noel who name-drops our *Monstrous Bubble* albums and krautrock, and who had hits with the Chemical Brothers' ran aground. Gallagher simply didn't have the courage, resources or curiosity of a Lennon or McCartney, or even a George Harrison. 'He obviously loves that kind of music, but has no idea how to make it,' concluded Cobain. Oasis were always destined to fall away from the centre. That space was now clear for electronic dance music.

In 2007, Dave Clarke, aka the 'Baron of Techno' (John Peel), performed a DJ set at the annual Lowlands Festival in Amsterdam, a city with which he eventually fell in love and settled in. I acquired it many years ago via a now-defunct Internet service. It may not be the best hardcore techno set of that era; it may be well down the list of the greatest sets by Dave Clarke. I've only ever heard a section of it. However, it is a section I know extremely well, one I've played many times on headphones at the gym to mask the invariable soundtrack of turbo-charged, Auto-Tuned Europap, with its ultra-predictable drops and tedious starbursts of synth. It also seems to tell a story. Clarke claims never to prepare his sets, but this one follows a quite definite arc.

Clarke left his Brighton home at sixteen, was temporarily homeless, worked part-time and, fired by his early love of punk and hip hop, began to scratch a living in the music industry, eventually establishing himself as a DJ of the highest rank. His high-metabolic determination is reflected not just in his love of speeding down autobahns, where there are no speed limits, but also in the thudding kinetic metal heartbeat of his sets.

The Lowlands set, bathed throughout in colour, flash and fog, begins with a fury of scratching. It's not vinyl scratching; by 2007, that human act is no longer adequate to match the speed, density and relentlessness Clarke requires and he's using technology such as CDJs and Serato Scratch Live. The opening minutes are a jumbled frenzy of electro-funk, Man Parrish and Afrika Bambaataa-style riffs and percussive apparatus; a faster, harder, laser-cut reminder of the likes of Captain Rock, the Extra T's, the Jonzun Crew, punctuated by pneumatic-drill-like diagonal interventions and a scratch of Queen's 'Flash', diced and stuttering almost beyond recognition. A burst of Space Invader warfare, a verbal instruction – 'Time to land' – then a mutation of the opening of Bambaataa's 'Looking for the Perfect Beat', then 'Fasten your seatbelts – 'cos I'm about to flow,' and we're through a wormhole to the year 1988 and Eric B and Rakim's 'Follow the Leader', delivered here with a new rhythmical chassis of Clarke's own choosing. Listen to the left and right speakers and relics from what might be old Mantronix cuts fly about in the mix. It's a trip back, but coming fast forward. Next, past and future meld with Miss Kittin's '1982', a homage to Steve Strange and the New Romantics – 'I see your face fade to grey / imagine you're dancing / you're a robot, man-machine.' Now fast back to the future posited by Kraftwerk on 1981's *Computer World*.

Then, around thirteen minutes, a bass boost, a switch to seventh gear, and we're catapulted out of the referential zone into the deep, black space of the now, propelled at the warp speed of pure techno. Reverb, backwards taping, stereopanning, violent, European, a blur of light like the final scene of *2001: A Space Odyssey*. Arpeggiator sirens, a meteor storm of obsolete rhythms, then onward; except, despite the progress implied by the bpm, we're at a sort of terminus. A single-note stabbing riff makes it feel as if time itself has been left behind; we're going going nowhere at the speed of whooshes of Hubble gas – 'Somebody give the Lord a handclap' – and then the gruelling bass crescendo of the piece. Clarke sounds like he's cutting into a disc with a lathe, trying to saw through to the turntable rubber – a ruthless, vicious scratching action, a scrawl, blackening reams of club space the way the Futurists blackened reams of paper in their founding manifesto; blackening 'White Noise, White Noise . . .' – a plug for the show he presents. By now, among the crowd, white flesh melts, puddles form; the rat-a-tat-tat woodpecker of the looped riff evolves and spirals upwards into an acid-bass whiplash assault, one which fades into the cosmic distance and then, with a sudden flick of the volume, is back gnashing in your face, a threshing black hole of a riff . . . which then tapers off as the set hits cruise control.

The set tells the story of how dance music got past the stage of merely referring to its past, as it blasted beyond orbit into the sheer amnesiac, hi-tech, concentrated HERE and NOW.

Two years earlier, in 2005, Daft Punk at last agreed to play the annual Coachella Valley Music and Arts Festival, which had been held in Indio, California, since 1999. Its founders and organisers had long been aware of the burgeoning interest in dance music, despite the discophobia that still coursed deep from left to right across the spectrum of rock fans. But Disco Sucks was a long time ago, and among American college-radio kids the understanding that music with a 4/4 beat could be more than a banal commodity, could be 4-real, was growing by the year.

By this stage, as far as long-term European followers of the group were concerned, Daft Punk were a little faded. I had attended the playback for their 2005 album *Human After All* at Fabric in London and been less than underwhelmed. This was what they'd spent four years doing? Actually, they hadn't; they'd spent six weeks making the record, valuing the improvisational corner they'd forced themselves into. They'd thrown a few guitars into the mix as well, so at pains were they to stress the very human and very real aspects of their work. It felt like another case of techno musicians themselves falling victim to a sort of technophobia in relationship to their own work – something Kraftwerk had always resisted, thereby accounting for their immaculate preservation. Drearily, it appeared Daft Punk were, indeed, human after all.

So it seemed from London. The album received only lukewarm reviews, but America was moving on a different track. Punk had only happened properly there with Nirvana, and even then it made only a limited tear in the nation's cultural fabric. Rave, as a national explosion, had yet to happen at all. Daft Punk's Coachella appearance, however, would prove transformative.

Their set was kept well under wraps. Curious fans came flooding over from the main stage, where Depeche Mode had just finished playing. What greeted the stream of heady punters was a reminder of Daft Punk's black funk/white soft rock duality: a giant pyramid atop a spaceship that reminded one of George Clinton's P-Funk stage pomp. Inside this were Thomas Bangalter and Guy-Manuel de Homem-Christo, preserving their spectacular anonymity in their robot guises. The music was fine – their trademarked, more-than-human vocoderising, their deceptively simple but perfectly pared 4/4 concussion pumping sweet, exquisite, scaffolded softness into the night air. The context was all. Not only diehard fans but a wider industry of more distant cultural onlookers had been drawn to this set by Daft Punk's coyness. What they understood was that all their preconceptions of rave as dank, muddy, subterranean, a mere sleazy stream of beats in which swam society's drug-addled jetsam, were junk. Daft Punk's 2004 Coachella set established before the very eyes of the industry's movers and shakers that dance music could work as a clean, huge, crowd-pleasing spectacle, in the tradition of, and supplanting, rock music. Son et lumière. It was legitimate. Furthermore, qualms about pop versus rock, us versus them, underground versus overground, real versus fake, guitars versus synths, were dead. The Internet, iTunes had razed such assumptions to the ground. These were the binaries of old men. What was left was a flat landscape. And, appropriate to the technology-driven times, the primary beat was electronic.

> I remember seeing the full Daft Punk pyramid show in 2007. I went alone, drove up in my Honda Fit, bought a ticket off a scalper for $150, got on the floor, and had the best time of my life. I didn't have a drink, no drugs. But I was high out of my mind. It changed my life. This is gonna sound really lame, but try to take it the right way: There have been a couple times where I've been so proud of what I've done live, like I feel like I've given someone the same kind of feeling I got at that Daft Punk show. And that feels so good.
> *Skrillex,* Pitchfork *magazine*

Skrillex is onomatopoeic. A case in point: his remix of Avicii's 'Levels'. Every knob on the board is twisted as far right as it will go. Every last pixel is shrieking with maximum sound, light and energy. This mix shreds, the way metal used to. It serrates and claws. It eats alive the space it occupies. It Skrillexes: shrill, skirling, post-Aphex (Skrillex's hero). In a music industry that is elsewhere utterly occupied with its own past, it exists entirely in the present, like an iPhone upgrade that will itself be obsolete in a matter of months. Nuance, shade, reflection, retrospection are trampled in this mix, with its white broadsides of digital treble and twisted, enema basslines. This is music for a generation that is post-postmodern, no longer steeped in the recent past, out of its shadow. They're in an audio/techno/visual culture where everything happened in the last few months. For a while, everything in the chart rundown on Radio 1 sounded like this – the garish, unpretty blare of the obliviously new.

Skrillex himself, aka Californian Sonny Moore, is 4-real, however, a fugitive from the basements of punk/grunge/emo who spent his formative years soaking up Warp Records' output – not just Aphex but Squarepusher. He comes across in interviews as engagingly nerdy, as much a fan as a musician, and looks like the sort of specky kid whose autograph book is always in the back of his trousers. No airs, pretensions, smooth graces or ambitions beyond playing and making records. 'Every decision I make, I want to feel honest about. I'm not chasing opportunity. I don't wanna do something for money if I'm not interested in it. Not to say a phone company or whatever is bad, but I'm not excited about it. That's not what I do,' he told *Pitchfork*. And from him, you believe it. He's driven. The discovery at the age of sixteen that he was adopted – and not only that, but that all of his friends knew – seemed to trigger something in him that set him on the road, a road he has travelled hard ever since. Such a specimen has been improbably vaulted to the apex of the EDM pyramid, not revered like a guitar hero, but more of a cypher; a high priest, not to be revered in his own right but as one who channels a higher power. For many, he is at the gauche, clichéd, vulgar end of dubstep – what Kiss are to rock – yet the power he commands doesn't come from sculpting esoterica for a handful of after-hours taste police but from drawing the crowd by whatever means necessary, harder, faster, stronger, if not necessarily better, than the rest.

Deadmau5 is an altogether smoother, more progressive, chromium proposition than Skrillex. Cases in point: 'Faxing Berlin' (2007) and 'The Veldt' (2012). On 'Faxing Berlin' there is space aplenty, delineated patiently by a looped house rhythm and rattlesnake wisps. In fades the arpeggiator, bouncing like an orb of spotless metal, windowless and featureless, as a giant, gaping maw gradually opens behind it – the Daft Punk device of simulating the opening of a nightclub door applied slowly and solemnly. Who faxes a city? Who still uses a fax in 2007? It doesn't matter. This is a content-less, vocal-less exercise, the orb bouncing back and forth and creating a vast, irresistible awning, before receding, its work done. 'Faxing Berlin' is about nothing but its own existence, as wondrously meaningless as the motions of the cosmos – pure spectacle. Clean as a whistle.

'The Veldt' is not content-free. It is based on a 1950 Ray Bradbury short story, 'The World the Children Made', a disquieting, ultimately grisly tale of children escaping into a virtual reality zone within their own nursery and creating an African veldt, to the mystification of their parents, George and Lydia. When the parents enter the virtual veldt themselves to see just what their children are getting up to, they are killed by lions, their kids looking on with apparent indifference.

Again, the arpeggiator, a gentle, undulating fabric on which a beat hammers softly and warmly. This is pure seduction, like the scent of a just-bought car to the power of ten. Rhythms shower and burst in cascading shards, as vocalist Chris James gives a husky-sweet lyrical précis of the key moments and phrases appertaining to Bradbury's story, while falling short of the carnage of its conclusion. The long version fades out, then fades back in again, so in love with the way it is.

So deceptively benign was 'The Veldt' that Justin Trudeau, the Canadian Liberal campaigning for prime minister on a platform of handsomeness, actually used it as part of his soundtrack while out on the stump, his team doubtless finding in its 'world the children made' a Whitney Houston-style message of hope for the future. Trudeau and his people may have read too little into it; perhaps it's reading too much into it to connect the untroubled, sun-kissed air of the track's progressions with the serenity of the children as their parents are killed and eaten by wild animals, victims of their own overbearing surveillance. The happiness of EDM, the soundworld the children made, is similarly indifferent to the indignant qualms of an older generation.

Seeing Deadmau5 at the Brixton Academy in 2010, I remember thinking two things. Firstly, how the mouse's head had a Shamanic quality. The identity of Joel Zimmerman, born in

Toronto in 1981, was known but unimportant; what mattered was his accepted role as high priest, in the course of whose duties it was necessary to take on another masked identity. This was not how rock superstardom had worked; it was a great means of taking advantage of the anonymity of the DJ/auteur, supposedly their drawback. Secondly, I was struck by how skinny, how very white his arms were, and that such a frail, faceless Caucasian was able to defy the old *Übermensch* pretensions of rock yore and fill such a huge hall with people and noise. These were new rules, new rulers.

Skrillex and Deadmau5 were just two among many artists performing under the banner of EDM – there was also Calvin Harris, Swedish House Mafia, David Guetta and a host of wannabes excoriated by older hands like Carl Cox for reducing the art of DJing to the press-button expedient of an on-cue bass drop. But both were North American, proof that the taboos long harboured by that continent regarding dance music – the Disco Sucks movement in particular – had been utterly scotched.

Or maybe not quite. Deadmau5 was a very different sort of character from Skrillex, pricklier in interviews. Ironically, musically he was a product of smoother influences – Steely Dan and Tears for Fears, alongside Canadian anti-vivisectionist avant-industrialists Skinny Puppy. His father's record collection included U2 and Metallica, and he was drawn to these groups rather than the piano lessons forced on him. He played Microsoft Golf and Minesweeper as a kid. But he never seems to have had any interest in rave or its names, and shamelessly declared he had never heard of Pete Tong. 'I don't care for the who's whos and what's whats,' he said in an interview with *Resident Advisor*. 'I'm interested in two things: music and technology. I'm not interested in clubs, I'm not interested in being in the middle of a 80,000 person crowd and "having the time of my life." That's my idea of hell. Being in the middle of a dancefloor like that.'

'But you're often playing to that dancefloor,' protested the interviewer.

'Right. But I've got my little area, in my own little world. I'm having a fun time – and helping other people to have a good time. That's great. That's a cool situation. But I could never go to a club and be that guy in the middle. Every gig, it's packed like sardines and you look at the dude in the middle and he's got the biggest shit-eating grin on his face and it's like, "What's wrong with you?"'

Deadmau5 was disdainful of the wave of EDM artists who came after him, and received criticism for apparently slagging off his own constituency. You sense a kernel of grudging grunginess about Deadmau5, a little bit of shame at the role into which he has been cast, one that has made him millions. Is EDM just depthless noise, surface blare, a mere push to the max for the sake of the max? A sell-out, a white-out, a massive stadium-swelling cliché? Is it a genre that has stalled because it has left itself nowhere to go?

There was a worry that EDM marked the point where rave and club music had become over-legitimised through sheer commerciality, far too acceptable to the sort of white-jock constituency whose forefathers would once have burned twelve-inch vinyl in baseball arenas. We'd come a long way from Castlemorton, that was for sure. It's tempting, indeed, to regard Castlemorton as the last time that popular culture and the authorities were at loggerheads, when actual legislation was used in an attempt to strike down a musical movement.

For black British artists working on the UK live scene, however, it's long been a different story. In 2009, Kode9 and the late Spaceape cut a version of the Specials' 1981 hit 'Ghost Town'. 'All the clubs have been closed down,' intones Spaceape with slow, solemn emphasis over a post-apocalyptic, razed dubscape of ghostly peals of brass, sirens and a subdued bass pulse. That same year, reported Dan Hancox in the *Guardian*, the live-music community was protesting against the police's use of the infamous risk assessment form 696, which demanded information from licensees as to the performers and audience members at any club night or gig they were planning to stage, on pain of a hefty fine if they failed to comply. One of the questions asked on the original form was: 'Is there a particular ethnic group attending? If "yes", please state group.' This somewhat blatant racial profiling was removed from the form in December 2008, but mentions elsewhere on the form of musical styles to be played ('bashment, R&B, garage') gave strong hints as to the kind of events the police were looking to circumscribe. Grime DJs protested that despite the combative nature of their music's lyrics, the amount of trouble at events was no worse than you might get at the average pub; that grime was being penalised for its blackness and its newness.

Several years on, things hadn't changed. In 2016, the owner of the Dice Bar in Croydon, south London, was told that the music he featured was attracting 'the wrong sort of clientele', while a licensing officer from the local borough made reference to 'unacceptable forms of music' – those considered synonymous with blackness, with violence.

The Grenfell Tower tragedy of 2017 made this sort of exclusionary tactic, an attempt to suppress cultural expression based solely on prejudice, even more repugnant. Many insisted that the word 'tragedy' was not adequate for what was a criminal act of state and local authority negligence, whose victims were people of colour left behind in a London ruthlessly bent on gentrification and social cleansing. Grime artists such as Skepta, Stormzy and Ladbroke Grove's AJ Tracey were already becoming engaged at this point, finding in Jeremy Corbyn's Labour Party a reason to engage with mainstream politics. Interviewed by the *Guardian*, Tracey excoriated the continued suppression of London, the 'most multicultural place in the world', and the attempt to shut down its celebratory music 'because the rich people don't like the noise or seeing brown people outside their window'. The Grenfell tragedy did not surprise him, nor the pitiful lack of response from central government. 'If this had been a Tory constituency in Hampshire, they'd have sent the army in,' opined Tracey's brother. The whole country was moved by the efforts of the emergency services and communities themselves – if not the abysmally inert local council – to rally and lend assistance in the face of the disaster. Still, when an attempt was made to organise a fundraiser for Grenfell at the Trapeze Bar in Shoreditch, London, the general manager wrote back and said the music they intended to play – bashment – was 'crap' and would attract a 'poor quality demographic' to the venue.

In fairness, the manager in question was subsequently relieved of his position. What's more, at this time live-music venues of all kinds were under threat of closure as new people moved into hip city areas and attempted to close down the 'vibrancy' that was supposedly their selling point, complaining with far too frequent success about noise and enabling property developers to swoop and create yet more new apartments. Even the urbane Fabric looked to have closed its doors for the last time following a drugs scare, before its licence was reinstated.

However, while the gradual acceptance of rave as a mass music that had come to supplant rock made it an overground, mostly white and Euro-American phenomenon, the excluded, illegitimate beats of the black underground would provide the rhythmical accompaniment to a protest against a post-neo-liberal, post-prosperous and fatally polarised society: Grime4Corbyn.

On the face of it, grime's endorsement of Corbyn is a little puzzling, as there's little in the lyrical content itself, with its brags and beefs, its ruthless top-dog materialism, that seems to share any kinship with Corbyn's personal and political ethos: a 'kinder, gentler' approach, but one unequivocally pitted against the ravages of the capitalist free market on the welfare state. Jeremy Corbyn is perhaps the least grime-y person on the planet. The best way of making sense of this undoubted phenomenon is to regard the motions of grime as having as much to do with ritual as reality. It is inadmissible in the genre to talk about social deprivation, personal vulnerability, theft of pride, poverty, much as it has been in African American music since 1990. But that does not mean that feelings of racism, of disadvantage and exile from mainstream concerns and discourse are not felt. And when a Corbyn comes along professing that he will at least turn around a system that is stacked against black and ethnic minorities, there will be no pretence that they are anything other than 4 him and 4 that.

17

CONCLUSION

When Kraftwerk released 'Expo 2000' at the turn of the twenty-first century, it wasn't just a reminder of how, despite having barely recorded anything new since 1986, they still hadn't lost, above all, the uncanny knack to pick out simply but perfectly plotted and weighted electropop tunes. It was also a reminder of how all they had proposed had come to pass. *The Man-Machine* and *Computer World* in particular were prophetic; *Computer World* more so than they could have dreamt, as communications technology evolved way beyond mere programming and surveillance into the vast, generally unanticipated web of the Internet.

While this had a paralysing effect on Hütter and co., it liberated electronic music, whose dissemination has mushroomed in the twenty-first century. It's nearly impossible to contrive straight narrative lines to summarise the explosion of micro-genres and their worldwide reach. To list every modern practitioner worthy of mention would require a telephone directory. Here, culled at random from the playlists on my iPhone, is but a cross-section of electronica artists all worthy of investigation and devotion, tiny, disparate lights pulsating away in an era dominated by the yawning complaint that 'nothing is happening'.

There's ACTRESS, the Wolverhampton-based artist whose cuts, hooks, edits and beat sketches deliberately isolate him from any particular micro-genre. AKATOMBO, aka Paul Thomsen Kirk, Scottish-born, Hiroshima-based, the grey, industrial washes of whose work reminds one of Gerhard Richter brought alive in sound. Philadelphia's BEE MASK, whose lengthy, granular explorations break down to atomic-level relationships between ambient and techno, bleep and drone. THE BUG, aka Kevin Martin, who transitioned from avant-rock to a tuff re-reading of dancehall. CIO D'OR, the Berlin 'sound architect' whose own creations and DJ sets bristle with a delicacy and drama only she could bring to the party. MATTHEW DEAR, an upfront, tortured presence in his songwriting, as if existentially tangled in the wires of his electronica-based settings. VLADISLAV DELAY, the Finnish artist whose work at times sounds as if it is undergoing a constant, churning process of processing and fermentation; glitch reduced to its very quarks. DJ ELMOE, star of the Chicago-based footwork movement, responsible for 'Whea Yo Ghost at, Whea Yo Dead Man', which is technically crude in its tweaking and rep-rep-repetitions yet somehow exquisite in its outcome.

There's EMIKA, English but of Czech origin, responsible for 'Drop the Other', a transcendent and bladed specimen of electropop. GAGARIN, aka Graham Dowdall, former drummer for Ludus and Nico, now with Pere Ubu, whose work has moved beyond the confines of IDM into new galaxies, and whose moniker epitomises a mourning for the loss of a certain kind of exploratory spirit that may never be truly reinvoked. Tennessee-born HOLLY HERNDON, who has found a way of making a music which establishes a meaningful relationship with her laptop, rather than one of mere portable convenience, in recognition of how much of her life she spends on the machine. PETER VAN HOESEN, who continues Belgium's singular tradition of diamond-hard, on-point electronic music, preceded by Front 242 and R&S Records, among others.

KLARA LEWIS, the daughter of Wire's Graham Lewis, who has elaborated on the proto-ambient 4AD work he and Bruce Gilbert generated under the Dome moniker, producing improvised, abstract electronic works of colour, depth and detail which exceed the capability of visual representation. MATMOS, aka

M. C. Schmidt and Drew Daniel, two of the most intelligent musicians in the world, whose collaborations show a telepathic mutual understanding and whose range of work, from straight-up pop to sound art to a reworking of Robert Ashley's TV opera *Perfect Lives*, is incomparable. JOHN MAUS, from Austin, Minnesota, a former professor of philosophy and Ariel Pink collaborator, whose frantic neo-electropop, as evidenced on *We Must Become the Pitiless Censors of Ourselves*, sounds like he is caught in a long tunnel of 1980s electropop reverb; it's deceptively well-judged outsider pop. Parisian sound artists BÉRANGÈRE MAXIMIN, whose best work sounds like meditated, artificially generated additions to the world of nature. The Sri Lankan-born M.I.A., jealously maligned at times but whose initially hip hop-inspired work is acid-tipped with militancy, best evidenced on 'Born Free', which was built around the riff to Suicide's 'Ghost Rider'. BARBARA MORGENSTERN, whose 2005 album *Tesri*, with Robert Lippok, is the sort of consistently strong electropop album that makes the genre sound recently minted. OH ASTRO, whose ingeniously conceived 'Candy Sun Smiles' is made up of macro- and micro-samples from Electronic's 'Getting Away with It' and sounds capable of inducing a sort of epilepsy. SCUBA, the British-born sometime dubstepper who honours the memory of massive, anthemic house by creating works like 'Adrenalin' that are even more massive and anthemic than the originals. SHACKLETON, founder of Skull Disco, whose use of Arabic and African percussive styles shoots through his technoscapes with a sense of nameless anxiety akin to that produced by Cabaret Voltaire's *Red Mecca*. ANDY STOTT, the Mancunian with an impressive lack of a need to adopt a snazzy, name-masking moniker, whose *Luxury Problems* inhabits caverns of deep-house bass and benefits from collaboration with his former music teacher, the operatically trained vocalist Alison Skidmore. TERRE THAEMLITZ, aka DJ Sprinkles, a giant, both cerebrally and as a beatmaster; her vast output, ranging from ambient to dancefloor, embracing grand pianos and queer theory, hobo rhythms and decayed FM pop, rewards total dedication on the part of the listener. Finally, but not finally, YOUNG ECHO, a Bristol collective who pace the history-laden dub back alleys of their home town, which were formerly traipsed by Portishead, Massive Attack, Tricky.

This is a barely adequate list; another consisting entirely of different names would make the same point. There is a worthy abundance of electronica in the twenty-first century, venturing further, adding incrementally but significantly to the works of the pioneers, achieving greater detail in terms of granular breakdown, technical capability and intelligent use of the weight of musical history than its makers' more famous and celebrated twentieth-century predecessors ever could. In addition to these names, and those unmentioned, there is a veritable periodic table of genres and sub-genres; moreover, the democratising effect of new technologies has led to the proliferation of flourishing underground electronic scenes in China, Egypt, Iran, Algeria, Uganda, Liberia and Angola, among other places, each with its local imprint. It is so much, so much more than the market can bear, the sort of abundance that sends the casual pop consumer, always inquiring of music journalists at parties what the next big thing (singular) is, scurrying back to the certainties of the stadium-filling tried and obvious.

And yet, shooting through all of this music – explicitly in the case of Burial – is a deserted village air, a sense that we are in a permanent state of aftermath, as first noted by Tricky on his 1994 track of the same name, which was constructed around a decelerated sample of Marvin Gaye in his Motown pomp. Mark Fisher was preoccupied by a feeling that something of the twentieth century's politic hope and utopianism had been irrevocably lost in the twenty-first, snuffed out by disappointment and a too-well-developed inkling that utopia was a political impossibility from which we should sensibly avert our intentions. For him, it was no source of satisfaction that electronic music was so well woven into the weft of modern music that it was hardly noticeable. He lamented the days of Roxy Music, for example, when Brian Eno's snyth interventions on 'Virginia Plain' were a startling, zigzagging interruption, applying an alien, unexpected, electric shock to the pop system. It is hard to know how to go about addressing that sort of despondency.

The technologies of the twenty-first century were undreamt of in the twentieth, but many believe that they have not significantly advanced the ways and means of music-making, merely making things more press-button convenient. Communications technologies have contributed to a global shrinkage, made everyone and everything connectible. However, following the transformative leaps of the early twenty-first century, even communications technologies began to plateau. As the 2020s approached, it felt as if Apple had exhausted their supply of innovations, that all they had to offer were mere upgrades rather than game-changing, life-changing devices (for better, for worse) such as the iPod or iPhone. The word 'bloatware' has been coined – big companies pushing more and more needless functionality into their products.

Once more, however, there has been a big resurgence in the future and a feeling that it is about to come at us in a huge wave. Nano-technology, genetic manipulation, AI and quantum computing. In terms of the capitalist paradigm, Elon Musk's off-grid house. Driverless cars. Big data and machine learning. Graphene and 3D printer technology. Augmented reality.

No one is exactly throwing their hats in the air about all of this. There is a fearful inkling, expressed in volumes like Curtis White's *We, Robots*, that all of this presents a threat to humanity rather than the prospect of enhancing our lives. This isn't based on Luddite ignorance or superstitious loathing of the mechanical but a strong sense that all of this R & D is at the behest of greedy corporations rather than visionary civilisations; that all of this will create mass unemployment and mass alienation as a global elite seek to create still greater social and economic inequality, to push the vast majority of mankind towards obsolescence.

Futurology is an invidious game; hardly anyone ever gets it anything like right. Predictions of How the World Will Look in the Year 1990 were delivered in earnest, either with inappropriate optimism or undue pessimism, but always with risible inaccuracy. But if all of the above, all of it much documented, has anything to it, what might the response of an electronic musician be in such an impending world? Benign Kraftwerkian embrace? Absorb the new tech and divert it towards creative ends?

Maybe not. The tendency towards analogue and vintage electronic equipment might feel like a passing fad, indulged by musicians and audiences of a certain age who would, if they could, opt out of the twenty-first century altogether. For them, these instruments represent more equitable, pre-neo-liberal times, a period coated, moreover, in the grainy fuzz of nostalgic hankering for youth and a time when there was a future at which to gape in awe. A 1980 of Thatcher and Reagan, of socialism and outer space.

However, maybe what is required is for the analogue vogue to become a permanent principle. Preserve and reuse discarded technologies, not just for their retro cuteness but as an ecological protest against the coercive, wasteful aspects of technological 'development' and ceaseless upgrades designed more to engineer obsolescence than increase the quality of lives. Maintain a tactile, physical relationship with your equipment, while taking full advantage of the infinite variety of sounds it opens up once you get past the presets. Make the work that you do feel more like 'play' rather than the retina-burning, screen-fixated mundanity of everyday office work. Avert your gaze, if possible, from the thrall of the screen. Of course, the laptop itself might join the heap of former technologies discarded by capitalism in its ruinous pursuit of a technology that is increasingly invisible, increasingly remote and out of reach, yet increasingly, insidiously hard-wired in all of our

lives to exploit us, our hopes and vulnerabilities in ever more subtle ways. We need to keep our hands on the means of production.

A case in point: looping. Ed Sheeran might be regarded by many
as a vastly talented goblin from hell for his many pop misdeeds,
but it's one small thing to his credit that he uses a loop pedal.
Looping, either using a pedal or tapes or processors, has a long
tradition, particularly among female practitioners and vocalists,
from Meredith Monk to Laurie Anderson to, in the present day,
Georgina Brett and my own partner, the musician Roshi Nasehi.
The loop pedal in particular is a simple, much-used piece of hardware which I have seen used to great effect in tiny improv venues,
filling thirty-seater rooms with overlapping ripples of instantly
ghostly reverb, triggering real-time sound multiplications in space;
as a mode of expression, this is no more dated a gadget than a flute.

It is, however, a piece of technological equipment, and such
things resonate when used in a therapeutic setting. Neil Young
understood this when he made *Trans* in 1982, using a Sennheiser
vocoder VSM201 in the hope of making a music that would reach
his young son, who was born with cerebral palsy and unable to
speak. My partner, who has worked with elective mute and autistic
children, has spoken of the joy of introducing a boy with elective
mutism to her battery of looping equipment. He broke his near-
permanent silence, excitedly declaring into a VE20 vocal looping
and effects processor, 'Look at me! I'm a robot!' Such devices are
used in a discreet and commonplace way in conventional everyday
music, but it's only when they are used indiscreetly, in a way that
displays their eerie, mechanical strangeness, that you get this sort
of impact.

Both of these are indicators of the sort of cultural work that
can be done with existing technologies in a future economy in
which the prospects of making a living as a commercial musician
are decreasingly likely. Some of the most absorbing and rewarding
concerts I've been to in recent years have been by performers using

banks of well-used modular equipment, tablefuls of modified objects filtered and treated using basic but perennial hardware, the musicians packing and going home with a fistful of fivers and whatever they can make on album sales. Their music is exploratory, forged in the moment out of sheer electric curiosity, and is utterly uninhibited by any sort of commercial expediency. Meanwhile, the uses to which actual existing, tangible and tactile hardware can be put for therapeutic purposes remain yet to be fully explored.

As I type, I'm listening again to Laurie Anderson's 'O Superman'. Filed by some as a novelty hit, a surprise number one in 1981, it remains matchless. Has any piece of sound art ever tickled the curiosity of the public so successfully? Much as Anderson could step into the street today looking as she does in the video and not seem out of time, the only thing that dates the piece is the reference to 'smoking or non-smoking'. With its devastatingly simple looped vocal pulse, achieved using an Eventide Harmonizer, it feels like it has achieved eternal life through artificial respiration, floating free having jettisoned all the extraneous obligatory baggage you are supposed to carry with you to the top of the charts. It was supposedly inspired by a calamity of technological failure – Operation Eagle Claw, the attempt to rescue American hostages taken after the 1979 revolution in Iran, which resulted in the crash of a military helicopter, killing eight servicemen. However, as a piece of music, it is, conceptually, artistically and thematically, a triumph of technologically enhanced pop – an example of using technology itself to highlight and comment on its own alienating effects.

'O Superman' is not alone in reminding us that, ultimately, it's important not to regard the 'future' as meaning simply 'the 2050s and beyond'. There may be no future at all if we simply drift acquiescently with the times. The 'future' may have already been with us for some time, scattered in fragments like rocket parts from a failed Apollo mission, buried and embedded but still retrievable, still vital.

Mars by 1980 was still on in 1981. It's still on today.

NINETEENTH- AND TWENTIETH-CENTURY MUSICAL TECHNOLOGY: A TIMELINE

1876 The 'Musical Telegraph', invented by Elisha Gray, arguably the world's first synthesizer.

1877 The phonograph, invented by Thomas Edison, enabling the recording and mechanical reproduction of sound, originally recorded onto tinfoil sheets wrapped around a rotating cylinder.

1895 The pianola, or player piano, invented by Edwin S. Votey. Able to play pre-programmed music on perforated paper. It falls out of production following the Wall Street Crash of 1929, but is revived in the late 1930s and beyond by the American-born composer Conlon Nancarrow.

1906 The Telharmonium, developed by Thaddeus Cahill. The triode, the first usable electronic amplifier, is invented by Lee de Forest. This represents the birth of the electronic age.

1910 The Futurist painter Luigi Russolo develops the intona-rumori, sound-generating machines intended to add to the lexicon of sounds available to music in the twentieth century, as expounded in his *Art of Noises* manifesto of 1913.

1916 The Cubo-Futurist painter Vladimir Baranoff-Rossiné builds his Optophonic Piano, a 'synaesthesic' instrument in which sounds and revolving patterns are triggered by a keyboard, creating a combination of music and colour, as dreamt of by composers like Alexander Scriabin.

1917 The first theremin, named after its Soviet inventor, Leon
      Theremin, is built. Featuring two metal antennae, it
      generates sounds without the player's hand touching the
      instrument.

1928 Maurice Martenot invents the ondes Martenot, similar to
      the theremin. Used by Edgard Varèse on *Ecuatorial*.

1930 More Soviet invention: the Variophone, invented
      by Evgeny Sholpo, an optical synthesizer that uses
      soundwaves transcribed onto cardboard discs rotating
      synchronously with 35mm film.

1935 The Magnetophon, the first tape recorder, developed by
      Fritz Pfleumer, is demonstrated at the Berlin Radio Show.

1940 The 'voice synthesizer', developed by Karl Wagner and
      precursor to the vocoder.

1941 The Ondioline, invented by Georges Jenny and
      popularised by his fellow Frenchman, Jean-Jacques Perrey,
      in the early 1950s. An electric keyboard, the Ondioline's
      sound can be varied by shifting it manually from side to
      side, creating a range of vibrato effects more diverse than
      the ondes Martenot.

1944 Halim El-Dabh produces *The Expression of Zaar*, the first
      known piece of electroacoustic tape music.

1946 The 'Orchestra Machine' is developed by Raymond Scott,
      who no longer wished to work with human musicians, if
      possible. He later follows this up with the Clavivox.

1947 The clavioline, an electric keyboard featuring a vacuum
      tube oscillator, is invented by French engineer Constant
      Martin. It features on Del Shannon's 1961 hit 'Runaway',
      and during the 1960s is used extensively by jazz man Sun
      Ra.

1952 The RCA synthesizer, aka 'Victor', developed by Herbert
      Belar and Harry Olson, is conceived and eventually
      installed at Columbia University in 1957. Despite the

initial popularity of the complex notational sequences of which it is capable, beyond those of any acoustic instrument, the instrument falls into disrepair and is last used in 1997.

1955 'Selective Synchronous Recording', developed by Ampex, introduces the possibility of audio overdubbing, which guitarist Les Paul develops to create eight-track recordings.

1957 The ANS synthesizer, developed by Evgeny Murzin between 1937 and 1957, is unveiled. The computer is named in honour of the composer Alexander Scriabin. Eduard Artemyev uses the ANS extensively in his scores for the movies of Andrei Tarkovsky, including *Solaris*.

1959 Oramics, Daphne Oram's programming system, based on an idea she had as a child.

1963 The DA-20 drum machine, developed by Keiko (later known as Korg). It features a rotating disc system with a choice of sounds.

The mellotron, developed by the company Mellotronics, which was founded by Frank, Norman and Les Bradley, bandleader Eric Robinson and magician David Nixon. It is based on an earlier instrument that was developed by and named after the Californian Harry Chamberlin. The mellotron is popularised by the Beatles, notably on 'Strawberry Fields Forever'.

1964 The Ace Tone R1 Rhythm Ace, developed by Ikutaro Kakehashi.

The Moog synthesizer, invented by Robert Moog, is released. First demonstrated at the Monterey Pop Festival in 1967, it transcends its initial novelty status to become an integral part of the electronic furniture.

1970 The ARP-600, developed by Alan R. Pearlman and Dennis Colin, a simplified version of the ARP-500. Pete Townshend is an early adopter, but it's Stevie Wonder who

makes extensive and popular use of the instrument, with
the assistance of Bob Margouleff and Malcolm Cecil.

1973 The Yamaha GX-1, a prog-rock staple used by Emerson,
Lake and Palmer, among others, and later the Aphex Twin
on the track 'GX1 Solo', after he acquired the instrument
from the estate of the late Mickie Most.

1979 The Casio VL-1, released in June 1979, a digital
synthesizer available for just $69.95.
The Fairlight CMI, a seventy-three-note keyboard,
consisting of a central unit with two eight-inch floppy-
disk players, an alphanumeric keyboard, a monochrome
monitor and a light pen for graphic editing purposes. The
first instrument to include digital sampling.

1980 The Roland TR-808 analogue drum machine, popularised
by the Yellow Magic Orchestra on their 1980 album *BGM*,
but discontinued in 1983. It enjoys a lengthy afterlife both
in sound libraries and as a valued second-hand instrument,
and is particularly popular in hip hop.
The Yamaha GS-1, the first digital synthesizer. More
expensive than the Casio VL-1, it becomes a popular and
ubiquitous feature of 1980s pop, from Talking Heads to
Duran Duran.

1981 The Roland TB-303 Bass Line, later a key element in the
acid-house sound. However, its first use is by Heaven
17 on 'Let Me Go', and it doesn't feature on a hit until
Orange Juice deploy it on 1983's 'Rip It Up'.
The Toshiba LMD-649, the first digital sampler, used
extensively on the Yellow Magic Orchestra's *Technodelic*.

1982 The Roland Jupiter-6, one of the first MIDI synthesizers,
later popularised by Blue, Inner City, the Human League
and Orbital, among others.

1984 The first Macintosh computer by Apple, later taken up by
musicians in laptop form as a musical instrument.

Sound Designer, developed by Berkeley graduates Evan Brooks and Peter Gotcher. Later renamed as Pro Tools.

1985 The Atari ST computer, designed by Shiraz Shivji, an image of which can be found on Fatboy Slim's album *You've Come a Long Way, Baby*, on which the Atari features extensively.

1995 The Doepfer A-100, an analogue modular synthesizer system introduced by German manufacturers Doepfer. This 'rack-mounted' system enables different companies to integrate their modules into each other's systems under the 'Eurorack' standard.

1999 The creation of Ableton Live, a digital audio station that can also be used during performance. Goes live in 2001.

A *MARS BY 1980* PLAYLIST

Some of this I regard as canonical, some personal. To be used as a journey to take you down many other wormholes.

23 Skidoo, 'Just Like Everybody'
A Guy Called Gerald, 'Voodoo Ray'
Luke Abbott, 'Modern Driveway'
The Advisory Service, 'Civil Defence Is Common Sense'
Laurie Anderson, 'O Superman'
Aphex Twin, 'Didgeridoo'
The Art of Noise, 'Close (to the Edit)'
Edward Artemiev, 'Dedication to Andrei Tarkovsky'
Robert Ashley, *Your Money My Life Goodbye*
Autechre, 'Second Scepe'
Arseny Avraamov (arr. Miguel Molina), *Symphony of Sirens*
Afrika Bambaataa and the Soulsonic Force, 'Looking for the
    Perfect Beat'
Basic Channel, *Arrange and Process* (various artists)
William Basinski, *The Disintegration Loops*
Luciano Berio, *Omaggio a Joyce*
Boards of Canada, *Geogaddi*
David Bowie, 'Beauty and the Beast'
Gavin Bryars/Alter Ego/Philip Jeck, *The Sinking of the Titanic*
The Bug, 'Superbird'
Burial, *Untrue*
Cabaret Voltaire, *The Voice of America*, 'Slugging fer Jesus'

John Cage, 'Williams Mix'
Can, 'Moonshake'
Carter Tutti Void, 'f=(2.7)'
Suzanne Ciani, *Concert at Phill Niblock's Loft*
Dave Clarke, *Live at Lowlands Festival*
Cluster, 'Rosa' (from *Zuckerzeit*)
Coil, 'Sex with Sun Ra'
Holger Czukay, *Movies*
D.A.F., *Gold und Liebe*
Daft Punk, *Homework*, 'Digital Love'
Miles Davis, 'Yesternow' (from *Jack Johnson*), 'He Loved Him
    Madly' (from *Live/Evil*)
De La Soul, 'Eye Know'
Deadmau3, 'The Veldt'
Deathprod, *Morals and Dogma*
Depeche Mode, 'A Pain that I'm Used To' (Jacques Lu Cont
    remix)
Delia Derbyshire and Barry Bermange, 'There Is a God'
J Dilla, *Donuts*
Terrence Dixon, *From the Far Future*
Todd Dockstader, *Eight Electronic Pieces*
Einstürzende Neubauten, 'Engel der Vernichtung'
Halim El-Dabh, *The Expression of Zaar*
Brian Eno, *Music for Airports*, *On Land*
Faust, *Faust*, *Faust So Far*
Fennesz, 'Rivers of Sand'
Luc Ferrari, *Music Promenade*
Foul Play, 'Open Your Mind'
John Foxx, *London Overgrown*
Front 242, 'Headhunter'
The Future Sound of London, 'Papua New Guinea'
Gas, *Königsforst*
Godley and Creme, 'Under Your Thumb'

Goldie, 'Jah the Seventh Seal' (from *Inner City Life*)

Manuel Göttsching, *E2–E4*

Laurel Halo, 'Jelly'

Herbie Hancock, *Sextant*

Harmonia, 'Sehr Kosmisch'

Heaven 17, '(We Don't Need This) Fascist Groove Thang'

Tim Hecker, *Ravedeath, 1972*

Matthew Herbert, *One Pig*

Holly Herndon, *Movement*

Human League, 'The Dignity Of Labour', 'Love Action'

Humanoid, 'Stakker Humanoid'

Janet Jackson, *Rhythm Nation 1814*

Japan, 'Life in Tokyo'

Philip Jeck, 'Fanfares'

Joy Division, *Closer*

Leyland Kirby, 'Stralauer Peninsula'

KLF, *Chill Out*

Kode 9 + the Spaceape, 'Ghost Town'

Kraftwerk, *Autobahn, Trans-Europe Express, The Man-Machine,*
    Computer World

LA Style, 'James Brown Is Dead'

Ladytron, 'Playgirl'

Thomas Leer, *Four Movements* EP

Letherette, *Space Cuts*

Liaisons Dangereuses, 'Los Ninos del Parque'

György Ligeti, 'Artikulation'

Madlib, 'Shadows of Tomorrow'

Mantronix, 'Megamix (in Full Effect 1988)'

Matmos, *The Civil War*

John Maus, *We Must Become the Pitiless Censors of Ourselves*

Derrick May, 'It Is What It Is'

Joe Meek, 'I Hear a New World'

Merzbow, *Merzbient*

Metamono, 'Warszawa'

M.I.A., 'Born Free'

Jeff Mills, 'Cubango'

Janelle Monáe, *The ArchAndroid*

Luigi Nono, *Omaggio a Emilio Vedova*

Gary Numan, 'Cars'

Pauline Oliveros, 'Bye Bye Butterfly'

Daphne Oram, *Four Aspects*

The Orb, 'A Huge, Ever Growing Pulsating Brain that Rules from
the Centre of the Ultraworld'

Edith Pade, 'Faust'

Man Parrish, 'Hip-Hop Be Bop (Don't Stop)'

Annette Peacock, 'I'm the One'

Pere Ubu, 'Non-Alignment Pact'

Lee 'Scratch' Perry, 'Soul Fire'

Pet Shop Boys, 'Rent'

Henri Pousseur and Michel Butor, *Paysages Planetaires*

Prince, 'If I Was Your Girlfriend'

Jamie Principle, 'Baby Wants to Ride'

Pyrolator, 'Happiness'

Éliane Radigue, *Trilogie de la mort*

Steve Reich, 'Come Out'

Robert Rental and the Normal, *Live at West Runton Pavilion*

Porter Ricks, 'Port Gentil'

Roxy Music, 'Virginia Plain'

Rufige Kru, 'Ghosts of My Life'

George Russell, *Electronic Sonata for Souls Loved by Nature*

Pierre Schaeffer and Pierre Henry, *Orphée*

Conrad Schnitzler, 'Fata Morgana'

Paul Schütze, 'Tears'

Raymond Scott, 'Lightworks'

Scritti Politti, *Cupid & Psyche 85*

Scuba, 'Adrenalin'

DJ Shadow, *Endtroducing*
Skinny Puppy, 'Harsh Stone White'
Soft Cell, 'Memorabilia'
Mark Stewart, 'Forbidden Colour'
Karlheinz Stockhausen, *Gesang der Jünglinge*, *Kontakte*, *Hymnen*
Morton Subotnick, 'Silver Apples of the Moon'
Suicide, 'Frankie Teardrop' (from *Suicide*), 'Touch Me'
Donna Summer, 'I Feel Love'
Sun Ra, *Media Dreams*, 'I'll Wait for You'
Supercollider, 'Gravity Rearrangin''
Tangerine Dream, *Zeit*
Telex, 'Moscow Discow'
This Heat, '24 Track Loop'
Throbbing Gristle, 'Tesco Disco', 'Discipline'
Underground Resistance, 'Afrogermanic'
Edgar Varèse, *Déserts*, *Poème électronique*
Video-Aventures, 'Tina' (from *Musiques pour garçons et filles*)
Ricardo Villalobos, 'Bank Brotherhood'
White Noise, *An Electric Storm*
Stevie Wonder, *Music of My Mind*, *Innervisions*
Iannis Xenakis, *Orient/Occident*
Xhin, 'Vent'
Yello, *You Gotta Say Yes to Another Excess*
Yellow Magic Orchestra, *Technodelic*
Young Gods, 'Jimmy'
Zapp, 'Computer Love'
Zomby, *Where Were U in '92?*

INDEX